D1562661

COMMODITY OPTIONS:

A USER'S GUIDE
TO SPECULATING AND HEDGING

Terry S. Mayer

New York Institute of Finance

Library of Congress Cataloging in Publication Data
Mayer, Terry S.
  Commodity options.

  Includes index.
    1. Commodity exchanges—Handbooks, manuals, etc.
I. Title.
HG6046.M373   1983   332.64'5   83-13293
ISBN 0-13-152298-1

HG
6046
.M373
1983

To my mother and father,
who made this book possible.
Thank you.

© 1983 New York Institute of Finance

All rights reserved.
No part of this book may be reproduced
in any part or by any means
without permission in writing
from the publisher.

This publication is designed to provide accurate and authoritative information in regard to the subject matter covered. It is sold with the understanding that the publisher is not engaged in rendering legal, accounting, or other professional service. If legal advice or other expert assistance is required, the services of a competent professional person should be sought.

—From a Declaration of Principles jointly adopted by a Committee of the American Bar Association and a Committee of Publishers and Associations

Printed in the United States of America

10   9   8   7   6   5   4   3   2   1

New York Institute of Finance
(NYIF Corp.)
70 Pine St.
New York, New York 10270

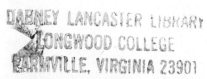
DABNEY LANCASTER LIBRARY
LONGWOOD COLLEGE
FARMVILLE, VIRGINIA 23901

CONTENTS

10 THE SPECULATOR—PUT BUYING STRATEGIES, 145

11 THE SPECULATOR—STRADDLE AND COMBO BUYING STRATEGIES, 156

FOREWORD

The cost of meddling is what it is all about. Meddling is what we want to do. Meddling helps us to actualize ourselves, to be that uniquely human thing—the animal that has input into his destiny. And so we act and decide and act some more. But maybe that's where we go wrong, maybe that's what the kids mean when they tell us just to "go with the flow." It's the meddling that gets us: When we change one city block, the urban development theorists tell us, we change the whole city and almost never for the better. Any drug we prescribe for disease works for only one reason: It disturbs some preexisting physiological mechanism and, by so doing, makes it harder for the disease to flourish. Yet it often—very often—does as much damage as the damage it is meant to avert. That is why the drug companies, hospitals, and doctors keep getting sued. Practice is malpractice.

What has all this to do with options? Everything. All the meddling we do has a cost. Options are a way of making that cost measurable. We want to meddle because it makes us feel that we are in charge of our otherwise hapless destinies. We want to meddle because we fear we would otherwise float. We must choose a school, a career, a business, and whether to cross the road. But when we choose, we know how imperfect our choosing equipment is and wish that we will, if wrong, be permitted to turn the clock back and do it all over again. Choosing has, then, a cost: the risk of error. And so does not choosing: the risk of floating or of missing our chance. Is there, then, a third choice? There is. It is the option. The right to do it all differently. And it too has a cost. Yet that cost is finite, measurable, knowable, and an ideal vehicle for those who are impressed by—no, overwhelmed by—the inadequacy of our choosing equipment in this accident-prone world on the one hand and the terror that our train—our only train, our only love, the only career in which we could become what we were meant to—has left the station while we watch its fading tail-light and feel our empty despair.

And so the option is what we want. It is the right to go one road and then another as if we had never gone the first. And we would pay for it in all of life if we could. The cost, however, so Goethe tells us, is dear. When the Devil grants Faust the right to let the moments flit past until he finds the one he wishes would stay, the cost for that right is dear; it is infinite—his ever-lasting soul.

In economics, we are saved. Or at least we are saved that cost, for we must merely pay the premium, the term Terry Mayer will soon introduce to describe the amount that the option costs. And it is a premium; it is often more than—in pure economic or probability theory terms—the option is "worth." People pay it because they get the right to review what they've done and do it over again. They get the right to walk the economically prudent road of not dissipating all one has to back one's imperfect market hunch but still to have the opportunity of seizing the "main chance" and making the "big score." Economists use the term "marginal utility" to describe man's willingness to invest a bit of his substance, even at imperfect odds, because a great increase in wealth means so much more. This is, of course, one aspect of gambling and also of investing in a way that gives one leverage over more of the invested-in object than one's money will buy—so much more that even a little change means a lot. This right to retread one's path, conjoined with the wish to be leveraged in one's investments, gave scope almost a decade ago to securities option trading. Around the same time—1971, to be exact—Mocatta started to offer commodity options as well.

At first, we thought only of the professional's needs to slake and/or be protected from greed or fear:

- the hedger's need to buy an option to secure himself against a loss when the market moves against him or to sell an option in order to cut the extent of that possible loss;
- the financial institution's willingness to view commodity price movements actuarially and to grant options as a way of maximizing the return on the funds they have at risk;
- the miner's need to be sure that he will not have to sell his production at a price so low that he will have to shut his mine, put his miners out of work, and set them amarch on his nation's capitol;
- the contract tenderer's fear of going wrong when he has to set a firm price long before he knows if he will get the contract;
- the fabricator's need to issue a catalog with real prices without having to fear that the commodity of which this product is made will sub-

sequently fall in price so that his catalog prices are high and he thus loses the sale to a competitor or that the commodity's price has gone up so that he will sell too much of the now-too-cheap product and must either denounce his catalog price or keep taking a loss.

I wondered how we could meet these needs and realized that the market needed the everyday speculator to give it the depth it required for the professional to have a counterpart. I could not in those days understand why individual investors were willing to trade commodities, why they were determined to pit their understanding of the world against that of their fellows and engage in the short-term form of investment known as speculation. I still cannot fully understand it. Greed, perhaps. A desire to test themselves; a desire to feel themselves a significant part of the world's stream of commerce and economics. Perhaps it is a more realistic concern: the feeling that the little they have will buy little now and less later on, so they might as well risk it in the effort to augment it.

True enough, it is not by any means a given that the odds are stacked against the speculator. Lord Keynes was persuaded that the professionals have so pressing a need to avert risk that they are willing to pay speculators a premium for carrying it. That, in and of itself, is probably true. In the ideal world there might well be an ideal relationship between the ideal hedger who needs price insurance and the ideal speculator who is willing to provide it. In the real world, the two have a hard time finding each other and so, between the two of them, they must take care of all the folks in-between: the shareholders, managers, and account executives of the brokerage firms they use; the floor traders and market-makers who provide the liquidity; and the exchange or market personnel that provide the meeting place and the rules for the two to meet. The two pay for all this in transaction costs: bid/offer differentials, brokerage commissions, and exchange fees.

As a result, each individual change of mind is extremely expensive. And this, too, has given impetus to the use of the option. If, having taken a view on the price of gold, the speculator changes his momentary attitude as often as each of us do on our careers, friends, and investments, the option protects him not only against the self-reproach that follows having been right and having then gone wrong, but also against the repeated cost of conforming is position to his mood.

Bill Baumol of Princeton told me years ago that the option's success comes from the fact that it repackaged risk so that those who wanted to take just one segment of it could do so and would not have to pay for all the risks there are. That is what options do, then. They let the investor decide just what risks he wants to take and, if he is right, they maximize his profit.

Terry Mayer has in this most comprehensive manual for the investor provided so thorough an outline of the field that each investor can maximize his use of and profit from option trading. In this book and in the five years I have been privileged to work at his side at Mocatta, he has shown me an aspect of option trading I had not seen before: the investor's vantage point. Had I not had those years of exposure, I would on reading this book have felt as if I had just discovered that my local librarian, with whom I have for years been talking about European literature, was a champion cha-cha dancer after library hours. His work and this book helped me—and the hundreds of men and women he has trained in option dealing—to understand the investment aspects of option trading—an activity that helps us to meddle in our own economic lives at the lowest possible cost. I and those who read this book have good reason to be grateful for this.

DR. HENRY JARECKI
Chairman
Mocatta Metals Corp.

PREFACE

On October 1, 1982, U.S. exchange-traded commodity options became a reality. Whether your background is commodities, security options, or debt investing, you will find these new markets of interest. If you have an in-depth background in commodities, you may wish to only scan Chapter 1. If you are well versed in security options, you may wish to take the same approach with Chapter 2.

Today we can take for granted a sophisticated market instrument like a commodity option only because of what has gone before. On April 26, 1973 an event took place that was destined to change the way we looked at investing. On that day the Chicago Board Options Exchange commenced trading. On the surface, this event was not apparently different from the opening of any new exchange. Yet from its inception most knowledgable people in the securities industry believed that the concept of exchange-traded options was doomed to failure.

To appreciate the significance of the Chicago Board Options Exchange (CBOE), you must understand how security option trading had existed prior to this genesis. Before the CBOE existed, investors who wished to purchase or grant options on a security would contact their brokers, and brokers would then contact one or more of the members of the Put and Call Broker's Association. The put and call brokers might attempt to find the other side of the transaction. Or perhaps they would act as principal themselves, on an interim basis, with the thought that they would eventually be able to find someone who would be interested in the transaction. This means of doing business was somewhat cumbersome and less than efficient. Due primarily to the ineffiencies and lack of liquidity in this type of transaction, the option market never accounted for a significant percentage of the total equity security business in the United States. In fact very few brokers, let alone investors, knew anything about option trading. It was no wonder that few were optimistic about the potential success of the CBOE.

On the first trading day the CBOE had forecast that, with options trading on only sixteen different securities, they would do only about ten options. To their surprise they traded several hundred.

Why had knowledgable people so grossly underestimated the potential of this market? Options serve a very useful purpose, and they never achieved their potential due to their lack of liquidity and the inability of brokers to rapidly disseminate price and volume information. These factors—along with the standardization of striking prices, maturity dates, and quantities—allowed option trading, in the next five years, to become one of the largest segments of the equity markets in the United States. The next five years saw the formation of additional option exchanges along the lines of the CBOE. The American Stock Exchange, the Pacific Coast Stock Exchange, the Mid-West Stock Exchange, and the Philadelphia Stock Exchange all eventually began trading options on equity securities.

Today the commodity exchanges find themselves in a situation very similar to that encountered by the security exchanges in the early 1970s. That is, commodity options have traded for hundreds of years in a fashion very similar to that of security option trading prior to the CBOE. The volume of traditional commodity option trading has only amounted to about 2% to 3% of the total volume of commodity futures. Why do we need listed commodity options and will the market be successful?

Over the last decade, the commodity futures market in the United States has grown to a level that the contract value of the commodity futures traded exceeds $1 trillion annually. As these markets continue to grow, there will be an ever increasing demand for speculative capital to support the needs of the commercial hedger. Commodity futures transactions, by definition, expose the investor to losses that are great, in many cases much greater than the dollar amount of the initial commitment. A limited number of investors are willing to assume this kind of risk, and consequently the pool of risk capital for commodity futures trading is limited. As our economy continues to grow and the prices of the basic commodities continue to remain volatile, there will be an ever increasing need for speculative capital. When properly employed, commodity options offer the individual a means of participating in commodity futures with a predetermined risk. There is, potentially, a much larger pool of risk capital for transactions wherein the total risk can be defined, than there is for open-ended risk transactions.

TERRY MAYER

ACKNOWLEDGMENTS

I would like to thank the many people who read various drafts of this book and supplied numerous useful suggestions. I would also like to thank Joseph Stefanelli for starting my option education. Dr. Henry Jarecki must be thanked not only for adding to that education, but also for writing an introduction to this book.

I would also like to thank my administrative assistant, Bonnie Ryan, for her patient proofreading and advice, my publisher Ben Russell for his patience and help, and Fred Dahl for his copy editing and pointed questions.

This book would not have been anywhere near as easily done without the friendly folks at Atari. Their 48K Atari 800 and word processor made the job much easier.

And lastly but not leastly, thanks to my wife and children for their patience, understanding, and support.

1

COMMODITY FUTURES—
AN OVERVIEW

While this chapter is not designed to teach you the commodity markets or even the commodity futures markets, it is designed to be a brief review of material that should be second nature to registered representatives or sophisticated investors. Regardless of your background, you must be familiar with the subject matter discussed in this chapter because later chapters are based on a thorough understanding of the commodity markets. If you are uncomfortable with any of the following material, pick up any of the better books on commodity futures trading. (See References.)

If you were looking for a textbook definition of a commodity futures contract, it would be something like this:

> *Commodity Futures Contract:* A legal contract that provides for the delivery of a specific item, at some future time.

Yet simple textbook definitions often do not tell us enough about what we are trying to understand. To appreciate where commodity futures trading fits into a total investment program, we must look at the background of commodity trading, the development of contract markets, and finally the natural progression to commodity options. A thorough understanding of futures trading is critical to the understanding of the purposes of commodity options.

WHAT ARE COMMODITIES?

In this country, commodity trading can be traced back to our earliest industry, agriculture. The farmer, always the backbone of the American

1

economy, plants, grows, harvests and sells the foodstuffs that have, past and present, been the lifeblood of our economy. As a result, the initial commodity trading in the United States was agricultural in nature. Interestingly, prior to the Commodity Exchange Act of 1936, commodity options were also actively traded in the Chicago grain markets.

Today, with our economy changing its emphasis, the spectrum of commodities traded is much broader. In addition to the traditional agricultural products, commodity trading now includes such diverse items as metals, financial instruments, stock indexes, petroleum products, and livestock, to name a few. All these products are exchange-traded in the form of futures contracts. In fact, over 40% of the futures volume trading done today is done in futures contracts that did not exist prior to 1975.

For the purposes of our discussion, a *commodity* is any basic item (agricultural, financial, etc.) either that is traded on and subject to the rules of a designated contract market (that is, an exchange) or that is traded in the physical or forward form by and among commercial entities. All of the basic terms of the commodity futures contract are determined by the exchange with the exception of the price, which is determined by the forces of supply and demand. In other words, the buyers and sellers of the commodity determine what the contract is worth by the amount they are willing to pay if they are buyers and by the amount they will accept if they are sellers. Because the participants determine price, it is free to rise or fall and, as a result, gives rise to risk.

Risk is the actual reason that commodity trading, in contract form, exists. Because commodity trading began with agricultural commodities, let us use the farmer as our example. Although the farmer's risks can be paralleled in almost any industry, the risks in the agricultural industry are perhaps the easiest to understand.

Farming is associated with many risks about which the farmer can do nothing: weather, blight, fire, flood, vermin, and the like. Farmers are investors. They plant crops, which represent the investment of capital and time, in an effort to harvest and sell these crops at a profit. This, as I am sure you will agree, is a high-risk form of investing. Farmers, however, make this investment in the hope of being able to sell their crops at a price high enough to justify the risk inherent in this form of business. Assume that a farmer plants corn in the spring, with the hopes that by fall the harvest will return sufficient profit to justify the risks and show a reasonable rate of return on the investment. This approach to farming has one additional risk, which is market price fluctuation. The farmer knows the current market price of corn at the time of planting, but not the price at harvest time. How does a farmer deal with this problem? How does the farmer achieve price insurance? The missing ingredient in this equation (or solution) is the speculator.

THE ROLE OF THE SPECULATOR

The speculator is the person to whom the farmer turns for market price insurance. The farmer sells the corn to the speculator at the time that it is planted, through the use of commodity futures. The speculator assumes the risk that is inherent in the ownership of the corn from when it is planted until it is harvested. Why would the speculator pay the farmer for such a "right"? The speculator has analyzed the market factors that he deems important to the price of corn, and believes that the price of corn will rise over the period involved. If the assumption is correct, the speculator will reap a profit when the actual corn is sold. In so doing, the speculator has fulfilled two roles:

1. The speculator assumes the risk that the farmer is unwilling or unable to accept.
2. The speculator is available to the farmer at the time of need.

In other words, the speculator assumes some of the commodity producer's risk and thereby fulfills an economic function.

This economic purpose, along with the related storage, insurance, and opportunity cost, is the basis for the establishment of commodity futures and commodity option markets.

As a final note, the speculator must be distinguished from two other types of people. First, a speculator is not a hedger. The risk to the farmer is very real, and the speculator allows the transfer of that unwelcome risk. In that a commodity futures contract is a binding legal contract for the delivery of actual merchandise, it has value and can be freely traded. The commodity option contract is also a risk-transference vehicle, as will be seen later. As such, it can, in many cases, be used as either a replacement for or in addition to the traditional futures contract. The exchange's role is to provide liquidity by bringing buyers and sellers together in a business environment. Various versions of these types of contracts have been traded throughout American history.

The hedger, another type of participant in the market, is traditionally the participant who deals in the physical commodity in the normal course of business activity. The speculator participates in the commodities markets for profit potential only. Second, the speculator is speculating, *not* gambling. Whereas speculation is the assumption of an already existing risk for the purpose of profit, gambling is the creation of risk for the purpose of profit.

COMMODITY TRADING

Transactions in commodities today take place in one of several forms. They are traded:

1. for *cash*,
2. for *forward delivery*,
3. as *futures contracts*, and
4. in the form of *options*.

Each of these markets is separate and distinct, but closely related, with a definite and useful purpose. Let us briefly describe the first three forms, as a background to the fourth, which the rest of the book treats.

Cash Market

In some industries referred to as the "spot" or "actuals" market, the *cash market* is the market in which the physical commodity is bought or sold for immediate delivery. Traditionally, commercial entities use this market to make and take delivery of the physical commodity for immediate use, such as physical gold to fabricate jewelry. The agreement entered into by the participants in this market is unique to them and usually results in an actual delivery. The agreement can be cancelled only by mutual agreement of the parties involved.

Forward Delivery Market

In the *forward delivery market*, the commodity is bought and sold for delivery at some specific time in the future, in much the same manner as exchange-traded futures contracts. The major difference is that the contract is custom-tailored to the specific needs of the participants in the transaction. The contract may call for the delivery of a commodity that is or is not exchange-traded. The delivery may be at an unusual location, or it may call for an uncommon quantity or grade. Perhaps payment is to be made in a foreign currency. As a result, this contract is unique to the participants and can be cancelled only by mutual consent. A large portion of the commodity transactions that result in actual delivery are done via the forward delivery contract.

Futures Contracts Markets

The *futures markets* are distinguished from both the cash and forward markets in several ways. The futures markets are markets for *contracts* that call for delivery, whereas the cash markets are markets for the delivery of an actual commodity. The futures markets differ from the forward markets in that an exchange sets the terms of a futures contract. These future contract terms are standardized, and the contracts may be freely traded. In contrast, the terms of forward contracts are unique and may be terminated or changed only by mutual agreement of the parties involved.

Going Long or Short. The buyer of a futures contract is said to be going long. That is, the buyer agrees to take delivery of the specified commodity at some time in the future. The seller of a futures contract is said to be going short, that is, agreeing to make delivery of the specified commodity at some future time.

As you can see, the transaction itself between the buyer and the seller of the futures contract creates the contract. By definition, for everyone who buys, someone must sell. In securities, one party usually purchases shares (stock) from someone who owns them. In commodities, one may purchase the contract from someone who currently owns a contract. This is a *long* liquidating transaction. The buyer may also purchase from someone who is creating a new contract, such as a farmer who is *going short*. In commodities, unlike securities, there must be a short for every long.

Fulfilling Contracts. Futures contracts may be fulfilled by one of two methods:

1. by the making or taking of delivery of the physical commodity, or
2. the offsetting (liquidating) of the futures contract prior to the delivery period.

Example: Mr. Smith, a speculator, has purchased a contract of March corn, thereby obligated himself to take delivery of 5,000 bushels of corn during the month of March. He need not, however, fulfill this contractual obligation. At any time prior to the actual delivery, which would take place in March, Smith may sell a contract of March corn and thereby *offset* his position. Since Smith is long, this sale may be to one of two buyers: (1) to an individual who is currently short and wishes to offset a short or (2) to another investor who wishes to be long. Despite the fact that the contract calls for the delivery of the actual commodity, only about 2 to 5% of all futures contracts result in actual delivery. The old tales about winding up with a backyard full of wheat may be great material for cocktail party conversations, but they bear little relationship to reality.

The offsetting transaction does not negate any profit or loss; it merely terminates the delivery obligation. Assume that corn, for delivery in the month of March, is selling at $2.50/bushel at the time Smith purchases the contract. Further assume that corn is selling at $3.50/bushel at the time the contract is liquidated. On a contract of 5,000 bushels, Smith would realize a $1.00/bushel profit or a total profit of $5,000.

THE EXCHANGES AND THEIR FUTURES CONTRACT RULES

The Exchanges

The exchanges on which futures contracts are traded are referred to as "designated contract markets." These exchanges are subject to the supervision and regulation of the Commodity Futures Trading Commission (CFTC). The CFTC also bears the responsibility for the supervision of commodity option trading both on and off exchanges. For exchange-traded commodity options, the designated exchanges play a larger role in the supervision of sales and trading practices than they do in the futures markets.

The Rules

A futures contract has standardized terms that call for the delivery of a commodity in a way that is subject to the rules of an exchange. Understanding these rules is important because many commodity option transactions are done in conjunction with futures, and the exercise of a futures contract option results in the creation of a position in the commodity futures markets. Let's look at some of these rules:

The Trading Months. The exchanges and their members designate some months as delivery months, and these months then become exchange-traded contract months. This designation is based, in agricultural commodities, on the normal planting, harvesting, and marketing months of the commodity involved, for the locale served. In agricultural commodities, it is unusual for a contract more distant than 18 months to be traded. In industrial and financial commodities, the months traded are normally based on industry-related criteria. In nonagricultural commodities, futures contracts are in some cases traded as far forward as 36 months, reflecting the hedging needs of the users. With the advent of "index" futures (commodity future contracts on stock indexes), the concept of very long-term maturities is even more justified because the underlying securities exist perpetually.

> *Example:* A given commodity might have such trading months as January, April, July, and October. If the commodity trades up to 36 months forward, the months are duplicated in the following years. January, for instance, of the most nearby year is referred to as "Jan." January of the following year, would be referred to as "Red Jan" or "Pink Jan," and January of the succeeding year would be referred to as "Green Jan."

The Quantity. The exchange and its members determines the actual size of the contract. The quantities normally traded are those that are common for industrial usage in the corresponding industry. As an example, the grain contracts traded on the Chicago Board of Trade (CBOT) are traded in 5,000 bushel quantities, while silver traded on the Commodity Exchange Incorporated (COMEX) is traded in 1,000 and 5,000 troy ounce units. These are the standard sizes in their respective industries. The exchange may change these quantities from time to time as industry standards and market conditions dictate.

Exchange-traded commodity option contracts are the same size as the futures contract to allow their exercise to result in the creation or liquidation of a standard futures contract.

The Grade. The grade that is normally deliverable against the futures contract is the grade that is most common to the industry in the part of the country that the exchange services. For instance, gold, as traded on COMEX, must be at least 99.5 fine; that is, 995 out of each 1,000 troy ounces must be pure gold. This grade reflects the normal fineness from which a jeweler would begin the alloying process.

Exercise. With exchange-traded commodity futures options, the delivery period may be any time the option is outstanding. This is acceptable, because the item deliverable is the futures contract itself. Normally the option expires prior to the first notice day on the underlying futures contract. This phenomenon minimizes market congestion and allows for the liquidation of the underlying futures contract without having to resort to making or taking delivery of the physical commodity.

The Delivery Period. Ultimately, if the futures contract is not liquidated prior to the delivery period, a commodity futures contract results in the delivery of the physical commodity. The exchange determines, the period during which the short may make delivery. The period for delivery varies from exchange to exchange, but it is normally defined as the period starting from *first notice day* (a day set by the exchange) and ending with last delivery day.

The Delivery Point. Again, the exchange determines this contract term, based on commonality of its use within the industry, as well as on the locale of the industry and the members served. In the case of the grains traded on the CBOT, delivery is called for in the Greater Chicago Area, while on COMEX delivery of copper may be in any approved warehouse in the United States.

The Delivery Terms. These terms normally parallel the practice of the relevant industry. For example, in the physical metal markets, metals are normally delivered and paid for two days after the transaction. In metal futures contracts, the procedure also calls for a two-day delivery and settlement in most cases.

Trading Hours. Each exchange determines its normal trading hours, although these can be changed from time to time. Under unusual circumstances, trading may be suspended for a finite period. Because any change could inhibit the liquidity that investors have grown to expect, exchanges do not treat trading hours lightly. Trading in commodity futures contracts may be done only "on the exchange," and as a result the investor is limited to instituting and liquidating positions during trading hours. There is no over-the-counter (OTC) market for futures contracts.

Price Quotations. Although the exchange takes no part in the determination of the price at which a commodity will trade, their responsibility is to disseminate both price and market data to the news media and to the various market data services. This data includes last sale, opening price, closing price, settlement price, open interest, and volume of trading, to name just a few. This data is most important to both the broker and the customer because it is the basis for many investment decisions and technical analysis. (See Chapter 3.) Price quotations in options are handled in the same fashion, and they are normally quoted in the same unit terms to allow the option investor to easily relate one contract to the other.

Carrying Charges. Though not an amount set by the exchanges, carrying charge costs are involved in the ownership of a commodity, and as such they constitute a fact of commodity trading. Under normal conditions, commodity contracts for more distant delivery trade at a higher price than the more nearby deliveries. This price difference normally approximates the cost of storing, financing, and insuring the commodity from the time the trade is consummated until the physical commodity is actually delivered. These are the costs that would have to be borne by an investor who owned the physical commodity, and they are thus reflected in the futures contract price.

Settlement Price. In many cases the settlement price is synonymous with the closing price. In some instances, however, a given contract either does not trade at all or does not trade close enough to the end of the day for its price to fairly reflect its market value. In such cases, the exchange, through either a computer model program or a settlement price committee, determines the fair settlement price for the contracts involved. This method assures investors that the market prices of the various months fairly reflect carrying charges and that margin requirements will be based on the fair market value of the contracts. Options are also given a settlement price for margin purposes. In some cases an econometric model (see Chapter 20) is used to determine the settlement price for months not traded or for months whose last price did not take place at about the close of trading.

Price Fluctuations. The exchanges establish both minimum price fluctuations and maximum price fluctuations, the latter of which are referred to as daily trading limits.

The *minimum price fluctuation* is the smallest amount by which the price of a given commodity may change from trade to trade. In grains traded on the CBOT, the minimum fluctuation is 1/4¢/bushel and therefore $12.50 per contract (.0025 × 5,000 = $12.50). In gold futures traded on COMEX, the minimum fluctuation is 10¢/troy ounce, which is a contract equivalent of $10 (.10 × 100 = $10).

The maximum fluctuation, or *daily trading limit*, is the maximum amount the price of the futures contract may increase or decrease, during the current trading session, above or below the closing (or settlement) price of the prior day. The intent of this type of rule is to allow the individual investor some time to digest and evaluate the impact of major market news without the price of the commodity futures contract changing dramatically. The intent of the rule is admirable, and it is successful in most cases. Yet there is no such limit in the cash market where prices may fluctuate wildly in response to the same news. The negative result of this disparity between futures and cash markets is that the futures may be "up the limit" due to a major upward move in the cash market. If the investor is short futures and wishes to liquidate the position, maybe no one is willing to sell futures at the limit price, thereby forcing the investor to remain short in the market. It is not at all uncommon for a market to be limit up or limit down several days in a row. This type of market condition can expose an investor to losses substantially larger than the initial commitment or than the amount that the investor had intended to risk on the transaction.

In most cases, the exchanges also have a *daily trading range*, or the maximum amount by which the futures contract can move both up *and* down during one trading session. Although the daily trading range is normally twice the daily limit, the daily limit and the daily range are the same amount on some exchanges.

> *Example:* The daily limit on sugar futures is 1¢, and the daily range is 2¢. If sugar futures closed last night at 12¢, then today it could trade as high as 13¢ and as low as 11¢. If, however, both the daily limit and the daily range are 1¢, and if sugar begins by trading up to 13¢, it could not trade below 12¢ for the balance of the trading day.

The phrases "daily trading limit" and "daily trading range" do not apply to all option contracts. Some of the exchanges have imposed daily trading limits on their options, and some have not. (In Chapter 6, exchange-traded commodity option contract specifications are discussed in detail.)

Commissions. Although commissions are not set by the exchanges, they are of importance to any trading program. In most cases, commissions are omitted throughout the book since they add nothing to the clarity of the examples and in some cases might confuse them. They are, however, significant and must be considered because, in many cases, the commission is the difference between a profitable and unprofitable trade. In some instances, commissions are included when they play an important part in a computation.

Commissions vary from one brokerage house to another. In most cases you get what you pay for. You might decide to make all your own trading decisions, to subscribe to all your own research reports, and to look to the broker only for executing your orders and carrying your account. If so, you are not asking for much service and should not pay much commission. If you want more than order execution service, you have to pay for it, and you do so in the form of commission.

Margin. To the investor with experience in trading stocks and bonds, margin is nothing new. If you purchase securities, at some time or another you have to decide if your transactions will be cash transactions or margin transactions. In the securities business, when investors purchase on margin, the brokerage firm is lending them the money that represents the difference between the amount they invest and the total purchase price of the securities involved in the transaction. The brokerage firm, in exchange for lending customers this money, is paid interest on the borrowed funds, and the amount of the loan is reflected in the customer's account as a debit balance. Although the brokerage firm does not normally do so, it may require the customer to repay the loan at any time.

Customers use margin for several reasons, including being able to purchase more securities or more expensive securities with a given amount of capital than they could on a cash basis. Of course, the customer has the right to repay the loan at any time and need not use margin in the first place.

MARGIN IN COMMODITIES

In commodities, the term "margin" has an entirely different meaning. Because a commodity futures contract is nothing more than a promise to perform, the dollars deposited by the customer do not really buy anything; they are, in effect, "good faith" or earnest money. The funds deposited assure the contra party in the transaction that the other party will perform as the contract provides at the time of the actual delivery. By definition of the commodity contract itself, neither party, at the time the contract is entered, is aware of the potential profits or losses that might accrue. Therefore, neither party could or would be willing to put up the total dollars reflected by the transaction. By their very nature, then, commodity transactions *must* be margin transactions, and they must be done in a margin account. The exchanges are responsible for establishing the margin requirements which the participants must meet. Margin is therefore the money deposited by the participants to the transaction to assure that, when called upon to perform, they will do so.

The Clearing Corporation

The clearing corporation is in most cases a separate legal entity from the exchange that is responsible for the margining, bookkeeping, and recordkeeping of all the transactions done on a particular exchange.

At the end of each trading day, all the brokerage firms submit to the clearing corporation a summary of all the trades that they have done for their customers. That evening, the clearing corporation takes the data supplied by all its members and verifies it by a process called *matching*. This process assures that for every long there is a corresponding short, and that the specific trade information (price, maturity, etc.) is identical for both parties to the transaction. After this matching process has taken place, and any discrepancies have been resolved, the trades are considered *cleared*.

Once the trade has been cleared, the clearing corporation interposes itself between all longs and all shorts. That is, from that point forward both the long and the short look to the clearing corporation as the entity from whom they demand performance of the commodity futures contract. The clearing corporation does, in fact, become the issuer and guarantor of all cleared contracts. The margin that customers deposit with their brokerage firms and that the brokerage firms deposit with the clearing corporation provides the clearing corporation with the resources to assume this responsibility.

In exchange-traded commodity options, the same clearing corporation that is responsible for the clearance of the futures contracts for a given exchange assumes the responsibility for the clearance of the options. It also handles the exercise notices and the futures contracts created thereby.

Types of Margin

When we speak of margin in relation to commodities, we are speaking of several different types of margin. Original margin, maintenance margin, hedge margin, speculator margin, exchange minimum margin, and house margin are just a few.

Original Margin. This type of margin is deposited with the brokerage firm by both parties to the transaction, at the time they institute their position. Both the long and the short parties deposit original margin. Depending on the exchange involved, this margin may be deposited (posted) as cash or as acceptable United States government securities. If the exchange's rules permit doing so, using government securities is usually advisable, because the investor earns interest on the original margin deposit.

Exchange Minimum Margin. The exchanges establish the minimum amount that must be deposited by any investor who deals in commodity futures on a given exchange. This amount of money is referred to as *exchange minimum margin*. The exchange further divides this type of margin into minimum speculator margin and minimum hedge margin.

Minimum hedge margin is normally set at a lower dollar amount or eliminated entirely, because the hedger is assumed to have a position in the physicals market. This hedge position, to a greater or lesser degree, offsets any profits or losses that the hedger may realize in futures. Since on most days the price of a given commodity fluctuates, both the long and the short have unrealized profits or losses on their futures positions.

Variation Margin. In securities, for a profit to be realized, the position must be liquidated because one owns the actual security; the profit is realized only when one succeeds in physically selling it to another person. In commodities, if the price of the contract increases, the long has an actual profit and the short has an actual loss. The reason for this lies in the fact that neither party to the commodity futures contract has yet bought or sold anything but the contract. The margin that they have deposited is only earnest money. In that the price of the commodity has risen, the long is more likely to perform, because, at delivery, he or she has an unrealized profit. The short is less likely to perform because he or she has an unrealized loss.

To assure that the short will perform at delivery, the clearing corporation asks that the short deposit an amount or money equal to this unrealized loss. The clearing corporation is aware that the unrealized loss of the short is an unrealized profit to the long and that the long is likely to perform. In an advancing market, the clearing corporation finds itself holding too much earnest money from the long, and it refunds to the long an amount equal to that deposited by the short. In a declining market, money is refunded to the short.

This passing of money through the clearing corporation from the long to the short and vice versa is referred to as *variation margin*. Each night, as part of the clearing function, the clearing corporation reevaluates each long and each short position. Prior to the market's opening on the following day, the clearing corporation either pays to, or receives from, its members the appropriate variation margin.

The daily flow of funds between participants who have sustained profits or losses is referred to as *variation margin*. It is imperative that this variation margin flow on a timely basis to allow the participants with profits to realize those profits. It follows, then, that market participants who are losing money must also deposit those funds on a timely basis. Because the clearing corporation is obligated to remit profits to the brokerage firms involved in profitable transactions, it must demand variation margins from brokerage firms involved in losses. The brokerage firm, of course, has the same relationship with its clients. The time frame within which this variation margin must be deposited varies from exchange to exchange, but in all cases it is timely.

Normally the customer deposits variation margin in one to two days. If the customer does not deposit the variation margin when required, the broker, after notifying the customer, will liquidate the position. When the liquidation is of a "long," it is referred to as a *sell-out*; in the event of a "short," it is referred to as a *buy-in*. If the sell-out or buy-in results in a loss greater than the amount the customer has on deposit with the brokers, the customer must still pay this *debit*. Brokerage firms will not continue to deal with customers who do not meet their margin calls on a timely basis.

COMMODITY OPTION MARGIN

Commodity option margin falls into a grey area between security margin and commodity margin. In some cases, the monies deposited are original margin in the commodity sense, but in other instances, the brokerage firm is actually lending the customer money in the securities sense. When the customer is actually borrowing money, a debit is created and the customer must pay the broker interest. (See Chapter 8.)

House margin is the amount of money that individual brokerage firms charge their customers for each commodity futures position that that customer has outstanding. The dollar amount of house margin on a given contract will usually be higher and, in many cases, substantially higher than exchange minimum margin for that contract. This variation can occur even from account to account within the same brokerage firm.

The reason for the variation has to do with the clearing operation. On the morning following any unfavorable price movement, the brokerage firm is required to deposit variation margin with the clearing corporation prior to the opening of business on the exchange. It is virtually impossible for the brokerage firm to inform their client of the amount of the needed variation margin and then to collect it within such a short time. The surplus funds in the customer's account, as represented by the difference between the exchange minimum margin and the house minimum margin, supplies the necessary funds to the brokerage firm for depositing with the clearing corporation. In setting house minimums for an individual account, the brokerage firm therefore looks at the diversity of positions within the individual account. An account with many different positions, both long and short, normally qualifies for lower minimum margin, because it is unlikely that all the positions would move against an individual at the same time. So the profit on one position would be available to offset the loss on another. The brokerage firm also considers unusual concentrations in a given account. If an individual's account has large positions in a specific commodity, the magnitude of potential loss is higher in the event of an adverse market move. As a result, the brokerage firm would likely charge a higher house margin on that position.

The primary point is that the level of margin set by the exchanges, by the clearing corporation, and by brokerage firms is a function of the risks involved. In turn, the risks involved are not only a function of the price change of the commodity, but also of how rapidly the individuals are capable of depositing the variation margin involved. Obviously, the margin levels required by the exchange and the clearing corporation of the brokerage firm may be, by reason of their close proximity, lower than the levels required by the brokerage firms of their customers.

Day Trades

The transactions discussed thus far are ultimately cleared by the clearing corporation, and they remain outstanding for some period of time. The nature of commodity trading, however, gives rise to instances where the customer both institutes and liquidates a position on the same day. This type of transaction is referred to as a *day trade*. The customer receives any profit from the transaction or deposits any loss sustained.

Since this type of transaction results in no position remaining at the end of the day, however, the customer, from the clearing corporation's point of view, need not post any original margin. Because no position is outstanding at the end of the day, the clearing corporation is never directly involved in this type of transaction as principal and does not require margin. The brokerage firm, however, requires margin from the customer, apart from the profit and loss, as a good faith deposit. The required level of this margin is usually substantially lower than for positions held overnight.

Commodity Spreads

Like the day trade, the spread transaction also qualifies for a reduced level of margin. A basic understanding of this type of trade is important because spreading is a very common type of commodity transaction. Spreads normally fall into three categories:

1. *interdelivery*,
2. *intercommodity*, or
3. *commodity/product*.

Interdelivery (Intracommodity) Spread. In this type of spread, an investor goes long in one month and short in a different month for the same commodity on the same exchange. This type of transaction normally qualifies for some type of reduced original margin.

Example: Jones goes long March wheat and short December wheat on the CBOT. Because the prices of March wheat and December wheat are related, it is not likely that the price of one would go up dramatically while the other went down.

Intercommodity Spread. This type of spread involves going long in one commodity while going short in a different but related commodity. This transaction too has a smaller risk than either side individually, and it therefore normally qualifies for spread margins.

Example: The purchase of February gold is coupled to the sale of March silver on COMEX.

Commodity/Product Spread. In this type of spread, the trader couples a long or short position in a raw material with a contra position in a related byproduct. Because the prices of raw materials and their byproducts must be related, they also qualify for spread margin.

Example: The purchase of soybeans is coupled by the sale of both soybean oil and soybean meal on the CBOT.

Although similar to futures spreads, commodity option spreads are normally done for totally different reasons. Because spreads account for a very large portion of the total commodity option volume, Chapter 16 has been devoted to this topic.

CUSTOMERS' FUNDS

Cash and securities on deposit in a customer's commodity account are handled slightly differently than they are for similar transactions in stocks and bonds. The Commodity Futures Trading Commission regulations require the *segregation* of all cash and securities on deposit with a futures commission merchant (FCM) (broker) to secure commodity transactions. That is, the brokerage firm must maintain separate accounts for commodity transactions and securities transactions. Further, the customer must authorize, in writing, the removal of any funds from a segregated commodity account. In other words, to have surplus funds in a commodity account paid out or even transferred to a securities account, a customer must give the broker written instructions. This requirement is not as cumbersome as it appears. Most brokerage firms provide a "blanket" authority for this type of payout or transfer in their customer agreements. The same protection afforded customers on futures funds also applies to deposits made as margin in commodity options. The brokerage firm holds the funds deposited for both futures and commodity options transactions in the same segregated account. Funds deposited for futures and options are commingled with each other, but in no case are they commingled with the funds of the brokerage firm itself. Each customer's funds are accounted for separately.

TYPES OF ORDERS

Of the numerous types of commodity orders, some have parallels in security transactions. Some of the more common orders are: market, limit, stop, spread, scale, all-or-none, immediate-or-cancel, fill-or-kill, market-if-touched, and contingent. Not all of these orders are usable on all exchanges, and neither are they all usable for commodity option transactions. One or more exchanges, however, accept some or all of these types of orders.

Market Order. A market order tells the broker to execute a buy or sell order immediately at the best price then available.

Limit Order. A limit order tells the broker to execute an order only, if in the case of a buy, at or below your stated price, or conversely, in the case of a sell, at or above your stated price.

Stop Order. Stop orders are one of two types: stop-buy or stop-sell. Many customers refer to stop orders as stop-loss orders because they are, in many cases, used to limit a loss. This view is an oversimplification of the stop order and minimizes the order's true flexibility.

1. A *stop-sell order* is placed below the current market price and tells the broker to sell the commodity if the commodity trades at, or is offered at or below, the stop price. The order is normally placed to protect a previously established long position; however, it can also be used to institute a short position.
2. A *stop-buy order* is placed above the current market price and instructs the broker to buy the commodity if it trades at or is bid at or above the stop price. This order is normally used to protect a short position, but it may also be used to institute a long position.

In securities, for a stop order to be executed, there must be a trade at a price that "triggers" the stop order. In commodities, a stop is triggered if there is a trade or, on some exchanges, an appropriate bid or offer. As a result, in commodities, the broker may be unable to execute your order due to limit moves. Suppose you have a long position in a given commodity and have entered a stop-sell (sometimes called sell-stop) to protect that position. Further assume that the market price of the commodity opens offered "down the limit." Even though your stop has been triggered, your broker may be unable to find any buyers willing to buy your long position at a price equal to down the limit. This situation could result in no execution that day and perhaps for several days, with substantially larger losses than you had envisioned.

Spread Order. Like market, limit, and stop orders, spread orders are as common in option transactions as they are in futures, but the spread order has totally different meanings in futures and options. This discussion of the spread order is from the futures point of view. The option application is discussed in Chapter 16.

Spread orders are orders that result in two executions, such as the purchase of one month's wheat and the simultaneous sale of another month's wheat. In this type of order, the customer is not normally concerned with the actual execution price of either the buy or the sell, but rather with the relationship between the two prices.

Example: A spread order might say, "Spread-buy 1 March wheat; Sell 1 December wheat, March 50¢ under." This order tells the broker to buy March wheat and sell December wheat if March wheat can be bought at a minimum of a 50¢ discount to December wheat.

Scale Order. A scale order is used either to institute or to liquidate a multiple contract position.

Example: This order might read: "Buy 1 May pork bellies, market, 1¢ scale down, total 5." This tells the broker to buy one contract of May pork bellies at the market, and for each 1¢ drop in price to buy additional contracts until a total position of five contracts is accumulated. If the market goes up instead of down, one would buy only the first contract.

All-or-None. An all-or-none order directs the broker, on multiple contract orders, to execute all of the contracts or none at all.

Example: The order might say: "Sell 10 January platinum $525, all-or-none." Your order would be executed only if all ten could be sold at a price of $525 or better.

Immediate-or-Cancel. An immediate-or-cancel order tells the broker to fill any portion of a multiple contract immediately and cancel the unfilled balance.

Fill-or-kill. A fill-or-kill order tells the broker to fill the entire order immediately or cancel it. A fill-or-kill order is a combination of an immediate-or-cancel and an all-or-none.

Market-if-Touched. A market-if-touched order is a stop order placed on the wrong side of the market price. Stop-sells always go below the current market, and stop-buys go above the current market. Conversely, a market-if-touched buy goes below the market, and market-if-touched sell goes above the current market.

> *Example:* A market-if-touched order might read: "Buy 1 March wheat $3.87, market-if-touched." This tells the broker that if March wheat trades down to $3.87 or is offered at $3.87, buy at the market because it has been touched.

Contingent. Contingent orders are executed due to the occurrence of an event.

> *Example:* An order might read: "Buy 1 February gold, market, contingent January platinum $525." This tells the broker to buy 1 contract of February gold at the market if January platinum is trading at $525 or lower.

Not all exchanges accept or allow all these orders, nor do all brokerage firms accept them even if the exchanges do. To be assured of the best execution in a given situation, being familiar with the orders that are available in the commodities being traded is important. In an effort to be of service to their clients, brokers in many cases accept some or all of these complex order instructions, but they do so only on a *not-held* basis. In other words, the brokers use their best efforts to fill your order, but they do not want to be held responsible if they are unable to do so.

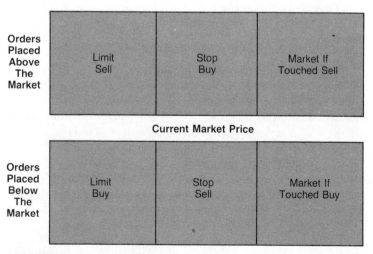

Orders Placed Above The Market	Limit Sell	Stop Buy	Market If Touched Sell
Current Market Price			
Orders Placed Below The Market	Limit Buy	Stop Sell	Market If Touched Buy

FIGURE–1. Order Placement.

WHY COMMODITIES?

All forms of investing exist because they serve an economic purpose. The public investor ultimately determines if a given investment vehicle will be successful or not. The equity and debt markets exist because corporations, as well as municipalities and the federal government, must look to the public as their source of capital. The public demands a liquid aftermarket in which to trade those securities. The security exchanges exist to provide this market place.

The purpose of the commodity futures markets is similar. With these markets, commercial entities that are involved in the commodity industry can transfer risks that they are unwilling or unable to assume to investors who are willing and able to assume these risks, in exchange for the profits that may accrue. This philosophy is little different from that of investors who purchase common stock and hope to profit from the earnings of the corporation of which they become part owners.

The commodity markets have grown and flourished over the past years as a result of the growth both of the economy in general and of the role that these markets themselves fulfill. The lure of commodity trading encourages many investors to become involved before they investigate the risks that go with the potential rewards. Investors encounter problems when they falsely assume that their many years of experience in trading equities and debt securities qualify them to trade commodities. The similarities are very deceiving: yes, commodities trade on regulated exchanges; yes, they are regulated by a government agency; yes, they are, in most cases, handled by the same brokerage firm and possibly even by the same broker. But that is where the similarities end. Unfortunately, most investors who venture into the commodity markets know little more about commodities than what is contained in this chapter.

In any business venture, investors must be comfortable, as well as knowledgeable, before becoming involved. The balance of this book is designed as an introduction to the commodity and the commodity options markets. If you have not previously dealt in commodities, further reading would be prudent. For that reason, a bibliography has been provided in "References."

2

SECURITY OPTIONS—
AN OVERVIEW

The review of option concepts in this chapter is based on the assumption that at some point you have either traded security options or gained a fairly complete understanding based on reading. If, after reading this chapter, you are not comfortable with all the terms and concepts, refer to the bibliography at the end of the book for suggested additional reading.

THE CHICAGO BOARD OPTIONS EXCHANGE

In the late 1960s, commodity trading did not represent as large a percentage of the total investment spectrum as it does today. Of the several reasons for this lower interest, the most important was the limited selection of commodities that traded in comparison to the multitude now available. At that time, we were not yet trading financial instruments, currencies, or precious metals. Most commodity trading was centered in agricultural commodities. The commodity futures business, because of its limited scope, was somewhat cyclical.

The Chicago Board of Trade commissioned a management consulting firm to study and recommend what additional commodities the Board of Trade might add to its then current list that would behave counter cyclically in volume. The result of the study, surprisingly, was that the Board of Trade should develop a market for security options. On the surface, this recommendation might not appear very logical, until you assess the similarities between options and commodity futures contracts.

Interestingly, the creation of an options market on securities offered the securities investor a means of dealing in securities on a high-leverage basis. In the past, the use of margin allowed the investor only 2:1 leverage, at best. With options traditionally costing only 10% to 15% of the value of the underlying securities, the leverage became 7:1 to 10:1.

In 1969 the Chicago Board of Trade made the decision to proceed with the concept of listed security option trading, forming a wholly owned subsidiary called the Chicago Board Options Exchange. Even though the Chicago Board Options Exchange was a subsidiary of the Chicago Board of Trade, the new "commodity" in which they were to begin trading was legally a security. The Chicago Board of Trade felt that they should be able to commence trading rapidly, but the Securities and Exchange Commission felt otherwise. Trading did not commence until April 26, 1973. Although initially only call options were traded, today put options are traded on all of the securities. Many felt that trading in listed options, a new concept, would be totally unsuccessful. Time showed that listed option trading filled a void in the investment spectrum.

RIGHTS AND OBLIGATIONS

To intelligently discuss security option trading and later commodity option trading, we must begin with the question, What is an option? An *option* is the right but *not the obligation* to buy or sell a given item at a specific price at some future time. A *call* option is an option that gives its owner the right to buy, while a *put* option is an option that gives its owner the right to sell. The word "option" is difficult in itself because it doesn't say anything. Many countries that deal in options refer to them as *privileges*, a term that is perhaps easier to understand than the word "option." Individually the most important single attribute of an option is the fact that, to its owner, it is a right and not an obligation. An option is a contract between two people, wherein one of the participants, the buyer, has rights and no obligations, and the other participant has obligations and no rights. This type of contract is referred to as a unilateral contract. Most contracts are bilateral, wherein both parties have rights and obligations.

Even if you have not traded options, you are more familiar with options than you realize. Let us assume that a corporation is considering relocating its headquarters and must decide which of several office buildings it will buy. This is not a simple decision, as many items must be considered. Perhaps the moving costs to each location are different; perhaps the degree of modification to the facilities is different; perhaps the commutation time for employees is different. These factors require a substantial amount of study before a final decision can be made. One of the problems that the corporation will encounter is that, while the decision is being made, one or more of the facilities may be sold or leased, invalidating all of the study. The solution is rather simple. The corporation pays each of the property owners a fee for the right, but not the obligation, to purchase the building at a fixed price within a fixed period of time. This privilege, which the corporation is purchasing, is called an option. The only difference between this option and a security option is what will be delivered in the event of exercise.

OTC OPTIONS

Prior to the existence of the Chicago Board Option Exchange (CBOE), all security options transactions were done in the over-the-counter (OTC) market. If you wished to purchase an option, your broker had to find someone who was willing to sell the option. You, who wished to purchase, were referred to as the *buyer* or *taker*, while the person who sold the option to you was referred to as the *grantor, writer, seller,* or *maker*. If you, for instance, wanted to purchase a call on American Telephone and Telegraph, you would ask your broker, and it was your broker's job to find the seller. Through the facilities of the Put and Call Broker's Association, your broker would find someone willing to grant the option. The actual terms of the option would be negotiated between the buyer and the seller.

Options were normally traded at-the-market. That is, the striking price of the option (the price at which the owner of the call may take delivery of the underlying security) was the same as the market price of the underlying security at the time the transaction was consummated. The normal duration for options was either 30 days, 60 days, 90 days, or 6 months and 10 days. Usually, though not necessarily, the option was on 100 shares.

> *Example:* Suppose the broker finds someone willing to sell an AT&T call. Ultimately, you might purchase a 6-month-and-10-day call on American Telephone and Telegraph with a striking price of 52¼ per share. This option would give you the right but not the obligation to take delivery of 100 shares of AT&T at $52.25 per share within the next 6 months and 10 days. You paid the grantor of this option a premium of, say, $500. (The logic of a specific premium is discussed in Chapter 4.)

In OTC option trading, you, the buyer, were tied directly to the seller and could exercise or abandon only that option. Logically, you would exercise the option if it were profitable or allow it to expire if it were worthless. You could not resell or transfer the option in the normal course of events. In specific cases, a Put and Call Broker might be willing to attempt to resell your option to a third party, but doing so was the exception rather than the rule. Occasionally these types of special offerings were made in the newspapers and were referred to as *specials*. The Put and Call Broker charged a fee for this service. As you can see, each option was unique to its participants and, for all practical purposes, illiquid.

LISTED OPTIONS: STANDARDIZATION

The genesis of the CBOE brought standardization. On the surface, standardization does not appear important, but singularly it made exchange traded options possible. The concept of standardization has also been carried into the area of commodity options for the same reason as will now be discussed for security options. Any security option has five items that could be subjected to standardization: the security itself, the striking price, the type of option (put or call), the expiration date, and quantity. If these contract terms could be standardized, then the option could take on a life of its own and become *fungible*, or freely transferable. The listed options exchanges have standardized these contract terms.

Security Itself

Part of the standardization process is the concentration of options trading on a limited list of actively traded and popular underlying securities. Although literally thousands of securities are traded, the list of actively traded and widely held securities is much more limited. This concentration of trading activity on a more limited list of securities adds to liquidity.

As a result, listed options were initially available on only 16 securities, but, as the exchanges and number of participants in the market grew, the list expanded to several hundred.

Striking Price

Striking prices are set in logical increments. For securities that sell for less than $50 per share, $2.50 increments are normal. For securities above $50 per share but below $100 per share, $5 increments are used. For securities between $100 per share and $200 per share, $10 increments are used. Finally, for securities selling above $200 per share, the normal increment is $20. For a security currently selling for $72 per share, it would be likely to have $60, $65, $70, $75, and perhaps $80-per-share striking prices.

Adding Striking Prices. New striking prices can be added as the price of the underlying security changes. In practice, the exchanges normally add a new striking price if the security trades at the highest or lowest striking price then traded.

Example: Company X is trading at $40/share; you might have $35/
share and $40/share as striking prices currently trading. If "X" began
trading at $40/share there would be a need for higher striking prices.
The exchange would normally list a $45/share striking price at such
time as "X" traded at $40 per share.

The number of striking prices that can be trading is limited only by the
magnitude of price change to which the security is subject while a given
maturity is outstanding. In some cases, more than 15 striking prices of a
given maturity were trading at one time.

Expiration Dates

Expiration dates are set at quarterly intervals with each security trading in one of three cycles. The first group of options listed had a trading cycle
of January, April, July, and October. As more options were listed, a second
cycle was established with February, May, August, and November expirations. Eventually a third cycle with March, June, September, and December expirations was established. Each security has four expirations, each
three months apart; however, only three expirations are trading at any one
time.

Example: A security has a January, April, July, and October cycle. It is
February. At this time, April, July, and October expirations are trading. At such time as the April option expires, the exchange will list and
allow trading in the maturity for January of next year. When the next
maturity commences trading, it has an expiration of approximately nine
months.

All options with the same maturity expire and cease trading at the same
time. The last trading day is the third Friday of the expiration month, with
expiration officially the following day, but public customers must make their
determinations of whether or not to exercise by 5:30 P.M. on the last trading
day.

Quantity

Quantity had traditionally been 100 shares in OTC options, and a
round-lot of trading in securities was also 100 shares. So it was decided that
listed security options would also be for 100 shares.

TERMS

Each industry has its own jargon or specialized vocabulary, and the
option business is no exception. Let's look at some of the other terms with

which you will have to be familiar in order to feel comfortable with the product.

Class and Series

Two such terms are "class" and "series." A *class* of option is all the puts and call on the same underlying security. A *series* is all the options of a given class, puts and calls, with the same expiration date and the same striking price.

Opening and Closing Transactions

The terms "buy" and "sell" do not by themselves completely define the intent of a transaction. Security option transactions therefore have to be designated as either "opening" or "closing." A buy order may establish or add to a long position, or it may serve to close out or reduce a previously established short position. In either case, the buy order would be an *opening transaction.* Conversely, a sell order can create or add to a previously established short position, or it can liquidate or reduce a previously established long position. In either capacity, the sell order serves as a *closing transaction.*

Options exchanges require that all orders be designated as either "open" or "close." This information is equally important in both security and commodity options. In security options, however, all exchanges require the information be included at the time the order is transmitted to the trading floor. This requirement exists for the purpose of clearing the trade. In commodity options, all of the clearing corporations require the same information, but only some of them require that the information be on the order ticket.

As an additional requirement, orders involving option-writing transactions must be designated as covered or uncovered. This information, which is used in the option clearing process, in many cases minimizes possible errors.

The exchanges also require that each option order must designate if the transaction is being done for a public customer or for the brokerage firm's account. This requirement assures that the public has priority in execution of orders.

Example: If you, the public, were selling a covered option, the additional or "trailer information" on the order would read, "open (covered) customer." This information shows that the sell creates a new short (or written) option position, that the option position is covered, and that the transaction is being done for a member of the public.

Straddles

A *straddle* is a transaction in which you purchase or sell both a put and a call on the same security, with the same striking price and the same expiration date. Even though the put and the call transactions may be individually executed, the "package" is called a straddle. You are said to be a *straddle buyer* if you buy both the put and the call, and you are a *straddle grantor* if you sell both the put and the call. If you buy a straddle, you have the right to buy and sell the underlying security at the striking price until the expiration date. Either half may be liquidated or exercised independently with no effect on the remaining half.

A *combination option* or *combo*, is another "package" in which you purchase or grant both put and call options on the same security but with different striking prices. The terms "straddle" and "combo" are of great importance to the option grantor because the margin requirements (discussed later) take into consideration the risk involved in straddle or combo granting.

Spreads

Some investment strategies require the purchase of one option and the sale of another option. (We will cover these strategies in detail in the strategy section of this book.) In a *vertical spread*, you purchase a call option on a given security and simultaneously sell a call option on the same security with the same maturity but with a different striking price. If the striking price that you have purchased is lower than the striking price of the option granted, then the spread is also referred to as a *bull spread* because it is designed to be profitable in a rising market. If you purchased the option with the higher striking price and granted the option with the lower striking price, the transaction is referred to as a *bear spread* because it is designed to be profitable with declining prices. All these spreads use only call options.

Similar transactions can be done with put options. If your transaction involves the purchase of a put on a security and a sale of a different put on the same security and maturity, this too is a *vertical spread*. If the put option purchased has the higher striking price and the put option sold has the lower striking price, the transaction is said to be a *bear spread*. If the lower striking price is purchased and the higher striking price sold, the transaction is a *bull spread*.

Spreads are not limited to differences in striking prices. You can just as easily purchase an option on a given security for a future maturity and grant an option for a more nearby maturity. This type of transaction is referred to as a *horizontal* or *calendar spread*. While the majority of these types of spreads are done with identical striking prices on both the long and the short options, this is not mandatory or in all cases desirable.

Exercise and Assignment

To *exercise* an option is to take advantage of its privileges. If you exercise a call, you may demand delivery. In other words, you are buying the underlying security at the striking price of the option. If you exercise a put, you may make delivery. That is, you are selling the underlying security at the striking price. The concept of exercise is the same in commodity options as in security options, except that a commodity, as opposed to a security, underlies the option.

On the opposite side of the transaction is, of course, the grantor. *Assignment* is the notification to the grantor that an option is being exercised. When an option holder exercises, the grantor is assigned a notice of exercise and must perform according to the terms of the option. If a call is being exercised, the grantor must deliver the underlying security. If a put is being exercised, the grantor must receive and pay for the underlying securities.

A listed security option allows its owner to exercise the option at any time from the point of ownership until 5:30 P.M. on the last trading day. To exercise an option, you notify your broker any day during this period. Your broker notifies the Options Clearing Corporation, and the OCC determines which option grantor will be required to perform. The OCC allocates assignments by means of a weighted, random method.

> *Example:* Broker A has 100 customers who are short options of a given series, while Broker B is short only 1 option of the same series. If you are Broker A's customer, you have 100 times more of a probability of being assigned than Broker B's customer.

In reality, however, Broker A has 100 times the probability. Each brokerage firm, after receiving its assignment notices, must then assign those notices to its customers according to its own internal assignment procedures. These procedures must be "fair and nondiscriminatory," and they must be approved by the Option Clearing Corporation. Most brokerage firms use some form of random assignment. This procedure determines when your number comes up before expiration, or when you are likely to be assigned before expiration. At expiration, you should assume that, if you have granted an option and that option is in-the-money, you will be assigned.

On expiration day, the Option Clearing Corporation follows a procedure called *automatic exercise*. According to the Option Clearing Corporation's regulation, all options that, on expiration date, are 1/2 point or more in-the-money will be exercised for the account of the option holder. This procedure is based on the assumption that, if an option this far in-the-money is not exercised, it is an oversight. This regulation is an added protection to the option holder, who might forget to exercise an in-the-money option. If you are the holder of a sufficiently in-the-money option, it will be exercised on expiration date. If you don't want your option exercised, you must notify your broker not to exercise. If you forget and your broker does not have a protective procedure, you could wind up owning and having to pay for 100 shares of stock that you don't want. It is important that you and your broker have a clear understanding of what action should be taken under various market conditions. The same concept is valid in commodity options. Options that are in-the-money at expiration should also be exercised. Each of the exchanges has taken its own approach to automatic exercise. Some exchanges have automatic exercise, some do not. Check with your broker so that you don't have any unpleasant surprises.

Open Interest

The term *open interest* is used in options and it has approximately the same meaning as in commodities. In commodities, it is the number of futures contracts outstanding. In options, it is the number of options outstanding.

Position and Exercise Limits

Exchange-imposed *position limits* serve to eliminate market congestion and illiquidity. These rules preclude an investor, or a group of investors acting in consort, from being long or short more than 2,000 options on a given security on the same side of the market. So if you happen to be long 2,000 calls on a given security, you cannot be short even one put on that security, because long calls and short puts are both on the same side of the market. Long call is a contingent long position in the underlying security, and short put is also a contingent long position in the underlying security.

Exercise limits are designed to limit an investor or a group of investors from causing congestion in a security. These rules limit the number of options that an investor, or a group of investors acting in consort, can exercise in a limited period of time. Such rules minimize the effects of attempts to "corner" a market. In other words, you couldn't buy 2,000 options, exercise them, buy 1,000 options, exercise them, and so on.

In commodity options, because there is the same concern about market congestion, position limits are imposed. In addition, reporting requirements oblige investors to file reports with the exchanges upon reaching a certain position level. At certain times, filing reports on the number of options exercised during a given period is also necessary.

Parity

Usually, "parity" is used as a synonym for intrinsic value (the value that could be received if the option is exercised and the resulting position immediately liquidated). In other words, when an option is trading for a price that is equivalent to its intrinsic value, it is said to be trading at parity. This, however, is not a common occurrence. Parity is most commonly encountered when the option is deep enough in-the-money to command no time value, but not deep enough to trade at a discount to parity.

Let's spend a moment on this concept. Basically, an option has two basic purposes: either to obtain leverage or to minimize the risk of owning the underlying security. At-market options are generally thought to be the best balance of these two investment objectives. They offer a reasonable amount of leverage, and their cost is usually low enough to be substantially lower than the price of the underlying security. Options that offer the greatest investment utility also command the highest price above intrinsic value. Options that are deep in-the-money offer reduced leverage and a higher dollar risk; they therefore trade at a smaller premium to parity. Deep out-of-the-money options, although offering good leverage and limited downside risk, have a small probability of profit, and as such they do not command much "time value," which is the term discussed next.

Time Value

Time value is the amount you pay for an option above what you could receive were you to exercise it and immediately sell the underlying security. (See Chapter 4.) Time value has to do with how people behave in relation to the view they hold of the market, and it derives from the price they will pay for a given market projection. When the price of a security moves above the strike price of a call option, the option gains in intrinsic value as it becomes further and further in-the-money. Yet it loses time value due to the reduced leverage and risk protection. As the price of the security declines in relation to the striking price, the option becomes more out-of-the-money and loses investment utility.

Calls. The chart in Figure 2–1 depicts the price behavior of an option as the market price varies in relationship to the striking price. This chart depicts the price behavior of 3-month, 6-month, and 9-month call options on a hypothetical security. The striking price of the option is $50/share. Notice that a 45-degree line originates at the $50/share market price and increases as the price of the underlying security increases. This is the dollar-for-dollar increase in intrinsic value as the market price of the security exceeds the striking price. The curved line marked "3 month" is the actual price of the option. You can see that an option trades at the greatest premium to parity when the striking price of the option and the market price of the underlying security are the same. The reason is that, at this point, the option offers the greatest investment utility, that is, the best balance between leverage and downside risk protection. Notice that deep out-of-the-money options trade

FIGURE 2-1. $400 Gold Call—Price Curves

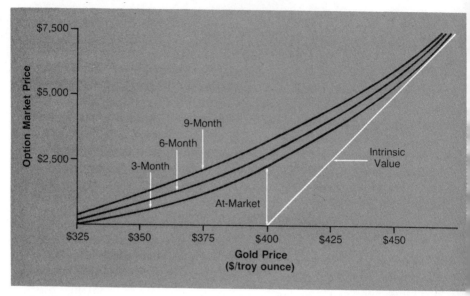

for almost no time value because investors consider them almost worthless. Deep in-the-money options, although expensive, command very little time value due to the low leverage and high dollar risk. Options of greater duration—the curves marked "6 month" and "9 month"—also follow the same pattern. Finally, deep in-the-money and deep out-of-the-money options, regardless of expiration, trade for very similar prices in terms of time value.

Puts. The chart in Figure 2–2 is nothing more than a mirror image of the call chart. A put's intrinsic value increases as the market price of the underlying security declines. As a result, the 45-degree line originating at the strike price of the put moves toward the left, reflecting the increase in intrinsic value as the market price of the underlying security declines. The curves that reflect the actual market price are reversed, because the market utility of the option declines with a decrease in market price, and the probability of profit decreases with an increase in market price. The psychology and logic of this phenomenon are discussed in greater length in Chapter 4.

There is no restriction on the trading of deep out-of-the-money options, but, by regulatory requirement, customers must be made aware of the risks involved in this type of transaction. Deep out-of-the-money options may appear inexpensive, but their usefulness is very limited. Think twice before becoming involved in deep out-of-the-money transactions as either a buyer or a grantor.

Delta

The rate at which the price of an option changes in relation to the price change of the underlying security is referred to as *delta*. Delta is a dynamic number, that is, it constantly changes. Delta varies not only from security to security but also as the option becomes more in or more out-of-the-money. If our hypothetical security has a delta of .5, we would expect that for each dollar of price increase in the underlying security, we would see a 50¢ increase in the market price of the option.

Price

The prices of options are quoted in a fashion similar to that of securities. Securities are quoted in dollars per share, and options are quoted in premium per share.

> *Example:* An option is offered for 3½, or $3.50 per share. Since most options are on 100 shares, an option offered at 3½ would cost $350.

Dividends

Cash Dividends. Many of the securities on which options trade pay dividends, and in some cases these dividends are substantial. Owners of

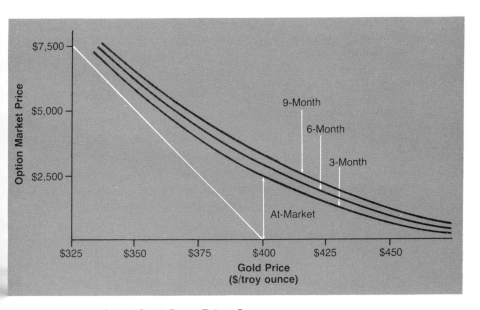

FIGURE 2–2. $400 Gold Put—Price Curves

options are not entitled to receive dividends unless they have exercised their options, thereby owning not the option but the underlying security itself.

This fact gives rise to a potential problem. Because deep in-the-money options trade at parity and in some cases at a discount to parity, the grantor of the option may be subject to premature exercise. This discount to parity allows an investor to purchase a deep in-the-money option at parity or perhaps at a discount, immediately exercise it, receive the dividend, sell out the underlying security, and still realize a profit. This type of transaction is not normally economically possible for the public customer. For professional arbitrageurs, however, who pay substantially reduced commissions, it is not only possible but a very common occurrence. If you are a call option grantor, expect to be exercised when the option you have granted is trading at parity or below as a result of market action and a dividend is about to be paid. This situation is neither good nor bad, but it is a fact of deep in-the-money call options when dividends are paid.

Although commodities do not pay dividends, their options may be subject to premature exercise when they get deep in-the-money. This occurrence is most likely when the commodity market involved is either bid or offered at the limit.

Stock Dividends or Stock Splits. These two types of dividends also have an economic effect on the option holder and the option grantor.

Example: Company X is currently trading at $50/share, and the company declares a 2-for-1 stock dividend. Outstanding options must be adjusted to reflect this occurrence. At the time the stock goes ex-dividend, the exchange splits the option. The original option gave its owner the right to purchase 100 shares at $50/share. This option now splits into two options, each of which gives its owner the right to purchase 100 shares at $25/share. The option split results in a position economically equivalent to that of the underlying security. Two options at $25/share are the equivalent of one option at $50/share.

If you are the option holder, you now have two options, each of which you can dispose of individually. You may sell, exercise, or abandon either option. The grantor is short two call options and has the contingent liability to deliver 200 shares of the new stock at $25/share.

All such dividends, however, do not always work out equally.

Example: Company X declares a 10% stock dividend. In this case, the outstanding options would have become options for 110 shares at $45.45/share. Actually the price is rounded to the nearest 1/8th or $45.375. This too represents an economic equivalency, but only one option remains, not two.

Each type of dividend is treated differently. All dividends must be considered whether they are stock dividends, stock splits, rights offering, warrants, and the like. The adjustment is based on the details of the dividend, with the decision made at the time of the announcement.

In many ways, security options are more like commodities than they are like securities. You will see that some of the exchange and clearing corporation rules and procedures appear more common to a commodity than to a security.

The Floor

Trading on the floor of an option/security exchange is a combination of security and commodity trading. Depending on the exchange, trading may take place at a "post," as in securities, or at a "pit/post," more like commodities.

In trading normal equity securities, orders are executed by means of the specialist system. The specialist system is also common in options, but it is not the only system. Certain employees on the CBOE, called *board brokers*, fulfill half of the specialist function. They are responsible for holding public customers' limit and stop orders and assuring that customers' orders have priority over proprietary orders in the execution process. The other half of the specialist function is fulfilled by *market-makers*. Market-makers are individuals who, on the floor, buy and sell for their own account to maintain an orderly market, as well as adding to depth and liquidity.

Trading Rotations

The fact that option trading has different maturities and different striking prices, which securities trading does not have, gives rise to *trading rotations*. When trading commences at the beginning of the day, all options do not commence trading simultaneously. The options of the shortest maturity and the lowest striking price are opened first. Only orders that can be executed immediately are filled, and that series is closed. The next higher series is then opened. This procedure is repeated until all the striking prices of a given maturity have traded. After the highest striking price of a given maturity has been traded, the next maturity is opened in the same manner. After all the series have been traded on the rotation, all series are reopened and trade simultaneously for the balance of the day. If trading is halted during the day, reopening the options by rotation is sometimes necessary. During rotational trading, spread orders cannot be executed, because a spread requires the simultaneous execution of both a buy and a sell in different series. Spreads will be dealt with in great depth in the strategy chapters.

MARGIN

Margin requirements for the customer are different from those for the brokerage firm. The reason for this difference is much the same as it is in commodities. Customers dealing in security options should be aware of the assorted positions that have margin consequences. Let's look at some of these positions.

Purchase of a Security Option

The purchase of a security option, whether a put or a call, requires the full cash payment of the premium. As a result, it is not a margin transaction. The margining of long option positions is precluded by the Federal Reserve as part of Regulation T, which controls the extension of credit on security transactions. For the same reason, the sale of a security versus a long call or the purchase of a security versus the ownership of a put does not qualify for any special margin treatment.

Sale of a Covered Option

The sale of covered options itself is not a margin transaction. For instance, if you sell a call option and you own 100 shares of an underlying security that is fully paid for, there is no margin consideration.

Sale of Naked Options

Margin first becomes a consideration with the sale of uncovered, or naked, options. This is the sale of a call without a position in the underlying security. You have agreed to deliver 100 shares of a given stock at the striking price at some point in the future, and you do not currently own the stock. The margin required in this position is very similar to the money deposited in a commodity futures transaction, that is, it is earnest money. You are putting up "good faith" money to assure both the brokerage firm and the clearing corporation that, when called upon to perform, you will do so. The margin actually required is 30% of the market value of the underlying security. This amount would be increased by any in-the-money value or reduced by any out-of-the-money value. The premium received for granting the option may be used to meet this margin requirement. Regardless of the computed figure, you must deposit a minimum of $250 per option granted. This becomes the significant figure on out-of-the-money options in some cases.

Example: You are selling a call option on X common stock with a striking price of $60/share, and the premium is $4/share or a total of $400. If X common stock is selling at $50/share, the margin computation looks like this: 30% × $5,000 ($50/share × 100 shares) equals $1,500. Since this option is $10 out-of-the-money, the margin requirement is reduced by $1,000 ($10/share × 100 shares). So the requirement is $500. With the option trading for $400, you have to deposit an additional $100.

In security options, both the initial margin and the maintenance margin are computed the same way. As with commodities, the margin involved does not produce a debit balance, because the broker is not lending you anything. No debit balance means no interest on your margin account. Accounts are marked-to-market daily, which means your margin requirement is recomputed daily, and you either get or pay variation margin. It is normal not to issue margin calls for amounts of less than $100.

Spreads

In spread transactions, you purchase one option and sell a different option of the same type (put or call) of either a different striking price or a different maturity. The logic of this position is in strategy. So let's look at just the margin ramifications of the three possibilities.

Example 1: You purchase a call on X with a striking price of $50/share at a price of $7/share, and you simultaneously sell a call on X at $60/share for a premium of $4 with the same or shorter expiration. What is the margin? Spread margin, very logically, is always the maximum amount you can lose. In this case, you purchased an option for $700 ($7/share × 100 shares) and sold an option for $400 ($4/share × 100 shares). If the option you have sold is exercised, you can exercise the option you own at a lower striking price; if both options expire, the net difference in premium has been paid. Your risk is therefore limited to the difference in premiums between your purchase and your sale. Since you purchased for $700 and sold for $400, you need only deposit the difference of $300. There is no variation margin, because the total potential loss has already been deposited.

Example 2: If on the other hand, you purchase the call with the $60 striking price and sell the call with the $50 striking price, the risk is different. If exercised, you are obligated to deliver 100 shares of stock at $50 per share, and you would, through exercise, have to pay $60 per share. So your risk is $1,000 [($60 × 100)−($50 × 100)]. Therefore your margin requirement is $1,000. For the option you sold, however, you received $700, while for the option you bought, you paid only $400. This $300 positive cash flow, or credit, can be used as part of the margin requirement, thereby reducing your initial cash requirement to

$700. Once again there is no variation margin as the total risk has already been deposited.

Example 3: You purchase an option of one maturity on a given security and sell another option of a different maturity, with the same or different striking prices. You receive no consideration if the option purchased is of shorter duration than the option sold. To qualify for reduced margin, the option you purchase must be of the same or greater duration than the option sold. If you buy the nearby and sell the deferred, the nearby must be fully paid for, and the deferred is a naked option. Assuming that you buy the more distant option and sell the more nearby option, you will qualify for lesser margins.

This last type of spread, which is generally referred to as a *calendar* or *horizontal spread*, is margined based on the difference in striking prices as were the first two examples which reflect the true risk involved. The case difference is, of course, applicable to the margin requirement. This particular treatment will vary substantially from commodity option calendar spreads to be discussed later.

SETTLEMENT

Settlement has been discussed on several occasions in relation to both commodities and now options. In options all settlements are one day. In other words, options must be paid for in one day, and the premiums due you on liquidations are available in one day. Due to the short settlement time, most brokerage firms require good faith funds in your account prior to the entry of an order to purchase options that will create a long position.

TYPES OF ORDERS

Most of the orders that can be used in commodities and securities can also be used in options. These orders, however, do not necessarily have precisely the same meaning. When there is a difference in either the meaning or manner of execution, I will point it out.

1. A *market* order means the same in all markets. It says to the broker: "Fill my order at the best available price at the time you receive the order."
2. A *market-not-held* order tells the broker to execute at the best available price but to use judgment. If in using judgment, the broker does

not execute the order, he or she is not held responsible. This type of order is normally used on large orders that require delicate handling.

3. *Limit* and *stop* orders have the same meaning as in commodities, but they can be triggered only by an execution not by a bid or offer.

4. A *stop-limit* order says to the broker: "If the option trades at my stop price, execute it on the very next trade provided you can execute it at my limit or better."

5. *Good-till-cancelled* orders, also referred to as "GTC," tell the broker that the order is to remain outstanding until it is either filled or cancelled. Good-till-cancelled orders do expire if the underlying option expires.

As you can see, commodities and security options bear more similarities than they do differences. Commodities, in the natural course of events, led to security options, and security options led to commodity options. In some cases, drawing a clear distinction between the three investment vehicles is hard.

3

TECHNICAL ANALYSIS

There are basically two approaches to the analysis of any market, be it security or commodity: fundamental analysis and technical analysis or charting. Generally, fundamental analysis, which in commodities is a price forecasting analysis based on supply and demand, tends to be longer-term in nature; it is designed to identify major price moves. Technical analysis is viewed as more short-term in nature, to be used as a short-term trading tool. Nothing is ever as simple as it appears, and such is the case when it comes to the market forecasting of commodity prices.

FUNDAMENTAL APPROACH

If your investment background is primarily in the securities markets, you may tend to favor the fundamental approach to price forecasting. The reason for this tendency is that the securities markets make up a market of primarily one type of security, namely common stocks. Once you have achieved a basic understanding of the factors that influence individuals' perception of the value of one common stock, you can apply this knowledge and logic to projecting all common stock prices. The implication is not that the forecasting of stock prices is an infallable science, but that the tools and techniques used to evaluate one common stock are basically the same for the next common stock.

In analyzing a common stock from a fundamental point of view, you normally begin with readily available information, such as the company's annual report. You review the report in light of such recognized standards as gross sales, total revenues, working capital, earnings per share, debt-to-equity ratio, new products, and so on. The next step is to compare this company to other companies in the same industry to determine if this company will be a leader. Will its common stock outperform other companies in the same industry? Will the industry lead or lag the economy? Finally, you will make overall judgment of how the securities markets will fare in light of general economic conditions, such as interest rates, Federal Reserve policy, unemployment, inflation, and the like. The fundamental tools applied to one security may be readily applied to the next security, and the sources of information for all of these judgments are available.

WHY TECHNICAL ANALYSIS?

Fundamental analysis is equally applicable to the commodities markets, but each of these markets is a market unto itself. The fundamentals that would affect the price of interest rate futures would be almost irrelevant to forecasting the price of cocoa. Each commodity, or at least each group of commodities, has its own set of fundamentals.

Commodities may be subdivided in a number of ways, but the following will give you some idea of a logical breakdown: financial instruments, grains, livestock and their byproducts, metals, and perhaps other comestables. Even this subdivision does not deal with such problem commodities as cotton, heating oil, and perhaps rubber. Each of these markets and, to a lesser degree, each commodity has its own fundamentals, which, in turns, affect its supply/demand and the public's perception of it. This affects futures prices.

There are a couple of ways to deal with the variety of commodities markets. The easiest approach is, of course, to disregard these markets, taking the view that "they are too complex" and not worth the effort. This approach, however, forces you to eliminate one of the potentially most profitable and dynamic sectors of investing.

The second approach, which is used by some commodity investors, is to limit investments to one commodity or to one group of commodities. This approach is valid, and it has a great many reasons for its use. For example, some investors limit their trading to the grain complex. Doing so, however, is not as simple as it sounds, because even this group includes such items as wheat, corn, oats, barley, flaxseed, grain sorghums, and most likely the bean complex of soybeans, soybean oil, and soybean meal. The difficulty arises from the fact that most grain commodities are grown both domestically and internationally.

For the domestic portion of these crops, The United States Department of Agriculture accumulates and makes available tremendous quantities of statistical information. This information includes: planting intentions, estimated yield per acre, government price supports, carry-over, shortfall, import and export intentions, and other good information. But a large portion of these grains are raised by small farmers, who do not participate in any government programs and who therefore need not supply any information. As a result, the reports sometimes miss their estimates by "a country mile."

As a further complication, the statistics on international production and consumption are not as readily available for two reasons. First, most countries do not maintain the same extensive research capabilities as the United States. Second, some countries don't wish to make the information available. Take, for example, the Soviet Union. If this year's Russian wheat crop is going to be exceptionally small, the Soviets will be forced to buy large quantities of grain in the world markets. It would serve the Soviet Union's purpose to release information that the Russian wheat crop was large and thereby depress prices. This puts the Soviet Union in a position to make its initial purchases in a depressed market.

Although this second approach to commodity investing has nothing inherently wrong with it, it has two weaknesses. The obvious first weakness is that your investments are limited to one group of commodities, which may or may not be active over an extended period of time. The second is that the information, on which your fundamental analysis is based, is neither as readily available nor as reliable as in the fundamental analysis of securities.

THE TECHNICAL APPROACH

The third approach is technical analysis, also referred to as charting. Many people with a background in securities disregard charting, not because it is unreliable but more because it is not as relatively important in securities as it is in commodities for the reasons discussed.

Technical analysts take the view that "price is everything." They believe that the current market price and the history of that price will provide all the answers. The logic behind this approach is that price is determined by the cumulative view of all the participants in the market and that each of these participants brings with them their own market knowledge. Inasmuch as the market is presumed to be the sum total of the speculators, growers, refiners, hedgers, and others, and the market price is really the best source of market information, everything that everyone knows is already reflected in the price.

The chartist believes that market prices and their daily changes reflect the views of the participants. These daily changes, as well as the related volume and open interest figures, form patterns that, by comparison with similar circumstances in the past, indicate trends and future prices.

Whether you are an ardent adherent to this philosophy or you believe that it is totally fallacious, you have to realize that, to many commodity investors, it borders on religion. All you need do is pick up an issue of the *Wall Street Journal*, the *Journal of Commerce*, *Commodities Magazine*, or *Barrons* to realize the importance of charting. In each of these publications are numerous articles on technical analysis as well as, more importantly, many "ads" for commercial chart services. The chart services cost anywhere from several hundred to several thousand dollars per year. If people were not purchasing these services, they would not be offered, and they would certainly not command the prices they do. People who spend that kind of money on chart services *believe*. These people believe and act on their beliefs.

The heavy reliance of believers on market price behavior, however, involves a traditional "chicken-and-egg" problem. Does the market behave the way it does because the charts forecast it? Or do the chartists cause the market to behave the way it does because of their actions? Whatever the cause, it is immaterial. Charting is important in commodities because enough people use it that it has become a market force of its own.

How do you use technical analysis? How technical analysis is used is ultimately up to the judgment of the user. It is foolish however, to institute a buying program at a time when the technical segment of the market is sellers. It is equally foolish to begin selling when the technicians are buying. If nothing more, technical analysis is at least a good timing tool. In most investing, it is more important to know when to get in and when to get out than what to get into. Because technical analysis looks primarily at price, volume, and open interest, it allows investors to trade all of the market, with limited background in the fundamentals of the specific market traded.

Remember one thing about using technical analysis in commodities options. You do not use technical analysis on the commodity option itself. Technical analysis is of the commodity not of the option. Options are nothing more than a means of investing in commodities. Even though there is a supply and demand for the option itself, the major influence over the market price of a commodity option is the public's view of the future price of the underlying commodity. So first establish a market view of the underlying commodity—be that by fundamental analysis or technical analysis—before you view the means of investing, the option.

Graphics

Technical analysis uses graphic representations of the price, volume, and open interest history of a commodity or security over a given period of time. This graphic representation is then analyzed to determine the future price of the underlying market instrument.

The technician uses two types of charts: (1) bar charts and (2) point and figure charts.

Bar Charts. The *bar chart*, sometimes referred to as a "vertical line chart," is a graphic representation of a given commodity's high price, low price, and closing price on a particular day. The scale of price is placed on the left side of the graph paper along the vertical (or *y*) axis. The time sequence, or period of time to be covered, is placed along the horizontal (or *x*) axis. Each day's high price and low price are entered on the chart as dots above the appropriate date. These two points are connected by a vertical line, which now represents the commodity's trading range for a given day. Finally, the closing price for the day is entered as a small horizontal "tick" mark on the right side of the vertical line.

In Figure 3–1, you can see that we have entered the high price, the low price, and the closing price for one hypothetical week of gold trading. In some commodities, a split-close is not uncommon, that is, the commodity closes at two prices. This type of close occurs when trades are done at different locations in the trading ring at or near the close. Chartists would enter these two closing prices as two horizontal tick marks on the vertical line, or in some cases the chartist uses only the lower of the two prices.

Having done this for a week, you have a picture of the market's price activity, which may prove useful in determining the trend of the market as an indication of future price movements.

Point and Figure Charts. The point and figure tends to be more useful, more sensitive, and possibly more accurate because it also shows the value of intraday moves. From the bar chart we get the high, the low, and the close, but this information does not include the trading activity of the day. We are at a loss to determine where intraday price changes took place. This type of information can be useful in determining at what specific price levels the buyers became more aggressive than the sellers and brought about a price change.

> *Example:* The bar chart in Figure 3–1 shows that on the first day gold had a low price of $382, a high price of $396, and a close of $395. We know that the trading range for the day was $14, but this is all the information that we have. This chart gives us no information about what happened during the trading day, which might give us some indication of either a continuation or reversal of trend. The market, perhaps, opened at $384, rallied to $387, declined to $385, rallied to $392, withdrew to $390, rallied to $396, declined and closed at $395. We don't see any of this intraday activity on the bar chart.

Figure 3–2 is referred to as a $1.00 reversal chart. Notice that the graduations on the left side (*y* axis) of the chart are in one-dollar increments.

FIGURE 3–1. Gold Bar Chart

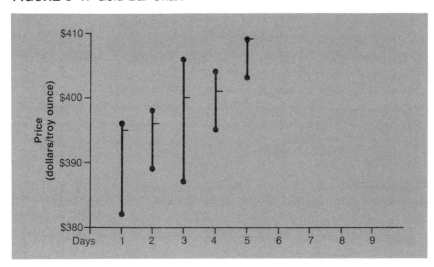

On this type of chart, you enter only $1.00 moves. Disregard fractional portions of a dollar, such as 10¢ or 20¢. You plot only full dollars, and you plot to the nearest full dollar. If gold moves up $11.70, you plot $12.00, but if gold moves down $5.10, you plot only down $5.00. There is nothing magical about a $1.00 reversal chart. You could just as easily use 50¢, $2.00, $5.00, or even a $10.00 reversal chart. The smaller the increment, the more sensitive—and the more difficult to keep—the chart becomes. Smaller increments tend to be used for short-term trading, while larger increments are quite satisfactory for longer-term trends.

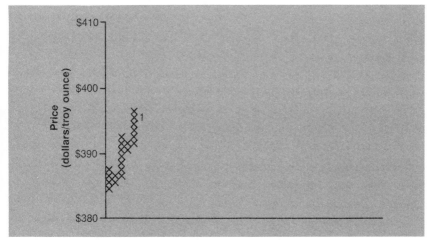

FIGURE 3–2. $1.00 Reversal Gold Point and Figure Chart

Example: The chart in Figure 3–2 is the point-and-figure equivalent of the bar chart in Figure 3–1. The market opens at $384, so we place an "X" in the $384 box in the leftmost column of the chart. The market then rallies to $387. We place "X"s in the boxes above $384, up to and including $387. At this point, the market turns around and begins its decline. Since the boxes below $387 are already filled, we must move one column to the right. Our first "X" would be placed in the $386 box, and we continue to insert "X"s as the market declines. The decline ends at $385, which is our last "X." On the next series of trades, the market rallies to $392. Once again we move one column to the right, entering "X"s from $386 to $392. This advance is followed by a decline to $390. We move one column to the right and enter "X"s in the $391 and $390 boxes. The next rally carries the market to $396. Again we move to the right and enter "X"s from $391 to $396. On the close, the market declines to $395. Once more we move one column to the right and enter an "X" in the $395 box. This concludes our first trading day.

Scale and Time

Note several things about this chart. First, there is no specific time scale across the bottom of the chart. Although horizontal movement indicates time, the number of reversals during the day determines the magnitude of the movement to the right. Second, although this chart contains all "X"s, some chartists use "X"s for rising markets and "O"s for declining markets. In addition the price box, where the commodity closed is normally occupied by a number, representing the trading day. In our chart, this was the first trading day, and consequently the number "1." Finally, the commodity need not trade at every intervening price for the box to be filled. For example, if the price of gold had traded at $394, and the next trade was $397, you would have filled in all the boxes from $394 to $397.

Why not try your hand at constructing a point and figure chart? Use the following trading sequence for four days. Use both "X"s and "O"s, remembering to show the end of each trading day with a number. You can then compare your chart with Figure 3–3:

Trading Data											
Day 2:	394,	393,	392,	389,	393,	395,	396,	395,	396,	397,	397,	396
Day 3:	390,	391,	393,	395,	397,	400,	402,	399,	398,	397,	398,	400
Day 4:	400,	401,	401,	402,	401,	399,	397,	396,	397,	395,	398,	401
Day 5:	403,	404,	405,	406,	406,	405,	406,	405,	406,	407,	409,	409

How did you do?

Many chartists believe—and act on the belief—that charts can predict the future of commodity prices. What the chart does is show the interaction

FIGURE 3–3. $1.00 Reversal Gold Point and Figure Chart

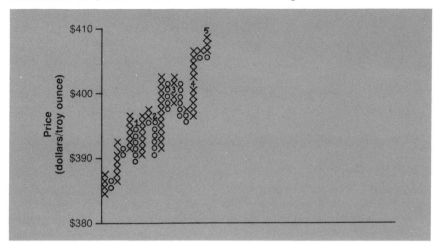

of the participants in the market. By looking at Figure 3–3, you can see the price level at which the sellers become more aggressive and stem a further price advance, or provide a level of *resistance*. You can also see the levels at which the buyers become more aggressive and overcome selling pressure, thereby providing *support*. Markets tend to meet resistance after rallies as these rallies give rise to profit-taking, and they tend to meet support after declines due to both "bargain hunting" and short covering. If the selling pressure and the buying demand are in relative balance, the market tends to trade in a range limited by these two diverse opinions. This type or range is called a *trading range*. If the buyers are consistently more aggressive than the sellers, prices work their way higher, and we are in an *uptrend*. If the sellers are the more aggressive market factor, and prices work their way lower, we are in a *downtrend*.

Trends

Uptrends. An *uptrend* is a market condition wherein both the daily lows and highs are at ever increasing price levels. A line connecting the low points of an uptrend would be referred to as an *uptrend line*. The line is particularly useful because it not only indicates the direction of future prices, but it is also a reference to determine when the uptrend has terminated. As long as the price remains above this line, the buyers are more aggressive than the sellers, and any price decline will be limited. Regardless of your fundamental view of the market, if you are going to trade in this type of market, you should trade from the long side. If you are bullish and wish to be long, you can count on the support of the technical traders to further the price advance. If you are bearish, it is time to stand aside and await technical

FIGURE 3–4. Uptrend Chart

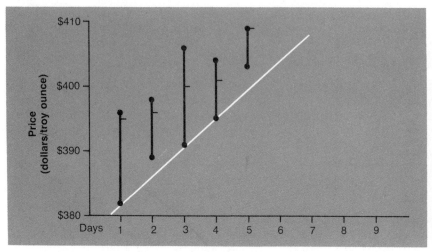

confirmation of your fundamental view prior to entering the market on the short side.

An uptrend is terminated when the highs cease to make new highs. If failure to make new highs continues for any period of time, the uptrend line, through the passage of time, is also penetrated. All this penetration shows is that the uptrend is terminated; the penetration is not necessarily indicative of a downtrend. At this point the market may continue to trade in a sideways pattern, reestablish its uptrend, or in fact go lower and establish a downtrend.

Downtrends. A *downtrend* is a market condition wherein both high and lows are at progressively lower levels. Drawing a line connecting the high points is often useful. This line, referred to as a *downtrend line*, indicates the future direction of the market, and it serves as a reference to determine if the downtrend is intact at any point in time. A market that is in a downtrend is one where the sellers are more aggressive than the buyers. Each attempt at a rally is met with renewed selling pressure that drives the market still lower. The buyers are not firm enough in their conviction to overcome the aggressive market view of the sellers. This market should be traded from the short side, with rallies used as points either to establish or to add to short positions. If fundamentally you wish to be long, this is a good time to stand aside and await a change in technical market conditions. Buying when everyone else is selling is not wise.

Congestion Areas. At times, a market has no direction. Neither the buyers nor the sellers have the courage of their convictions, and consequently the market goes nowhere. Such markets normally occur after

FIGURE 3–5. Downtrend Chart

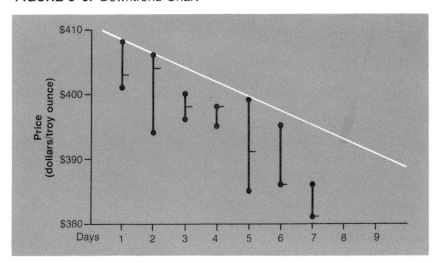

either a protracted advance or a protracted decline. If the market has been in a sustained uptrend, the buyers are looking to take profits, and the short sellers (who have been repeatedly wrong) show no tendency to be aggressive. The longs may have held a fundamental view about price level, and that level has been reached. In a declining market the opposite is true. The shorts have been taking profits and do not see further potential on the downside, thus withdrawing. In looking for a place to go long, buyers have been burned so many times that they have a total lack of interest.

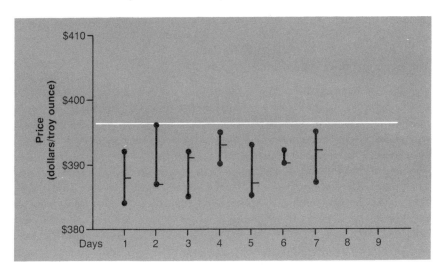

FIGURE 3–6. Congestion Area Chart

What develops in a congestion area is a market of balanced buying and selling pressure. On each decline the buying interest improves, but not to a substantial enough level to sustain a major rally. After a small rally, the buying interest dries up; the longs become disinterested and liquidate, thus possibly generating some short selling. A small decline follows, but not sufficient to start a downtrend; the shorts lose interest and cover.

The technician believes that the longer a market trades in a congestion area, the greater is the magnitude of the ensuing move. If you think about this philosophy, you will see that it is founded on logic. A congestion area is a market characterized by disinterest, and as such it has no direction. Neither the sellers or the buyers have strong views. It is a market of distribution, where most people hold small positions for short periods of time. It is a market where people with losses are looking to get out, and people with profits are looking for a slightly better price. No one is anxious to do business, except at their price. The longer this congestion pattern exists, the more participants experience either small gains or small losses.

Once the congestion area is violated, on either the upside or the downside, the participants must take some action. If the market "breaks out" on the upside, you have a scurrying of activity of the shorts to cover their positions. Buyers who felt they should be long, but who did not establish their positions while the market was in the congestion area, now buy. Technicians buy solely because of the breakout. If the market breaks on the downside, the longs rush to cover (liquidate). The shorts add to their position, and those people who refrained from going short within the congestion area will do so. Technicians also sell because of the technical "breakdown." Such is the logic of the premise that the longer the congestion, the greater the following move. Once a market has either broken out or broken down, a move is likely to follow.

Support and Resistance Areas

But the importance of the congestion area does not cease after its limits have been violated. A congestion area, once violated on the upside, becomes a *support* level on the next market decline. A congestion area, once violated on the downside, becomes a *resistance* area on the next market advance. Let's look at support and resistance.

Support areas are price ranges in a declining market, in which you would expect to see an increase in buying interest. The nature of the logic behind the support area is largely psychological. In Figure 3–7, the last advance of the market, the support is a congestion area that is eventually violated on the upside. When the market breaks out of the congestion area on the upside, some investors were short. Others either are not quick enough to cover their short position or do not believe that the breakout is valid, and as such they are still short. These shorts are just looking to get out

FIGURE 3–7. Support Area Chart

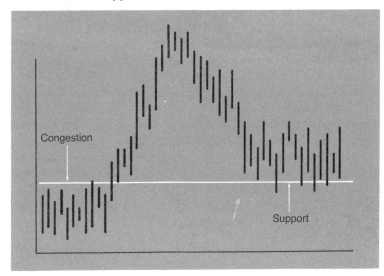

even, and they become buyers when the market nears the price at which they established their position. Still others "knew" the market was going to break out and go up, but they "missed it." These people are looking for a chance to "get in." They too become buyers if the market comes down just a little. Some people got in a little late or with a smaller position than they had wanted, and they look on this decline as an opportunity to add to their

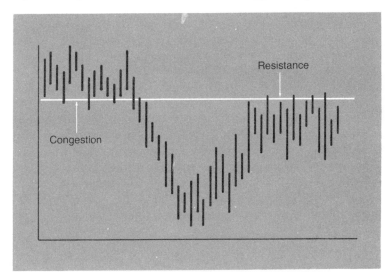

FIGURE 3–8. Resistance Area Chart

existing position or to improve their average cost. Other people had a profit on their long position at a higher price and want to add to that position, so when the market goes back up, the profit will be bigger. As a result, what was a congestion area on the way up becomes a support area on the way down. Resistance areas are also a psychological phenomenon.

When the congestion area is violated on the downside, some investors "knew" that they should have gotten out, but they were either too slow or not sure that the market was really breaking down. These people look for any opportunity to get out even. As the market starts to rally, they just want to save their hides. Some people wanted to go short on the breakdown, but they missed the opportunity; this rally gives the potential shorts another opportunity. Other people are short but do not cover their shorts at the bottom, and they use this opportunity to add to their short position for additional profits on the continued downtrend. For all these reasons, when a market rallies and that rally approaches a former level of congestion, resistance develops to further price increases.

Pattern Identification

A market in a trend is something like the "object in motion" in Newtonian physics. An object in motion tends to remain in motion, in a straight line, unless acted upon by outside force. So it is with a market in a trend. Such a market tends to remain in the trend, unless acted upon by an "outside force." We know that the trend will end but not necessarily that it will reverse itself. We know only that support and resistance levels tend to inhibit the continuation of the market in its "chosen" direction. When a trend ends, all we know is that the trend has ended—not necessarily what is likely to follow. Does the breaking of the trend indicate that the market is going to reverse direction? Is the uptrend "topping out" (that is, about to go lower)? Or is the downtrend "bottoming out" (about to go higher)? When the turn comes, will it be slow or swift? And what will be the magnitude of the move that follows?

Although technical analysis does not speak to these questions directly, pattern identification helps in the formulation of answers. Patterns are split into two distinct groups: reversal patterns and continuation patterns. A *reversal pattern*, when completed, indicates a market that will reverse its current direction. A *continuation pattern*, when completed, indicates a market that will resume its previous direction. Reversal patterns include tops and bottoms, while continuation patterns are characterized by triangles, flags, and pennants.

Tops and Bottoms. The *double top*, or "M" formation, represents a reversal pattern. This particular pattern indicates the end of an uptrend and, in most cases, when completed, the beginning of a downtrend.

FIGURE 3–9. Double Top Formation

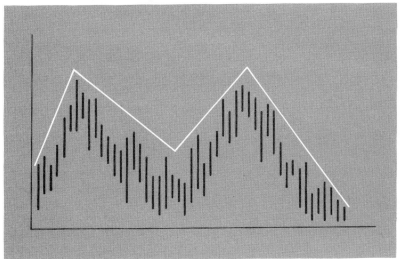

As you can see in Figure 3–9, a double top is a rally followed by (1) a downward price correction, (2) a second rally, and finally (3) a second selloff. The enthusiasm of the first rally is a continuation of the uptrend, with new highs being established in the market forming the left peak of the double top.

After the first peak, the price correction of itself is not significant, but if the correction violates an uptrend line, it is grounds for caution. Longs would look to exit the market because the uptrend line has been violated.

The second rally forms the right peak of the double top. In this rally, prices are unable to make new highs, and the rally is at a lower level than the left peak. An aggressive short seller should consider establishing a position when the market fails to make new highs, and any remaining longs should get out. One of the nice things about the double top is that it gives the short seller a valid place to enter a buy-stop order at a price above both peaks. An increase in volume on the second selloff over the first is also usual. This increase is a combination of the longs exiting and the shorts entering the market.

The double top is not truly completed until the price of the second selloff is below the lowest price of the first selloff. More conservative short sellers might await this confirmation before establishing their short positions, especially if fundamentals are not in agreement with the technical observations. The weakness of this approach is that one winds up short at a lower price and should still use a stop above the double top.

A *double bottom* or "W" formation is the inverse of a double top. This formation too, when completed, indicates a reversal in market direction.

FIGURE 3–10. Double Bottom Formation

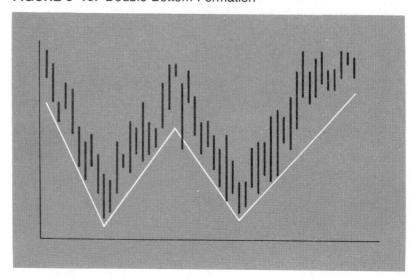

However, whereas a double bottom follows a market decline, a double top is found after a rally.

The market first sells off to new lows, which attract buyers and cause a rally. The first rally cannot be sustained, and the market once again sells off but does not make new lows. At this point, if the sideways movement of the market has penetrated the downtrend line, short sellers should be covering their positions as a protective measure.

With the market not making new lows, buyers once again enter the market but with more determination. When this second rally carries above the first rally, the formation is complete and signals a market turnaround. Aggressive longs could consider establishing their positions when the market fails to make new lows, but a more conservative approach is to wait for the second rally to carry to a level higher than the first. Either type of longs should use a stop-sell order below the double bottom to protect their long positions.

The volume pattern is also significant. While nothing unusual occurs on the initial selloff and the first rally, the volume on the second selloff is usually smaller and the second rally shows a substantial increase. Volume is normally quite heavy as a price above the first high is exceeded. This is a combination of new long positions and of shorts covering.

Head and Shoulders. Two widely recognized reversal patterns are the head and shoulders top and the head and shoulders bottom.

The *head and shoulders top* is sometimes called "triple top" due to the complexity of its formation, as well as the time it takes to form. This pattern is considered to indicate a major reversal of trend. It is generally conceded that the magnitude of the ultimate reversal is in direct proportion to the length of time that the formation takes to be completed, as well as to the magnitude of the moves during formation.

As with the double top, this formation take places after a market rally. The head and shoulders top is more commonly encountered after a long and sustained uptrend. The first indication of this potential formation is a sharp rally followed by a substantial decline. This decline, when followed by a second rally, in many cases brings in short selling, especially if the uptrend line has been broken. The difference is that this second rally carries to new highs, and often the newly established shorts cover or are stopped out when the market attains new highs. The second rally, although to new highs, cannot sustain itself, and a second selloff ensues, usually with heavier volume than the first. A third rally ensues, but on very light volume, followed by a selloff on heavy volume. The first rally is referred to as the *left shoulder*, the second rally *the head* (as it went to a higher level, and the third rally the *right shoulder*. The technician would draw a line connecting the low points of the two selloffs and refer to this as the *neckline*. When the neckline is breached on the downside during the third selloff, volume normally increases substantially. This volume indicates an increase in longs liquidating and shorts establishing new positions. A low volume rally to the neckline follows a small selloff on moderate volume. As the market price approaches the neckline on light volume, it turns down on heavy volume, with many new shorts and much long liquidation. The formation is now complete. The dollar value of the price change, indicated by the measurement from the top

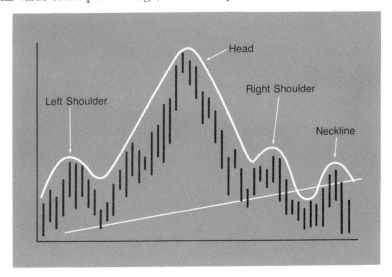

FIGURE 3-11. Head and Shoulders Top Formation

of the head to the neckline, is held to be equivalent to the magnitude of the selloff below the neckline.

The *head and shoulders bottom*, like the head and shoulders top, is normally encountered after a major market moves. The head and shoulders bottom, or triple bottom, comes after a major market decline, signaling a market turnaround of major proportions.

In this pattern, the market usually sells off sharply and then rallies weakly. If this rally violates the downtrend line, volume may increase as shorts cover and aggressive longs establish positions. A second selloff ensues, with the market making new lows and showing slightly greater volume. This volume consists of longs being stopped out and some individuals shorting in the belief that the downtrend is reestablishing itself. This time the market makes new lows on light volume and rallies sharply. These two moves have established the left shoulder and the head.

Next are another selloff on light volume and a rally on heavier volume. This rally continues above the neckline, which was drawn across the top of the two previous rallies. After a slight downward correction to the neckline comes a substantial rally with high volume. The formation is complete. Depending on their degree of aggressiveness, shorts would either cover when the market broke through the neckline coming out of the right shoulder or on the pullback to the neckline. Longs would also use these two points to establish positions. Again, the magnitude of the expected upward move is the equivalent of the measured distance from the top of the head to the neckline.

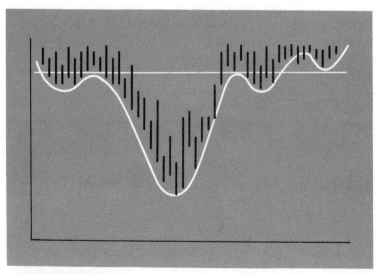

FIGURE 3–12. Head and Shoulders Bottom Formation

FIGURE 3–13. Ascending Triangle Chart

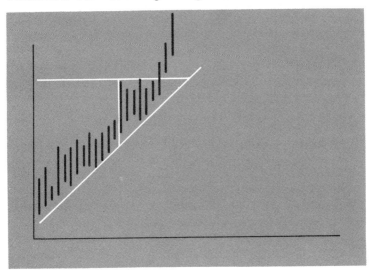

Triangles. There are three types of triangular patterns: ascending, descending, and symmetrical. The first two types of triangles are continuation patterns.

The *ascending triangle* is encountered in an uptrending market. As the chart in Figure 3–13 shows, the market is showing consistently higher lows and relatively equivalent highs. The triangle is formed by the uptrend line and a line drawn across the highs. The actual market movement may not— and usually will not—continue all the way to the apex of the triangle. This formation indicates a market that will move higher. For someone who is not currently in the market, the institution of a new long position when the market makes new highs is technically sound.

The psychology of the formation is that longs who are willing to institute new positions on any pullback encounter selling pressure at a given level (the equivalent highs). This selling pressure may be profit-taking of other longs or short sales based on some fundamental price value. Eventually the longs overcome the selling pressure, and the market breaks out. With new enthusiasm from the longs and some short covering, the rally that follows is usually sharp.

The *descending triangle* is encountered in a downtrending market, and it reflects a situation of ever decreasing highs and approximately equivalent lows. The triangle is formed by the downtrend line and a line drawn connecting the equivalent lows. The market may be expected to break out of the bottom side of the triangle (break down) somewhere before the apex of the triangle. The technician often enters a stop-sell order just below the bottom

FIGURE 3–14. Descending Triangle Chart

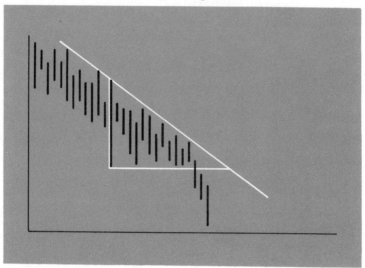

extreme of the triangle for the purpose of creating or adding to a short position.

Again, the psychology of the formation consists of aggressive sellers who are willing to sell at lower and lower levels but who meet support at a consistent price. The buying support may reflect new longs or profit-taking on other shorts. Eventually, the buying interest dries up, and the market breaks down. Any longs attempting to get out, of course, add to the rapidity of the market break. In this formation too, it is unusual for the market to continue all the way to the apex of the triangle before breaking down.

The *symmetrical triangle* cannot truly be called a continuation pattern, because it does not always indicate a market continuation. The symmetrical triangle may be encountered in either an uptrending or downtrending market. In this situation, each high is at a successively lower level, and each low is at a successively higher level. The triangle is constructed by drawing a line connecting the highs, which is, in effect, a downtrend line, and a line connecting the lows, which is an uptrend line. These two lines must, of course, cross and thus form the triangle.

This formation has a psychological base similar to the mechanical equivalent of a coiled spring. The sellers are more and more aggressive, and they are willing to sell at lower and lower prices. Meanwhile, the buyers, as aggressive as the sellers, are willing to buy at higher and higher prices. Eventually something or someone must "give." If the buyers become the dominant trend, the market breaks out on the upside. If the sellers become the dominent force, then the market breaks on the downside. The eventual break is sharp because the people on the "wrong" side of the market quickly

FIGURE 3–15. Symmetrical Triangle Chart

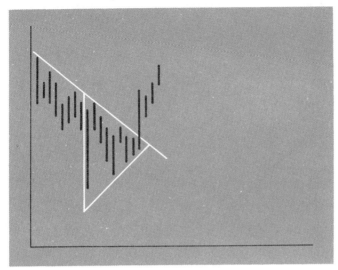

cover their positions, adding to the rapidity and sharpness of the ensuing move. Technicians often place stop-buy orders above the downtrend line and stop-sell orders below the uptrend line as a means of instituting a position. Rarely does the triangle reach the apex before either the uptrend line or downtrend line is violated.

Remember two things about this type of chart. On occasion these triangles occur under the "wrong" market conditions. That is, an ascending triangle has been known to signal the bottom of a downtrend, and a descending triangle has signaled the end of an uptrend. This may be a fact, or just a function of how carefully the triangle has been drawn. In reality, the interpretation of a chart is not always as easy as in our sample charts. Two technicians looking at the same chart may have different views depending on how the formation is defined and the period at which each is looking.

Flags and Pennants. Flags and pennants are two other types of continuation patterns. In addition to being continuation patterns, flags or pennants are in many cases repetition patterns. That is, they repeat themselves and form a second or third time. You will encounter upward flags, downward flags, upward pennants, and downward pennants, all of which indicate that the market will continue in the same direction.

The staff, or "flag pole," of an *upward flag* is formed by one or more sharp extended rallies. After these rallies, the market consolidates its gains. Existing longs are looking to take profits, and on each succeeding rally they

FIGURE 3–16. Upward Flag Chart

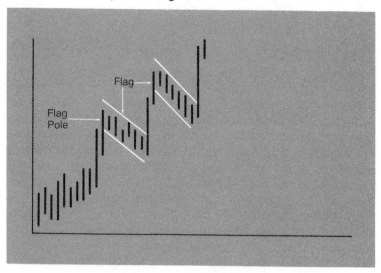

settle for lower and lower prices. With no enthusiastic buying interest, the market drifts lower. Graphically, an upward flag is a sharp rally followed by a gentle downtrend. Because there is no technical reason to establish a short position, the selling pressure dissipates rapidly. With no overhead supply and an uptrending market, another series of sharp rallies usually follows.

There is no method for determining how long the flag portion of the formation will continue. The technician normally places stop-buy orders above the flag portion of the formation. The technician's being stopped into a long position normally accounts for the succeeding staffs or flag poles.

A *downward flag* is the inverse of an upward flag. A sharp selloff forms the flag pole or staff, followed by short profit-taking, accounting for the ensuing rally. Again there is no valid method for determining how long the profit-taking and the resulting flag formation will continue. The technician places stop-sell orders below the ever increasing uptrend in an effort to go short on the next breakdown. These stop orders account for the staff or flag pole that follows.

Upward pennants are very similar to upward flags in their initial formation. The market has a sharp rally to form the staff or flagpole. At this point, instead of going into a minor downtrend, the market forms a symmetrical triangle. The longs are taking profits and doing so at ever decreasing levels; however, new longs are buying to establish long positions. The combination of decreasing highs and increasing lows gives rise to the symmetrical triangle, which forms the pennant. The pennant, contrary to the flag, can exist only for a finite period of time as the downtrend line and the uptrend line must cross. Many technicians place stop-buy orders above the ever

FIGURE 3–17. Downward Flag Chart

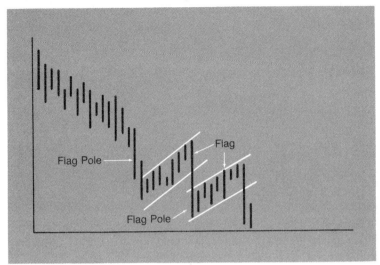

decreasing downtrend in an effort to establish a long position when the market breaks out of the flag. This action causes the succeeding staffs.

A *descending pennant*, the inverse of an upward pennant, is similar to a downward flag. The market initially has a sharp selloff forming the down flag pole. Then the market, instead of going into a minor rally as in the flag, forms a symmetrical triangle. The shorts begin taking profits at ever increasing levels, and new participants begin going short at ever decreasing levels. With descending highs and increasing lows, the consolidation has a finite lifespan. Technicians again place stop-sell orders below the ever increasing lows to establish a short position. These shorts account for the second and succeeding staffs. The participants in the market cause the repetition by their action.

Gaps. In addition to the line and related formations on charts, the technician also attributes importance to the vacant areas. When a market makes sharp moves, in some cases up or down the limit, it leaves blank areas on the chart. These blank areas are referred to as *gaps*. An *upward gap* occurs when the low for a given day is higher than the high of the previous day. A *downward gap* occurs when the high for a given day is lower than the previous day's low.

These moves very often occur when a news item occurs during the night or after the market has closed for the day. For example, should a news item cause the price of gold to rally in London or Paris prior to the opening of the New York market, a gap would quite likely occur at the opening in New York. If the gap is an upward gap, the technician continues to trade the market from the long side until the gap is filled, if filled. The logic is that, if the gap is filled, the news that caused the gap in the first place is no longer affecting market psychology and can now be disregarded. The converse holds true for down gaps.

Volume and Open Interest

Both volume and open interest are of significance to technicians, and they play a major role in their market judgments. Inasmuch as these two factors are not solely part of technical analysis, they are to some degree fundamental in nature. Having made a market judgment, either technical or fundamental, you should look for confirmation in the form of volume and open interest, or perhaps reconsider the judgment.

Volume is the total purchases *or* sales, while *open interest* is the number of contracts outstanding at any one time. These figures are supplied and compiled by the various exchanges. Neither volume nor open interest in a specific month is important; it is the total volume and total open interest for all the contracts in the same commodity that is of importance.

In some commodities, both the volume and open interest are seasonal in nature, especially in the grains and livestock commodities. Seasonal variation must be disregarded in making evaluations of changes in volume and open interest figures. When we look at open interest, we must also look at the price environment in which the open interest changes.

There are four possible combinations of increased and decreased open interest and price:

1. *Increasing open interest and increasing prices:* This market condition indicates new buying. The increase of open interest is showing that, even though there are old buyers and old sellers, the new buying entering the market is the dominant force. When both volume and open interest are increasing, the market is said to be "technically strong."

2. *Increased open interest and decreased prices:* Here we have the converse of the first situation. There is an increase in open interest, showing both new buyers and new sellers, but, despite action by old buyers and sellers, the new sellers are the dominant force. This condition is considered to be "technically weak."

3. *Declining open interest and declining price:* This market condition is dominated primarily by long liquidation. Despite any new participants, the factor most influential is the long liquidating. The net effect is that part of the supply (the previously existing long positions) is being removed from the market. This removal of supply is "technically strong."

4. *Declining open interest and increasing prices:* In this market, the predominant activity is short covering, which is a removal of demand. With a constant supply and reduced demand, you have a market that is "technically weak."

In the evaluation of volume and open interest figures, knowing who is trading is often as important as knowing what is trading. The Commodity Futures Trading Commission publishes *Large Trader Reports.* These reports do not list the specific participants, but they do quantify the number of contracts held by individuals and companies when that quantity exceeds specified amounts. Many of these large participants have taken positions out of commercial necessity, and they are not influenced to change those positions by either technical or fundamental considerations. Because they are less susceptible to change, these positions are said to be in "strong hands."

There is no such thing as a small trader report. But if one subtracts the numbers of contracts held by the "large traders" from the open interest, you have the small traders. Small trading positions are thought to be held by "weak hands" because they are susceptible to change due to fundamental and technical considerations. These small positions are of greatest significance in evaluating open interest. Most brokerage firms and some financial publications routinely supply this information to their customers.

In conclusion, although many security investors subscribe to technical analysis, the complexity and diversity of the commodities markets warrant an even greater use of technical analysis. Whether you use technical analysis as nothing more than a timing tool or as a second check on your fundamental opinions, you will find it of tremendous value. This chapter just touches the surface of technical anslysis, and once again I refer you to the bibliography for suggested further reading.

4

PRICING COMMODITY OPTIONS

Why does one option cost $3,000 and another option cost $4,000? Why does an option sell for $5,000 today when a year ago it cost $2,500? If the commodity goes up or down a given amount, why doesn't the option go up or down the same amount? As you become involved in commodity options, you encounter what you believe to be a never-ending list of questions. Almost all such questions, however, generally can be restated as one of two essential questions: Why does an option cost what it costs? Why does the price of an option behave the way it behaves? When you know the answers to these valid questions, you will be able to answer most other questions that cross your mind.

Prior to the existence of the Chicago Board Options Exchange, option trading was more of an art than a science. When you wanted a quotation on a security option, your broker would check with several members of the Put and Call Broker's Association for a quotation. If you had asked for a quotation and your broker checked with five different dealers, almost all of the dealers would quote approximately the same price in most cases. This agreement on prices was not collusion; the dealers just "knew" what the option was worth. You could wake up these dealers in the middle of the night for a quote, and they would come up with the "right" price. If, however, you asked *how* they came up with the price, they couldn't tell you. They only "knew" it was the right price. For many years, some of the highest-priced traders on Wall Street were the traders who determined pricing for the various put and call brokers.

In the late 1960s there were no clearcut criteria for pricing. If you asked someone knowledgeable in option trading what an option costs, you most likely would have received a response like, "An option on an average security for six months and ten days will cost fifteen percent." If you think about this response, it's great! Regardless of what price the option actually costs, the statement is true because who knows what an "average" security is?

Part of the problem with determining how options were priced was that, with such small volume, very little data was available and the available data was not published anywhere. The advent of the CBOE changed this situation dramatically. Suddenly, virtually all of the security option business done in the country was done on the floor of an exchange with the corresponding price reporting and recordkeeping. With data available and with the sudden surge in option volume, many mathematicians and engineers became involved in econometric research on options. Such noted mathematicians as Dr. Fischer Black and Dr. Myron Scholes became involved. From their interest and research came the first, and probably most widely accepted, econometric model of option pricing, the Black-Scholes model (discussed later). This original work, as well as the work of many others, became the basis for a more scientific option pricing theory.

THE NEXT BEST THING TO A CRYSTAL BALL

What is the "fair price" of an option? The question is the starting point of all option pricing theory. Depending on your point of view, each participant in the market would have his or her own answer. If you are a buyer, you would feel that any option on which you made money was fairly priced. On the other hand if you were an option grantor, you might feel any option that generated an attractive rate of return was fairly priced. For the sake of this discussion, let's say that an option is fairly priced when the buyer and the seller, after having done an infinite number of trades, have broken even. This definition may not be great, but you will see that it works admirably for our purposes.

The starting point is then, How do you determine the fair price of an option? To be able to determine the fair price, you would have to be able to look into the future and see the price of the security or commodity at some point in time. Doing so, of course, is not possible. So we have to do the next best thing, which is to look at the past price history of the security or commodity and make the assumption that past price behavior is indicative of future behavior. For the most part, this approach works out to be relatively satisfactory, or, as the statisticians would say, "There is a high degree of correlation."

For our discussion, let's say we want to know the fair price for a 30-day call on a hypothetical commodity called X at-the-market. First we must look at the price behavior of X over every 30-day period throughout history. Although we can look at fewer 30-day periods, the fewer we look at, the less accurate the data becomes. We will find that, in most 30-day periods, the price of X changed very little, but in a small number of instances the price of X changed dramatically.

Now we should look at perhaps every 60-day period in history to see what happened to the price of X in each 60 days. What we learn from doing so is that the price of X is likely to move up or down more in a period of 60 days than in a period of 30 days. On the surface, most of this work appears worthless, since common sense would have told us that a 60-day option should cost twice as much as a 30-day option because we have control of the commodity for twice as long. Common sense does have some flaws, however, and tends to lead us astray. This conclusion, for instance, appears very logical, but it happens to be totally wrong. What our research into the price history of X shows us is that X *does* move more in 60 days than it does in 30 days—*but not twice as much.* A 60-day option should not then cost twice as much as a 30-day option.

Think of it this way. When you buy an option, you are leasing the profit potential of the commodity for a given period of time. By way of analogy, someone who buys a 1/4″ drill wants a 1/4″ hole, not a 1/4″ drill. When you buy a contract of corn, you want a profit on the price of corn, not the corn itself. If you have ever leased a car, you already know that the monthly cost on a three-year lease is less than the monthly cost on a one-year lease for the same car.

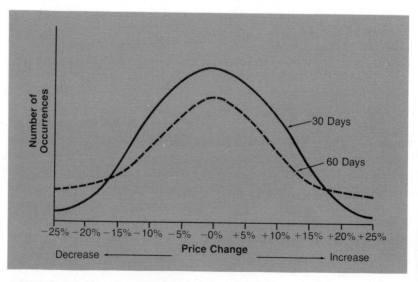

FIGURE 4-1. Price Distribution Chart

THE "FAIR PRICE" FACTORS

Five factors influence the price of an option:

1. duration,
2. relationship of striking price to market price,
3. volatility,
4. interest rates, and
5. supply/demand.

Duration

As you study actual option prices, you will find that the price of an option does not increase proportionately with the increase in time. The price of an option increases as a function of the square root of the time involved. Again, common sense fails us. Common sense tells us that, if a 1-month at-the-market option costs $1,000, then a 4-month option should cost $4,000 and a 9-month option should cost $9,000. In reality, if the one-month option costs $1,000, then the 4-month option will cost $2,000, and the 9-month option will cost $3,000. The reason is that the square root of 4 is 2, and so a 4-month option will cost twice what a one month option cost. Correspondingly, a 9-month option will cost 3 times that of a 1-month option.

What are you really buying? A lease. Assuming that a 1-month option costs $1,000, a 4-month option costs $2,000, and a 9-month option costs $3,000, you must decide how long a lease you want.

The 1-month option seems to be the least expensive. Is it?

Example: If you purchase a 9-month option today and hold it for a period of 5 months, you will then own a 4-month option. Assuming that the price of the underlying commodity has not changed, the price of your 9-month option, in 5 months, must be what a 4-month option is today. Therefore, if you purchase your option for $3,000 and nothing else happens except time passes, your option in 5 months will be worth $2,000. In other words, your 5-month "lease" has cost you $200/month. If you continue to hold your option for an additional 3 months, you would then own a 1-month option. Further assuming that nothing had changed, your option should now cost what a 1-month option had cost 8 months before, $1,000. Your "lease" for this 3-*month* period cost $1,000 or a monthly cost of $333.33/month. If you continue to hold the option until expiration, and the price of the commodity remains unchanged, your option will expire worthless with a monthly cost for the last month of $1,000.

As you can see, although options of greater duration have a higher absolute cost, their monthly cost is substantially less. In Figure 4–2, the straight line depicts common sense: a 9-month option depreciating approximately 1/270th of its value for each day it is outstanding. Common sense is based on the purchase of a "real" asset and its depreciation. As we have seen, this is not the case at all. The curved line depicts the way the price of an option actually depreciates with the passage of time. In the early days of an option's existence, its price depreciates very little. While later in an option's life the price depreciation becomes much more rapid. In fact, during the last 30 to 45 days of an at-the-market option's existence, its time value depreciates very rapidly.

At some point, having decided to buy an option, you face the question, What maturity or duration should one buy? The answer is connected with the fact that, when you purchase an option, you do so because you anticipate some event to occur. For example, you expect the price of gold to go up, interest rate to come down, or the like. With such a judgment, you generally also make some evaluation as to the time frame in which you expect the event to take place. Needless to say, you must purchase an option whose duration is great enough to allow the event to take place. The "key," however, is to purchase an option that will still have 30 to 45 days remaining to expiration at the time you intend to liquidate.

Many option theoreticians use the term *random walk* to describe the price behavior of both securities and commodities. The term relates the price change of the security or commodity to the random walking patterns

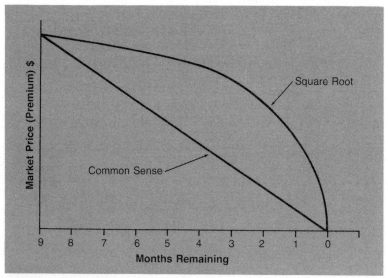

FIGURE 4–2. Square Root of Time

that might be demonstrated by a drunk left unattended in an open field. The question is, if you leave a drunk in an open field for a period of one hour and then return, where would he most likely be found? The answer is: on the spot you left him, because it is the only spot you are sure he occupied at least once. All other spots in the field are less likely. If you left the same individual in the field for two hours, the likelihood of the drunk being twice the distance from the point of origin does not double, because drunks do not move in straight lines at constant speeds.

Striking Price/Market Price

The second factor in option pricing is the relationship of the striking price of the option to the current price of the commodity for delivery at expiration. More succinctly, is the option in-the-money, at-the-market, or out-of-the-money? Most people feel that this factor is the most difficult to comprehend. In reality, if you consider your own behavioral patterns, it is rather simple. To understand option pricing, just realize that any econometric model tries only to explain how people will behave under a given set of circumstances; the actual price that an option is worth is what someone is willing to pay for it at any point in time.

Let's look at several hypothetical options and determine what they are worth to us as individuals. When you make these pricing decisions, think with your own dollars. What would I pay for this option? You will quickly find that you are willing to pay more for options that appear to have greater profit potential (or that are more in-the-money) than for options with less profit potential (out-of-the-money).

Example: Physical gold for immediate delivery is selling for $400/ounce. What would you be willing to pay for the following two options?

Call 100 ounces gold at $2,000/ounce expiring in 30 days $_____?
Call 100 ounces gold at $1/ounce expiring in 30 days $_____?

Common sense, which in this case is correct, would probably tell you that the first option is worthless. Why? Gold is selling for $400/ounce. The expectation that it will be selling for $2,000/ounce within 30 days is very unrealistic. This option is, by definition, a *deep* out-of-the-money option. The second option, at first glance, appears to have tremendous value. First of all, it is *deep* in-the-money. An option that gives you the right to buy gold at $1/ounce when gold is selling for $400/ounce, is $399/ounce in-the-money and worth, you think, at least $39,900.

This view appears valid, but it is not correct. You were looking at theory and not at how you, *as an investor*, would really spend your own money. The price of an option is what people are willing to pay for it, and not many people would buy this option because it has no investment utility (it serves no purpose). Would *you* really pay $39,900 for this option? Of course not. Why? An option offers an investor only two advantages: leverage and downside risk protection. This option is so deep in-the-money that it offers virtually no leverage and does not minimize your risk of ownership to any appreciable degree. You could buy 100 ounces of physical gold for $40,000, so why buy the option at all?

In fact, the only persons who would be willing to buy this option are arbitrageurs. They would buy the option, exercise it, and simultaneously sell the gold. They would do so only if they could make a profit and would pay some amount less than the option's intrinsic value, perhaps $39,800 or less.

How does price relate to time? Let's say that each of these two options has an expiration of 6 months instead of 30 days. Would they have been worth any more? The answer is very little, if any. This answer appears to contradict what was said about the effect of time. The word "time," as used in the expression "time value," is misleading because it intimates that, in all cases, the price of an option is related to time. Such an implication is not correct, as we have just seen.

A term that is perhaps easier to deal with than time value is *extrinsic value*. Extrinsic value is the portion of an option's price that is not included in intrinsic value. The first option had very little, if any, greater value for 6 months than 30 days because the probability of gold appreciating to $2,000/ounce in 6 months was not appreciably greater than it was in 30 days. The second option had no greater value, because the option's high price was already dysfunctional, and an increase in time only added to the dysfunction.

Extrinsic (or, if you prefer, time) value has a bearing only in a limited number of circumstances. The further the striking price of an option is from an at-the-market striking price, the less extrinsic value it has regardless of the time remaining until expiration. This phenomenon is a little easier to understand if you realize that you can expect only an option which has the investment merits of an option to behave like an option. At-the-market options offer leverage and downside risk protection—they have investment merits—and thus they behave as you would expect. Longer-term options cost more. As an option becomes further and further out-of-the-money, it becomes less and less like an option due to its probability of profit (less chance of being exercised). It therefore does not reflect an increase in extrinsic value for an increase in time. It is more like a $2 bet on a long-shot than it is like an option. A deep-in-the-money option approximates the investment characteristics of the physical commodity and, as such, does not have an increase in extrinsic value reflecting an increase in time remaining until expiration. An understanding of this relationship is crucial to dealing in options. At-the-market options command the greatest extrinsic value, and options that are either deep in-the-money or deep out-of-the-money command very little if any extrinsic value.

Example: Gold is at $500/ounce. You call your broker and ask for a quotation on a 6-month call on gold at-the-market. The broker responds that the option will cost $7,500. You purchase the option for $7,500. During the night, the Klingons invade earth, the San Andreas fault makes beachfront property out of Phoenix, and the polar ice caps begin to melt. The following morning, gold commences trading at $1,500/ounce. After congratulating yourself for your wise investment decision, you call your broker for a quotation on your option. You assume that your option is $1,000/ounce in the money and therefore has an intrinsic value of $100,000 ($1,000 × 100). You further assume that, because only one day has passed, your option should have approximately $7,500 in extrinsic, or time, value. Your broker informs you that the only bid for your option is $99,500. You ask your broker, "What happened to the time value?" It disappeared. Why? You really know the answer to your own question.

What happened is this: Yesterday you purchased an at-the-market option, and today you are liquidating a *very* deep in-the-money option, which has no extrinsic value. In fact, the only purchaser will be the arbitrageur. As the price of a commodity fluctuates, existing options become more in- or out-of-the-money. Consequently, the extrinsic value dissipates regardless of the passage of time.

The chart in Figure 4–3 reflects only the extrinsic value and not the

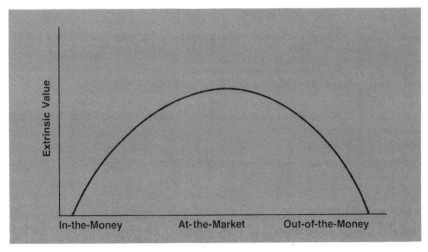

FIGURE 4–3. Extrinsic (Time) Value Chart

intrinsic value of the option. As you can see, options that are "struck" at-the-market have the highest extrinsic value, and options that are either deep in-the-money or deep out-of-the-money have no extrinsic value. As the price of a commodity increases, your call option becomes more in-the-money and loses extrinsic value, even though you are experiencing a move in your favor.

On the other hand, if the market moves down, your call option is moving out-of-the-money and you are losing extrinsic value. For small moves, perhaps 5%, you can generally expect the option either to appreciate or to depreciate about half as fast as the increase or decrease in extrinsic value.

> **Example:** You own a call on gold with a striking price of $500/ounce, and gold appreciates to $510 with very little time passing. You can expect the option to appreciate about $500 in market price ($10 × 100 ounces × 1/2). If gold continues to appreciate and the option gets further and further in-the-money, the sensitivity of the option continues to increase because your investment is becoming more like physical gold and less like an option. The chart in Figure 4–3 shows that you can expect the option to appreciate by .5, .6, ...9, and eventually 1.0.
>
> Conversely, if the price of gold moves down from the $500 level and you own a call struck at $500/ounce, your call becomes further out-of-the-money. Initially the option would depreciate 1/2 (.5) as fast; that is, if gold dropped $10/ounce, you could generally expect your option to depreciate about $500. As gold continues to drop, your option becomes less and less sensitive to this further depreciation. The option depreciates .4, .3, . . . and ultimately 0.0. There is very little difference in the value of an option that gives its owner the right to buy gold at $500/ounce, if gold is at either $50/ounce or $75/ounce.

Volatility

Another way of expressing *volatility* is asking, How much is the price of the underlying commodity likely to change over the duration of the option? If you have dealt in security options, you are aware that, in percentage terms, options of like durations generally cost more on Polaroid than on American Telephone and Telegraph. Historically, the percentages of price fluctuations of Polaroid have been far greater than those of American Telephone and Telegraph.

This same phenomenon holds true—indeed is of even greater importance—in commodities. Although the volatility of a given security does change over time, it is the exception rather than the rule. When the change does take place, it is in many instances more moderate in degree than corresponding changes in commodities. When you purchase a commodity, you in effect speculate as to the direction the commodity will then move. Most people fail to realize that they are also speculating that the commodity will continue to move at the same rate it has been moving in the recent past.

Yet beware! The concept of volatility is very similar to the famous tortoise and hare race. If your call option allowed you to profit based on which participant covered the greatest distance in the shortest time, you should willingly pay more for a call on the hare than on the tortoise. Hares are historically far more capable of rapid ground coverage than turtles. If you had purchased an option on the hare, the weakness of this approach would have become obvious. Past performance is the only criterion on which we can base our judgment, and yet it is not always a reliable indicator of future results.

Volatility is the measurement of price change over a given period of time. Most people measure this volatility as the change in price of the commodity from day to day, using the closing price as the basis for any calculations. Options on commodities that have historically had large price fluctuations over limited periods of time will tend to command higher premiums than options on commodities whose price fluctuations have been narrower over similar periods of time. It is impossible to know how much the price of a commodity will change over the next 24 hours, let alone how it is likely to change over the duration of an option. However, this rate of change is perhaps the most important factor in option pricing over limited periods of time.

As already mentioned, the volatility of commodities changes regularly. As a result, the premium levels of commodity options can and will change as the volatility changes without much change in the actual price of the commodity.

Example: You purchase a call option on platinum when the price of platinum for the past few weeks has not fluctuated more than $2 to $3 a day. You pay a premium of $2,000 for a 3-month option. On the day following your purchase, the price of platinum declines $25/ounce, and on the next day it rebounds the same $25/ounce. In such a case, your option would most likely show a profit. This appreciation in premium is a recognition of the fact that something has happened to the volatility of the price of platinum. As such, platinum has become more like a hare and less like a tortoise. These expansions in premium would effect both put and call options.

The converse can also occur. Let's say that you purchase a call option on platinum when its price is fluctuating an average of $20/ounce/day and the price of platinum continues to increase but at a decreased rate of perhaps \$2/ounce/day. In this case, you might actually see a decrease in the price of the option, while the price of the metal increases.

Under ideal circumstances, you would like to purchase an option at a time when the commodity has historically shown low volatility and the premiums are relatively small. You would like to liquidate positions when volatility is high and premiums are generally inflated.

As the price of a commodity increases, the price of call options on that commodity generally increases. As an option moves further in-the-money, intrinsic value increases and extrinsic value decreases. The decrease in extrinsic value is caused partially by the passage of time but more so by the decreased utility of the option. That is, as the premium increases, the option affords less leverage, and the higher dollar price of the option entails higher risk.

If, after having purchased an option, you see an increase in the volatility of the underlying commodity, there will most likely be an increase in the premium in the form of extrinsic value. (See Figure 4–4.) This expansion in extrinsic value has two results: First, the option appreciates in value more rapidly than you had forecasted. Second, the option goes further in-the-money before the extrinsic value is dissipated.

The converse occurs if the volatility of the underlying commodity contracts after an option is purchased. A contraction in volatility is evidenced in the contraction of the extrinsic value of options on that commodity. If you own a call option on a commodity that experiences a contraction in volatility, upward moves in the price of that commodity result in moves in the option premium of a lesser magnitude than you have forecast. You could actually see a declining premium with an increasing commodity price. This contraction is a result of the public's perception of reduced investment utility to the option. Options on less volatile commodities are less attractive than options on highly volatile commodities.

As an important factor in option pricing, volatility is incorporated into all option pricing formulas. Yet it is the most difficult to deal with because it must be entered mathematically and in reality is a subjective judgment on the part of the option purchaser and grantor.

FIGURE 4–4

Volatility	*Effect On Premium*
Increase (+)	Increase (+)
Decrease (−)	Decrease (−)

Interest Rates

Interest rates represent the first instance in which there is a substantial difference between security and commodity option pricing. In security options you are always dealing with the right to either buy or sell the underlying security at the cash price. In commodities you are dealing with the right to buy or sell at a future price. This difference appears to make the behavior of option premiums reversed for securities and commodities as they relate to interest rates. In securities, an increase in interest rates generally causes an increase in option premiums, and a reduction in interest rates causes a decline in premiums. In commodities, as interest rates go up, the extrinsic portions of option premiums come down; as interest rates come down, the extrinsic portions of option premiums go up.

The reason for this reverse behavior is carrying charges. The cash price of a security does not recognize the carrying costs involved in the ownership of a security for the period of time that the option is outstanding. If you purchase a security that pays no dividend and hold the security for a year, you might believe that you have incurred no loss if the price of the security is unchanged. This, of course, is not true because you have an opportunity loss on the money invested. You could have put the money into the bank and collected interest.

Commodity futures contracts normally reflect at least a portion of the carrying charges involved in their ownership. If you purchase a commodity futures contract that calls for delivery of the commodity in one year, the price of that commodity for future delivery will approximate the current cash price plus the approximate costs involved in the ownership of that commodity for the ensuing year. If the price of the cash (spot) commodity does not change over the course of the year, the price of the commodity for future delivery will, in a linear fashion, decline reflecting the costs of ownership. At the delivery time, both the cash and the futures price will be the same. The buyer of a call option must pay the carrying costs. In securities, the buyer pays the carrying cost by paying a higher premium when interest rates are high. In commodities the call option buyer pays the carrying cost because the price of the commodity for future delivery is higher.

Let's look at a commodity option from the grantors' point of view. In granting options, grantors receive two things: first the premium and second the use of the premium before the obligation is discharged. If the option is a 1-year option, the grantor gets the premium immediately but has not fulfilled the obligation until the option obligation is discharged, probably one year later. The grantor therefore has the premium and the interest on the premium over the next year.

Example: An option is granted for a premium of $4,000, and the prime rate is 20%. At year end the grantor will have the $4,000 and the interest on $4,000 at 20% for a year, or an additional $800. The total return on the investment is $4,800, not $4,000. Had the prime rate been 10% instead of 20%, the grantor would have received only $4,400, as opposed to $4,800. If the grantor believes that $4,800 is the proper compensation for the risk involved in granting the option, he or she will grant the option for $4,000 when the prime rate is 20%, but will demand approximately $4,365 if the prime rate is only 10%.

The purchase of an option is much the same as the purchase of a magazine subscription, in that you are paying for a product you have not yet received. This prepayment is more valuable to the person who will deliver the product when interest rates are high.

Another way to look at interest rates is the economic benefit derived by the commercial entity who uses options as part of a hedging program. Let's say that you are in the copper business and have in inventory a substantial quantity of copper wire bars. Traditional hedging strategy says that you will take an equal and opposite position in the futures market from your position in the cash market, which means that you will sell or go short a like quantity of futures. The broker will require the commercial to deposit original margin on the short futures position. If the commercial is also a grantor of call options, this granting is the equivalent of a contingent short position and would be hedged by a long futures position requiring margin. The net result of this strategy is: long physical copper, short futures, long futures, short options. You can see that the futures portion of the total position will "net out" to zero, thereby eliminating the need for futures margin. The commercial will still have to meet margin requirements on the short options, but the margin requirements on the options may be more advantageous than corresponding margin on futures. Any cash savings in a high interest rate market are attractive, and this positive cash flow becomes more advantageous as interest rates increase. As interest rates go up, options writing becomes more and more attractive to the commercial who will grant options at lower and lower premiums due to the offsetting economic benefit.

In security options, the grantor must receive higher premiums during higher interest rates to compensate for the higher cost of capital committed to the venture of option granting.

FIGURE 4–5

Interest Rates	Effect on Premium
Up (+)	Decrease (−)
Down (−)	Increase (+)

Supply/Demand

How specifically do forces of supply and demand affect the price of an option? For instance, why does a price go up? The common response is that there were more buyers than sellers. Yet obviously there must be as many buyers as sellers for the transactions to take place. Actually, prices go up because the buyers are more aggressive than the sellers, and prices go down when the opposite is true. The real question is what makes an option buyer or grantor willing to transact business at a given price?

Buyers are perhaps the easier to understand because a willingness to buy at a specific price is nothing more than a market judgment. When buyers believe that the purchase of an option will result in a profit, they buy regardless of the price. The more bullish the buyers, the more they will pay for a call option. The more bearish the buyers, the more they are willing to pay for a put.

Because the majority of option granting is done by either commercial (institutional) entities or individuals with an eye to return on invested capital, the granting side, as it relates to price, tends to be more specific. Let me show you with an example how an individual might view an option-writing program.

Example: Ms. Baker has $1,000,000 to commit to attractive business ventures. (Let's assume that there is no such thing as inflation, which would only complicate the example and add nothing to the understanding.) Baker runs an advertisement in the local paper offering venture capital, or money in search of a business. The first respondent to the ad states that he is interested in 6-month, at-the-market calls on gold; depending on the price, he will decide as to whether he wishes to buy or write the options. Baker must decide at what price she will be a writer and at what price she will be a buyer.

Price is the total determinant in this case. There is a "right" price to buy and a "right" price to sell. If gold is selling for $400/ounce and a 6-month call option can be purchased for a total price of $10, it should obviously be bought. If, on the other hand, the option cost $50,000 (far more than the total value of the gold), it should obviously be sold. Through whatever tools at her command, our venture capitalist determines that she would be a buyer of these options for $3,500 and a grantor for $4,000.

The respondent, reviewing the $3,500 bid and $4,000 offer, determines that he will be a buyer of 5 options at $4,000 each. The respondent, now an option buyer, pays the venture capitalist, now an option grantor, $20,000 for the 5 options. Baker is now in the option-granting business.

Baker's risk situation has changed dramatically. Prior to granting the options, she has no risk whatsoever because her assets were all cash. Now she has the obligation, at the buyer's discretion, to deliver gold if called upon to do so. Assuming that the options are each for 100 ounces of gold and that these at-the-market options have a striking price of

$400/ounce, the grantor has the contingent liability to deliver $200,000 worth of gold.

Without discussing the reasoning (covered in later chapters), let's assume that Baker elects to purchase 500 ounces of gold immediately to protect herself in the event that the buyer exercises the option. Having purchased $200,000 worth of gold, the grantor is now the proud(?) owner of an asset on which she has no profit potential, due to the call granted, and the assumption of the related risk inherent in the ownership of that asset.

Baker has received $4,000 per option in premium for assuming the risks of granting. This is the equivalent of $40/ounce ($4,000/100) ounces). If the price of gold declines by more than $40/ounce, the grantor will have offset any profit potential and will have the risk of the continued ownership of the gold until the option obligation is discharged. You can see that the option grantor has assumed a very real risk in granting the five options.

As the day progresses, many additional respondents propose business ventures to our venture capitalist. Some are accepted, some rejected. Later in the day another individual says that he is interested in 6-month, at-the-market call options on gold. He too does not know if he wishes to be a buyer or sell; price is the only determinant.

Given that the day commenced with no risk and that the price of gold has remained unchanged, Baker should be a more aggressive purchaser and a less aggressive grantor. This is because the sale of the first five options increased the venture capitalist's risk from zero to some higher level (although this level is still undefined). The sale of more options would commit the venture capitalist to the purchase of more gold and consequently to more risk, while the purchase of options might allow the venture capitalist to reduce her gold holdings and reduce her risk. The way that one becomes a more aggressive buyer and a less aggressive seller is to raise both one's bid price and one's offer price for the option. Under these circumstances, with no change in the price of gold, the venture capitalist might bid $3,700 for the options and offer options for $4,200. This change in price is nothing more than risk aversion on Baker's part to the further concentration of risk in the vagaries of the gold price.

From Baker's point of view, the market price for options fluctuates as a function of the risk that the participants, in total, are willing to accept. Notice that the price of the options increases without any increase in the price of gold. As the total risk increases to the grantor, the price she demands increases in an effort to compensate for the perceived increase in risk.

This magnitude of move and the inclusion of only one grantor were done for the sake of our example. But the logic is valid in a large liquid market with many grantors, only to a lesser degree.

Summary

These five factors are the mathematical input to determine the "fair" price of an option, which is a theoretical number. The interaction of the buyer and seller in the market place determines at what price transactions will take place. A formula serves only as a benchmark against which to make market judgments. Similarly, these mathematical formulas are means by which one attempts to predict price based on historical factors. Yet the past is not always indicative of the future, and, as a result, the concept of over-priced and underpriced options is questionable in relationship to fair value. Options will in many cases be overpriced in relationship to a fair value formula due to the nature of the participants in the market. Speculators, who are traditionally buyers, base their fair value on market projections that are what they anticipate will happen. Grantors, on the other hand, base their thinking on history, which is what has happened.

OVERPRICED OPTIONS

To understand why most options are overpriced and why this must be the case, we have to look at options from a slightly different point of view.

Example: A buyer pays a grantor $30/ounce for a 6-month, at-the-market call on 100 ounces of gold. The grantor sells for $3,000, and the buyer buys for $3,000. They have made a deal, whose terms read something like this: If the price of gold goes up, the grantor will receive the first $30/ounce because the buyer will ultimately exercise, and all the grantor will have received as profit is the premium. The buyer, on the other hand, will receive all the profit attributable to the gold price increase, minum the premium paid the grantor. If gold goes down, the buyer has agreed to assume the first $30/ounce risk in the form of the option becoming worthless, and the covered option grantor has agreed to assume any further risk.

We have been calling this transaction an option when in fact it is actually collision insurance—on commodity trading. The buyer wishes to trade gold with a $30/ounce deductible on the outcome, and the grantor is insuring this risk for a premium. The fact that options must be overpriced is far easier to understand if we follow the insurance analogy to its logical conclusion. Let's relate this insurance to a type of insurance with which we are all more familiar, life insurance.

Insurance companies are pecuniary ventures; that is, they expect to make a profit on their investments. Let us assume that the insurance company, through actuarial research determines that it can sell life insurance to a 30-year-old male for $4/$1,000 face value. Because the insurance company's intent is to make money, they sell the policy for perhaps $7/$1,000 face value. Death is a certainty, and as a result the insurance company will have to pay out the face value of the policy. If their actuarial assumption is correct, they will make $3/$1,000 face value, on average for every policy they sell. As insurance buyers, we are generally aware that we are overpaying for our life insurance, but we willingly do so. Why?

The least expensive way to insure any risk is to self-insure. If you want $100,000 of life insurance, the cheapest way to do it is to deposit $400 in a bank on your way home tonight, and each year do the same thing. If you live to your actuarial assumption, your insurance will have cost you nothing. The problem is, if on the way home tonight, you get hit by a truck and killed, your spouse is going to question your financial planning. We therefore, almost willingly, pay $7/$1,000 for something that we know is worth only $4/$1,000 because we want someone else to assume a risk which we are unwilling or unable to assume.

When you buy an option, you are doing exactly the same thing. You have said that you wish to trade commodities, but, beyond a defined point, you are unwilling or unable to accept the risk associated with it. You want an insurance company (the grantor) to assume that risk in exchange for a premium. If you are buying insurance, then the grantor must be selling insurance and, as such, must behave in much the same fashion as an insurance company would under like circumstances.

Let's look at how the grantor "plays" insurance company. The grantor, in granting the option, has assumed the risk inherent in owning the commodity, and this risk is mitigated only by the premium received from the buyer. Insurance companies reduce risk by selling policies to people of different ages, in different occupations, in different locations, as well as by transferring a portion of this to other insurance companies through pooling of risk. Grantors may transfer part of their risk in similar fashion. They can write many different options, at different times, at striking prices, and in different markets, as well as by using different hedging strategies.

As you can see, options are overpriced for much the same reason that insurance is overpriced.

Hedging

Why must options be overpriced? To appreciate why, you must understand the approaches taken by the grantor. (The strategy chapters deal with option writing in greater detail.)

Most people believe that all things are black or white. So they do also in option writing. They believe that you are either a covered option writer (you own the underlying commodity), or you are an uncovered/naked option writer (you don't own the underlying commodity). Along with this perception has gone the view that covered option writing is "good" and naked option writing is "bad." This perception makes about as much sense as "good guys wear white hats, and bad guys wear black hats." Let's look at the mathematics of both covered and naked option writing.

Covered Writing

Example: The grantor sells a 6-month call on gold at $400/ounce, on 100 ounces of gold, for a total premium of $3,000 ($30/ounce). At the time the option is written, the grantor purchases 100 ounces of gold at $400/ounce, thereby investing $40,000. This is a classic covered writing situation. Once the position is established, three things can happen: (1) gold can go up, (2) gold can remain unchanged, or (3) gold can go down. Let's look at the results of those three possibilities.

If gold goes up, at some point in time, the buyer will exercise the option, take delivery of the gold, and pay the grantor $40,000 for the delivery of the gold. The grantor will have sustained neither a profit nor a loss on the gold and will get to keep the premium of $3,000. This equates to a 7.5% ($3,000/$40,000) return on capital invested for 6 months, or 15% annualized. This rate of return is actually slightly understated as the grantor received the premium at the beginning of the transaction and therefore had to commit only $37,000 to the transaction. The rate of return is therefore, approximately 16.2% annualized.

If gold remains unchanged, through the passage of time, the option will expire. For the simplicity of the example, we will assume that the option grantor liquidates the gold position. In this case the economics are identical to gold moving up. The grantor receives $3,000 on an investment of $37,000 for 6 months' commitment.

Finally, let's say gold goes down and the buyer does not exercise. Thus the option expires. Let's assume that gold drops to $370/ounce. In this case, at expiration, the grantor might liquidate the gold position, sustaining a $3,000 loss, having purchased 100 ounces for $40,000 and liquidating them for $37,000. The grantor, on the other hand, gets to keep the $3,000 premium, thus breaking even with gold at $370/ounce at expiration. Were gold to decline below $370/ounce, the grantor would lose $100 each time gold declined by $1/ounce below the breakeven price of $370/ounce since the premium would be insufficient to cover this additional risk. The grantor has a $30 range in which he or she will not lose money. This range is from $400/ounce to $370/ounce.

These are the parameters for covered option writing with this set of circumstances. Now let's look at the parameters for the same set of circumstances when the grantor decides to be a naked option writer.

Naked Writing. In a naked writing situation, grantors assume the same obligations—that is, to deliver the gold—but they have decided not to purchase the gold at the time that the option is granted. The same three things can happen: gold can go up, remain unchanged, or go down. Let's look at the financial consequences.

> *Example:* If gold goes down, the option will expire, and the grantor will get to keep the $3,000 premium for which he really did nothing. He did not purchase gold, had only the risk of not owning it, and received $3,000 in exchange for this risk. Quantifying the rate of return on no investment is impossible. In the real world, if this option were granted, there would have been some sort of margin deposit, and we could compute a rate of return on invested capital.
>
> If gold remains unchanged, the option will expire, and the grantor will again retain the premium. The exposure to the naked grantor takes place in a market when the price of gold rises.
>
> If gold appreciates, at some point in time, the option will be exercised, and the grantor will be called upon to deliver the 100 ounces of gold at $400/ounce in exchange for the payment by the buyer of $40,000. Let's assume that gold is at exactly $430/ounce at expiration and the buyer exercises. In this case, the grantor goes into the open market, purchases 100 ounces of gold at $430/ounce for a total cost of $43,000, and delivers the gold to the buyer in exchange for $40,000. The grantor has sustained a loss of $3,000 on the gold portion of the transaction. He has, however, gotten to keep the premium, which was also $3,000, and therefore breaks even at $430/ounce. If gold continues still higher (above $430/ounce), the grantor will lose $100 for each dollar that gold is above $430/ounce at expiration. This grantor also has a $30/ounce range in which he will not lose money ($400/ounce to $430/ounce).

You can see that the difference between being a "good guy" and a "bad guy" is whether gold goes up or down. In reality, naked writing and covered writing have identical risks. In this example, the risk is that the market moves counter to your projections by more than $30/ounce. Factually, naked writing is a better investment purely from the point of view of "rate of return on invested capital." It takes less investment to generate the $3,000 premium.

The option writer tends to be the professional, that is, either a commercial user of the commodity or an investor who approaches the option market with the thought of generating a return on invested capital. As such, neither the covered nor the naked approach to option writing offers a purely neutral view of the market. The granting of either covered or naked options carries with it an implied market judgment. Covered call option writers are generally saying that the market will not go down much, while naked option writers are saying that the market will not go up much.

Variable Ratio Option Writing

Most professional option writers use the strategy referred to as *variable ratio option writing*. An example will perhaps best demonstrate the parameters of this strategy and thereby define it. The so-called ratio writer would, at the time the option was granted, buy part of the amount of the commodity required for delivery.

Example: In the same set of circumstances as in the previous example, the grantor would buy 50 ounces of gold at $400/ounce as a partial hedge for the delivery obligation. The same three market possibilities exist: gold up, gold unchanged, or gold down.

If gold remains unchanged, the option will expire through the passage of time, and the grantor will liquidate the gold position, having received a $3,000 premium on a $20,000 investment. The grantor purchased only 50 ounces of gold at $400/ounce, thereby investing only $20,000 in the metal. The grantor receives the premium immediately and thereby has an out-of-pocket cost of only $17,000 to buy the gold. If the option expires worthless, the grantor has received a $3,000 premium on an investment of $17,000 for 6 months. This is 17.6% for 6 months or 35.2% annualized. So if gold remains unchanged, the hedging procedure makes no difference except that it affects the rate of return on invested capital because the option will expire worthless, and the grantor will experience neither profit nor loss on the hedge.

If gold goes up, the grantor has risk because he owns only a portion of the gold that may ultimately have to be delivered. If, at expiration, gold is at $460/ounce, the option buyer will exercise, and the grantor will be obliged to deliver 100 ounces of gold for a total price of $40,000. The first 50 ounces poses no problem because the grantor acquires those 50 ounces for $20,000 at the time the option was granted. If at expiration, gold is at $460/ounce, the grantor has to purchase an additional 50 ounces at $460/ounce with a related cost of $23,000 (50 ounces × $460/ounce). These two purchases (50 ounces at $400/ounce and 50 ounces at $460/ounce) give the grantor a total cost of $43,000 for the 100 ounces of gold to be delivered. The grantor receives $40,000 at the time of delivery, thereby sustaining a $3,000 loss on the gold portion of the transaction. The grantor, however, keeps the $3,000 premium and therefore breaks even. If gold continues still higher (above $460/ounce), the grantor sustains a $50/ounce loss for each dollar of gold appreciation above this price. The reason is that the protection afforded by the premium has been exhausted, and the option obligation still exists. It is interesting to note that a naked writer would be sustaining a loss of $100/$1 move, while the ratio writer is sustaining only a $50/$1 move above breakeven.

Let's say gold moves lower, and the option expires worthless. If, at expiration, gold is trading at $340/ounce, the grantor liquidates the 50 ounces of gold, receiving $17,000 on the gold sale (50 ounces × $340/ounce). The initial purchase was $20,000, and the liquidation is $17,000. The loss on the gold portion of the transaction is $3,000, but the grantor gets to keep the $3,000 premium and thereby breaks even with gold trading at $340/ounce at expiration. Below $340/ounce, the grantor loses $50/$1 drop in the gold price because he owns 50 ounces, and the protection afforded by the premium has been exhausted.

Note that a covered option writer loses $100/$1 drop in the gold price below breakeven. The $340 per ounce is a substantially lower breakeven than the $370 breakeven for the covered writer in the earlier example. The ratio writer, through the use of this strategy, has a range from $340/ounce to $460/ounce on the price of gold at expiration in which to make money. This is a substantially larger range than that afforded to either the covered or the naked option writer.

All three of these strategies direct themselves at what the option writer does at the instant the option is granted. They overlook action that may be taken by the grantor between the date of granting and expiration. Most covered option writers do not change their "hedge" during the period that the option is outstanding unless they experience a change in their view of the market, and it is impossible to say what approach they would follow not knowing their change in view. Ratio writing is, however, an active, as opposed to a passive, strategy, and it requires a constant alteration of the hedge during the period that the option is outstanding if the price of gold does or does not change. As the price of gold appreciates, the probability of the option being exercised improves, and as a result the ratio writer adds to the gold position. As the market price of gold moves lower, or as time passes, the probability of exercise declines, and the ratio writer reduces the number of ounces held as a hedge against the commitment. The ratio writer's strategy is therefore to buy when the market goes up and to sell when the market comes down. In other words, counter to the aged dictum to buy low and sell high, the ratio writer buys high and sells low. How do you make money buying high and selling low? You don't!

The option writer knows that ratio writing is designed to lose money on the underlying commodity. Don't forget: Options must be overpriced, but buyers buy regardless of this fact. Knowledgeable option writers realize that the fair price of an option is the price that equals the trading losses sustained by the ratio writer during the period that the option is outstanding. Ratio writers, in much the same fashion as the insurance company, write options for amounts that exceed their value by enough to compensate them for the time, effort, capital, and risk committed and sustained by option granting.

> *Example:* If an option is offered for $3,000, it is perhaps bid $2,600. The $2,600 price is quite close to the fair value. If $2,600 is the fair price and the option grantor succeeds in granting the option for $3,000, the losses sustained in a ratio writing program should be about $2,600. The option writer then realizes the difference between the bid and the offer as the real profit for entering the transaction.

This is very nearly the fact. Over a period of time, this spread is the option grantor's potential profit. If the spread is the grantor's real profit, then the spread is also the buyer's real cost. Let's look at this concept.

The Bid/Offer Spread

When you purchase an option, your cost is not truly the offer premium but the difference between the price at which you purchase and the price at which that option could be resold immediately. The only time that your true cost is the purchase price is when the option that is purchased is not fungible (cannot be resold). The magnitude of this spread is a function of many variables, of which some are inherent in all commodity transactions and some are peculiar to options.

In commodities and in options, liquidity is a major determinant of the bid/offer spread. A majority of the activity (volume) is normally concentrated in the first few contract months, and the more distant maturities (the back months) entail progressively less volume and open interest. This lack of volume and open interest causes a larger spread in the bid and offer. The reason is that a person, having purchased a futures contract in a back month, finds fewer people trading that month and therefore a wider bid/offer spread. When there are many participants in a contract, each is attempting to either bid slightly higher or offer slightly lower to improve his or her chance of execution with a resulting narrow bid/offer spread.

This phenomenon also has a bearing due to the difference in exchange rules for the trading of futures and options. Futures contracts in this country are subject to limit moves, while most exchanges have not imposed the same limit restriction to options. That is, the futures may be bid up the limit or offered down the limit, and the option contract will continue to trade. In these market conditions, the bid/offer spread on the option widens due to the reduced liquidity in the underlying commodity. Regardless of your approach to hedging a short option, the inability to either purchase or sell futures to alter the hedge increases the risk. This disability is expressed by grantors' demanding a higher price due to the inability to hedge. The buyer, on the other hand, pays only lower price due to his or her inability to offset the position with futures (hedge). These two attitudes taken together result in a wider spread. Therefore limit moves in futures widen spreads and decrease liquidity.

5

THE REGULATORS
AND REGULATIONS

THE BACKGROUND OF COMMODITY OPTION REGULATION

Commodity options are not new. Even commodity options trading on commodity exchanges is not new. Shortly after World War I, the commodity business in the United States experienced tremendous growth, primarily as a result of speculators entering markets that commercial interests had previously dominated. By the 1930s, market manipulation, "corners," and fraud were common occurrences. Under the Department of Agriculture, the Commodity Exchange Authority (CEA) was created with the purpose of regulating the then existing commodities. The legislation that created this agency was very narrow in scope and therefore provided only for the regulation of the commodities that were then exchange-traded. These "regulated" or "reg" commodities, as they became known, were primarily the comestibles, such as grains and livestock.

In regulating these markets, the CEA decided that commodity options served no economic purpose and were being used primarily for market manipulation. As a result the CEA banned the sale of commodity options on the commodities over which they had authority.

The commodity industry continued to grow, and additional commodities became exchange-traded. Such commodities as coffee, cocoa, sugar, silver, copper, and platinum became very active with substantial public participation. The CEA had no authority to regulate these new commodities, and these commodities were therefore free to trade encumbered only by the regulation of the exchanges on which they traded. These commodities came to be known as "nonregulated" or "nonreg" commodities.

This was not all bad, since the exchanges on which these nonreg com- modities traded, provided much the same customer protection and trading supervision required by the CEA on reg exchanges. In that the CEA had no authority over nonreg commodities, there was also no band on the trading of commodity options on those commodities.

The governmental agency set up to regulate commodities therefore did not have any control. But there was some control over nonreg commodities. Many states regulated commodity trading under their own commodity, se- curity, or fraud laws. Though designed to protect the customer, these laws caused a lack of uniformity throughout the country.

With the passage of the Commodity Futures Trading Commission Act in 1974, Congress created a new regulatory agency, the Commodity Futures Trading Commission (CFTC). The CFTC was charged with the responsibil- ity of regulating all commodity futures transactions done in the United States, including commodity options. The only exception was an exclusions for "off-exchange" transactions between commercial entities. The CFTC was further charged with determining whether commodity options served an economic purpose: if so, it was to regulate them; if not, ban them. With this charge, the CFTC was also given "exclusive jurisdiction," which meant that the CFTC was the only entity that could regulate commodities. This exclu- sive jurisdiction precluded the various states from having and enforcing their own commodity regulations.

The CFTC was one of the first governmental agencies to be created under what is referred to as "sunset legislation." This sunset legislation provided that newly created governmental agencies would exist for only a predetermined time, unless "reauthorized" for an added period of time by Congress. The CFTC, which was created or "authorized" in 1974, was given an initial "life" of four years, with their initial authorization expiring in 1978. Since then, Congress has routinely reauthorized the CFTC.

One of the early activities of the CFTC was to form a Committee on Market Instruments. The committee was asked to review all the commodity-type market instruments that currently were trading, stressing the economic purpose that each instrument served. The committee, among other things, made the determination that commodity options served an important economic purpose and therefore should not be banned.

The CFTC was a new agency charged with large responsibilities. With commodity options representing only a very small portion of the overall commodity transactions done in the United States, they did not get any substantial attention from the CFTC initially. Although most major broker- age firms had dealt in London commodity options over the years, the busi- ness had been very small with no measurable problems.

In 1975, a new type of commodity firm became popular. This new entity was the commodity option sales firm. The company would buy commodity options in London and then sell them to American investors at grossly inflated prices. This business was initially small-scale, but, when coffee prices went up dramatically as a result of a freeze in Brazil, many investors who had bought coffee options made "small fortunes." These "windfall profits" gave rise to two events: (1) The profits drew many new, unspecting investors into the commodity options markets, and (2) they encouraged the organization of many new commodity option sales firms.

As the business continued to grow, fraud made an appearance. Firms that called themselves London option dealers were charging enormous markups. As a result, option purchasers were not at all likely to make enough money to cover the markups, let alone profit on the entire transaction. At some point, many of these dealers realized that, if customers stood no chance of making a profit on the option, why hedge their commitments at all? Many of the dealers started selling "London options that never got to London." These dealers were "bucketing" the orders; that is, customers who thought they were buying London options were not. The dealers merely took the risk themselves as principals. This is fraud. Granting an option as principal and accepting the risk has nothing legally wrong with it—provided that this fact is disclosed to the customers. These dealers told their customers that they were buying London options, and such was not the case. The dealers did not disclose that, in most cases, 75% to 80% of the customer's funds were going for commissions and markups—not toward premiums. In addition, the dealers made outlandish promises about profit potential and often guaranteed profits. Before long, these fraudulent activities came to the attention of the press and the CFTC.

Commodity options suddenly achieved national recognition through extensive exposé articles in such publications as The *Boston Globe*, the *Washington Post*, and the *New York Times*. The publicity reached a point that most people knew more about commodity option fraud than they knew about commodity options. The CFTC reacted by passing what later became referred to as "Part A" regulations. These commodity option regulations were passed to eliminate fraud and protect customer funds.

The "Part A" Regulations

These regulations required the following:

Disclosure: The CFTC required that each customer who wished to deal in commodity options, receive a disclosure statement that "fairly" disclosed the risks, as well as the commissions and related charges involved. This disclosure was to include all material facts including the customer's breakeven price.

Segregation: The option dealer was required to segregate 90% of the funds received from the option customer until such time as the obligation, under the option, had been fulfilled. This meant that only 10% of the funds received from customers could be used to meet overhead expenses (commissions telephone, etc.). It also meant that new funds could not be used to pay off previous "winners."

Option Identification Number: Each option sold had to carry with it a unique identification number, which would provide an "order trail." That is, the option could be traced back to London, if it was in fact purchased there.

Registration: The option dealer, selling to the public had to be registered with the CFTC as a Futures Commission Merchant (FCM). This carried with it a minimum capital requirement of $50,000. Each employee of an FCM who was dealing with the public (salesperson) had to be registered as an Associated Person (AP). One could not be registered as an AP if one were a convicted felon.

These requirements, on the surface, do not appear especially onerous or unfair, but to the participants in this new scam, they were fatal. Most commodity option firms closed their doors, because, if they did not comply with the regulations, they faced federal prosecution.

Several (approximately 10) of the larger commodity option dealers formed an organization called the National Association of Commodity Option Dealers (NASCOD). NASCOD took the CFTC to court and obtained a "temporary restraining order" (TRO), which enjoined the CFTC from enforcing its regulations until the CFTC could prove that the regulations were not unconstitutional. Each time that the CFTC won its case, NASCOD would appeal the case to a higher court. This litigation dragged on for the better part of a year, during which time the members of NASCOD could legally continue to sell commodity options and not have to adhere to the Part A regulations.

By now it was 1978, the year that the CFTC would have to return to Congress to be reauthorized. This request for reauthorization could be based, in part, on the CFTC's record as a regulator and on the degree to which it had fulfilled its Congressional mandates. About the time the CFTC was preparing for reauthorization, the television show *60 Minutes* aired an exposé on commodity options. The negative repercussions and unfavorable publicity that the CFTC received were unimaginable.

The CFTC took the only action open to it. It banned the sale of commodity options to Americans by American firms. This action had been authorized by Congress in the original CFTC authorization, and it was therefore not subject to the same court challenges as the Part A regulations. One of the great weaknesses of a democracy is that it protects the "bad guys" as well as the "good guys." The ability to challenge the Part A regulations in the courts forced the CFTC to ban the sales of all commodity options by all firms. On balance, this was not bad since the majority of "good guy" brokerage firms did not do much commodity option business, and they were willing to have the ban if it succeeded in putting the "bad guys" out of the business.

The ban also had the potential to put out of business "good guys" who were doing substantial business. Two of the firms who were doing a large commodity option business were Mocatta Metals Corporation (MMC) and Metals Quality Corporation (MQC). Although neither MMC nor MQC dealt with the public, several major and many smaller brokerage firms sold MMC and MQC commodity options to the public. This ban would have precluded the sale of these options, called "dealer options." Mocatta Metals Corporation asked the CFTC for an exemption from the ban on the grounds that there had been no abuses in the sale of MMC or MQC options. The CFTC was in the difficult position that, although there had been no abuses, the granting of an exemption was the equivalent of granting a monopoly, which was beyond their authority and legally arbitrary and capricious. The CFTC realized that the request was not unwarranted but beyond its authority.

During the CFTC's reauthorization hearings, Mocatta petitioned Congress for rules that would allow the CFTC to grant exemptions to the commodity option ban. The reauthorization legislation, when completed, provided legislation that allowed the CFTC to draft rules providing exemptions to qualified dealers.

Shortly after reauthorization, the CFTC published what was called "Part B" regulations, which provided the guidelines under which a commodity option dealer could qualify for an exemption to the ban. These regulations, which are today included in Part 32 CFR, included all of the requirements of Part A plus the following:

Capitalization: To be qualified for the exemption, each dealer had to be capitalized at $10 million. In other words, two firms, such as Mocatta Metals Corporation and Metals Quality, had to each meet this capital requirement.

Aggregate Excess: Each firm that granted options was required, at such time as a customer's option was profitable, to set aside this unrealized profit for the benefit of the customer.

Grandfather Date: For a firm to qualify for the exemption, the firm had to have been both in the physical commodity business and in the business of granting commodity options on May 1, 1978.

Joint and Several Liability: Each dealer requesting an exemption from the ban had to assume liability for the actions of both the brokerage firms and the brokers selling their options.

The "joint and several" liability, although designed to protect the customer, also had the effect of discouraging large commercial companies from becoming option grantors. The "grandfather date" also had this undesirable effect. The CFTC, however, made it known that they would consider applications individually and allow variance from the regulations when warranted. Ultimately five firms qualified for an exemption from the ban.

Throughout this period, the commodity exchanges and the dealers were petitioning the CFTC for a regulation that would provide regulations allowing commodity options to trade on regulated commodity exchanges. Finally, in 1981, the CFTC published proposed rules that would provide both for exchange-traded commodity options and for permanent regulations for dealer options.

In November of 1981, seven major commodity exchanges filed proposals with the CFTC for the commencement of commodity option trading on their respective exchanges.

Today, non-U.S. commodity options are still banned. Americans cannot buy any foreign commodity options from a U.S.-based commodity brokerage firm. An American can, however, buy a London commodity option, for instance, from a London-based brokerage firm.

COMMODITY OPTION REGULATION TODAY

From the public customer's point of view, there are few noticeable differences between commodity futures and commodity options trading. The most apparent differences are the amount and types of disclosures made by the account executive prior to the first trade and in conjunction with later trades.

The CFTC requires with all commodity trading that customers receive a disclosure statement prior to their first futures trade. This disclosure statement is rather brief and cautions customers as to the general risk involved in futures trading. A similar requirement calls for the delivery of a disclosure statement for commodity options, but this statement is much more extensive and detailed. The brokerage firm is also required to receive written acknowledgment from customers that they have read and understood the disclosure statement. Both disclosure statements have specific language required by the CFTC, but the option disclosure statement also requires that the brokerage firm include any material fact that might affect the customer's option trading.

Most brokerage firms use a standard disclosure statement prepared by the Futures Industry Association (FIA). They then include an appendix covering any special procedures, policies, and the like that apply to their firm only, along with their commission schedules.

In addition, the broker is required to make specific disclosures verbally if the transaction contemplated involves deep out-of-the-money options. On purchase transactions, the customer must be informed that, although the option is inexpensive, the probability of profit is very low. On granting transactions, the grantor must be informed that even though the chance of exercise is small, the premium received is small in comparison to the potential risk. In addition, the broker must keep written records reflecting that these required disclosures have been made for each and every deep out-of-the-money trade.

Apart from disclosure, the customer is unlikely to be aware of the other regulatory differences. The primary regulatory responsibility rests with the CFTC in commodity options as it does with commodity futures, but the CFTC has delegated to the exchanges a greater degree of direct oversight responsibility. The exchanges have a far greater responsibility for the supervision of sales practices and advertising in commodity options than they do in commodity futures. Many more detailed reports must be filed by the brokerage firms with the exchanges and by the exchanges with the CFTC relating to trading activity and customer positions in commodity options than in commodity futures. To a great degree, this additional reporting is necessary because commodity option trading is a "pilot" program. At the end of the three-year pilot program, the CFTC will have to make determinations relating to the continuance, enlargement, or cancellation of the program. In addition, there have historically been more regulatory problems with options than with futures.

The next three chapters deal with U.S. dealer options, foreign options, and U.S. exchange-traded commodity options.

6

DEALER OPTIONS

As of early 1983, five dealers had received an exemption from the ban on the sale of commodity options: Mocatta Metals Corporation, The Mocatta Corporation, Dowdex, Comark, and Valeur First Boston Corporation. All these companies are legally qualified to sell dealer options. These companies sell their options only through brokerage firms appropriately registered with the CFTC. The discussion of dealers will be limited to the options granted by Mocatta Metals Corporation and The Mocatta Corporation because they are the largest and the oldest, with the largest number of brokers and the largest selection of options. As such, they account for the vast majority of the volume.

MOCATTA METALS CORPORATION

Mocatta Metals Corporation issues options on gold and silver, as well as gold and silver coins. The Mocatta Corporation issues options on copper and platinum. Although these options are legally dealer options, the term "Mocatta Option" has almost become generic and synonymous with "dealer option." Also, each company issuing an option is solely responsible for its own options; therefore Mocatta is responsible only for options issued by Mocatta, Metals Corporation; and The Mocatta Corporation is responsible only for its options, and so on. Regardless of what an option is called, the individual grantor is ultimately responsible.

Mocatta options differ from U.S. exchange-traded commodity options in several aspects. In some instances, these differences are minor, and in some cases they affect your entire approach to trading. The following paragraphs discuss the differences, where major, as well as the advantages and disadvantages.

Mocatta options are options on physical commodities as opposed to futures contracts. If you exercise a Mocatta call option, you receive the physical commodity in the form of a warehouse receipt, as opposed to a futures contract. If you exercise a put option, you are expected to deliver the physical commodity in the form of a warehouse receipt. Mocatta deals in options on gold, silver, copper, platinum, Krugerrands, Maple Leafs, silver dollar bags, and silver-clad bags. In the gold, silver, copper, and platinum, Mocatta trades both puts and calls; in the coin options, Mocatta deals only in call options. The dealer sets, not an exchange or regulatory agency, all of the contract terms and procedures. The dealer must, of course, abide by the regulations set by the Commodity Futures Trading Commission.

Maturity

Mocatta options have standardized maturities in much the same fashion as exchange-traded options. Each Mocatta option expires on one of eight days a year. Each different commodity has its own series of expiration dates. For example, gold options expire on the first banking day of either January, March, April, June, July, September, October, or December. In each quarter, two of the three months are traded, and in no situation are two back-to-back months without a contract traded. All Mocatta options expire at 12:00 noon New York time, on the first banking day of the contract month. At any point in time, Mocatta trades five contract months. Although Mocatta has, at times, traded options of up to sixteen months' duration, they now offer options of no greater than ten month's duration.

Trading Hours

Mocatta normally does business from its New York trading facility from 9:00 A.M. New York time until 10:00 P.M. New York time. During these hours, Mocatta deals in its options. It should be noted that most brokerage firms have nine-to-five office hours and do not offer the same extended trading that is actually available. As an option grantor, Mocatta uses, among other methods, the futures markets as a means to hedge the options that they grant. As a result, Mocatta's ability to hedge is limited during those hours when the futures markets are either not trading or trading at the limit. Under these situations Mocatta continues to deal in options, but at a slightly wider bid/offer spread. These extended trading hours offer the investor the ability to trade when news or preference dictate, not just when the futures markets are open. In addition, Mocatta, through its Hong Kong and London trading facilities, deals in Mocatta options during normal business hours in those markets. This facility allows the investor to trade Mocatta options 24 hours a day, approximately six days a week.

Exercise

Mocatta options are exercisable only during a specific period of time, that is, during an exercise "window." They expire at 12:00 noon on the first banking day of the contract month. A Mocatta option may be exercised on expiration date or on the five preceding banking days. The exercise of the option results in the delivery of the physical commodity in warehouse receipt form and obligates the person taking delivery to pay for the total value of the commodity including all weight adjustments based on the striking price value. A very small percentage of Mocatta options are exercised (perhaps 2% to 5%). When exercises do take place, it is usually the coin options, because the call owner wants to actually own the coins.

Contract Size

In most cases, the size of a Mocatta option is equivalent to the unit amount that is dealt in industrially. Gold options are for 100 troy ounces. Silver options are for either 1,000 or 5,000 troy ounces. Copper options are for 25,000 pounds, and platinum options are for 50 troy ounces. The actual quantity of metal delivered is within industry-recognized tolerances, such as plus or minus 5%. In the coin options, Kruggerand calls are on 50 coins, Maple Leaf calls are on 10 coins, and silver dollar and silver-clad bags are one bag. The coin bag options are on bags containing $1,000 face value of the stated coin. These coin bag contracts trade because the coins contain either 90% or 40% silver. In the case of silver dollar bags, a $1,000 face value bag contains approximately 795 troy ounces of silver, while a clad bag contains approximately 265 ounces of silver.

Grade

The grade of metal delivered is such that it would be acceptable for delivery against an exchange-traded futures contract. If you owned a Mocatta gold call and exercised, you would receive a warehouse receipt whose specifications would satisfy the delivery requirements of either the Commodity Exchange Incorporated (COMEX) or the Chicago Mercantile Exchange (CME). Not only would the gold be the proper grade, but it would also be within the required weight tolerances and on deposit at an exchange-recognized depositry. This grade requirement can be important to an investor if future resale is contemplated. Gold in unusual sizes, grades, or locations may be difficult to dispose of at a future date.

Striking Prices

Mocatta sets striking prices at logical increments, as do the exchanges, and follows a prescribed format. In gold, for instance, Mocatta uses $10 increments up to $200/ounce, $25/ounce up to $700, and $50/ounce thereafter. At any one time, Mocatta is trading 10 to 15 striking prices in each commodity. With five different contracts, with puts and calls, and with 10 to 15 striking prices, you can see that Mocatta is trading over 1,000 options at any given moment.

Two-Way Market

Although Mocatta is under no obligation to do so, it has always been willing to repurchase any option that it has ever sold. Throughout its 300-year existence, no Mocatta group company has defaulted on any contract into which it has entered.

Pricing

Mocatta sets the prices for its options. The factors that they consider are those outlined in Chapter 4. It would be difficult, if not impossible, to maintain a two-way market in over 1,000 options without a computer-automated system of pricing. On all the aforementioned options, Mocatta maintains a bid/offer market. Mocatta is not only the grantor of options, but it will also be a buyer of options granted by the public through brokerage firms. Mocatta's offer price may be used by a customer to establish a long position or to liquidate a previously established short (granted) position. Conversely Mocatta's bid price may be used to liquidate a previously established long position or to create (grant) a short position. When a broker asks Mocatta for a quotation, Mocatta responds with a two-way quotation, that is, both a bid and an offer. Mocatta asks brokers neither whether they wish to buy or sell nor whether the transaction is option-buying or option-granting in nature.

Automated Trading

Approximately 90% of Mocatta's option business is done via their proprietary computer system, the Mocatta Automated Quotation System (MAQS).^{SM} Most people are accustomed to using the words "quotation" and "indication" as equivalents. But the meanings of these terms are different in automated trading. An *indication* shows where a market was trading, and it is the type of information available on most broker's desk terminals. A *quotation* is a price at which a trade may be done. The MAQS terminal gives brokers "firm" prices at which they can trade at that instant. All brokers need do is depress either the "buy button" or the "sell button," and their orders are immediately executed at the stated price. Mocatta's computer does not know if it has bought or sold until the broker has depressed the appropriate button!

Special Options

The exchanges, because they are appealing to the general public, have created a standardized option that appeals to the largest audience, as does the standard Mocatta option. Exchanges, however, are limited in their flexibility, attempting to appeal only to this market. General Motors has the same problem in building cars. If buyers want something unusual, they go to Ferrari or BMW. Mocatta realizes that there are special interests in the option market, and it has therefore created special options to meet these needs and interests. Some of the specialized options are:

1. Lookback Options^SM (or dints),
2. Donts,^SM
3. Contango Options,^SM
4. Trading Range^SM options, and
5. Stellages.

Not all brokerage firms deal in all types of options. In many cases, customers have to contact the dealer directly to determine which brokers in the area deal in the type of option in which they are interested.

Lookback Options. Mocatta offers lookback options on gold, silver, and platinum. There are both lookback calls and lookback puts. A *lookback call* gives its owner the right to buy the underlying metal at the lowest price at which that metal trades between the effective date of the option and the day the option expires. A *lookback put* offers its owner the right to sell the metal at the highest price at which the metal trades from the effective date of the option until the option is either exercised or expires. Either type of option may be exercised any time from the effective date until the expiration date.

Example: You purchase a lookback call of approximately 6 month's duration. You have the right to purchase 100 troy ounces of gold at the lowest London gold fixing from the effective date until the expiration date or the day the option is exercised.

A lookback gold put gives its owner the right to sell 100 troy ounces of gold at the highest price of gold achieved on the London gold fixing from the option's effective date until either exercise or expiration. This option gives its owner the benefit of "20-20 hindsight"; that is, you can look back and determine what strike price was the best for you.

Naturally, the added benefits of this option are reflected in the premium. A lookback option is substantially more expensive than a standard put or call, but the benefits are also substantially greater.

Out-of-the-Money Lookback Options are substantially similar to the lookback option already described. The difference is that the out-of-the-money amount raises the purchase price in the event of a call, and it lowers the sale price in the event of a put. Out-of-the-money lookback options have differential prices in $10 increments for gold and platinum and in 50¢ increments for silver.

> **Example:** You purchase a $10 out-of-the-money lookback call. This call gives you the right, from the effective date until the expiration date, to purchase gold at $10 above the lowest price that gold achieved between the effective date and the date of exercise or resale.

Conversely, a put would give its owner the right to sell at the stated increment below the high achieved for the applicable period. Mocatta offers lookback options with identical expiration dates to those for the same metal in the standard Mocatta option.

Dont Options. The word "dont" comes from the French word *donner*, to give. Dont options (or donts) are normally offered only to commercial entities, because they find their greatest usefulness with such entities. A *dont option* is an option that you don't pay for unless you don't exercise. Mocatta might offer a jewelry fabricator a dont call option on gold with a striking price $30 out-of-the-money. The jewelry fabricator would pay nothing for the option but is obligated to exercise the option. If the fabricator does not wish to exercise the option, he or she must pay Mocatta a cancellation fee to negate the obligation.

This is not a free option: Either the obligation to exercise or the cancellation fee is, in fact, a premium. The commercial entity is, in this case, buying insurance to provide an available supply of gold at a predetermined price if gold were to go up substantially. If, at the time the option is due to expire, gold is either $50 higher, or up by an amount less than the cancellation fee, the jewelry fabricator would exercise and take delivery. Only in the event that the cancellation fee is greater than the amount by which gold is out-of-the-money would the jewelry fabricator not exercise.

This option is especially attractive to commercial entities because it does not require the payment of a cash premium at the time the option transaction is consummated. All costs are deferred until expiration or exercise. This feature is very attractive when interest rates are high and working capital is "tight."

Mocatta also grants dont puts, which obligate the buyer to deliver a fixed quantity of the commodity at expiration or pay a cancellation fee. It should be noted that the striking price of a dont option must be out-of-the-money, or it would always be exercised and there would be no premium. Due to the credit and utility issues of this option, it is available only to commercial entities.

Contango Options. Carrying charges (Chapter 1) constantly fluctuate as a function of interest rates, storage charges, insurance, and the relationship of supply for various deliveries versus demand for those deliveries. Because the relationship between the prices for various delivery months changes, there is the potential for profit or loss by speculation on this pricing relationship. The difference between the prices for various delivery months is referred to as the *contango*. When distant months are trading at a premium to the nearby months in a futures market, the market is referred to as a contango market. If the nearby months are at a premium to the back months, the market is said to be in *backwardation*.

If a speculator were to purchase a contract for future delivery and sell a contract for the same commodity but for a different delivery, a change in the contango would generate either a profit or loss. Trading done for the purpose of benefitting by the change in the contango is referred to as *switch trading*. For the sake of an example, let's say that you, a speculator, believe that interest rates will go up and that all other factors affecting the contango remain unchanged. To benefit from this view, you could sell a nearby futures contract and buy a more distant contract. If you are correct in your judgment, the increased interest rates would cause the more distant contract to appreciate relative to the nearby contract. This price change would be beneficial, and you could close out the position at a profit. If you are incorrect in your judgment and interest rates decline, the price difference between the two months would narrow and you would have a loss. This particular strategy—selling the nearby and buying the deferred—is referred to as *buying a switch*. If you buy the nearby and sell the deferred, this strategy is referred to as *selling a switch*.

Switch trading carries with it risks very similar to other types of commodity trading, that is, a substantial risk in exchange for substantial profit potential. The ability to benefit from the profit potential of switch trading, and still retain a defined risk, exists through the use of contango options. Mocatta offers both contango call options and contango put options. A *contango call* gives its owner the right, at some time in the future, to buy a specific switch. A *contango put* gives its owner the right to sell a specific switch at some time in the future.

Contango options are offered on gold, silver, copper, and platinum. Both in-the-money and out-of-the-money options are offered. The options expire at 12:00 noon New York time on the second banking day preceding the first banking day of the expiration month. The expiration month is the first month of the switch on which the option is granted.

Example: Silver is at exactly $6 per ounce, and interest rates are at exactly 13%. You believe that interest rates will shortly appreciate to 17%. You might purchase a hypothetical 3-month contango call that would allow you to purchase a 6-month switch. At 13%, the difference between nearby silver trading at $6/ounce and silver for delivery 6 months later is 39¢/ounce. In effect, you have the right to sell a given amount of silver for one delivery at $6/ounce and buy the same amount of silver for a 6-month later delivery at $6.39/ounce. If interest rates appreciate to 17%, the difference between nearby silver at $6 per ounce and silver for delivery 6 months later will widen to 51¢ per ounce. If you exercise your option, your profit would be 12¢/ounce (51¢–39¢). This amount times the size of the contract would be your profit. Your total exposure would be the premium you paid for the option.

Trading Range Options. When you purchase an option and pay a premium, you pay for the right to benefit from the unlimited profit potential that could be realized were the market to make an enormous move, when, in fact, the probability is small that the market will make an enormous move. It is not that markets do not make enormous moves, only that the probability is smaller than a move of lesser magnitude. A *trading range option* is one that gives you the ability to profit from the potential move of the commodity over a limited trading range.

Example: A gold 325/350 July call option gives its owner a call on gold at $325/ounce, but it limits the maximum resale price of the option to the difference between $325/ounce and $350/ounce times 100 ounces. This option could never be worth more than $2,500. In reality, you have purchased a call at $325/ounce and granted a call at $350/ounce. So if gold appreciates to $325/ounce, the call you own is $25/ounce in-the-money and worth $2,500. If gold continues to appreciate above $350, the $325 call continues to appreciate, but you lose a like amount on the $350 call that you are short.

The maximum amount that can be made on a trading range option is the difference in the striking prices of the two sides, times the quantity of commodity involved, and less the original premium paid. The maximum amount that can be lost is the dollars paid to the dealer at the time the option is purchased, provided that both "legs," or sides of the option, have the same maturity. Trading range options can be purchased with either two calls or two puts on the same commodity, with either different striking prices and/or the same or different maturities.

Depending on the combination of striking prices purchased, these options may be designed to be profitable in a rising, declining, or stationary market. The investment effect of a trading range option is much the same as bull spreads or bear spreads (discussed in greater detail in the spreading strategies chapters).

According to the striking prices involved, trading range options will have a lower cost and a lower breakeven price than outright long option positions. To some degree these advantages are offset by the limitation of profit potential. This option appeals primarily to the noncommercial entity because the commercial tends to use options to protect against the negative effect of major moves, whereas the trading range option is designed to maximize profitability on lesser moves.

Stellages. A stellage is a double-ended dont option; that is, it is both a put and a call. Mocatta grants stellage options to commercial entities.

Example: With gold trading at $325, Mocatta might grant a stellage with the call at $350/ounce and the put at $300/ounce.

Again, no cash premium changes hands, but the "buyer" of the option is obligated to exercise one side of the option. Normally, no cancellation fee is involved, because with both a put and a call, the cancellation fee would equal the loss incurred by exercising an out-of-the-money option. Both sides of a stellage are out-of-the-money at the time the option is granted.

Nonstandard Options

The commercial side of the option business dictates that users may require specific grades, specific locations, specific quantities, or possibly payment in non-U.S. currency. Such is the business that dealers are in that they will accordingly custom tailor an option to the needs of the commercial user. There is also the possibility that, at the time of exercise, the option holder's requirements may have changed. Perhaps the buyer of a gold call would rather take delivery of Kruggerands, or vice versa. The commercial options grantor is in a position to meet these needs and is usually willing to do so for the proper price differential. Dealers for commercial counterparts are also willing to grant options on many products in which they do not deal with the public, such as T-Bills, GNMAs, and currencies. This is where the dealer market fits into the overall option picture.

Option Granting

Dealers in general are as anxious to be buyers of options as they are anxious to be grantors. Dealers on both sides of the market maintain a substantial business. Although the dealers don't normally deal with the public in any fashion, they are willing to let the public be option grantors through brokerage firms. An individual or corporation may grant Mocatta-type options or perhaps trading range options. Whether or not such an investment is suitable for an individual is a function of the investor's market sophistication, risk-taking ability, and investment objective(s). (This will be discussed in greater detail in the sections on option granting.)

Margin-Free Hedging

Mocatta, through brokerage firms, will allow individuals to trade physical metals against in-the-money option positions without depositing margin.

Example: Mr. Edwards had purchased a gold call that is now in-the-money, and he believes that gold, from a short-term point of view, is going to go lower. Mocatta would loan Edwards a 100-ounce gold bar, which could be sold.

If Edwards is correct and gold does go lower, he will be able to repurchase the gold bar in the open market and return it to Mocatta. The investor's profit will be the difference between his purchase price and his sale price. Mocatta will hold the customer's option and the proceeds of the gold sale as security for the loan until the bar is returned.

If Edwards is incorrect and gold appreciates instead of depreciates, he can always exercise his call option as the method of returning the gold bar to Mocatta. This method of trading offers the investor the advantages of trading against an option without the necessity of depositing additional margin. Metals can be borrowed and sold against long in-the-money calls, or they can be bought and traded against in-the-money puts.

Most dealers have brochures explaining all the possibilities available with their options, and these brochures are available through your broker or through the dealer directly. Option dealers will gladly direct you to a broker in your area who can service your account in dealer options.

Special Deliveries

Most dealers, because commodities are international in scope, have the ability to arrange for delivery of the underlying commodity in almost any location and payment in almost any currency. If you need delivery in a tax-free location, such as Delaware, or in a European location, such as Switzerland or England, this can normally be arranged for a modest fee.

Now let's look at some of the exchange markets.

7

FOREIGN OPTIONS

Foreign options, or options not traded in the United States, are traded on exchanges in London, Amsterdam, Paris, and Winnipeg to name a few. London options are the oldest exchange-traded commodity options, with Winnipeg and Amsterdam being recent additions. Currently, these options are banned by CFTC action. In 1978 the CFTC banned the sale of all commodity options to U.S. customers by American commodity brokerage firms (FCMs). Some Americans have continued to deal in foreign commodity options by dealing with nonresident brokerage firms. At some time in the future the CFTC is likely to reauthorize the trading of foreign options in the United States. A discussion of these options is important, if you are to fully comprehend the avenues of investment available in commodity options, as well as the arbitrage possibilities that exist.

LONDON COMMODITY OPTIONS

Exchange trading of commodities and of commodity options in London is divided into two general areas: the metals and the "softs." Metals trading, logically enough, is done on the London Metal Exchange, and the nonmetals or "softs" are traded on the various individual terminal markets. The exchanges on which the commodities are traded are the same markets on which the commodity options are traded.

The London Metal Exchange

The London Metal Exchange (LME) can trace its formal existence back to late 1876, even though many of the exchange's members had done business with each other for many years before that. The metals traded on the LME are copper, silver, lead, tin, zinc, nickel, and aluminum. For each metal traded, there is a corresponding option market.

In the United States, when we think of a commodity exchange, we think of a market for futures contracts, with those contracts guaranteed by a clearing corporation. We also think of a marketplace where all commodities are traded all day long. Such is not the case on the LME.

The LME is not a market for futures contracts, but rather a market for both spot and forward transactions on physical metals. If you, for instance, were to purchase a contract of silver on the LME, it might be a contract calling for delivery in three months. The date on which the contract will expire and the delivery will be made is referred to as the *prompt date*. A 3-month contract purchased tomorrow will have a different prompt date from a 3-month contract purchased today. Because the contract is a contract for the physical metal, no profits or losses are realized until the prompt date.

> *Example:* If you purchased 3-month silver on January 1, you would have a prompt date of April 1. If several weeks later you wished to liquidate your contract, you would not sell 3-month silver, but April 1 prompt silver.

Any profit or loss, although actual, will not be settled until the prompt date. If you, as an American dealing through a brokerage firm, deal on the LME, your account will be debited for any losses, but you will not be able to withdraw the profit until prompt date because the metals dealer will not have to pay these profits until then. Dollar losses are retained by the brokerage firm for their protection, since these losses will not be paid to the metals dealer until prompt date.

The options that trade on the LME are puts, calls, and "doubles." Were you to exercise a call, you would take delivery of a forward contract on the underlying metals. The exercise of a put, conversely, requires the delivery of a forward contract on the underlying metal.

The *double* option is really an either/or option. At the time a "double" is purchased, it gives its owner the right to either call or put the metal, but not both. A double and a straddle are not the same thing even though many people, incorrectly, use the words interchangably. If you exercise either the call or the put portion of a double, the remaining side is terminated. With a straddle, the exercise of the call or the put has no effect on the remaining side.

London options are not fungible or tradable like American options. Once a London option has been purchased, you have only two alternatives: exercise it if profitable, or abandon it if unprofitable. There is no aftermarket in London options (either metals or softs). Because these options are not resalable, a large percentage of the options purchased are purchased as trading insurance. A call is purchased as insurance when the market is going to be traded from the short side, and a put is purchased as insurance when the market is going to be traded from the long side. The double is especially popular for the purpose of insuring trading positions because it protects either a long or a short position, and one side of the option must be in the money at expiration, with the exercise of that side helping to defray the cost of owning the double.

LME transactions are not cleared and guaranteed in the traditional sense. All transactions done on the LME are done by *ring-dealing members*. These members are, in fact, their own clearing corporation. All trades done are done between these ring-dealing members. Performance is guaranteed by the firms that the ring-dealing members represent. In the history of the LME, there has never been a default on an LME contract. Each ring-dealing member settles its own trades with the opposing ring-dealing member. A member of the public wishing to deal on the LME must deal either through a ring-dealing member directly or with a brokerage firm affiliated with a ring-dealing member.

The word "ring" has two meanings on the LME. The first meaning is the physical facility in which the trading actually takes place, as in "trading ring" or "ring-dealing member." The second meaning of "ring" is the time period during which each of the metals actually trade. The term "ring" in this sense come from the ringing of a bell which signals when trading is to commence or cease in a given metal. All metals on the LME do not trade at the same time. Each metal trades during official and unofficial times, which are signified by the sounding of a bell. Each metal trades four times a day (twice in the morning and twice in the afternoon). The morning session is referred to as the *official*, and the afternoon session as the *unofficial* session. Each session is followed by 15 minutes of trading in all metals, referred to as a *kerb* session. In addition, interoffice trading between sessions is referred to as *premarket trading*.

The official ring trading serves as part of the basis for the London spot or "fixing" prices in LME metals. One of the LME's primary functions is this price establishment. Much of the world's metals business is done in relation to the LME fix, even though the trades are consummated in other parts of the world and have no direct effect on the LME.

Although all profits and losses are normally realized as of the prompt date, such is not always the case. If you were to purchase 3-month silver, for instance, and then liquidate the position, and if the liquidation happened to be with the same ring-dealing member from whom the position was purchased, the ring-dealing member might be willing to pay out the profits immediately. This prepayment is at the discretion of the ring-dealing member. A prepayment, when done, is discounted by the ring-dealing member to reflect the current or project interest rates from the date of the prepayment until the normal prompt date. *This is an exception, not common,* and certainly not to be counted upon.

Despite the utility offered by LME options, with rare exception, option trading has never accounted for much of the total LME volume. This may well be because the option is not tradable (fungible) or not well publicized.

Non-LME Metal Options

Gold and platinum, though not traded on the LME, are actively traded in London. In addition, there is an active dealer market in silver bullion outside the LME trading. This trading is through bullion dealers whose policies and procedures are much the same as the trading on the LME. There are two fixings for these metals. The metals are dealt in for prompt delivery, and the options offered are similar to U.S. dealer options. The importance of this market is not to be underestimated. The gold fixings, for instance, serve as "benchmarks" for a large percentage of the world's gold dealings.

London "Soft" Commodities

The "soft," or nonmetal, commodities trade in London in much the same fashion that commodities trade in the United States. That is, they trade on organized exchanges in the form of futures contracts, and they are cleared by a clearing house that guarantees performance of the contracts.

The London Commodity Exchange

The London Commodity Exchange (LCE) is a trading facility in much the same sense as Commodity Exchange Corporation (CEC) in New York is a facility. Both the LCE and CEC provide their member exchanges with the trading floor on which to do business. As the CEC trading floor in New York is shared by four different commodity exchanges, so are the LCE trading facilities in London shared. The major London soft commodity exchanges are:

- The London Rubber Terminal Market Association
- The Coffee Terminal Market Association of London
- The London Cocoa Terminal Market Association
- The United Terminal Sugar Market Association
- The Grain And Feed Trade Association Limited

Each of these individual futures markets trades futures contracts similar in terms and procedures to American futures contracts. Each market has its own procedures and rules, as do its American counterparts. The area of greatest difference is that most of these soft markets do not have daily limits.

Each of these soft exchanges clears its trades through a clearing house, except that, in London, all the trades are cleared by one clearing house, called the International Commodity Clearing House (ICCH). This clearing house is a separate business entity from the exchanges, and it is a profit-making organization, in addition to being a service organization. ICCH also clears the trades on the Hong Kong futures exchange, the Australian futures trades and the currency and currency option trades done by Intex in Bermuda.

London Soft Commodity Options

The London soft commodity exchanges trade options on their futures contracts, and, in that sense, there is a similarity to the American exchange-traded commodity options. These options are options on futures contracts, and the exercise of an option results in the delivery of a futures contract. Call, put, and double options may be purchased on the commodities that are exchange-traded. The trades take place on the same floor as the commodity, and they are cleared and guaranteed by ICCH. These options are *London-type* options, that is, they are not fungible or tradable. As with the LME options, option holders may exercise or abandon the option, and these are the only alternatives.

Because the option traded on the LCE exchanges is an option on futures, any profits that result from the exercise of the option and from the liquidation of the thereby created futures contracts are immediately available. With ICCH clearing both the futures contract and the related options, an investor who has an in-the-money call can go short futures against the call option. The investor merely notifies the broker to "lodge" an option with ICCH against the futures position. No additional margin is required by ICCH because the option is a bona fide hedge for the futures.

This ability to lodge options with the clearing corporation and trade futures against them allows tremendous flexibility in futures trading. If you have lodged an in-the-money call with ICCH and have sold a futures position against it, you may close out the futures whenever you like. If the futures position is profitable, you may withdraw the profit. If the futures position is at a loss, you must deposit the loss to your account at the time of closeout. In either case, once the futures contract has been offset, your option is returned to you, and you can continue to do this type of trading over and over again.

Despite the flexibility offered by this modus operandi, option trading on the LCE exchange, except for limited periods of time, has not exceeded 2% to 3% of the total futures volume.

The Canadian Financial Futures Market

The Canadian Financial Futures Market is a division of the Winnipeg Commodity Exchange, The CFFM currently trades call options on both gold and silver futures contracts. The options dealt in are options of fixed striking prices and fixed maturities, but they are not assignable (or fungible) in the sense of a listed security or commodity option as traded in the United States.

Units of Trading

The gold option, when exercised, is converted into a futures contract calling for delivery of 20 troy ounces of gold while the silver option calls for the delivery of a 200-ounce silver futures contract.

Restricted Options

The exchange may limit the opening of new positions in options, if those options are restricted because they are deep out-of-the-money or for such other reasons as the exchange may determine. This limitation does not apply to exercises.

Premium Quotations

Both gold and silver options are quoted in dollars and cents per fine ounce.

Expiration

The option shall expire at the close of business on the sixth business day before the first delivery day of the underlying futures contract.

Last Day of Trading

Trading in gold and silver options ceases at the close of the market on expiration date.

Currency

Trading premiums, as well as the deposit of margin, are quoted in U.S. dollars.

Rights of Exercise

An option may be exercised by the holder on any trading day up to and including the expiration date of such option, by requiring the writer to exchange it for the underlying futures contract.

Contract Delivery Months

Gold options trade for March, June, September, and December delivery. Silver options trade for January, April, July, and October delivery. Options are normally traded for two successive delivery months. On the first exchange business day in the sixth month prior to the futures contract delivery month, options commence trading in that delivery month.

Trading Hours

Gold options trade from 8:25 A.M. until 1:35 P.M., and silver options from 8:40 A.M. until 1:30 P.M. Both times are U.S. Central time.

Limit on Daily Price Movement

Gold options are limited to $30/troy ounce, and silver is limited to 50¢/fine ounce above or below the previous day's settlement price. There are no limits on the last trading day.

Expanded Limits

When for two successive days any contract month closes at the normal limit in the same direction, an expanded daily limit price schedule goes into effect. On the third day, the limit is expanded to 150% of the normal limit. If the contract continues to trade at the limit, the limit is further expanded to 200% of the normal daily limit. If, while expanded limits are in effect, no contract month closes at the limit in the same direction, then the normal daily price limit will be reinstituted the following business day.

Margin Requirements

Long Call Options. The margining of premiums payable by the purchaser of an option on a gold futures contract or a silver futures contract is prohibited. Such premiums must be paid in cash.

Uncovered Short Call Options. The margin requirement is the sum of the current settlement premium for the option involved, plus the current maintenance for the underlying futures contract.

Covered Short Call Options. Where a customer deposits with the broker a gold certificate or silver certificate deliverable on the Winnipeg gold and silver futures contract, no margin is required against a short option covered thereby. No other margin value may be credited against the deposited gold or silver certificate.

When customers hold long positions in the underlying futures contract on the books of the same FCM with whom they hold the short option position, regular rates of futures margin are required for the underlying futures. But the full option premium margins are required only on the short option position. No underlying option margin need be required.

THE EUROPEAN OPTIONS EXCHANGE (EOE)

The European Options Exchange trades both put and call options on 10 troy ounce units of gold. This is the equivalent of approximately 310 grams.

Trading Unit

Put and call options on 10 troy ounces of gold, with 1 troy ounce considered to contain 31.1 grams.

Expiration Date

An option has a fixed expiration date, which falls on the third Friday of the expiration month, with the option expiring at 2:00 P.M. Amsterdam time.

Expiration Months

The expiration months are February, May, August, and November. Options are usually quoted for three expirations at one time, such as February, May, and August. When the February option expires on the third Friday of the expiration month, the November option would commence trading.

Striking Price Intervals

The normal intervals between striking prices is $50/troy ounce, but the exchange may introduce other intervals.

Currency

The currency of trading is in U.S. dollars per troy ounce.

Position Limits

The exchange has the authority to impose position limits. As of 1983, the position for one individual or individuals acting in consort is 5,000 option contracts on the same side of the market. Call options purchased and put options written are on the same side of the market, and together they may not exceed 5,000 contracts. Similarly, call options written and put options purchased are on the same side of the market.

Exercise Limits

Option owners are prohibited from exercising more than 5,000 options in a 5-day period. Puts and calls are not aggregated for this purpose.

Guarantees

In practice, there is no direct relationship between the buyer of a call and the writer. The European Options Exchange's clearing organization is responsible for balancing the rights and obligations. This organization guarantees the obligations will be met any time during the contract.

Cover and Margin Requirements

A writer of a covered option has to deposit gold in whatever quantity required to meet the obligation created by the option transaction. The writer of an uncovered option must deposit a margin equal to 300% of the premium or 20% of the value of the underlying gold, subject to a minimum of $1,000 per contract.

Special Rights

The European Gold Clearing Corporation reserves the right, in the event of an abnormal situation arising in the world market in gold, to declare that exercised options shall be settled in cash on the basis of price, which the EGCC shall set. For the duration of the abnormal situation, option exercisers and assignees lose the right to insist on settlement by delivery of gold.

8

U.S. EXCHANGE-TRADED COMMODITY OPTIONS

This chapter covers the contract specifications and regulations of the various exchanges that deal in listed commodity options in the United States. When exercised, the options in this chapter result in the creation or transfer of a commodity futures contract. Even though options on futures contracts appear identical when comparing one futures exchange with the next, such is not the case. Each exchange has its own set of definitions, rules, and procedures. Because these differences may have an economic impact on the investor, the specifications of each contract are covered.

COMMODITY EXCHANGE, INC. (COMEX)

Commodity Exchange, Inc. applied to the CFTC for permission to trade options on its 100 troy ounce gold futures contract in a filing submitted on December 9, 1981. The exchange's intention is to continue to broaden the breadth and depth of all its markets, and the gold option was a logical addition. Comex's gold option, like all futures options, represents a more complicated vehicle than most speculators have encountered.

Definitions

Call Option. This option gives its owner (buyer) the right but not the obligation to buy the underlying futures contract at a particular price, known as the striking price, at *anytime between the purchase date and the expiration date of the option*. The owner of a call option who elects to exercise receives a long futures contract position.

Put Option. This option gives its owner (buyer) the right but not the obligation to sell the underlying futures contract at a particular price, known as the striking price, at *anytime between the purchase date and the expiration date of the option*. The owner of a put option who elects to exercise receives a short futures contract position.

Strike Price. The price at which the holder (buyer) of a futures option may purchase (in the case of a call) or sell (in the case of a put) the underlying futures contract upon exercise. Also known as "striking price" or "strike."

Exercise. The conversion of an option position into the underlying futures contract through the Comex Clearing Association.

Expiration Date. The time and day on which a particular option may no longer be offset or exercised. The month in which the option expires is also known as the expiration month.

Premium. The amount the buyer agrees to pay for an option with a particular expiration month and striking price. This amount does not include any commission charge by a brokerage firm. Premiums are determined by open outcry at the Gold Futures Options Ring on the floor of Comex. Premiums are quoted in terms of U.S. dollars and cents per troy ounce.

Intrinsic Value. The amount by which the settlement price of the underlying futures contract exceeds a call option's strike price, or the amount by which the put option's strike price exceeds the futures price. (This may be expressed in dollars per ounce or in total value.) Options with intrinsic value are said to be "in-the-money"; options without intrinsic value are said to be "at-the-market" or "out-of-the-money."

Time Value. The portion of the premium that allocates value to potential changes in the price of the underlying futures contract prior to the option's expiration. The mathematical number for time value is premium minus intrinsic value (if any). This may be quoted in dollars per troy ounce or as a total dollar amount.

Writer. The entity who grants the option to the buyer and who is thus required to fulfill the contractual obligation should the option be exercised. Writers are of two types: covered, (or hedged) and uncovered (or naked). Covered writers have offsetting futures positions, while uncovered writers do not.

Spread (Straddle). A combination of option positions with other option positions or with futures positions such that there is offsetting risk. Thus a long call/short call position would be considered a spread, while a long call/short put position would not, since it does not contain the element of offsetting risk.

Contract Months. The option contract months that are traded correspond to the following delivery months for the underlying Comex gold futures contract: April, August, and December. Four consecutive option contract months are traded at one time; thus one "red" or "back month" will always be listed for trading. (A "red" or "back month" is the duplication of a current month in the succeeding year. March of this year is "March"; March of next year is "red March.")

Trading Hours. Gold options trade from 9:25 A.M. to 2:30 P.M. New York time. A warning bell is sounded one minute before the opening and one minute before the close of gold options trading.

Strike Price Intervals:

	Increments Between
Strike Prices	*Strike Prices*
Under $300	$10
$300 to $500	$20
$500 to $800	$30
$800 and Above	$40

Strike Prices for Newly Listed Months. On the first trading day of any gold option contract month, there will be five tradable strike price series: five for puts and five for calls. The strike price series created will include the one with the strike price nearest the previous day's settlement price of the underlying futures contract, plus the next two higher and the next two lower strike prices.

Addition of New Strike Prices. A new strike price series is added after the settlement price of the underlying futures contract moves halfway between the third highest and the second highest strike price or the third lowest and second lowest strike price. This will insure the availability of at least two out-of-the-money options at all times.

Expiration and Exercise. Trading in an expiring option ceases at 2:30 P.M. New York time on the second Friday of the month *prior to* the expiration of the underlying futures contract. Customers can notify brokers of their intention to exercise by 3:00 P.M. New York time on any business day on which the option is trading, including expiration day. The option will expire on its last trading day.

Payment of Premiums. All long options must be paid for in full by 11:00 A.M. New York time on the business day following the purchase. There is no margining of long options on Comex gold futures options.

Price Limits. There are no daily price limits for options on gold futures.

Margin Requirements
for COMEX Gold Futures Options

Grantor Margins. As with futures contracts, the margin deposited by the grantor is considered to be "good faith" money to assure performance of the option contract at the time of exercise. Premiums received from the granting of options are retained in the option grantor's account, though they need not necessarily remain in their original cash form. If the value of the premium declines, this decreased value is released to the options grantor's use. If the value of the premium increases, the option grantor must deposit additional funds to the account to secure this increased value (liability).

The concept of margin, as it relates to grantor options, is one of fluctuating original margin. The original margin is equal to the market value of the premium plus the normal futures margin. If the market value of the premium were to increase, the grantor would have to add this difference to the option account. If the market value of the premium were to decrease, this amount of decrease could be removed from the account. The marking-to-market of an existing option position is similar to the deposit and withdrawal of variation margin in the futures contract market. However, it is called "fluctuating original margin" because the grantor may add to the account, if required, collateral that is acceptable as original margin (not necessarily cash).

Example 8–1: An individual grants a March $400 gold call for $4,000 ($40/ounce), and the exchange minimum margin on gold futures is $2,000. In this case, the option grantor would deposit $6,000 ($4,000 + $2,000) with the broker as original margin. The grantor could then withdraw the $4,000 premium. If, as a result of market action, the option premium increases, the grantor would have to deposit additional margin. If the premium declines, the grantor could remove the then excess margin in the account.

Spread transactions involving options and futures are defined to exist *only* if the option is in-the-money and the futures constitutes an offsetting position.

Spread transactions involving two option positions, however, have only the requirement of an offsetting position. The option spread has the same offsetting character as a futures spread. Calls and puts need not be in-the-money to get spread treatment, but they must be actual offsets—i.e. call versus call, put versus put.

Long Call or Long Put. Buyer pays premium in full; there is no margin or marking-to-market involved.

Short Call or Short Put. (1) Grantor receives premium in full in cash. (2) Grantor deposits original futures margin plus the market value of the option premium, which will be marked-to-market daily. (3) Grantor meets margin calls in the form of additional original margin.

Short Call/Long Futures or Short Put/Short Futures. (1) Options must be in-the-money. (2) Grantor receives the premium in cash. (3) Grantor posts futures spread margin plus the market value of the premium marked-to-market daily. (4) Grantor meets margin calls in the form of additional original margin.

Example 8–2: An individual grants a March $400 gold call for $4,000 ($40/ounce) while long March futures. The exchange spread margin on gold futures is $1,000. In this case, the option grantor would deposit $5,000 ($4,000 + $1,000) with the broker as original margin. He or she could then withdraw the $4,000 premium. Later changes in the option's premium would result in margin calls (higher premium) or excess margin (lower premiums).

Long Call/Short Futures or Long Put/Long Futures. (1) Option must be in-the-money. (2) Premium on long option must be paid in full in cash. (3) If the option contract and the futures contract are the same month, the purchaser posts futures spread margin, which is reduced by the option's intrinsic value. (4) If the option and the futures are different months, the purchaser posts spread margin. (5) The brokerage house may grant the option holder (buyer) loan value on the long option's intrinsic value for the purpose of meeting margin calls on the offsetting futures position.

Example 8–3: An individual purchases a March $400 gold call for $4,000 ($40/ounce) when March gold is trading at $405/ounce. The grantor sells one March gold futures contract at $405/ounce. The individual must pay for the option in full ($4,000) and deposit spread futures margin (assumed to be $1,000) reduced by the amount, if any, that the option is in-the-money (has intrinsic value). In this case, the option is $5 in-the-money [($405 − $400) × 100 ounces] or has a $500 intrinsic value. Therefore, the dollars actually deposited are $4,500 [$4,000 + ($1,000 − $500)].

Short Put/Short Call. (1) Grantor receives both premiums in cash. (2) Grantor posts one original futures margin plus the market values of the two premiums which will be marked-to-market daily. (3) Grantor meets margin calls in the form of additional original margin.

Example 8–4: An individual grants both a March $400 gold call and a March $400 gold put for $4,000 each (total $8,000). The grantor would deposit $8,000 plus an assumed original futures margin of $2,000 for a total of $10,000 in original; and he could then withdraw $8,000 in cash.

Short Call/Long Call or Short Put/Long Put (with long call strike price greater than short call strike price, or short put strike price greater than long put strike price. (1) Long option premium is paid in full, and short option premium is received in full. (2) Grantor posts original futures margin minus the amount, if any, by which the short option is out-of-the money subject to a $250 minimum. This position is marked-to-market daily. (3) Grantor meets margin calls in the form of additional original margin.

Example 8–5: An individual purchases a March $420 gold call for $3,000 and grants a March $400 gold call for $4,000 with March gold futures trading at $405. The individual pays the $3,000 and receives the $4,000. The individual must deposit original futures margin ($2,000) minus the amount by which the option is out-of-the-money or $500 [$2,000 − [(420 − 405) × 100]]. The account already has a $1,000 credit; therefore the individual can withdraw all but $500.

a.	Sell March $400 gold call—receive	$4,000
b.	Buy March $420 gold call—pay	($3,000)
c.	Net credit on transaction—receive	$1,000
d.	Original futures margin—pay	($2,000)
e.	Credit for out-of-the-money-receive	$1,500
f.	Net margin requirement—pay	$ (500)
g.	Cash in account (c. above)	$1,000
h.	Margin requirement (f. above)	$ (500)
i.	Surplus margin in account	$ 500

Short Call/Long Call or Short Put/Long Put (with short call strike price greater than long call strike price, or long put strike price greater than short put strike price). Long option is paid for in full, and short option premium is received in full.

THE COFFEE, SUGAR & COCOA EXCHANGE INC.

The Coffee, Sugar & Cocoa Exchange Inc. currently trades both pu: and call options on its #11 world sugar futures contract. When permissible, i will list put and call options on both their cocoa and coffee futures contracts

Definitions

Call Option. This option contract provides its owner the right through exercise to buy one #11 sugar futures contract at the stated striking price at any time from the date of purchase of the option until its expiration.

Put Option. This option contract provides its owner the right through exercise to sell one #11 sugar futures contract at the stated striking price at any time from the date of purchase of the option until expiration.

Offset. The options contracts to be traded on the Coffee, Sugar and Cocoa Exchange will permit offset of like maturities and strike prices for options of the same class in a given account. This provision enables the market participants to liquidate existing positions without the necessity of exercise.

Price Quotations. Price quotation in sugar options is in cents per pound in the same manner as sugar futures are quoted. Minimum price changes are in one-one-hundredth of a cent per pound, providing for a minimum fluctuation of $11.20 per option contract.

Expiration Date/Last Trading Day. Option contracts cease trading on the last Friday of the month preceding the stated delivery month of the underlying futures contract. Thus a March contract ceases trading on the second Friday of February. The option contract expires at 12:00 noon New York time on the Saturday after the last trading day.

This early expiration provides for an orderly liquidation of the underlying futures contract. An option trader who exercises, or who is exercised against, has at least two weeks to liquidate the underlying futures contract. In some instances, the time involved is actually closer to three weeks.

Exercise Period. An option holder may exercise an option any time after the purchase of the option and before its expiration. The Coffee, Sugar and Cocoa Clearing Association requires of its members that they submit notices of intention to exercise by 3:00 P.M. New York time any business day, provided, however, that on the last trading day the clearing members have until 9:00 P.M. New York time to submit their exercise notices. Each brokerage firm has different procedures and cutoff times for public customers. The difference between the last exercise time (9:00 P.M. last trading day) and the official expiration time (12:00 noon on the Saturday following last trading day) is provided for the clearing members to resolve any back office problems. From the public point of view, the option actually ceases to be exercisable at 9:00 P.M. New York time on the last trading day, and most likely earlier depending on your brokerage firm.

Assignment of Notices of Exercise. The Clearing Association assigns notices of exercise to its clearing members by 8:30 A.M. on the business day following the day that the exercise notice was submitted. In the case of last trading day, these notices are assigned by 8:30 on the Saturday morning following last trading day. The clearing member notifies the option grantor prior to the opening of the market on the next following business day.

Strike Price Increments. The system of striking prices devised by the Coffee, Sugar and Cocoa Exchange provides a balance between diversification and liquidity. Striking prices are at more narrow increments in the nearby months and more divergent in the distant or back months.

Strike price increments are in multiples of 1/2 cent (50 points). The following is the actual system:

Futures Contract Price	2 Nearby Months	Deferred Months
Less than 15 cents	1/2 cent-50 points	1 cent-100 points
Between 15 and 40 cents	1 cent-100 points	2 cents-200 points
Above 40 cents	2 cents-200 points	4 cents-400 points

Each month always has striking prices listed at levels two above and two below the previous day's settlement price at a minimum. When an option month begins trading, five striking prices are listed: the striking price least out-of-the-money, the next two higher, and the next two lower. Other than these, additional striking prices are delisted if for ten consecutive business days there is no open interest or trading in such series.

Delivery Months. Option contracts are traded for the months of March, July, and October and the first of these months to be traded in the following year (the first such "red" month).

Trading Hours. Sugar options trade from 10:00 A.M. until 1:43 P.M. New York time. One exception, however, is that on the last trading day of an expiring option, trading in that option ceases at 12:00 noon New York time. A warning bell is sounded one minute before the opening and one minute before the close of sugar options trading.

Price Limits. There are no daily price limits for options on sugar futures contracts.

Margin Rules for CS&C Sugar Futures Options

Payment of Premiums. Long option positions are fully paid for with no margining of long positions. Options must be paid for in full prior to the opening of business the day following the day on which the long option position is instituted.

Long Position. When a account buys an option, the premium must be paid for in full at the time of purchase (three business days). If the market value of the option declines subsequent to the purchase, the option holder has an unrealized loss but is not marked-to-market because the total risk (the premium) was paid at the time of purchase. Thus margin calls cannot exist for an account with only long option positions. If the market value of the option appreciates, the option holder has an unrealized profit but cannot realize this profit without liquidating the position. This approach to margining, or to the lack of it, eliminates the cash flow feature of futures from options and allows both the option holder and the brokerage firm to determine risk precisely.

Short Position. An account that has granted an option position has risks substantially identical to the risk involved in an outright futures position. Unlike the risks of an option purchaser, these risks are virtually unlimited and must be margined accordingly. The margin requirements for a short option position are the requirements for the underlying futures contract plus the current market value of the option premium. (See COMEX Example 8–1.)

Grantors are credited with the cash premium at the time the option is sold, and they are required to post margin in a form acceptable to the exchange at the time the option is granted. This approach to margin serves two purposes: First, it provides for marked-to-market loss margining; second, it allows the grantor to earn the "time value" as it is earned over the life of the option through time value depreciation.

Maintenance margin for the grantor would be equal to the maintenance margin requirement for the underlying futures contract plus the current market value of the premium. This margin requirement is also adjusted for any add-on margin, such as increases for spot month trading.

Long Call Option/Short Future. If the long option is in-the-money, the margin requirement is based on spread margin requirements. If, on the other hand, the long option is out-of-the-money, the position is margined as if no option position existed. (See COMEX Example 8–3.)

With respect to long option/short futures positions, remember that the futures contract is continuously marked-to-market, and normal variation margin is required. To minimize the negative aspect of this variation margin, the brokerage firm (FCM) is permitted to grant loan value to the customer equal to the option's in-the-money intrinsic value once it is fully paid to fund any futures cash margin calls. Since the in-the-money value of the option is the least amount that would be realized from its exercise, the broker is carrying a secured loan, which becomes self-liquidating in the event of a market reversal.

Long Put Option/Long Future. This strategy carries with it risks that are similar to long call/short future but for opposite market movements. The difference is that the call versus short future strategy yields the most profit in a declining market, while the put versus long future strategy yields the most profit in a rising market. Accordingly, the margin bases for the two strategies are the same.

Short Call Option/Long Future. Were these positions margined separately, there would be two margin requirements, one on the short option and one on the long future. Two requirements constitute an unrealistic approach as the long futures, to some degree, mitigates the exposure on the short call. (See COMEX Example 8–2.)

The original margin requirement for this matched position is placed on the short option position, and it equals the margin requirement on the underlying position plus the current market value of the option premium. In a rising market, the variation margin generated by the long futures position offsets the additional margin requirement on the short option, which tends to appreciate more slowly due to "delta" (see option pricing theory). In a declining market, the losses incurred in the long future is to some degree offset by the reduction in option premium, but in most cases there would be a difference in the rates of decline, with the option grantor incurring margin calls on the futures position.

Short Put Option/Short Future. Once again, if these two positions were margined separately, there would be two margin requirements as with short call/long futures position. The relative risks are the same as short call/long futures, and they are margined in a like manner.

Call Option Spread Margin. The relative risk in option spreads is a function of the difference between the strike price of the long and short options, as well as the difference in the term to maturity of the options involved. The Coffee, Sugar & Cocoa Exchange's (CSCE) margin requirements take these factors into account. Spread positions are margined at a level equal to the margin requirements for a spread in the underlying futures contracts. The proviso is that the margin requirement is increased to the amount, if any, by which the long call exercise price exceeds the short call exercise price. This margin requirement, however, is never in excess of the outright margin on the underlying futures contract and is reduced by the amount that the short option is out-of-the-money. The margin requirement is also increased by any amount that the short premium market value exceeds the long premium market value. Further, if either leg of the spread position involves a futures contract month that is subject to add-on margin requirements, such as the spot month, the additional margin requirement is also applied to the spread.

In that long option positions must be paid for in full, whenever the long option has a strike price lower than the short option (in the case of a call or vice-versa in the case of a put), there is relatively little risk to the option position itself. Yet the spread relationship between the two underlying futures contracts must be satisfied by the deposit of margin. The add-on of the excess in premiums of the short over the long takes into account the time values of the two options. It requires the spreader to leave on deposit any excess premium received for selling an option with a longer maturity than the one purchased. (See COMEX Example 8–5.)

The risk is also reduced in a spread position when the long position has a higher striking price than the short position (in the case of a call or vice versa in the case of a put), for striking prices that are not significantly higher. CSCE has provided a margin requirement equal to the difference between striking prices subtracted from spread margin requirements; this requirement is subject to a minimum reflecting the reduced risk of such a position as compared to an outright short option position. The exchange's margin rules also provide that the margin requirement must never be greater than the spread margin, since penalizing someone for having a fully paid long position would be unfair. The risk can never be greater than no "cover" at all, regardless of the striking prices. (See COMEX Example 8–5.)

Put Option Spread Margin. Put option spreads are, in principle, margined in the same manner as call spreads. The only difference is that long put options provide greater protection when their striking prices are higher than the striking prices of the short put options.

Short Call/Short Put. An account that has granted both a put and a call option for the same underlying commodity is assuming the risk that the commodity moves in either direction by an amount in excess of the value of the premiums received for granting the options involved. A stable market may allow the grantor to realize one or both premiums, while a volatile market can cause substantial exposure on one or both short positions. To require full margin on both short positions would be unfairly restrictive and not truly representative of the risks involved. Accordingly, the margin requirement for the short put/short call position is equal to the outright margin for one underlying futures contract plus the market value of the premiums of the two options involved. (See COMEX Example 8–4.)

In a rising market, the call appreciates while the put declines. In a declining market, the put appreciates while the call declines. The extent to which the premium moves inversely or in consort is a function of the strike prices of the options and their terms to maturity. This tendency, however, is reflected in their market values and consequently in their margin requirements. The deposit of original margin protects the broker and the exchange from any relative variances in the two premiums; the variance can be caused by substantial movements in the price of the underlying future(s).

Conversions and Reverse Conversions. Whenever:

1. a granted exchange call option is matched with both a long position in the underlying futures contract with the same delivery month as the

call option and a purchased Exchange put option with the same option month and striking price as the call option, or

2. a granted Exchange put is matched with both a short position in the underlying futures contract with the same delivery month as the put option and a purchased Exchange call option with the same option month and striking price as the put option,

the total amount of margin required for an exchange option and exchange futures contract combined is equal to the amount by which the premium of the granted exchange option exceeds the premium of the purchased Exchange option.

NEW YORK MERCANTILE EXCHANGE

The New York Mercantile Exchange originally submitted an application to trade put and call options on its platinum futures contract. After due consideration, it elected to withdraw that application and trade both put and call options on its #2 Heating Oil-New York Harbor futures contract. Each contract has its own specifications. Once again, let's review those specific contract terms and definitions.

Definitions

Class of Options. All options of the same type (put or call) covering the same underlying futures contract.

Closing Purchase Transaction. A transaction wherein an individual with a short option position liquidates the position through an offsetting purchase.

Closing Sale Transaction. A transaction in which an individual with a long option position liquidates the position through an offsetting sale.

Opening Purchase Transaction. A transaction in which an individual purchases an option, thereby creating a long position.

Opening Sale Transaction. A transaction wherein an individual sells an option, thereby creating a short position.

Series of Options. Options of the same class that have the same striking price and expiration date and that relate to the same underlying commodity.

Expiration. An option contract on the New York Mercantile Exchange (NYMEX) expires at the close of trading on the second Friday of the month preceding the delivery month for the underlying futures contract unless prior notice of exercise is given. If that Friday is not an exchange business day, the option will expire the first business day thereafter.

Exercise. An option may be exercised until 5:00 P.M. New York time on expiration day or up until 4:00 P.M. New York time on any day prior to expiration day.

Notice of Exercise. The Clearing House notifies the brokerage firm by 8:00 A.M. New York time on the day following the submission of an exercise notice by an option owner that that exercise is for one of their accounts. The brokerage firm then promptly notifies their customer. The Clearing House allocates notices of exercise in a series of options for any given day among its clearing members carrying short positions in the same series of options according to a ratio. That ratio consists of the number of notices of exercise to be allocated compared to the percentage of short open interest in the said series of options held by that clearing member.

Trading Hours. The #2 Heating Oil futures options have the same trading hours as the underlying futures contract.

Margin Rules

Long Call or Long Put. Option must be paid for in full.

Short Call or Short Put. Seller of the option deposits the original margin for the underlying futures contract plus the market value of the premium marked-to-market daily. (See COMEX Example 8–1.)

Short Call/Long Futures or Short Put/Short Futures. If the option is in-the-money, the seller deposits the original margin for a spread in the underlying futures contract plus the market value of the premium marked-to-market daily. If the option is not in-the-money, the seller deposits the margin for the underlying futures plus the market value of the premium marked-to-market daily. (See COMEX Example 8–2.)

Long Call/Short Futures or Long Put/Long Futures. If the option is in-the-money, the purchaser deposits spread margin for the underlying futures contract. The customer's brokerage firm may grant the customer loan value on the in-the-money portion of the option's premium for the purpose of meeting any margin calls on the related futures position. If the option is not in-the-money, the customer must deposit original futures margin on the underlying futures contract. (See COMEX Example 8–3.)

Short Put/Short Call. The seller deposits original margin for one futures position in the underlying futures contract plus the market value of the two premiums marked-to-market daily. (See COMEX Example 8–4.)

Short Call/Long Call or Short Put/Long Put. When the long call's striking price is greater than the short call's striking price, or when the short put's striking price is greater than the long put's striking price, the seller/

purchaser deposits spread margin in the underlying futures contract, minus the net market value of the two option premiums, subject to a minimum marked-to-market daily. When the short call's striking price is greater than the long call's striking price, or when the long put's striking price is greater than the short put's striking price, the seller/purchaser deposits the cash difference in premium. (See COMEX Example 8–5.)

Contract Specifications

Trading Months. Trading in heating oil futures options is conducted in the contract months of February, July, October, and December. Trading in an option contract month commences fourteen months prior to the first business day of the delivery month for the underlying futures contract.

Striking Prices. Striking prices are in units of:

1. 1 cent per gallon, when the price is less than 70¢/gallon,
2. two cents per gallon when the price is equal to 70¢/gallon but less than $1.50 per gallon,
3. 3¢/gallon when the price is equal to $1.50 per gallon but less than $2.10 per gallon, and
4. 4¢/gallon when the price is equal to or greater than $2.10 per gallon.

On the first business day of trading in a contract month, trading commences for the striking price nearest the previous business day's settlement price for the underlying heating oil futures contract and for the two successive strike prices above and below that strike. Thereafter, on any business day through the first business day of the month in which the option expires, new striking prices are added whenever the previous business day's settlement price for the underlying heating oil futures contract is at least midway through the interval to the second to the most distant posted strike price.

No new striking prices for any heating oil option contract shall be added during the month in which the option expires.

Price Quotations. Prices are quoted in cents per gallon and are in multiples of .01¢/gallon premium.

THE CHICAGO BOARD OF TRADE

The Chicago Board of Trade currently trades both put and call options on U.S. Treasury bond futures contracts. These options are especially interesting because a Treasury bond is nothing more than an intermediate-term interest rate index. This particular option offers perhaps the greatest flexibility to both the speculator and hedger because all people in all walks of life are directly affected by interest rates and their changes.

Definitions

Trading Unit. The option contracts call for the delivery of one (1) $100,000 face value U.S. Treasury bond futures contract on the Chicago Board of Trade.

Striking Prices. Trading is conducted for options with striking prices in integral multiples of one (1) point per U.S. Treasury bond futures contract, with no new striking prices being added on the last day of trading.

Option Premium Basis. The premium for U.S. Treasury bond futures options is in multiples of one sixty-fourth (1/64) of one percent (1%) of $100,000 U.S. Treasury bond futures contract ($15.62). Note: A 64th is actually $15.625. The first through 63rd 64th is worth $15.62, while the 64th 64th is worth $15.94.

Option Expiration. Unexercised U.S. Treasury bond futures options expire at 10:00 A.M. Chicago time on the first Saturday following the last day of trading.

Months Traded. The option months currently traded are currently the same as the underlying futures contract.

Last Day of Trading. There is no trading in U.S. Treasury bond futures options expiring in the current month after 12:00 P.M. Chicago time on the first Friday that precedes by at least five business days the first notice day (first day the short may deliver) for the corresponding U.S. Treasury bond futures contract. If such a Friday is not a business day, or if a nonbusiness day Friday precedes by four business days the first notice day for the corresponding U.S. Treasury bond futures contract, the last day of trading shall be the business day prior to such a Friday.

Premium Fluctuation Limits. Trading is prohibited during any day in a U.S. Treasury bond futures option at a premium of more than the trading limit for a U.S. Treasury bond futures contract above and below the previous day's settlement premium for that option as determined by the Clearing Corporation.

Exercise of Options. The buyer of a U.S. Treasury bond futures option may exercise the option on any business day by giving notice of exercise by 8:00 P.M. Chicago time on such day.

Margin Rules

Long Put or Long Call. Premium must be paid in full.

Short Put or Short Call. Margin consists of the premium (marked-to-market) plus per contract, initial $2,000 ($3,000), maintenance or hedging $1,500 ($2,500). These dollar amounts are subject to change. (The dollar amounts in parentheses, such as $3,000 and $2,500 in this case, refer to the spot month add-ons.) (See COMEX Example 8–1.)

Long Futures/Short Call or Short Futures/Short Put. For an out-of-the-money option, margin is equal to the premium (marked-to-market) plus per contract, initial $2,000 ($3,000) maintenance or hedging $1,500 ($2,500). For an at-the-money or in-the-money option, margin is equal to the premium (marked-to-market) plus, per contract $500 ($750). (See COMEX Example 8–2.)

Short Call/Short Put (Straddle). Market value of both option premiums (marked-to-market) plus per contract, initial $2,000 ($3,000), maintenance or hedging $1,500 ($2,500). (See COMEX Example 8–4.)

Vertical Spreads—Long Call/Short Call or Long Put/Short Put (Same Expiration). If the long call (put) option strike price is less (greater) than or equal to the short call (put) option strike price, the long option premium is paid in full and no margin is required for the short option premium. If the long call (put) option strike price is greater (less) than the short call (put) option strike price, the long option is paid for in full; the spread margin is equal to the amount by which the short option premium exceeds the long option premium, plus the minimum of either per contract, initial $2,000 ($3,000), maintenance or hedging $1,500 ($2,500), or the difference between the strike prices. (See COMEX Example 8–5.)

Horizontal Spread—Long Call/Short Call or Long Put/Short Put (with different expiration dates). If the long call (put) option strike price is less (greater) than or equal to the short call (put) option strike price, then the long option premium is paid for in full. Margin equals $200 per contract for option positions involving months that are 12 months or more apart plus the amount, if any, that the short option premium exceeds the long option premium. If the long call (put) option strike price is greater (less) than the short call (put) option strike price, then the long option premium is paid in full. Margin equals the amount by which the short option premium exceeds the long option premium plus the minimum of the difference between the strike prices and, per contract, initial $2,000 ($3,000), maintenance or hedging $1,500 ($2,500).

Long Call/Short Future or Long Put/Long Future. The long option premium is paid in full. Margin equals per contract, initial $2,000 ($3,000), maintenance or hedging $1,500 ($2,250), minus any amount by which the market value of the option premium exceeds the appropriate futures spread margin of $200 per contract for positions involving months that are 12 months or more apart or $2,000 per contract for positions involving T-Notes versus T-Bonds or $1,000 per contract for positions involving GNMA versus T-Bonds. The future position may be in one contract unit of any Chicago Board of Trade U.S. government security future. (See COMEX Example 8–3.)

Long Call/Short Future/Short Put (reverse conversion) or Long Put/ Long Future/Short Call (conversion). This case's assumption is that the expiration months for all three positions and the strike prices for the two option positions are the same. The long option premium is paid in full. The margin equals the amount by which the short option premium exceeds the long option premium.

INDEX OPTIONS

Today the Kansas City Board of Trade (KCBOT), the Chicago Mercantile Exchange (CME), and the New York Future Exchange (NYFE) trade options on index futures contracts. The KCBOT trades options on the Value Line Index, the CME on the Standard & Poor's Index, and the NYFE on the New York Stock Exchange Index.

An index is a weighted or nonweighted average of the market price of a group of (in this case) stocks that gives investors regular "benchmarks" against which they can evaluate the performance of either individual stocks or groups of stocks.

Different indexes have different advantages and disadvantages, but their economic function is substantially identical. The G&P 500 Index futures options, as traded on the CME, is fairly representative of index options as a group and will serve as a good example. (See Table 8–1.)

CHICAGO MERCANTILE EXCHANGE (CME)

The Index and Option Market (IOM) of the Chicago Mercantile Exchange is currently trading both put and call options on the Standard and Poor's 500 futures contracts. This option is of particular interest due to its close relationship to the security markets.

Definitions

Size of Trading Unit. One option represents a right to buy in the case of a call, or to sell in the case of a put, one IOM Standard & Poor's 500 futures contract.

Price Quotation. Prices of options are quoted in basis points. The option premium dollar amount is equal to the number of basis points multiplied by $5.00. A premium of 1.00 (100 basis points) is equal to $500. Each minimum fluctuation of .05 equals a move of $25 of option value.

Striking Prices. Standard & Poor's 500 option strike prices are quoted on the Standard & Poor's 500 futures contract in intervals of 500 basis points from a round number base, such as 115.00, 120.00, or 125.00. As a new month commences trading, two strike prices for puts and calls in each contract month will be listed: one with an exercise price in excess of the then current underlying S&P 500 futures price, and one with an exercise price less than the current underlying S&P 500 futures price. If the underlying S&P 500 futures price is within 100 basis points of an exercise price, three options are listed: the strike price within 100 basis points of the futures price and one on either side of it. When a sale, bid, or offer in the underlying S&P futures contract occurs at, or passes through the highest (or lowest) exercise price of the currently listed option series, put and call options contracts at the next higher (or lower) exercise price commence trading at the next trading session. However, no new options are listed if less than 30 calendar days remain to maturity.

Daily Price Range. There shall be no trading at a price more than 500 basis points above or below the previous day's settlement price, except:

1. when on two successive days any S&P futures option contract closes at the normal daily limit in the same direction, or
2. when expanded limits are in effect on the underlying futures.

(Expanded daily limits go into effect on the option.

Termination of Trading. Option trading terminates on the last trading day of the underlying S&P futures contract.

Exercise Days. Exercise of an option contract may be made on any IOM business day during the life of the option contract. The discretion to exercise the S&P option contract rests with the holder of the long position and results in the appropriate long or short futures position. However, the exercise of an option on the last trading day results in a cash settlement as the underlying futures contract also ceases trading that day. Any option remaining unexercised on the last trading day shall be automatically exercised.

Assignment of Exercise Notices. The Clearing House randomly matches within a series a notice of exercise received from the buyer with that of an option writer. Exercise results in the short and short option position being cancelled. The exchange of the option for the futures position shall be effective on the date that the exercise notice is received.

Expanded Daily Price Limits. Whenever on two successive days any option contract closes at the normal daily price limit in the same direction (not necessarily the same contract on both days), or whenever expanded daily price limits are in effect for the underlying S&P futures contract, an expanded daily price limit schedule shall go into effect as follows:

1. The third day's price limit in all options contracts shall be 150% of the normal daily limit.
2. If any contract closes at its expanded daily price limit on the third day in the same direction, then the fourth day's expanded daily price limit, as well as each successive day thereafter, shall be 200% of the normal daily limit, so long as any contract closes at its daily expanded price limits.
3. Whenever the foregoing daily price limit schedule is in effect and the contract does not close at the price limit in the *same* direction that initiated or maintained the expanded schedule, then the normal daily price limit shall be reinstated for the following day.

Months Traded. Options trade for the months of March, June, September, and December.

Hours of Trading. S&P futures options trade from 9:00 A.M. to 3:15 P.M. (Chicago time).

Margin Requirements

Although all the contract specifications so far discussed are important, you should understand certain minor technical differences among the various exchanges. These differences affect rights and obligations, as well as the amounts of money received or paid under given situations. With regard to margin, most commodity exchanges have followed a similar route in establishing requirements. CSCE, CBOT, and NYMEX have what is substantially an identical system with minor technical differences. The CME too has generally followed the same approach.

TABLE 8–1. Customer Margins on S&P Futures Options

Naked Options

Long
 Premium paid in full

Short
 Premium marked to market *plus* futures margin on S&P futures contract (speculative or hedge as appropriate) *less* one-half the amount the option is out-of-the-money. Margin, however, shall not be less than the premium plus $1,000.

Option-Futures Spreads

Long Call-Short Futures or Long Put-Long Futures
S&P futures hedge margin *minus* option premium marked to market (cannot be negative). Cash loan can be granted on the position up to the amount the option is in-the-money to finance settlement variation on the futures contract. Such loan amounts are added to the margin required on the position.

Short Call-Long Futures or Short Put-Short Futures
Option premium marked to market *plus* S&P futures hedge margin less one-half the amount the option is in-the-money. Margin, however, shall not be less than the premium plus $1,000.

Option-Option Spreads

1. *Vertical Spreads*—Long call, short call or long put, short put with the *same* expiration date and different strike prices.
   a. *Bull Spread (Calls); Bear Spread (Puts)*—Exercise price on long leg is lower than exercise price on short leg for call spreads, or higher than exercise price on short leg for put spreads
      • No margin
   b. *Bear Spread (Calls); Bull Spread (Puts)*—Exercise price on long leg is higher than exercise price on short leg for call spreads, or is lower than exercise price on short leg for put spreads.
      • Difference in exercise prices on the options not to exceed margin on naked short option
2. *Mixed Spreads*—Long call, short call or long put, short put where the time to maturity and exercise prices are different.
   a. Exercise price on long leg is lower than exercise price on short leg for call spreads, or is higher than exercise price on short leg for put spreads
      • Futures spread margin + excess of short premium over long premium
   b. Exercise price on long leg is higher than exercise price on short leg for call spreads, or is lower than exercise price on short leg for put spreads
      • Excess of short premium over long premium plus the difference in strike prices not to exceed margins on naked short option
3. *Butterfly Spreads*—One vertical Bull Spread combined with one vertical Bear Spread. The four options are either all puts or all calls with a common exercise price for two long or short options. The common exercise price must lie between the exercise prices for the remaining two options.
   a. *Debit Spread*—Combined long premiums exceed short premiums and the middle strike price is exactly halfway between the remaining strike prices
      • No margin
   b. *Credit Spread*—Combined short premiums exceed combined long premiums or middle strike price is not halfway between remaining strike prices
      • Largest difference between two adjacent strike prices, not to exceed futures hedge margin plus amount by which short option premiums exceed long option premiums
4. *Box Spreads*—Long Call, Short Put with the same exercise price coupled with a Short Call, Long Put with the same exercise price. All four options have the same expiration date.
   a. *Debit Spread*—Combined long premiums exceed combined short premiums
      • No margin
   b. *Credit Spread*—Combined short premiums exceed combined long premiums
      • Difference in strike prices

5. *Straddles*—Short Call, Short Put with the premium on two short options marked to market plus S&P futures hedge margin.

Conversions and Reverse Conversions

Conversions—Long Futures, Short Call, Long Put

Reverse Conversions—Short Futures, Long Call, Short Put
   Short premium minus long premium marked-to-market (cannot be negative). Cash loan can be granted to finance settlement variation on futures as under B.

MID-AMERICA COMMODITY EXCHANGE (MID-AM)

The Mid-Am also trades a gold futures option similar to that traded on COMEX. This option calls for the delivery of a gold futures contract upon exercise. The only major difference is the Mid-Am gold futures contract is a contract on a kilo bar of gold (32.15 troy ounces), while the COMEX contract is a contract for 100 troy ounces.

CONCLUSION

Investor *must* have a thorough understanding of the margining of the various types of option and option/futures position before undertaking a discussion of strategy. Without such an understanding, they cannot discuss return on investment (ROI). The dollars committed to a given strategy often determine whether the economics make the commitment worthwhile.

This chapter is designed to discuss the general concepts that will continue to apply as the exchanges continue to "fine tune" their actual rules. Because margins are set by the exchanges and by their related clearing corporation, this book cannot be the final authority. Only the exchanges' rules can be relied upon for final answers. Since the exchanges and the clearing corporations are constantly changing and enhancing their own rules, only your broker can supply the latest rules and procedures.

The margin rules discussed have been "exchange minimum" requirements, and most brokerage firms have higher requirements than these minimums. The actual money you may expect to deposit is the minimum that your brokerage firm will allow. Different brokers have different minimum margins. You should carefully consider what minimums are available in light of your approach to option strategy.

9

THE SPECULATOR— CALL BUYING STRATEGIES

The use of options is a strategy in itself. The investor has numerous vehicles for investment in commodities, and options is only one of them. At the outset, therefore, the assumption is that the investor has decided that options are the proper vehicle.

The outright purchase of options offers the investor, in addition to the profit potential, only two things: leverage and risk protection. The chapter on option pricing theory (Chapter 4) showed that an at-market option behaves most like an option and that either deep in-the-money or deep out-of-the-money options held few similarities to our traditional view of options.

An option is a tool of investing, not an investment in itself. If options are used properly, they serve their investment purpose admirably; if used improperly, they will tend to do more harm than good. Whether your approach to commodity investing is "fundamental," "technical," or possibly a combination of both, you must make your investment judgment on the underlying commodity, not on the option. The underlying market decision is "strategic"; the option decision is "tactical." The concept that the option is "the tail of the dog," and the commodity is "the dog" itself is valid for all but the professional option writer (discussed later).

Having made the decision to purchase an option, you often encounter the comment that a given option is "overpriced" or "underpriced." These terms deal with the theoretical value of an option and have little bearing on day-to-day investing. Remember there is no such thing as an overpriced option to an investor who makes money or an underpriced option to an investor who loses money. In addition, because markets are generally efficient determinants of price, the degree of overpriced or underpriced option is not significant enough to affect market strategy or tactics.

BREAKEVEN

"Breakeven" is a term that is encountered frequently in discussing option strategies. Simply defined in relation to listed, fungible options, *breakeven* is the price at which the underlying commodity must be at some point in time for an investor to recover the purchase premium plus the commissions involved in the transaction. Breakeven is normally computed for expiration date because an economic model is necessary to come up with the number for an earlier date. To compute breakeven, take the total premium plus commission, and divide this sum by the size of the contract to come up with premium per unit volume.

Example: If you purchase a call on 100 ounces of gold for $3,000 in premium and pay $100 in commission, the total cost is $3,100. If the option is a call on 100 ounces, the premium is $31/ounce. You then add this premium in the case of a call or deduct this premium in the case of a put, in dollars/ounce, to or from the striking price of the option. If the striking price of the gold call is $300/ounce, your breakeven point, or price, at expiration is $331/ounce, neglecting any close-out commission.

BUYING CALLS AS A SPECULATION

The purchase of a call option, as an outright speculation (not in conjunction with another position), is made in anticipation of higher prices in the underlying commodity. This is perhaps one of the most difficult strategies because it requires correct market judgment as to market direction, magnitude of move, and timing. Having purchased a call option, one of three things can happen: the market can go up, the market can go down, or the market can remain unchanged. In two of these cases (unchanged or down), the call buyer normally loses money. In the third case (market up), the magnitude of appreciation must be sufficient to overcome the cost of the premium and the related commission(s). This investment vehicle therefore has an apparent dysfunction in that the probability of success is weighted mathematically against the investor. This is not to say that call buying is not a good strategy; it is merely a strategy in which the probability of success is against the investor.

In fact, call buying is outstanding for its intended purpose. Commodities are no more volatile than securities over any extended period of time; however, commodities offer the investor much greater leverage than is normally encountered in the purchase of securities. When you buy securities on margin, you deposit 50% to 80% of the market value of the security. The

leverage of buying securities on margin at best doubles the positive or negative effects of price changes. In commodities, margin is traditionally 5% to
10% of the value of the underlying commodity. The leverage factor is therefore between ten and twenty times the magnitude of the market price change
in the underlying commodity. A 5% to 10% change in the market price of a
commodity either doubles your investment or causes you to lose the entire
investment. Buying an option limits your exposure to the premium plus
commission—and nothing more. When you buy a commodity option, you
are buying fire insurance on commodity trading. The premium you pay may
be thought of as a "premium" in the insurance sense. The magnitude of the
out-of-the-money feature, if any, may be thought of as "deductible" in the
insurance sense. You want the right to trade commodities, but you wish
someone else (the grantor) to assume risk beyond a certain point.

In all the following examples, commissions have not usually been included, as they add nothing to the clarity of the point but only complicate the
mathematics. However, commissions play an important role in actual
strategies and must be considered.

> *Example:* The chart in Figure 9–1 depicts the economic effect of pur-
> chasing a call on 100 ounces of gold with a striking price of $300/ounce
> for a premium of $3,000.
>
> As you can see in the chart, at $300/ounce or below, at expiration,
> you would lose your entire premium because you would have at best an
> at-market option with no time remaining. Your breakeven point is
> $330/ounce, which represents your premium/ounce added to the strike
> price. Above $300/ounce your option is worth at least $100 for each
> dollar that gold appreciates above $300/ounce. Notice also, that your
> maximum loss is $3,000, which is sustained at a price of $300/ounce or
> below. Between $300/ounce and $330/ounce, you recover some of your
> initial premium depending on how far your option is in-the-money.
> Prior to expiration, you generally have a lower breakeven, and you're
> able to recoup some of the option's extrinsic value, depending on the
> time remaining and on the degree to which the option is in the money.
> Above $330/ounce, you have the same economic position as if you had,
> at $330, purchased a commodity futures contract, with the exception,
> that your risk with the option is always limited to the premium.

The option, in this case, offers leverage that is about equal to commodity futures. The option involved costs 10% of the value of the underlying
comodity, which is about the equivalent of the margin requirement to trade
the futures. What you give up is "probability of profitability" (the potential
profit times the probability of that profit occurring). What you gain is risk
protection.

FIGURE 9–1. Gold $300 Strike Call Buying Chart

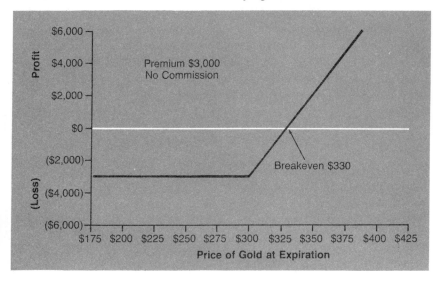

ADDING TO A PROFITABLE FUTURES POSITION

When you successfully trade futures, you have credited to your account the profits prior to the position being closed out due to the variation margin. As the position moves in your favor, there is always the temptation to add to the position (pyramid), in an attempt to further increase those profits. By adding additional contract to an already established position, you increase not only the potential for profit but also the potential for loss. Investors who traditionally trade one or two contracts may, because they are "winning," overextend themselves in the risk area through the addition of more contracts.

An alternative approach to the conventional pyramiding approach is to pyramid through the use of options. The buying of, say, call options in conjunction with a long futures position offers the possibility of additional profits with a further price increase (after the premium has been overcome) without a commensurate increase in risk. The added profit potential is unlimited, but the added risk is limited to the premium paid for the options.

> *Example:* You purchased 2 COMEX gold futures contracts when gold was trading at $250/ounce. Gold is now trading at $300/per ounce, and you have a very nice profit of $10,000 ($50 × 100 ounces × 2 contracts). Your trading capital allows you to take the risk associated with a two-contract position, but you are very bullish on gold. You might

"double-up" on your gold position by purchasing 2 $300 striking price calls at a cost of $3,000 each. If the market continues higher, you will continue to profit on your futures position as well as on your long call position. If the market moves lower, you have an acceptable risk on your futures position, but you are limited to a total risk on the two calls of only $6,000.

ADDING TO AN UNPROFITABLE POSITION
(Dollar/Cost Averaging)

Often you make a market judgment and take on a futures position that does not immediately work in your favor, but conversely moves the wrong way. In securities, when a position moves against investors and their market view has not changed, they commonly add to that position for the purpose of dollar/cost averaging. Additional shares bought at a lower price bring down the average cost of the entire position. Even though this philosophy is equally valid with commodities, the leverage imparted to the position by 5% to 10% margin discourages most investors from following what could be a second approach to commodity investing. Instead of adding additional futures contracts for the purpose of dollar/cost averaging, the purchase of call options serves a substantially identical purpose, but it does not subject the investor to margin calls of ever increasing magnitude. The major disadvantage is that the premium is a true cost that must first be overcome before the effect of the averaging can be felt.

Example: You have purchased 2 COMEX gold futures contracts when gold was trading at $325. Gold is now down to $300, and the thought of dollar-cost-averaging appears attractive were it not for the increased risk of the larger position. In lieu of additional futures contracts, you might purchase 2 $300 striking price call options, thereby achieving much the same advantages as the additional futures contracts but with a predefined risk.

AS A REPLACEMENT FOR A PROFITABLE POSITION

Occasionally you make a correct market decision. Having been bullish and taken on a long futures position, the market has moved up. The question becomes whether to remain with the profitable position or to take profits and look for more fertile grounds elsewhere. The old market adage of "cut losses short and let profits run" is not always easy to do emotionally. One approach is to take the profit in the futures contract and use a portion of that profit to reestablish a substantially identical position through the purchase of a call option on the same contract. This offers the advantage of "nailing down" the profit, while still leaving a chance to participate in any further move. If the move continues, you need only overcome the premium to continue to profit; if the move is truly over, your risk is limited to the premium expended.

Example: You purchased a gold futures contract when gold was $250 per ounce, and, with gold now at $300, you want to take your $5,000 profit. You would like to continue to profit on any further rise, but you don't want to risk all the profit you have already accrued. You might liquidate your futures position and use part of the profits to purchase call option(s). This approach allows you to participate in any further price increase, but it limits your exposure to the premiums paid.

REPLACING AN UNPROFITABLE POSITION

Sometimes you believe in a position that continues to move against you, but the margin calls force you to liquidate. In fact, many investors have been either stopped out of a market or forced to liquidate due to margin calls, only to see the market turn around and ultimately fulfill their projections. This tends to be very disheartening when you no longer have a position to participate in your correct judgment. If your views have not changed as to the correctness of your market view, liquidation therefore tends to be most uncomfortable. A valid approach is to liquidate the futures position and at the same time purchase a substantially identical option position. Thus you eliminate the possibility of further margin calls, but you can retain the benefits of the futures contract. This approach gives you "staying power."

Example: You purchased gold futures when gold was trading at $325 per ounce, and you have seen the price decline to $300 per ounce. You still believe that gold will go higher, but, if gold were to break below $300 per ounce, the risk involved might be greater than you were willing to accept. If you liquidate your futures position and perhaps buy a $300 striking price call, you can limit your risk to a $3,000 premium and still have the potential to profit should the market rally substantially.

PROTECTING A SHORT POSITION

The tradition in both securities and commodities has been to use "stop" orders as a means of limiting the risk exposure on a given position. Although this is a valid approach, it has several disadvantages. The first disadvantage is that a market may "gap" up or down thereby bypassing your stop order. The market may also be bid up the limit or offered down the limit, which would preclude the execution of your stop order. The second disadvantage is that a stop order, after being triggered, becomes a market order and does not guarantee at what price it will be executed.

As an alternative to the entry of a buy-stop to protect a short position, purchase a call option when you are considering the entry of the stop. This strategy offers several distinct advantages to the buy-stop order in many cases. The first advantage is that, by carefully selecting the strike price, you can predetermine the magnitude of exposure that you are willing to assume. This approach is much the same as deciding on the dollar amount of "deductible" you will accept on your car insurance. The second advantage is that both positions will continue to exist regardless of market gyrations.

If you have gone "short" and purchased a call to protect the position, even if the market rallies initially, you will not be immediately stopped out only to find that your long-term market judgment was later confirmed by a substantial decline.

LOCKING-IN A PROFIT

Assuming that you go short futures and the market works in your favor, a problem arises with regard to liquidating or retaining the positions for additional profits. Closing out the position does "nail down" the profits, but it also eliminates the possibility of incremental profits on any further decline in the commodity. One traditional approach has been the entry of a buy-stop order above the market in an attempt to achieve the desired result. In some cases this works. In many cases, however, after a market has suffered a protracted decline, it stages a substantial rally and the stop order is triggered liquidating the position. An alternative approach is the purchase of a call option, with a strike price somewhere near the price at which you would normally have entered a stop order. Except for the cost of the premium, this is the equivalent protection of a stop order, but if the market continues its decline before or after a rally, the short position remains intact and profits continue.

OPTIONS IN CONJUNCTION WITH TECHNICAL ANALYSIS

Several of the sections in the chapter on technical analysis (Chapter 3) deal with reversal formations. These types of formations, when completed, indicate a change in market direction. Depending on the type of formation, the magnitude of a move following a reversal may be substantial. The temptation is always to anticipate the completion of a technical formation, or to anticipate a "breakout" or "breakdown." The risk, of course, is that the market does not do as anticipated but continues in its original direction, and the investor has prematurely established a position on the wrong side of the market in anticipation of the projected move. A safer and more creative approach to the anticipation of a technical breakout or to the reversal of a downtrend is the purchase of a call option whose strike price is the equivalent of the technical breakout or reversal confirmation price. This approach allows one the same market potential, but it limits the risk to the premium.

DURING LIMIT FUTURES MOVES

All the designated contract markets in the United States have limitations on the maximum move that a futures contract may make in any one day. Some exchanges, however, have not imposed similar limitations in the options contracts. This allows unlimited entry to a market that is up the limit when you want to establish a long position. The purchase of a call is a contingent long position, and the subsequent exercise results in an actual long position. Perhaps more important than the ability to go long when a market is bid up the limit is the ability to close out a short in like circumstances. If you are short the futures and the market is bid up the limit, the purchase of a call option with the same maturity, followed by an immediate exercise, results in the liquidation (close-out) of the short position. Realize that, with the market bid up the limit, the call is quite costly, but you are assured of being out of an uncomfortable short futures position.

REVERSALS

Let's explain this strategy by way of example. You have purchased a call option in anticipation of an upward move in the commodity. Further assume that the move has taken place and that you have a nice profit on the long but now believe that the market is going to go lower. The sale of a futures contract, while holding a long call position, has much the same investment risk and benefits as the ownership of a put option. In some cases, this approach to reversing a position has a commission advantage, as most brokerage firms charge a different rate of commission on options than on futures. Second, the liquidation of the call, followed either by the purchase of a put or by the sale of a futures contract, involves a second commission and a second transaction. Last, the absolute dollar profit potential of the reversal may be greater, depending on the actual market prices of the instruments involved.

Reversals: When a short futures position held in conjunction with a long call whose strike price is identical to the price at which the short futures was established, it is economically a put. This position gives rise to profit potential. If the market price of a put is greater than the market price of a call with the same strike price and maturity, you can purchase the call, go short the futures, and simultaneously grant the put. Due to the difference between the call and put premiums, a profit results. This potential profit may not be achievable depending on the commissions you must pay for the transaction. Some of the exchanges have provided special margin requirements to allow this type of reversal to be done on an economic basis.

RATIO POSITIONS

All the discussion up to this point has dealt with single units, either on call or one futures contract short and one call long. In some instances, this 1:1 relationship is not the most advantageous.

Let's say that you are short a futures contract and that the market is up the limit. The purchase of one call limits the risk, and its exercise closes out the position. Yet the purchase of a second or perhaps third call effectively converts the short position into a long position. This strategy is most advantageous in markets in which the futures have limits and the options do not.

> *Example:* A gold call with a $300 striking price and a March maturity is trading for $3,000, while the $300 gold put for March is trading for $2,700. To execute the conversion, buy the $300 March put for $2,700, go long the March futures, and sell the $300 March call for $3,000, thereby realizing the $300 difference in premiums as a profit. If the market goes up and the call is exercised, the futures are delivered and the put expires. If the market goes down, the put is used as the means of liquidating the long futures, while the call expires.

A VIRTUALLY ALL-WIN, NO-LOSE WAY TO BUY CALLS: CALLS IN CONJUNCTION WITH T-BILLS

Some texts on options tend to imply that the purchase of options is generally foolish because the probability of success is weighted against the option purchaser. That implication may be correct at times. If you purchase a call, the market must move up enough to cover the commissions. If you hold the option for any period of time, the move must exceed the premium for you to make a profit. Yet the advantages of leverage and downside risk protection are why you are paying the premium. If one strategy "guarantees a profit" and has "no risk," it is the purchase of options in conjunction with the ownership of T-Bills or like investments.

> *Example:* Let's make several assumptions: (1) The yield on 6-month Treasury bills is 15% per annum; (2) U.S. T-bills are a riskless invest-ment; and (3) you have $10,000 to invest in the commodities markets.
>
> Because T-Bills are issued at a discount and mature at par, you could purchase a 6-month 15% $10,000 T-bill for approximately $9,250. This would leave you with $750 uninvested. If you use the $750 to purchase a call option on a commodity, you can't lose. If the commodity remains unchanged or goes lower, and the option expires worthless, you lose the premium. But in 6 months, the T-bills mature, and they may be redeemed for $10,000, which is what you started with. On the other hand, if the market moves higher, and the option is profitable, you will not only have the profit on the call, but your T-Bill will mature at par, and you will get that $10,000 back also.

Over any period of time, the purchase of calls should show some profit—hence the premise that you are guaranteed a profit. It would appear that this is an "all-win, no-lose" strategy. To a certain degree it is. In reality, however, there is a risk, and profits are not guaranteed. The reason is that you have a lost opportunity cost. That is, had you put all $10,000 into the T-bill originally, you would have had more than $10,000 at maturity. Nevertheless, this strategy is a way to trade commodites for the cost of simple interest.

SPECULATIVE CALL TRADING TACTICS

If the purchase of calls is the proper strategy for a given set of circum-stances, what maturity should you buy? What striking price should you buy? When should you buy? Most importantly, when and how should you take profits or losses?

Maturity

The purchase of a call options presupposes that some event will take place. If you purchase a call on heating oil, you have made the judgment that the price will go up due to perhaps OPEC actions, a cold winter, or a government-imposed import duty. Any event carries with it a time frame judgment. When do you anticipate the effects of this event to be reflected in the price? Obviously, you must buy an option whose maturity at least coin-cides with the event, if not postdates it. The "best" maturity to purchase is the one that still has 30–45 days remaining to maturity when the price change event takes place. The reason to pick this maturity is that, because extrinsic value (see the chapter on pricing) declines as a function of the square root of time, the greatest percentage of decline takes place in the last 30–45 days of an option's existence. This circumstance, of course, holds true only if at the time of liquidation the option is not so far in-the-money that it has no extrinsic value.

Striking Price

In determining the proper striking price, you must consider several things. For instance, an at-the-market option is only at-the-market for the maturity under consideration.

> *Example:* Gold for spot delivery is trading at $400/troy ounce. If the prime rate is 15%, gold for one-year delivery will be trading at approximately $460/troy ounce. An at-the-market call on spot gold would have a striking price of $400, while an at-the-market call on one-year gold would have a striking price of $460.

With this in mind, let's look at in-the-money, at-the-market and out-of-the-money calls.

In-the-money options are the most expensive in terms of actual dollars because a portion of their premium is intrinsic value. Yet if the commodity remains unchanged, the intrinsic value cannot dissipate. In-the-money options offer the least leverage (because they are the most expensive) and have the highest risk (because they cost the most). Their advantage is that they are the most sensitive to a price change in the underlying commodity—that is, they have the highest "delta." An in-the-money option is most like the underlying commodity itself; that is, in absolute dollar terms, if the commodity moves up (in the case of a call), the option gains in value most rapidly. If the commodity moves down, the option loses in value most rapidly.

Out-of-the-money options are the least expensive because they have no intrinsic value and have the lowest probability of ultimately being exercised. Out-of-the-money options have the lowest dollar risk because they are inexpensive; for the same reason, they offer the highest leverage. Because this type of option has no intrinsic value, if the commodity does not appreciate sufficiently to cover the premium plus commission added to the striking price, you lose money. If the underlying commodity remains unchanged, the option expires worthless.

At-the-market options, by definition, have no intrinsic value, but because they are not out-of-the-money, they command the highest extrinsic value. At-the-market options offer reasonable leverage and reasonable downside risk protection because they are the mid-point between being in-the-money and out-of-the-money.

Market statistics have shown that over the years the vast majority of options purchases are made in options that fall from at-the-market to slightly out-of-the-money. This most likely indicates a risk/reward relationship that is most representative of the temperament of the typical option buyer. There are no "absolutes" in picking striking price. For a given move in the price of the underlying commodity, the out-of-the-money option generally shows the greatest percentage increase in price, while the in-the-money option shows the greatest dollar change in price. This is offset by the leverage and risk factors of the in-the-money/out-of-the-money relationship.

Timing of Purchase

When to buy a call would appear to be a simple question: You buy when you think the market is going up. This answer, however, is only half true. Part of the price of an option is the volatility of the underlying commodity. Ideally, you would like to buy an option when the volatility is low because, at that time, the premium should be the lowest. In general, try to avoid purchasing calls immediately after the market has made a large move. In response to a large move (regardless of direction), premiums are usually inflated. After a large rally or a large sell-off, wait a few days for the premium to contract before instituting new positions.

Taking Profits

When and how to take profits is a function of both market view and technique. An option has the attributes of leverage and downside protection to the greatest degree when it is at-the-market. It begins to lose some of these advantages as it becomes profitable. As an option moves in-the-money, it becomes more expensive, both reducing the leverage and increasing the dollar exposure. Either when the underlying commodity, in your view, no longer has additional profit potential, or when the option has reached the point that it no longer offers leverage comparable to futures, it is the time to liquidate.

Another consideration is volatility. If the market has made an inordinately large move in a short period of time, the premium is overly inflated. The ideal time to liquidate a position is at a time of high volatility, because the inflated premium may more than compensate its owner for an early liquidation.

If you have purchased a call and the market has moved favorably, you may be in such a situation that you wish to remain in the market, but the option you own is so expensive that it offers little leverage and has substantial downside risk. At this point, you should liquidate the option you own, thereby nailing down a profit, and purchase a higher striking price. This transaction is referred to as *rolling up*. In many cases, the proceeds of the liquidation supply enough capital to purchase two or more at-the-market options of the same maturity. Realize that if you do this, you once again increase your leverage, but, because the same dollars are still committed, you maintain the same downside risk.

> *Example:* You purchased an at-the-market call when gold was at $250 for $2,500, and gold is now at $300. Your call can be liquidated for approximately $5,000. You might consider liquidating the $5,000 call and using a portion of the proceed to purchase a new at-the-market call for perhaps $3,000. This takes some of your profits out of the market, reduces your dollar risk, and increases your leverage.

If, after having purchased a call, the market moves lower and you liquidate what is now an out-of-the-money option in favor of purchasing an at-the-market, this is referred to as *rolling down*. The chapter on spreading deals with the mechanics of rolling up and rolling down in more detail.

10

THE SPECULATOR—
PUT BUYING STRATEGIES

The put is to the "bear" what the call is to the "bull." As an unrelated investment, the purchase of a put option is made in anticipation of declining prices in the underlying commodity. Historically, puts have not been a popular investment with the general public. Perhaps human nature leads people to think that something is "wrong" with making a profit based on a decline in prices. Exchange-traded and dealer put options have never, for any appreciable period of time, accounted for 50% of the overall volume, even in protracted bear markets.

The old market adage of "buy low, sell high" does not say which half of the transaction must be done first. It is just as easy in commodities to sell high and buy low. Traditionally prices tend to decline more rapidly than they advance. This is because a market price can decline of its own weight. In other words, a portion of the volume that causes a price advance is supplied by the short-term technical or fundamental trader who is looking for an active market regardless of the commodity. As prices decline, the volume generally tends to be lighter. This reduced liquidity and activity causes the short-term trader to move capital to more active or "fertile" fields. It can be argued that the withdrawal of this speculative trading capital adds to the rapidity of the decline. For this reason, profits are generally realized faster in a market of declining prices than they are in a rising price markets.

Traditionally, the public speculator has been thought to be a buyer of futures, and the commercial, who is the hedger, has been regarded as the seller of futures. The public view that the commercial is traditionally short out of necessity may be another reason why the public tends to be long. Also, over any extended period of time, inflation tends to favor a long position.

The put is only a means of investing. If investors' judgments dictate that profit will be made on the short side of the market, then investors, in addition to puts, may consider outright short positions in either futures, physicals, or forwards. The put's advantages are, as with calls, leverage and protection against adverse price movement, which in this case is upward. In exchange for these advantages, investors pay premiums that must be overcome before substantial profits are possible.

BREAKEVEN

As with the call, the breakeven number can be easily determined only for the expiration date. To breakeven on the purchase of a put on expiration date, the commodity futures contract must be below the strike price by an amount equal to the premium plus the commission.

Example: You purchased a put option on 100 ounces of gold with a strike price of $400/ounce for a total cost of $3,500. The commission was $200. The total cost of $3,700 is the equivalent of $37 per ounce. At expiration gold must be $37 below the $400 strike price for you to break even. Your breakeven price is $363. For any price below $400 per ounce at expiration, you recover all or a portion of your premium. Below $363, you begin to realize a profit. Generally, the greater the time until expiration, the greater the remaining extrinsic value and

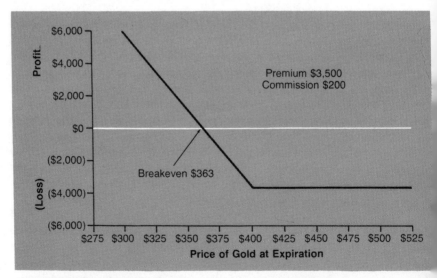

FIGURE 10–1. Gold $400 Strike Put Buying Chart

consequently the smaller the move necessary to achieve the same results.

The chart in Figure 10–1 shows graphically the economics of the purchase of this put. The advantage of the put is really the horizontal line representing the loss. At no price is the potential loss ever greater than $3,700. The position is approximately the equivalent of having gone short gold at $400 and then having had the market rally $37. The difference is that you now have a guaranteed stop-buy order at $437.

BUYING PUTS AS A SPECULATION

The purchase of a put option as an outright speculation (not in conjunction with another position) is normally done in anticipation of lower prices in the underlying commodity. The purchase of options, either puts or calls, is one of the most difficult strategies to employ successfully because it requires not only good market judgment as to direction and magnitude, but also good judgment as to the magnitude in relation to the time involved. Having purchased a put option, market prices can do one of three things: go higher, remain unchanged, or go lower. The probability of each occurrence is not equal. Obviously, if the market price goes higher or remains unchanged, at maturity the option expires worthless. In addition, if the market goes lower, it must do so by an amount equal to the premium plus the commission for the investor to realize a profit on the put option. The option purchaser is always working in an investment environment where the probabilities of failure are better than 2-to-1 against success. That does not mean that the purchase of a put option is not a good idea. This better-than-2-to-1 disadvantage is part of the cost for the limited risk and leverage offered by the instrument.

In recent years, we have seen futures markets move up the limit many days in succession. Markets, such as the New York COMEX silver market, have in recent years had limit upward moves 12, 13, or 14 days in succession. Investors who were short in these markets would have appreciated the limited risk feature of the put option. Moves of this magnitude are not the norm, but, when they do occur, the "insurance" offered by the put is most welcome. Most people never collect on the liability feature of their automobile insurance, but to drive a car without this protection is subjecting oneself to financial ruin if the unforeseen occurs.

In practice, the magnitude of market moves is no greater on the upside than on the downside, but, in theory, there is no limit to how far a commodity price may advance over a period of time. This possibility too, explains people's reluctance to be short the market, and it also adds to the validity of the purchase of put options.

ADDING TO A PROFITABLE
FUTURES POSITION

When you trade in the futures markets, profits are realized immediately as a result of the positive cash flow supplied by the variation margin on positions moving in your favor. There is always the temptation, correct or not, to add to the existing futures position with this variation margin and thereby increment profits on a further favorable move. This approach to investing (pyramiding) is satisfactory if the investor can withstand the margin calls of a larger position on a market reversal. If the contemplated position is too large in light of the investor's risk-taking ability, pyramiding is unwise. The put option offers a logical solution to this problem.

In lieu of the traditional pyramiding approach, a portion of the positive variation margin generated on a profitable short position may be used to purchase put options on the same underlying commodity. This approach offers the investor many of the same advantages as adding to the futures position, but it increases the risk only by the amount of the premium(s) involved. If the investor is correct and the market continues its decline, once the premium is overcome, the results are identical to having pyramided originally. If, however, the market reverses itself, the incremental loss of the enlarged position is the premium itself, not greater margin calls on the overall position. Depending on the strike price and maturity selected, the investor can also adjust the leverage and risk factors to the then current market environment.

ADDING TO AN UNPROFITABLE
FUTURES POSITION
(Dollar/Cost Averaging)

All investments do not necessarily turn out the way we anticipate. If, after having gone short the futures contract, the market rallies as opposed to declining, you must make a judgment. Do you remain with the position, liquidate the position, or add to the position?

Liquidating the position is perhaps mathematically the easiest approach to understand. In liquidation, you admit that you have made a mistake; you know the magnitude of the mistake and now rectify the mistake. In most cases, a move against you does not necessarily signal that you were incorrect in your market judgment, nor do you necessarily wish to liquidate the position. The real problem is that, if you are correct, the first portion of the market move in your favor will only overcome your current loss. Adding to a position to take advantage of dollar/cost averaging is common in securities. This is not commonly done in commodities because the leverage of futures is so tremendous that most investors could not withstand the added margin calls were the position to continue to move against them.

Put options offer a logical solution to the dollar/cost averaging dilemma. The purchase of a put option, in conjunction with an unprofitable short futures position, offers the advantage of an increased position size with a higher short price, but not an increased exposure to margin calls. The cost, of course, is the premium paid, but this cost may be more than warranted for the investment advantage offered by the increased position and the higher short price.

If the position continues to move against you, your risk is increased only by the premium, and your profit potential is incremented by the equivalent of an additional short futures contract once the options are in-the-money.

AS A REPLACEMENT FOR A PROFITABLE FUTURES POSITION

A profitable short futures position is in itself a problem. Do you take the profit, stay with the original position, or add to the position? As a position moves in your favor, a smaller and smaller percentage of your risk capital is committed to that commodity because the equity in the account is growing, but the position remains constant. Economics suggests that we add to the position, and greed tends to reinforce this view. The problem is that the additional risk inherent in the larger position may not be warranted, and we may give back all or a portion of the profit on any market reversal.

Put options offer a viable solution to these problems. Seldom is it wise to liquidate a profitable position, unless technical or fundamental considerations justify the liquidation. The put offers the ability to liquidate the futures, thereby "nailing down" the profit, yet retaining additional profit potential. The mechanics of the transaction are to liquidate the futures and use all or a portion of the profits to purchase put option(s). Depending on the portion of the funds committed, you may have limited your risk, you still have a short position, and you are not exposed to margin calls should the market reverse itself.

It is not uncommon for a market, after a long decline, to rally on an interim basis. Investors who are short futures may be either stopped out or elect to liquidate their futures rather than see their profits dissipate. Had you replaced the short futures position with put options, you could withstand these interim rallies because there are no margin calls. If the market continues lower, you can, on a regular basis, take profits on the puts and reinstate the position with lower and lower strike prices. This strategy, also used intelligently, can "nail down" profits and limit risk. This strategy, as with calls, is referred to as *rolling down*. This is a way to "nail down" profits and still retain profit potential.

PROTECTING A LONG FUTURES POSITION

The put option need not be used only as an outright position for speculation. One of the best uses of a put option is the protection of a long futures
position. It is common, when entering into a long futures position, to simultaneously enter a sell-stop order to quantify and limit the risk of the position.
The stop order, although useful, is limited in two respects. The first is that it
may not offer the desired protection if the market goes down the limit;
second, if it is placed at a "valid" technical price, the risk may be greater than
the investor can accept.

The purchase of a put option, in conjunction with a long futures position, overcomes both of the disadvantages of the sell-stop. What you have
done is akin to the purchase of collision insurance on your long futures
position with some magnitude of deductible. The deductible, or risk, is
limited to the premium plus a difference between the price at which the
futures contract was instituted and the strike price of the option. This position is very similar to the ownership of a call option. In deciding whether to
use this particular strategy, you must compare it to the purchase of a call
option as an alternative. For this strategy to have an advantage over the
purchase of a call option, the put is normally purchased with the striking
price out-of-the-money. If you purchase a put option with the striking price
either at-market or in-the-money, you actually purchase a call and generally
overpay due to the additional commissions.

LOCKING IN A PROFIT

Having taken a long position and seen that position become profitable,
you face the temptation to take the profit. To make profit over a long term in
commodities, you have to let profits run and cut losses short. The put makes
it easy to follow this dictum. The variation margin supplied by the profitable
long future offers the necessary capital to purchase a put option to lock in the
profit on the long futures position. If you are long futures and the position
has moved in your favor, consider the purchase of a put option as opposed to
the entry of a stop-sell order. The stop order, although a valid and costless
approach, exposes the long position to liquidation on any temporary market
setback, while the purchase of a put allows both positions to remain intact
during technical corrections. The purchase of a put carries with it a cost that
the stop order does not—that is, time value—but the added flexibility and
staying power may in many cases more than offset this disadvantage. If the
market continues higher, neither the put nor the stop-sell would have been
necessary. If the market goes lower, however, the put offers the means of
liquidating the futures at a predetermined price without the risk of limit
moves bypassing the stop order.

IN CONJUNCTION WITH TECHNICAL ANALYSIS

Many investors use technical analysis as the basis for determining which positions to institute, when positions are to be instituted, or when and where they are to be liquidated. Technical analysis is also one of the better methods for the determination of the price placement of stop-loss orders.

When analyzing the market technically, the temptation is to anticipate the completing of technical formations such as head and shoulder, double tops, and the like. If you are correct in this anticipation, the rewards can be outstanding. If, on the other hand, the anticipation is incorrect, the risk can also be outstanding. If you anticipate the completion of either a head and shoulders top or a double top, the purchase of a put option may be the best approach to implement this anticipation. If you are correct, the position was established early, and you should enjoy the benefits of the entire move. But if the anticipation is incorrect, the risk is limited to the premium.

Often the placement of a stop order is best dictated by a trend line, or a support area, or the like. If the technical price is within the dollar limits that the investor is willing to accept, perhaps the stop order is the best approach. Yet if the technically valid stop price carries too high a dollar risk, the purchase of a put may solve the problem. Puts also serve as protection in markets that go down the limit and bypass stop orders.

DURING LIMIT MOVES

Each of the futures exchanges that are currently trading commodity options have different rules. Most of the exchanges have not imposed a limit on the price change for a given day in the options contracts that they trade, even though such limits apply to the underlying futures contracts. This allows unlimited entry to a market that is bid up the limit or offered down the limit. As advantageous as this is, it is even more important that the same rule allows unlimited exits from the market.

You can go long a put option with the market down the limit in the futures because there is no limit to the option. In most cases the option is quite expensive, because most people do exactly the same thing, but at least that avenue is available. Having gone long the put, were you to immediately exercise, you would be short the actual futures contract despite the fact that the market was down the limit. This flexibility is useful when instituting a position, but it is even more useful when attempting to liquidate a position. If you are long the futures contract and the market is down the limit, you are inhibited from liquidating the position. The purchase and immediate exercise of a put option result in the liquidation of the long position. If you had a stop-sell entered in conjunction with the long futures, you must remember to cancel that order. If you do not, when trading resumes in the futures, the stop will be executed, and you will be short at what could be a very unattractive price.

REVERSALS

The purchase of a put not only offers profit potential, but, when used in conjunction with a long futures position, it takes on the economic characteristics of a call option.

Let's assume that you have purchased a put and that the market has moved in your favor, with the put now profitable. Your view of the market has changed and you believe, for at least the short term, that the market will rally. You really have several alternatives open to you. You could liquidate the put and buy a call, or you could liquidate the put and go long futures. If you use either of these two alternatives, you either pay a second premium or assume the open-ended risk of an outright futures position.

Another approach is the purchase of a futures contract while continuing to hold the put option. You have the upside potential associated with the long futures, and the position is hedged with the put, thereby limiting your downside risk. If you are correct and the market rallies sharply, you can liquidate your profitable futures position retaining your put to possibly benefit in any further market decline. This strategy is valid, provided that the put that you own still has sufficient extrinsic value so that the long futures appreciates substantially faster than the put depreciates in a rising market. An added advantage is that you pay only one commission to institute the futures position, as opposed to two commissions if the other strategies are employed. This strategy is most effective when the put is out-of-the-money, the futures position is instituted, and the ensuing move in the futures is rapid. The risk with an out-of-the-money put is the increased risk due to the difference between the current market price of the futures and the striking price of the option.

If the market happens to move against the futures position to the degree that the put becomes in-the-money, the brokerage firm can loan you money against the in-the-money value of the put to meet margin calls. The put can ultimately be exercised to liquidate the long futures position.

RATIO POSITIONS

As with reversals, the use of futures contracts in conjunction with options can economically reverse the investment attributes. The same is true when one or more options are used in conjunction with an outstanding futures position.

Let's say that you are long futures and that the market is down the limit. You are, of course, aware that the purchase of a put position limits your risk on the long position. Some of the exchanges do not limit their option trading, even though they limit futures. This is most advantageous because the in-the-money value of a put hedge can be borrowed from the brokerage firm to help meet the call on the long futures.

In addition, if one put effectively converts a long futures contract to a call option, the purchase of a second put option, in conjunction with the first, converts the position to a straddle (discussed later). The purchase of a third put effectively benefits from any further decline. This flexibility, of course, is available only when the options are not limited as are futures.

CONVERSIONS

As you are aware by now, there is a mathematical relationship between calls, puts, and futures contracts for the same commodity and the same delivery. Because no market is totally efficient, and even the most active arbitrageur misses some of these relationships, there is a potential for profit on what is sometimes a totally riskless basis.

The simplest example is when the put of a given strike price for a given maturity is trading at a premium to the call for the same maturity and strike price, and the futures are approximately at the strike price of the options. In this instance you would buy the call, go short the futures contract, and sell the put, thereby realizing a profit. If the call is trading at the premium, you would buy the put, go long the futures, and sell the call. These possibilities do not always exist, but on occasion they are there for the taking. Depending on the commissions involved, it is not always possible to make an apparent profit after all of the costs are covered. In some instances the relationship is sufficiently out of line that, by doing the conversion, if the market returns to normal, the position can be unwound for a profit.

IN CONJUNCTION WITH T-BILLS

One of the factors involved in option pricing is interest rates. When rates are high, premiums are low, and vice versa. This fact, especially with puts, offers some interesting investment potential. If you invest a fixed amount of money in a discount instrument, such as a T-bill, you get back more than you invest.

Example: You have $10,000 to invest when interest rates are 15%. A 6-month T-bill that would mature at $10,000 is selling for approximately $9,250. When it matures at $10,000, you receive $750 for the 6-month period or 15%. If you invest only $9,250 in the bill and use the balance to purchase a put option, you cannot lose money. The reason is that, if the commodity remains unchanged or goes up and the option expires worthless, you would still get your $10,000 back due to the interest. If the market goes down, you profit on the option in addition to the interest. If the option is not profitable, then the true cost is that you did not earn any interest on your money.

If commodity prices remain unchanged for a period of 6 months and the price of futures and spot must converge at maturity, then the 6-month futures contract must decline to the spot price over the 6 months. Because the mathematical probabilities of price increase and decrease are equal, carrying charges work in the favor of the futures short or the put owner.

There is a higher probability of profit in the T-bill/put game than there is in the T-bill/call game. Traditionally, puts have cost slightly less than calls, which adds to the potential profit of the strategy. Because the majority of speculators are call buyers, even in an efficient market, the put is more likely to trade at a discount to the put/call/futures mathematical relationship than is the call. This also works in your favor. As markets become more efficient over time, this may not continue to remain true.

SPECULATIVE PUT TRADING TACTICS

Having made the decision that the purchase of puts is the investment strategy that best meets your market objectives, which striking price should you select? When should you get in and out? What maturity is the best to buy? And so on. All the principles that apply to the purchase of calls apply equally well to the purchase of puts. They are therefore not repeated here. This is, however, the right time to discuss in-the-money, at-the-market, and out-of-the-money as they differ between calls and puts.

A futures contract is really a contract that calls for the delivery of the physical commodity at some time in the future. The future price approximates the costs that would have to be borne were the physical commodity purchased today and carried until the delivery month in question. The owner of the physical commodity would have to bear these costs—namely, interest, storage, and insurance—over the period involved. Therefore an at-the-market option is only at-the-market in relationship to the commodity price for the maturity under consideration.

Example: The spot price of gold is $400/ounce, and the costs of interest, storage, and insurance on gold are 15% per year. A one-year futures contract on gold is therefore selling for $460. Both an at-the-market call and an at-the-market put have the same striking price, namely $460. A call for one year that is $25 out-of-the-money has a strike price of $485, and a $25 out-of-the-money put has a strike price of $435. If you do not understand this thinking, you will not be able to make correct option cost judgments.

If spot gold is $400 and you look at the premiums of puts and calls on gold at $400, you find that the calls are far more expensive than the puts. The reason is that the call is $60 in-the-money and the put is $60 out-of-the-money. This must be the case due to the carrying charges. If you do not understand this point, you might be tempted to buy the put, go long the futures, and sell the call for the purpose of doing a conversion. In fact, if the market were totally efficient, you should break even, neglecting commissions, because the call premium should exceed the put premium by the carrying charges. This difference should be lost through the holding of the long futures position for one year.

When a put and call have the same expiration and the same striking price, the put must trade at a discount to the call in terms of extrinsic value, if both options are approximately at-the-market. The magnitude of this discount is a function of the time to maturity and the carrying charges involved: the greater the time or the carrying charges, the greater the discount.

As with calls, most activity in puts is centered in one to two striking prices out-of-the-money and in the first one to two maturities.

11

THE SPECULATOR—
STRADDLE AND COMBO
BUYING STRATEGIES

Neither the straddle nor the combo are options that exist in their own right; they are the creation of the speculator.

A *straddle* results from the purchase (or sale) of both a put and a call on the same underlying commodity, with the same maturity and the same striking price. A straddle is not one option; it consists of two, with either half purchased at the same or different times. Either half of the straddle may be liquidated separately.

A *combination option* (combo) is similar to a straddle, except that the put and the call have different striking prices. Typically, in a purchase of options to create a combo, the call has a higher striking price than the put, although this is not absolutely necessary.

STRADDLES

The straddle gives its owner the right but not the obligation to both buy and sell the underlying commodity at a fixed price for a fixed period of time.

Example: Gold is currently trading at $400/ounce, and both put and call options struck at $400/ounce are trading at $40/ounce each. By purchasing both the put and the call, you create a straddle with a striking price of $400 for a total premium of $80/ounce or $8,000.

The chart in Figure 11–1, summarizes the economics of this transaction including an imagined commission on the purchase of $400. If gold

FIGURE 11–1. Gold $400 Strike Straddle Buying Chart

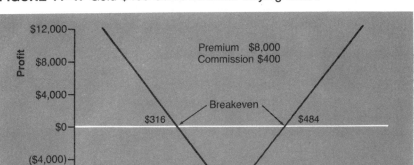

is at exactly $400/ounce at expiration, both options expire worthless, and your loss is the total premium plus the commission.

Since gold is highly unlikely to be at exactly $400/ounce on the expiration day, the total premium is therefore unlikely to be lost.

Example: You purchase both a March $400 gold call at $4,000 ($40/ounce) and a March $400 gold put at $4,000 ($40/ounce) plus $400 commission. The total premium is $80/ounce ($40+$40). For the call to be profitable at expiration, gold must be above $484 ($400+$80+$4). Conversely, for the put to be profitable, gold must be below $316 ($400−$80−$4).

Breakeven

To determine the breakeven price at maturity, you normally either add the premium to the strike price of the call or subtract it from the strike price of the put. To determine the two breakevens of a straddle, you must take the total cost of both premiums plus commissions, and add this total to the strike price of the call and subtract it from the strike price of the put. The reason is that, if the market is moving higher and the call is becoming more valuable, the put is becoming less valuable. Both premiums must be overcome before a profit results at expiration. In a declining market, the converse is true, with the put appreciating and the call depreciating.

Buying Straddles As A Speculation

Typically speculators purchase straddles when they anticipate a major move but are unsure as to the direction. Often the price of a given commodity has made a major move due to the anticipation of a major supply/demand imbalance. Having made this move, "the market" awaits confirmation of its perception. If the perception is confirmed, the market may continue in the same direction to a still greater degree. If not confirmed, it may have a substantial correction.

Example: In late 1979 and early 1980, as inflation and interest rate figures for gold and silver were released, the market would surge to new highs and await the next set of numbers. Eventually, when both inflation and interest rates abated, the market collapsed. Anywhere along the way, a speculator would have been justified to purchase either a put or a call due to the magnitudes of the moves involved. For the first six months, the call side of straddles purchased would have shown a profit; thereafter, the puts would have generated the profit. You could not wait for the statistic to become available, because the market move was too immediate to allow for a purchase at that time. Straddles purchased ahead of the release of the statistics offered the best chance of profit.

In purchasing a straddle, you purchase two options and therefore pay two premiums. You should expect moves of sufficient magnitude that, over relatively short periods, the large expense of straddle purchases can be justified for outright speculation.

Adding to a Profitable Futures Position

Regardless of whether the futures position is a long or a short, the purchase of a straddle dramatically alters the economics of the position.

Suppose that the profitable position is a long futures contract and that you purchase a straddle whose strike price is approximately the equivalent of the current market price of the long futures contract. The put portion of the straddle is effectively a stop order on the profitable long, and the call portion is an addition to the established long. The total profit on the long has been reduced by an amount equal to the purchase price of the straddle. Yet the remaining profit is locked in due to the put, and the profit potential has doubled on the upside due to the call.

Assume that the profitable position is a short and that you purchase a straddle whose striking price is approximately the equivalent of the current market price of the short futures position. The call portion of the straddle serves as a stop order for the short futures, and the put is an additional contract on the short side of the market. The total profit on the short has been reduced by an amount equal to the total cost of the straddle. The remaining profit on the short, however, has been locked in by the purchase of the call, and the profit potential on any further downside move has been doubled by the addition of the put contract.

The net effect of this transaction, in the case of a profitable long futures position, is to convert that long futures position into two calls. The net effect of the purchase of a straddle with a profitable short futures position is to convert that position into two puts. The negative aspect of this strategy is the time value cost on the two options.

Adding to an Unprofitable Futures Position

Unfortunately all positions taken do not immediately or even ultimately become profitable. When you take a long position in a given commodity and the position moves against you, you really have a two-sided problem. Should you remain with the position, hoping that the market will ultimately move in your favor? If so, what do you do to minimize the risk of further losses?

If you purchase a straddle, whose strike price is approximately the same as the current market price of your futures position, you economically convert the long futures into a two-call position. The put option portion of the straddle eliminates the possibility of further losses on the long futures contract, and the call effectively doubles the long position without in itself exposing you to larger margin calls. The major disadvantage to this strategy is that the premium paid for the straddle immediately increases the unrealized loss on the total position, and it requires a larger move in the upward direction to break even. This approach may, however, be best in light of limited risk-taking ability and available capital.

If the unprofitable position is a short position, and a straddle is purchased whose striking price is approximately the same as the short futures, the position is economically converted to two puts. The call portion of the straddle serves as a stop order for the short position, and the put doubles the downside potential of the short. This position also requires a capital commitment that immediately increases the unrealized loss and demands a greater downside move to reach break even.

Both of these positions, however, minimize the margin call impact of any further market deterioration. The option serving as the stop order, on a further negative move, goes into the money and has loan value for the purposes of meeting margin calls. The "stop order" option also offers a convenient means of disposing of the futures position, if the market continues in the "wrong" direction.

As a Replacement for a Profitable Futures Position

When you have a profitable position in futures and take the profit, the concern is always that the move that generated the profit is not over, and that additional profits are being given up. On the other hand, you don't want to give back the "winnings."

Example: Had you purchased a gold futures contract in 1979, you would have very quickly realized a $100/ounce profit. Yet all the market forecasters were calling for several hundreds, if not thousands, of dollars of additional appreciation. A profit of $100/ounce is $10,000 per contract. Emotionally, not to take this kind of profit is very difficult, if not impossible. A viable alternative to this dilemma is to take the profit on the futures position and use a portion of the profits to purchase an at-the-market straddle. History, of course, shows that the speculator was well rewarded as the market continued hundreds of dollars higher and, eventually, hundreds of dollars lower. With good market timing, you would initially profit on the call portion of the straddles and later on the put portion of the straddles through trading (discussed later).

The same philosophy can, of course, be applied in a down market, when you have a profitable short position, want to liquidate, and do not wish to miss any further move or give back the already realized profits.

Options In Conjunction With Technical Analysis

In both speculative call and put buying, an option may be the way to institute a speculative position before a "reversal" formation is technically completed. The logic behind this approach is that, if the formation does not complete itself, it is not indicative of a reversal.

A straddle is perhaps the most effective way to anticipate the completion of a reversal formation. If the formation is complete and the market reverses, you have an early position with either the put or the call. On the other hand, if the market does not reverse, you have the alternate option to profit from the continuation of direction.

Let's see how this approach works. The completion of a head and shoulders top would indicate a reversal of trend and possibly a downward move of major proportions. If the formation does not complete itself, it is indicative of nothing, and the market continues on the upside. If, in anticipation of the completion, you purchase a straddle whose strike price is approximately that of the neck line, you might have the best of both worlds. If the formation is completed, the put should be profitable; if the formation does not complete itself, the call should be profitable. The converse would also be true with such formations as head and shoulders bottoms, double bottoms, and the like.

The major risk with this approach is that the cost of the straddle exceeds in dollar terms the dollar magnitude of the ultimate move.

During Limit Moves

Options in many cases do not have limits as do the underlying futures contracts. The purchase of a straddle during limit moves offers speculators a means either of entering the market if they have no position or of hedging an existing profitable or unprofitable position during limit moves in the underlying futures contract. The one caution involved in this type of transaction is that the options tend to be very expensive. The person from whom you are purchasing the option is accepting the risk you are trying to transfer. Because the market is either up or down the limit, the grantor is unable to hedge the risk and consequently demands a far higher premium for transactions done in this environment. This additional cost may be justified, if your projection of the magnitude of the price move is large enough.

Trading Against Straddles

Most straddles are not created for the purpose of trading, but rather as a medium against which to trade. The straddle is normally held as a means to establish either a long or a short futures position. As you are aware from the prior sections, a straddle held in conjunction with a long position has the economic characteristics of two calls, and a straddle held in conjunction with a short futures position has the characteristics of two puts.

A straddle is most commonly purchased for trading purposes when a given commodity has been trading in a well established trading range.

Example: For some period of time sugar has been trading in an 11¢ to 12¢ trading range. On a given day, with sugar trading at 11½¢, the speculator purchases a straddle with a striking price of 11½¢. Normally no immediate futures position is established. Sugar continues its rally to about the top of the range. At this time, the speculator would go short one contract of sugar at approximately 12¢.

This trade has two advantages: First, the position has now become two puts at the top of the trading range; second, the margin requirement on the short futures is only spread margin because the short futures is hedged by an in-the-money call. In addition to the margin being only spread margin, it can be met with T-bills because it is initial margin. Were the position to move against the speculator (that is, higher), the in-the-money call would have loan value against which the brokerage firm could loan money to meet the margin calls.

Ultimately, if necessary, the call could be exercised to cover the short position. Although this scenario was not favorable, the exercise of the call at 11½¢ against the short at 12¢ would recoup $560 of the original premium (½¢ × 112,000 pounds of sugar).

If, on the other hand, the market behaved as projected and started down, the results are obviously more favorable. As the market moves lower, the speculator has the economic benefit of two puts. Money is actually being made on the short future and the long put, while money is being lost on the long call. As sugar reaches the bottom of the trading range, the speculator covers the short position in the futures contract and now goes long futures. The speculator is actually buying two futures contracts: one to cover the short and one to establish a long position. This transaction effectively converts the two-put position to a two-call position. The speculator can withdraw the profit realized on the short futures contract, as they are a realized profit.

The position is now long a straddle, and long a futures contract near the bottom of the trading range. Once again the speculator only has to put up spread margin on the futures contract, because the 11½¢ put is in-the-money and serves as a bonafide hedge against the long position. If the market declines, the loan value of the in-the-money put helps to meet the margin calls on the long future and also offers an "escape hatch" if it is necessary to ultimately deliver the long futures.

If the market rallies, the speculator repeats the process at the top of the trading range. This entire process continues as long as sugar continues to trade in the trading range and the straddle does not expire.

It is highly unlikely that, at expiration, sugar will be at exactly 11½¢. Therefore, either the put or the call will be in-the-money and liquidated for some intrinsic value. Depending on the actual date of liquidation, the other side of the straddle may also have recoverable residual value.

In this strategy, the straddle is primarily serving the purpose of trading insurance. Since the day-to-day cost of an option is lowest on longer-term options, the most cost-effective way to employ this strategy is to use more distant months for both purchasing the straddle and for trading the futures contract. The second advantage that this strategy offers is that it reduces the margin requirement from normal initial margin to spread margin. A third advantage is the in-the-money side of the straddle helps to meet margin calls on unfavorable market moves. Lastly, the straddle itself offers a means of disposing of the futures contract in either a limit-up or limit-down market, should that become necessary.

Although this strategy is ideal for a well established, broad trading range, it works well for a market with an established uptrend but trading in a broad channel, or for downtrends within the same constraints. This strategy works equally well for "double options" (see section on London softs). The added advantage is that, when the offsetting position is taken in futures, the clearing corporation requires no initial margin, even though the brokerage firm may require a token margin.

COMBINATION OPTIONS (COMBOS)

The *combo option* gives its owner the right but not the obligation to buy or sell the commodity at the prices represented by the put or call comprising the combo for a fixed period of time.

Example: Silver is currently trading at $6.00 per ounce, and both a $5.75 put on silver and a $6.25 call on silver are each selling for $.50 per troy ounce. If you were to construct a combo with the $5.75 put and the $6.25 call, the total cost of the combo would be $1.00 per troy ounce. On a 5,000 troy ounce contract of silver, this combo would cost perhaps $5,000. If we assume the brokerage commission to be $400, the total cost and risk would be $5,400. The following chart in Figure 11–2 summarizes the economics of this transaction including the commission. In situations such as this, where commissions can be significant, they should be included in your calculations.

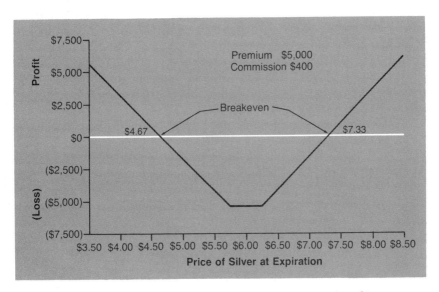

FIGURE 11–2. Silver Combo ($6.25 call/$5.75 put) Buying Chart

Like the straddle, the purchase of this theoretical combo carries with it two breakeven prices. Combos are generally purchased with both the put and the call out-of-the-money at the time the purchase is made. The computation of breakeven is done in much the same fashion as with the straddle. Without the use of a computer and an econometric/price-evaluation model, breakeven is normally computed for expiration day. With this approach, you take the total cost, which in this case is $5,400, and divide that cost by the quantity, in this case 5,000 ounces of silver. This calculation gives us a cost of $1.08/ounce premium. To determine the two breakeven prices of the combo, add this premium to the strike price of the call and subtract it from the strike price of the put. As the chart shows, the upside breakeven is $7.33 ($6.25+$1.08), and the downside breakeven is $4.67 ($5.75−$1.08). To make a profit on just the purchase of this combo at expiration, silver would have to either be above $7.33 or below $4.67.

A combo on a given commodity for a given month costs less than a straddle, if the striking prices of the combo are out of the money. This increased leverage and reduced dollar commitment are offset by higher and/or lower breakeven prices on the combo than on the straddle.

Buying Combos as a Speculation

For speculative purposes, the combo purchase is commonly used when a market has been trading in either a narrow trading range for some time or is perhaps approaching the end of a triangle formation. Due to the narrowness of the trading range or triangle, it appears impractical to attempt to trade within the range, but to establish a position prior to a breakout or breakdown would appear to be a substantial risk. The purchase of this combo allows the ownership of a call above the high point of the trading range and a put below the low point of the trading range. This, in theory, is an ideal position if the breakout or breakdown takes place.

The combo has the advantages of high leverage, small dollar commitment, and flexibility of striking price. It is an ideal strategy in the aforementioned case because, if the breakout or breakdown does not take place, you do not want an expensive, high-risk position already established.

Combination options, like straddles, are not normally purchased for their sole investment advantage, but are purchased for use in conjunction with other futures or option positions.

Adding to a Profitable Futures Position

Very often, after a sustained market rally, a profitable futures position enters a phase of consolidation. When this phase is entered, it is difficult, if not impossible, to determine whether the rally has ended and a reversal will follow or the rally will reinstate itself. In such a market condition, the use of a combo may be warranted. The purchase of a combo with the put's striking price just below the bottom of the congestion area and the call's striking price just above the congestion area is perhaps the most effective purchase. The put serves the purpose of a stop order on the long futures, and the call allows a form of pyramiding should the market reinstate the uptrend. This approach meets the objective of letting profit run and cutting losses short on a cost-effective basis.

The same approach could be used with a profitable short futures position in a declining market. After extended declines, it is common for a declining market to also enter a period of congestion and consolidation. If these are the circumstances of one position, a combo can also be used. In this case, you would purchase a combo with the strike price of the call above the congestion area, serving as a stop-buy order on the short futures position. The strike price of the put below the congestion area serves as a means of adding to the profitable futures position on a further breakdown.

Adding to an Unprofitable Futures Position

In this situation there are two logical uses of the combo option, depending on your market perceptions and risk-taking ability.

Example: You currently hold a long futures position that is unprofitable as a result of an unfavorable market move. You are still bullish and wish to remain with the long position. You really have two approaches through the use of a combo.

The first is to buy a combo whose lower strike price is just slightly lower than the current price of the futures contract, treating this put as a stop order against the futures and thereby limiting the magnitude of losses incurred through a further decline. The striking price of the call side of the combo should normally be placed closer to the original purchase price of the futures. This approach, though requiring additional capital, is weighted toward the minimization of risk.

The second approach, which is directed toward profit maximization with less thought toward risk, is the purchase of a call whose striking price is very close to the current price of the futures, and the purchase of a put at a lower price. This type of combo limits the risk to the strike price of the put, but it has the advantage of dollar cost averaging the existing futures position.

These two approaches can also be used with unprofitable short positions. Suppose the primary objective is to remain with the unprofitable short, but the minimization of risk is also important. In such a case, the call is purchased with a striking price just slightly above the current price of the short position. The put is purchased with a strike price approximately equal to the price at which the short futures position was put on.

On the other hand, the intention might be to maximize the profit potential with risk protection as a secondary objective. If so, the put is purchased with a strike price about equal to the current price of the short futures, and the call is purchased out-of-the-money as somewhat of a "trailing" stop order.

There is nothing absolute about the placement of the two striking prices. The two examples used are indicative of the extremes normally used. What is important to remember is that the relative position of the striking prices determines the economics of the combo. That is, is the combo designed primarily to achieve dollar cost average? Or is it designed to be a risk protection vehicle?

As a Replacement for a Profitable Futures Position

After either a sustained rally or decline, taking the profits from the futures position is often logical, because it may be some time before the market either reverses itself or continues. Having liquidated the futures, you may purchase a combo with the view that time can be more effectively spent trading elsewhere until the congestion period is over. The only major risk to this approach is that the market either reverses or continues before you have a chance to reinstate a position and a minimal time value cost. A combo with both legs out-of-the-money is really both a buy-stop and a sell-stop entered on a GTC basis with a limited risk. If the market were to break out on the upside, you would already have a position because of the call and, at that time, might liquidate the put. If the market were to break on the downside, you would already have a position because of the put and would most likely liquidate the call.

Trading Against Combos

Like straddles, most combos are purchased for the purpose of trading.

Example: Gold is trading in a well defined range of $350 to $400. One approach is, as gold approaches the bottom of the range ($350), purchase a call at about $400. As gold trades up toward the top of the range, purchase a $350 put. The combo has now been established, consisting of a $350 put and a $400 call. Notice that both options were purchased when the metal was trading at the opposite end of the trading range. This approach minimized the dollar commitment and the risk because both options were well out-of-the-money at the time of purchase.

Once the combo position has been established, futures trading can commence. As gold reaches the top of the trading range, a short position is taken in the futures contract. Each time gold reaches the bottom of the trading range, the short position is liquidated and a long futures position is taken. Both sides of the combo are being used as stop orders against the appropriate futures position. If the market breaks out on the upside while you are short, the call is available to cover the short position. If the market breaks down while you are long, the put serves as a protection and disposal mechanism for the long futures. In addition, if the protection of the put or call is actually needed from a margin point of view due to a breakout or breakdown, the appropriate put or call will be in the money and have loan value to help finance the margin calls.

If this position is implemented in the suggested fashion, it offers the benefits of at-the-market stop protection with out-of-the-money related costs. This strategy is less costly than trading against a straddle, but it does not have the advantage that one of the options may be in-the-money at expiration. It is quite likely that neither option will be in-the-money at expiration. The combo is serving as a trading insurance policy, and it is likely that the total premium will be expended for the insurance with no premium recovery.

During Limit Moves

When exchange regulations allow the trading of the option during limit moves, there is often profit potential. Most people who take advantage of this rule tend normally to purchase at-the-market options to protect a high-risk futures position. This activity tends to drive the price of the at-market options up in relation to more out-of-the-money options. If you are going to trade under these circumstances, combos with both legs out-of-the-money are far less expensive than comparable straddle positions.

12

THE SPECULATOR—
CALL GRANTING

For every option purchased, there must be an option granted. Up until this point, we have been looking at the long side of the market from the option purchaser's point of view. The investment objective of the option purchaser is normally one of "unlimited" profit potential. Buyers of options are normally aware that the probability of success is weighted against them, but the potential for unlimited profit, coupled with defined risk, is the motivation.

Option grantors (writers, sellers, makers) are generally more interested in generating a consistent rate of return on invested capital than in the possibility of reaping tremendous profits. Grantors tend to be better capitalized and more market sophisticated. The capitalization is probably a function of the minimum equity requirements imposed by the brokerage firms. The high level of market sophistication is perhaps a function of the complexity of the strategies involved. Option granting need not be complex. Some of the strategies require more time and thought than outright option purchases.

In the case of U.S. exchange-traded calls, the call option grantor assumes the obligation to deliver the underlying futures contract at any time at a fixed price between the date the option is granted and the expiration date. In exchange for undertaking this obligation, the option grantor receives the premium. The option grantor has a fixed profit potential, the premium, and a practically unlimited market risk. The option grantor assumes this risk/reward relationship due to the higher probability of profitability. Let's look at this probability from the grantor's point of view.

To those who are mathematically inclined, changes in a commodity over a period of time seem totally random. That is, prices are as likely to

FIGURE 12–1. Gold $300 Strike Covered Call Granting Chart

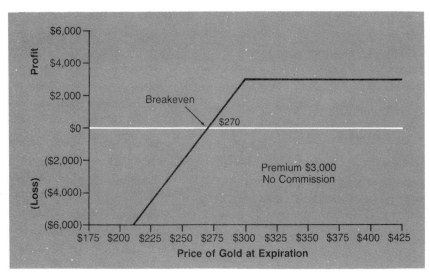

appreciate as they are to depreciate. The magnitude of the probable price change is a function of time: the greater the period of time involved, the greater the expected change in price.

Example: An option grantor grants a call on 100 ounces of gold at $300/ounce. The premium involved is $3,000. (This is the opposite side of the transaction referred to in Chapter 9; Figure 9–1 depicts the buyer's economic prospects.) The chart in Figure 12–1 depicts the grantor's prospects if the grantor, at the time the option is granted, purchases the underlying futures contract at a price equivalent to the strike price of the short option.

COVERED CALL GRANTING

The grantor in our example, having purchased a futures contract at the time the option is granted, is considered to be a covered option writer; he or she owns the item that must be delivered were the option to be exercised. The granting of the option generates a premium of $3,000, which is the equivalent of $30/ounce, in that the option is for 100 ounces of gold. Once the option is granted, the commodity can do one of three things: appreciate, depreciate, or remain unchanged.

Example: If the market remains unchanged, the option expires, and the grantor retains the premium. The grantor may then liquidate the futures contract or elect to write another option, but there is no economic impact as a result of owning the futures contract because it can be liquidated at the price purchased.

If the market appreciates, at some time the option grantor must assume that the option will be exercised. When the option is exercised, the grantor sells the futures contract at the strike price. Because the futures contract was purchased at the strike price, there is no economic disadvantage to liquidating it at the strike price. In this case the grantor also keeps the premium, and the premium is the profit.

If the market declines, the option grantor is losing money on the futures contract position. When the futures contract is trading below the strike price, it must be assumed that an option will not be exercised and will therefore expire. Because the grantor has received the equivalent of $30 per ounce for granting the option ($3,000/100), the futures contract could depreciate by $30/ounce and the grantor would break even. The grantor would have lost $30/ounce on the futures but received $30/ounce from the option. The futures contract could be liquidated at expiration with the $30/ounce loss, and the option would expire at a $30/ounce profit. The breakeven, from the grantor's point of view, is $270 per ounce.

Below $270/ounce, at expiration, the protection afforded the grantor by the premium is exhausted, and real losses begin to accrue. For each dollar below $270 that gold is trading at expiration, the grantor has a realized loss of $100, because a $1 decline on 100 ounces of gold is $100. The only limitation to loss is that gold cannot decline below $0. The true dollar exposure is $27,000 ($270×100 ounces).

Why will the grantor enter into a transaction that has a potential profit of $3,000 and a potential risk of $27,000? If the market goes higher, the grantor makes $3,000. If the market remains unchanged, the grantor makes $3,000, and, if the market does not go down by more than $30/ounce, the grantor breaks even. The grantor is in the position that the probability of success is substantially better than 2-to-1 in his or her favor, while the probability of the buyer's profiting is substantially worse than 1-to-2. Note: The probability of a market remaining exactly unchanged is negligible, but that does not materially affect the probabilities.

Overpriced Options

At this point, the concept of "fairly" priced options becomes important. While the chapter on option pricing discussed the concept, now we have the application.

In Chapter 4, a fairly priced option was defined as one wherein if the buyer and the grantor did an infinite number of trades with each other, they would both break even neglecting any commission cost. It is "fairly priced" because the option would fairly represent the magnitude of the moves to be expected in the underlying commodity over numerous experiences involved.

Options, in many cases, tend to be overpriced. In fact, if options were not overpriced, many grantors would be unwilling to grant them. Option buyers generally take a view of the market wherein they are either bullish or bearish, and, as long as the option does not cost more than the dollar value of the projected move, they buy options. On the other hand, a large percentage of the option grantors approach the market with the objective of consistently making small profits in exchange for accepting reasonable risks. Grantors are aware that, over any extended period of time, they must only sell overpriced options to make money. Due to this disparity in approach, options are normally overpriced or there would be too few grantors. In highly liquid, active markets, the magnitude of the overpricing is normally quite small, as many option grantors are competing to grant overpriced options.

Granting At-the-Market Covered Options

When you grant an at-the-market covered option, the only potential for profit is the premium to be received. Because the strike price of the option and the purchase price of the underlying commodity are the same, you cannot profit from any market appreciation in the underlying commodity, because this is ultimately taken by the buyer through exercise. Granting at-the-market options is a balance between rate of return on invested capital and downside risk protection.

Granting Out-of-the-Money Covered Options

When you grant an out-of-the-money covered option, in addition to the premium received, you also have the potential for appreciation in the underlying commodity.

Example: You grant a covered call option on gold at $320/ounce for a premium of $2,000. At the same time, you purchase the underlying futures contract at $300/ounce. This is equivalent to granting a $20 out-of-the-money call option. The grantor can now not only look to the premium for profit, but also enjoy market appreciation in the underlying commodity if the option is ultimately exercised.

If, at expiration, gold is above $320/ounce, the option purchaser exercises the option. The grantor has received a premium of $2,000 and liquidates the gold at a price $20/ounce above the original purchase price for an additional $2,000 ($20×100 ounces). The profit potential on this transaction is $4,000 as opposed to only $3,000 on our previous example.

If the market remains unchanged, the option expires and the grantor has received only $2,000.

If the market declines, the $2,000, which is the equivalent of $20/ounce, protects the grantor only down to $280, as opposed to our at-the-market grant, which supplied protection down to $270.

Between the purchase price of the futures of $300 and the striking price of the short call, $300, the option still expires, and there is some profit on the liquidation of the futures.

	Summary: *Granting Covered $320 Gold Call Having Purchased* *Gold at $300 Per Troy Ounce*		
Gold Price at *Option Expiration*	*Profit/(Loss)* *on Metal Owned*	*Premium* *Received*	*Total* *Profit/(Loss)*
360	$2,000	$2,000	$4,000
340	$2,000	$2,000	$4,000
320	$2,000	$2,000	$4,000
300	— 0 —	$2,000	$2,000
280	($2,000)	$2,000	— 0 —
260	($4,000)	$2,000	($2,000)
240	($6,000)	$2,000	($4,000)

In covered call option granting, the maximum profit is always achieved with the market at or above the strike price of the short option(s). The granting of out-of-the-money options is usually done by grantors who have taken a view of the market. In the case of a call, the out-of-the-money grantor is usually bullish and is willing to settle for less downside protection in exchange for greater potential should the market rally.

The mathematics of granting out-of-the-money options should not be carried too far. If you purchase a gold futures contract at $300/ounce and then grant an option with a striking price of $1,000/ounce for a premium of $1, the upside potential is terrific, but the option has no economic impact on the transaction. If the market remains unchanged, there is no rate of return; if the market goes lower, there is no protection. It is not that granting out-of-the-money or even deep-out-of-the-money options is not an attractive proposition, only that it is not a valid strategy if you are writing covered options, due to the low rate of return on invested capital.

Granting In-the-Money Covered Call Options

The grantor of an in-the-money covered call option can look only to the premium as potential profit, and even this amount must be reduced by the amount of the in-the-money value.

Example: You purchase a gold futures contract at $300/ounce and simultaneously grant a call option on that contract with a striking price of $280/ounce for a premium of $4,000. Again, the same three things can happen: The market can go lower, remain unchanged or go higher.

If the market remains unchanged or goes higher, the option is ultimately exercised because it is in-the-money. The grantor has purchased a gold futures contract at $300/ounce but must sell it at $280/ounce. On this transaction, the grantor realizes a loss of $2,000 ($20×100 ounces). The grantor retains the $4,000 premium and therefore has a realized profit of $2,000 ($4,000−$2,000).

If the market declines to $280 or below, the option is not exercised. At $280/ounce, at expiration, the grantor could liquidate the futures at a $2,000 loss, but this loss would be offset by the $4,000 premium leaving a $2,000 profit. At any price of $280 or above, the profit is identical—$2,000.

With a cost of $300/ounce on the futures contract and a premium of $40/ounce on the futures ($4,000/100 ounces), the downside breakeven for the grantor is $260/ounce. This strategy offers, in exchange for a lower downside breakeven, a lower overall rate of return on invested capital. Below $260/ounce, the grantor exhausts the protection offered by the granted option and loses $100 for each additional $1 decline in the price of the futures contract.

Summary: Granting Covered $280 Gold Call Having Purchased Gold at $300 Per Troy Ounce			
Gold Price at Option Expiration	Profit/(Loss) on Metal Owned	Premium Received	Total Profit/(Loss)
340	($2,000)	$4,000	$2,000
320	($2,000)	$4,000	$2,000
300	($2,000)	$4,000	$2,000
280	($2,000)	$4,000	$2,000
260	($4,000)	$4,000	— 0 —
240	($6,000)	$4,000	($2,000)
220	($8,000)	$4,000	($4,000)

Covered Call Granting Economics (Rate of Return)

To realistically appreciate the advantages and disadvantages of covered call granting, look at the potential rate of return in addition to the probable outcome of a given strategy. The use of the three previous examples with some assumed transaction costs should put the total picture into perspective.

Example Background: The futures contract for delivery of gold in approximately 6 months is currently trading at $300/ounce. Six-month

T-bills currently yield 15%, and the margin requirement on a COMEX gold futures contract is $2,000. The $280 call is trading at $4,000, the $300 call is trading at $3,000, and the $320 call is trading at $2,000.

Example 1—Covered At-the-Market Call: The speculator purchases the 6-month futures contract at $300 and deposits original margin in the form of T-bills that yield 15%. The speculator grants the 6-month option of the same futures contract with a striking price of $300 and receives a cash premium of $3,000. The roundturn commission on the futures contract is $100, and the commission on the option grant is $150.

The total potential profit is the premium ($3,000) minus the two commissions ($150+$100, or $250), for a net potential premium profit of $2,750. To this amount must be added the interest on the T-bills. The margin required on the futures is $2,000, and the margin required on the option is $3,000, but this too may be deposited in T-bills and therefore earns interest. The commission on the option is paid when it is sold, and the commission on the futures is generally paid when it is closed out. For the sake of simplicity, assume all commissions are paid initially, $5,000 is deposited initially, of which $2,750 is received in the form of premium less commissions.

If gold at expiration is $300, the option expires. Assume the futures position is liquidated at no profit or loss. If gold is above $300, assume the option is exercised, thereby liquidating the position. The total money committed to the transaction is $2,250. This is the $5,000 margin requirement minus the $2,750 cash premium received. You also earn $375 in interest on the T-bills [(15%×$5,000)÷2]. Therefore, your total earnings on the transaction are the net premium ($2,750) plus the interest on the T-bills ($375), equaling $3,125 on an investment of $2,250. This is a rate of return of 138.89% for only 6 months. On an annualized basis, this is 277.78%.

Rate of return is always a corollary to the risk involved in a transaction. The potential return is only this high because you, the option grantor, are assuming the risk of owning the futures contract for the 6 months involved. If the total maximum profit you can achieve is $3,125, this is an equivalent of only $31.25/ounce. If gold happens to drop more than this amount, you lose money. (During certain periods in very recent history, gold has dropped over $100/ounce in 6 days.) Your downside breakeven, with a purchase price of $300/ounce, is only $268.75.

Interest has been included on the T-bills in the calculation even though it is not truly correct. This has been done because many investors use total dollars in versus total dollars out as their basis for evaluating a given investment. The money committed to this transaction would have been collecting interest had you purchased T-bills and never sold the option. Your real rate of return is 122.22% ($2,750 ÷ $2,250) for 6 months or 244.44% annualized.

A second consideration in covered call writing is the market movement after the position has been instituted. If the market moves higher, positive variation margin is generated on the long futures position. As the short call moves higher, additional original margin is required to support the short option position. In an up market, this is generally favorable because the futures contract appreciates more rapidly than the short option due to the extrinsic value of the option. This excess cash flow is, in reality, an increase in the overall yield of the position, because part of the potential profit is being realized early.

In a declining market, margin calls are generated on the long futures position, but the original margin on the short option should also decline. The futures position generally declines at a greater rate than the option. This difference in depreciation forces the grantor to deposit additional margin to support the entire position. This effectively reduces the rate of return because the total capital commitment grows.

Example 2—Covered Out-of-the-Money Call: The speculator purchases the 6-month futures contract at $300 and deposits original margin in the form of T-bills that yield 15%. The speculator then grants the 6-month call option on the same futures contract with a striking price of $320 for a premium of $2,000. Assume that the roundturn commission on the futures contract is $100 and that the commission for granting the option is also $100.

The total potential profit for the transaction is a combination of the premium received plus the potential appreciation of the futures contract from its purchase price of $300 to the strike price of the short option, $320. Again, three things can happen: The market can appreciate, the market can remain unchanged, or the market can go lower. (Realize that each alternative does not have equal probability.)

If the market appreciates to a price above $320 at expiration, the option is exercised, and the futures contract is sold at $320. The original margin requirement on the position was $2,000 for the futures contract and $2,000 for the short option. The speculator received a net premium of $1,800 after the futures and option commission; therefore the true out-of-pocket expense was $2,200 ($4,000−$1,800). If the option is exercised, the grantor keeps the premium and has a realized profit on the futures contract of $2,000 ($320−$300×100), for a total profit of $3,800 on an investment of $2,200. The interest earned on the T-bills deposited represents an additional $300 [($4,000×15%)÷2], for a total return of $4,100, or 186.36% for 6 months.

If the market remains unchanged, the option expires and the futures contract is liquidated for the original cost of $300. The only profit is the net premium plus the T-bill interest for a total of $2,100 ($1,800 + $300), for a return on investment of 95.45% for 6 months.

If the market goes lower, the total cash flow generated by the net premium plus the T-bill interest is the only thing protecting the long futures position. This $2,100 is the equivalent of $21/ounce, and affords the grantor protection only from a decline down to a price of $279 ($300−$21)/ounce. Below $279/ounce, the grantor loses $100 for each $1 decline in the futures contract.

Between $300/ounce and $320/ounce, the option expires worthless with the grantor keeping the premium and the T-bill interest. But there will also be some profit on the futures position when it is ultimately liquidated.

As the market appreciates while the position is outstanding, the long futures contract generates positive variation margin and the short option possibly requires additional original margin. Yet the futures should appreciate more rapidly with no negative cash flow. In fact, you should be able to withdraw money from the account early, generating a higher overall return on invested capital.

If the market moves lower, the futures position creates a variation margin call. Very little reduction in the original margin requirement on the out-of-the-money option can be expected as a benefit. This requires the deposit of additional funds, thereby reducing the overall rate of return.

Example 3—Covered In-the-Money Call: The speculator purchases the 6-month futures contract at $300 and deposits original margin in the form of T-bills that yield 15%. The speculator then grants the 6-month option on the same futures contract with a striking price of $280 for a premium of $4,000. Assume the roundturn commissions on the futures to be $100 and the commission on the option granting to be $200.

The original margin on the futures position is $2,000, and the margin requirement on the short option is $4,000. The investor deposits a total of $6,000 in T-bills and withdraws a net cash premium of $3,700 [$4,000−($100+$200)]. The total actual investment is $2,300 ($6,000−$3,700).

As long as the market remains above the $280 level, the option is ultimately exercised and the futures position is liquidated at $280. This liquidation results in a $2,000 loss on the futures position ($300−$280×100); therefore the total profit is the net premium of $3,700 minus the loss on the futures position of $2,000 or $1,700. This is a rate of return of 73.91% ($1,700−$2,300) for the 6 months. To this you could add the T-bill interest of $450 for a total cash flow of $2,150 ($1,700+$450). This addition produces a rate of return of 93.48% ($2,150−$2,300) for the 6 months.

If the market moves lower, the protection afforded the futures position is a combination of the net premium received plus the T-bill interest. This total dollar amount of $4,150 ($3,700+$450) is the equivalent of $41.50/ounce. The futures contract is protected down to a price of $258.50 ($300−$41.50).

If the market moves higher, positive variation margin is generated by the long futures contract, but this is offset almost dollar for dollar by the increase in original margin on the in-the-money call option.

If the market moves lower, additional margin is required on the long futures, but this, to a large degree, is supplied by the reduction in margin requirement on the short in-the-money option.

Summary

Each of these three call granting strategies (at-the-market, out-of-the-money, in-the-money) are valid, but they have advantages and disadvantages. Each strategy carries with it a market view that is bullish, or at least not very bearish. All the strategies are designed to be profitable if the market remains unchanged or rises slightly. None of the strategies offer a meaningful level of protection if the market moves lower. These are speculative strategies, because they require the investor to make a market judgment; they reward good judgments and punish bad judgments.

UNCOVERED (NAKED) CALL GRANTING

Most option investors hold the view that covered call granting is "good" and that somehow the obligation of "nice" people is to cover the options they grant. The same investors hold the view that uncovered or "naked" option writing is "bad" or at least un-American. Uncovered option writing is a strategy, and, like all strategies, it has its good points and its bad points.

The sale of an uncovered or naked option is nothing more than option granting in which the option grantor has not purchased what underlies the option. If the option is a futures option, the grantor has not purchased the futures contract. The option grantor has undertaken the obligation to deliver a futures contract at the strike price for the period the option is outstanding, in exchange for receiving the premium. The only difference between covered and uncovered option granting is that the uncovered grantor does not have the futures contract, while the covered grantor does.

Example: Our option grantor grants a call option on 100 ounces of gold with a striking price of $300/ounce for a premium of $3,000 when the underlying futures contract is trading at $300/ounce. The grantor in this case does not purchase the underlying futures contract but is said to be granting the option "naked." This transaction could also be the opposite side of the transaction referred to as "buying calls as a speculation" in Chapter 9. The chart in Figure 12–2 depicts the grantor's prospects for various degrees of market movement once the naked option has been granted.

Having granted the call, one of three things can happen. As before, it can appreciate, depreciate, or remain unchanged. If the market remains unchanged, because this is an at-the-market option, the option expires worthless and the grantor has no further liability. If the market moves lower, the option also expires worthless and, because the grantor has no futures position, there is no risk of loss of the premium. If the market moves higher, the grantor is eventually called upon to deliver the underlying futures contract. The potential loss is the difference between the price that the grantor ultimately pays for the futures contract, minus the payment at the striking price, minus the net premium.

As you can see from the chart, the maximum profit, achieved at $300 or below, is the premium of $3,000. Above $300/ounce, the profit is reduced by $100 for each dollar increase in the price of the underlying futures contract; breakeven occurs at $330/ounce. For each dollar that

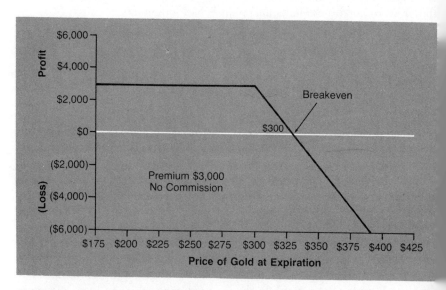

FIGURE 12–2. Uncovered Call Option Granting Chart

the futures contract (at expiration) is above $330, the grantor sustains a $100 loss.

Uncovered Call Granting Economics

To appreciate the dynamics of uncovered option granting, look to the potential profits to be achieved versus the risk exposure on the granting of various striking price options. The following examples use the same margin requirement, market price, and commission assumptions that were used in the covered option granting examples.

Example #4—Uncovered At-the-Market Call: The grantor sells the 6-month at-the-market ($300) striking price call option but does not purchase the underlying futures contract. The premium received for granting the option is $3,000, and the related commission on the option grant is $150. Granting a naked option requires the deposit of the equivalent of the normal futures margin, because the naked grant is the equivalent of a contingent short position. In addition, original margin equal to the market value of the premium must be deposited. Once this margin, which may be in T-bills, has been deposited, the cash premium may be withdrawn. The total margin requirement is $5,000 ($2,000+$3,000), which we assume is deposited in 15% T-bills. The net premium withdrawn was $2,850 ($3,000−$150). The actual capital committed to the transaction was $2,150 ($5,000−$2,850).

The risk in uncovered granting is if market prices move higher as opposed to covered granting where risk is associated with market prices moving lower. If the market at expiration is unchanged, the grantor has received a net premium of $2,850 plus the interest on the T-bills $375 [($5,000×15%÷2] for a total return of $3,225 on an investment of $2,150 or 150% for 6 months. This is an annualized rate of return of 300%. Note that this rate of return is actually higher than the comparable option sale when covered. This is so because there was no commission on the purchase and liquidation of the futures contract, which did not exist.

If the market moves lower while the position is outstanding, the margin requirement is reduced as the premium for the option declines. Conversely, if the market moves higher, the margin requirement on the option increases. Because no offsetting futures position is involved, there is no positive or negative variation margin on the futures itself. The increased or decreased margin requirements on the option are variable original margin and can be met with the deposit or withdrawal of T-bills. Additional bills deposited reduce the overall rate of return, while withdrawal increases the overall rate of return due to the smaller amount of dollars committed to the transaction.

Example 5—Out-of-the-Money Uncovered Call: The speculator grants the 6-month $320 strike price call option, when the underlying futures contract is selling at $300/ounce for a premium of $2,000. The margin requirement of the contingent short futures position is $2,000, and the margin on the uncovered call is also $2,000. After the $4,000, which can be met in T-bills, has been deposited, the premium can be withdrawn. Assuming the commission on the option grant to be $100, the net premium withdrawn will be $1,900, and, as a result, the total dollars committed to the transaction are $2,100 ($4,000−$1,900). The profit potential is the net premium of $1,900 plus the 15% interest on the T-bills, which will be $300 [($4,000×15%)÷2] for a total potential of $2,200 ($1,900+$300).

As long as the market price of the underlying futures remains at or below the striking price of the short option ($320), the option expires worthless and the potential profit is the anticipated amount of $2,200. You would realize $2,200 on an investment of $2,100 or 104.76% for 6 months.

Like the strategies discussed so far, the maximum profit occurs at the strike price of the short option. In this case that point is $320 and the profit is $2,200. Above $320 the profit is immediately reduced to $2,100 because a futures transaction has to be done and that carries with it a commission of $100. So the breakeven point is $21 above the striking price of the short option, or $341 ($320+$21). For each dollar increase in the price of the underlying futures contract above $341, the grantor would lose $100.

There is no downside risk in the transaction because no futures contract must be protected by the premium and interest received.

If the market moves higher, additional margin is required on the uncovered short option; if the market moves lower, margin is reduced. Increased margin requirements decrease the overall rate of return; reduced margin requirements increase the overall rate of return on the position.

Example 6—Uncovered In-the-Money Call: The grantor sells the 6-month $280 striking price option for a premium of $4,000 when the underlying futures contract is trading at $300/ounce and does not buy the related futures contract. The margin requirement on the contingent short futures contract is $2,000, and the margin on the short option is $4,000. Once this amount has been deposited, most likely in T-bills, the net premium can be withdrawn. If you assume that the commission on the option granting is $200, the net premium to be withdrawn is $3,800 ($4,000−$200); the dollars committed to the transaction are $2,200 ($6,000−$3,800).

The maximum potential profit that can be achieved is the premium

($3,800) plus the interest on the T-bills, which is $450 [($6,000 × 15%)÷2], for a total of $4,250. This potential is achieved if, at expiration, the underlying futures contract is at or below the strike price of the short option ($280). If the market declines, and the option expires, the profit of $4,250 is achieved on an investment of $3,800 for a rate of return of 111.84% for 6 months.

If at expiration the underlying futures contract is above the strike price of the short option, the profit must be immediately reduced by $100 because a futures transaction is necessary. This means that, above the striking price of the short option, only $4,150 protects the short option. For each dollar above $280 that the futures contract is at expiration, the profit is reduced by $100. Consequently the breakeven price is $41.50 above the striking price of the short option or $321.50. Above this price, each additional $1 increase in the price of the futures contract results in a $100 loss to the naked option grantor.

Summary

Like covered granting, each of the approaches (at-the-market, in-the-money, or out-of-the-money) have advantages and disadvantages. The grantor of uncovered options must hold a view that varies from very bearish to slightly bearish. These strategies are designed to be profitable if the market remains unchanged or goes lower. Risk begins to accrue if the market rallies. The rates of return available to the uncovered grantor tend to be slightly higher than those achieved by the covered grantor due to lower commissions. There is, however, an unlimited risk to uncovered granting, because there is not even a theoretical limit to the magnitude of a price rise.

THE MONEY-MAKING LIMIT ORDER

The granting of a naked call option can be used as an alternative to the entry of a limit sell order.

Example: Your investment judgment dictates that you would like to go short gold were it to rally to $330 basis the futures contract that is 6 months away. If the market rallies to the $330 level, your limit sell will be executed, and you will be short the market. If, on the other hand, the market remains unchanged or goes lower, your limit order will never be executed.

As an alternative to the entry of the limit sell, consider the granting of the 6-month $300 striking price call for a premium of $3,000 on an uncovered basis. If the market at expiration is above $300, your call will be exercised, and you will be short effectively at $330. Even though you sold at $300, you have a $3,000 premium that makes your position equivalent to having gone short at $330 and then having the market move $30 in your favor.

If the market remains unchanged or goes lower, your option expires. This is the equivalent of not having your limit sell executed, but you are $3,000 richer for having granted the option. This is a far superior strategy to the entry of a limit sell order as a means to establish a short position.

This strategy is equally valid if you are long the futures and looking to enter a limit sell to exit the market. You could sell at the market and have your futures contract sold at $300/ounce right now. If, however, you were going to enter a limit sell at $330, it makes more sense to grant the $300 call option using your existing futures contract as cover. If the market at expiration is over $300, your call is exercised, and you sell at $300 having collected a $30 premium. This is the equivalent of a $330 sales price. If the market remains unchanged or goes lower, at least you have the $3,000 premium as protection for your futures position.

13

THE SPECULATOR— PUT GRANTING

The grantor of U.S. exchange-traded puts assumes the obligation to accept delivery of the underlying futures contract at any time between the date of granting and the option's expiration date. In exchange for undertaking this obligation to receive the underlying futures contract at a fixed price, the option grantor receives the premium. The option grantor has a fixed profit potential, the premium, and a practically unlimited market risk. The reason the grantor assumes this risk/reward relationship is the improved probability of profitability. This is the same reason that the call grantor is a call grantor, as discussed in previous chapters.

> *Example:* An option grantor grants a put on 100 ounces of gold with a striking price of $400/ounce, with gold at approximately $400. The premium involved is $4,000. (Note: This is the opposite side of the transaction referred to in Chapter 10 as "Buying Puts as a Speculation." The chart in Figure 10–1 depicts that buyer's economic prospects.) The chart in Figure 13–1 depicts the grantor's economic prospects on the other side of the same transaction, if the grantor had gone short the underlying futures contract at a price equivalent to the strike price of the short put option. The difference of the two participants' profits and losses for a given commodity price change are only the commissions involved.

As with call options, after a put option is granted, a commodity can do only one of three things: appreciate, depreciate, or remain unchanged.

FIGURE 13-1. Put Option Granting Chart

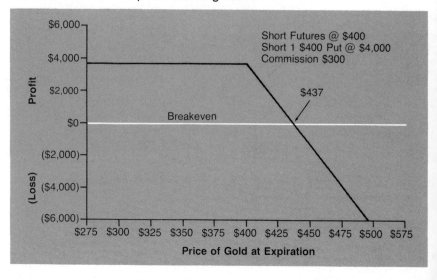

COVERED PUT WRITING

The grantor who has gone short a futures contract at the time the option was granted is considered to be a covered option writer; the item the investor is short is the item that will be delivered in the event that the short option is eventually exercised.

Example: An option is granted on 100 ounces of gold, generating a gross premium of $4,000. This premium, minus an assumed commission of $200, leaves a net premium of $3,800 or $38/ounce.

If the market remains unchanged, the option expires, and the grantor retains the premium. The grantor may then liquidate the futures contract or once again elect to grant another option. There is no economic impact to the ownership of the futures contract, except perhaps an assumed $100 commission, because the contract could be liquidated at its original price.

If the market appreciates, the grantor must assume that the option granted will expire worthless, as the option's owner would have no economic purpose in exercising. The grantor, however, sustains a loss on the short futures position. The grantor has received the equivalent of $3,700, including the commission on the futures contract, for undertaking the entire position. This $3,700 is the equivalent of $37/ounce insurance from the grantor's point of view. If the futures contract were to appreciate exactly $37/ounce, the grantor, at expiration, would liquidate the futures contract. The resultant $3,700 loss [($437−$400)×100] would be totally offset by the net premium received. Above $437/ounce, for each additional $1 that gold appreciates, the grantor sustains a $100 loss. There is no limit to the magnitude of the potential loss since there is no limit to the potential loss on any short position.

If the market depreciates, eventually the option is exercised. The grantor is called upon to purchase one futures contract at $400/ounce. Since this is exactly the same price at which the short position was instituted, the put grantor has neither a profit nor a loss on the underlying futures position. The total profit on the transaction is the time premium, but that is why the grantor entered into the transaction in the first place.

If the market remains unchanged, the grantor retains $3,700. If the market goes lower, the grantor retains $3,700. If the market goes higher, the first $37 move is not a loss for the grantor. The grantor is in the position that the probability of success is better than 2-to-1 in the grantor's favor, while the buyer invests with the probability far greater than 2-to-1 against him or her. Both players generally understand the relationship and can live with it because the strategies suit their own profit anticipation in relation to their risk-taking abilities.

Striking Price Determination

Having made the decision that put option granting best suits your investment objective, it is time to look at the aspects related to granting at-the-market, in-the-money, or out-of-the-money puts.

Granting At-the-Market Covered Puts. When you grant an at-market covered put, the only profit potential is the time premium. Because the strike price of the option and the market price of the commodity are one and the same, there is no potential for profit, to the grantor, for a decline in the price of the underlying commodity. Any downward movement in the price of the underlying commodity is ultimately part of the profit realized by the option purchaser. Granting at-the-market options is a balance between rate of return on invested capital and upside risk protection.

Granting Out-of-the-Money Covered Puts. When you grant an out-of-the-money covered put, in addition to the premium received, the grantor also has the potential to profit from the decline of the underlying commodity to the extent that the price of the short futures position is above the strike price of the short put option.

Example: You are able to grant a $380/ounce put option on gold for a premium of $3,000 when the underlying futures contract is trading at $400/ounce. If you were to go short the underlying futures contract at $400/ounce, then you would be granting a $20 out-of-the-money, covered put option. The grantor has not only the premium for potential profit but also benefits from any depreciation in the price of the underlying commodity. The put buyer profits only on a decline below the strike price. This situation offers a potential of an additional $2,000 ($20×100) profit.

If at expiration gold is below $380/ounce, the put purchaser exercises the option. The grantor covers the short futures position through the delivery received via the exercise. The grantor went short at $400/ounce and covered at $380/ounce, thereby realizing a $2,000 trading profit plus the premium. With this type of market action, the granting of out-of-the-money put options offers a far higher return than at-the-market options.

If the market remains unchanged, the grantor can only look to the premium for total profit. In this instance, granting at-the-market options shows a higher rate of return.

If the market rallies, the put expires worthless and the option grantor has some degree of loss on the futures position. This loss is offset by the premium received on the option. In our example, neglecting commissions, the premium received was $3,000, which is the equivalent of $30/ounce. Between $400/ounce and $430/ounce, the premium received is greater than the loss sustained on the liquidation of the futures contract. If the price of gold surpasses $430/ounce, the protection afforded by the premium is exhausted, and each additional $1 appreciation in the price of gold above $430/ounce results in a $100 loss to the put option grantor. This, as you may remember, is a lower breakeven than the granting of an at-the-market covered put option.

The granting of other than at-the-market options is usually predicated upon the market view of the grantor. At-the-market options favor neither a bullish nor bearish market. The granting of out-of-the-money covered put options is usually based on a grantor's view that the market declines following the option granting. This is the case because the greatest profit accrues to the grantor only through price deterioration.

The granting of an option is a balance between profit potential and risk protection. In determining how far out-of-the-money to grant, the mathematics of the situation must be taken into consideration. The granting of a put option with a striking price of $100/ounce when gold is trading at $400/ounce generates only a negligible premium, perhaps $1. This $1 affords no upside protection to the short futures position and in consequence inhibits the downside potential of the futures position. That is not to say that the granting of deep out-of-the-money options is not an attractive strategy; it is just not a strategy that makes economic sense to a covered writer.

Granting In-the-Money Covered Put Options. The grantor of an in-the-money covered put option can look only to something less than the premium as a potential profit, because part of the premium is intrinsic value and disappears upon exercise.

Example: You go short a futures contract at $400/ounce and simultaneously grant a $420 put option for $5,000. Again the same three market moves can occur. The market can appreciate, depreciate, or remain unchanged.

If the market appreciates to a price of $420 or above, the option expires because there is no economic purpose for the option purchaser to exercise. The premium is kept by the option grantor, but there is a loss on the futures position. At exactly $420/ounce at expiration, the futures position is liquidated for a $2,000 loss, which is more than offset by the $5,000 premium. In fact, this leaves a profit of $3,000 on the overall transaction. The $5,000 premium originally received is $50/ounce insurance on the short position. Were gold at $450/ounce at expiration, the futures contract would be covered for a $5,000 loss, but this would be offset by the $5,000 premium. Above $450/ounce, each additional $1 appreciation in the price of gold results in a $100 loss to the option grantor, because the protection afforded by the premium has been exhausted.

If at expiration, the price of gold is below $420/ounce, the option purchaser exercises the option. The grantor is forced through exercise to purchase gold at $420/ounce to cover the short position established at $400 per ounce. This transaction results in a loss on the futures position of $2,000 ($20×100). This loss is, of course, more than offset by the $5,000 premium received for having granted the option. Below $420, the grantor is always left with a profit of $3,000, neglecting commission costs. This protectionist strategy is normally used by an option grantor who is bearish on the market, but who feels that there is the potential for a substantial upward move, and therefore wants the maximum protection.

Caution must be used in granting in-the-money options because once an option gets well in the money, it commands very little time/extrinsic value. What is a large premium in total dollars is small in profit potential. If, for example, one were to grant an option that was $100 in-the-money for $10,000, there would be no profit potential at all. Granted there is also a very small risk, but any position that shows no profit potential and has risk is unattractive.

Covered Put Granting Economics

To make intelligent judgments in relation to covered put granting, you must be aware of the economics of risk and profitability as they relate to the granting of covered put options, be they at-the-market, in-the-money, or out-of-the-money. One must look at the potential rate of return in addition to the probable outcome of a given strategy. The previous examples and some assumed transaction costs will put the total picture into perspective.

Example 1—Covered At-the-Market Put: The speculator goes short the 6-month futures contract at a price of $400 and deposits original margin in the form of T-bills that yield 15%. The speculator then grants the 6-month option on the same futures contract with a striking price of $400/ounce and receives a cash premium of $4,000. The roundturn commission on the futures contract is $100, and the commission on the option granting is $200. The assumed original margin on the futures position is $2,000, and the original margin on the short option is the premium.

The total net premium received by the grantor is the $4,000 minus the two commissions (futures and option) for a net of $3,700 or $37/ ounce. For the sake of simplicity, all commissions are assumed to be paid at the outset of the transaction. For both the futures and the option, the margin is original margin and can be met with T-bills. The actual out-of-pocket commitment to the transaction is the $6,000 margin requirement ($2,000+$4,000) minus the net premium of $3,700 ($4,000−$300) or $2,300.

If the commodity price at expiration is unchanged, the option expires worthless. The grantor retains the premium and earns the interest on the T-bills. The total return is therefore the net premium ($3,700) plus the T-bill interest of $450 [($6,000×15%)÷2] or $4,150 ($3,700+$450). This $4,150 on an investment of $2,300 is the equivalent of 180.43% for 6 months.

If, at expiration, the market price of gold is above $400/ounce, the option also expires worthless, but in this case the speculator has a loss on the short futures position. The premium received for granting the option serves as insurance for the speculator's short futures position. The net premium of $3,700 is the equivalent of $37/ounce; this is the magnitude of the protection. If at expiration gold is $437/ounce, when the speculator liquidates the futures position, he or she realizes a loss of $3,700. This loss is exactly offset by the net premium. Above $437/

ounce, each additional $1 rise in the price of gold subjects the speculator to a real $100 loss on the total position.

If the market moves lower, the option is ultimately exercised and the speculator closes out the futures position at $400 as a result of the exercise. There is neither a profit nor a loss on the futures, and the total profit is still the net premium of $3,700.

This is basically a neutral strategy, wherein the speculator expects the price of gold neither to rise nor to fall by an appreciable amount during the time that the option is outstanding. The high rate of return potential on this position is a corollary of the risk. The total amount of protection is only $37/ounce, which is not a very large move in 6 months on a $400 commodity. The T-bill interest is important in determining the overall rate of return, but it should not be considered as part of the risk protection because this interest could have been achieved without the option or futures position.

Additional considerations come into play once the position has been established. If the market moves higher, in addition to the possibility of loss, there are also margin calls. The variation margin required on the futures position accrues at a rate faster than the original margin on the short option declines. This deposit of additional cash must be available, and its deposit reduces the overall rate of return on the total position. If the market moves lower, additional original margin is required on the short option, but this is easily met by the positive variation generated by the short futures position. This excess variation margin increases the overall rate of return on the position.

Example 2—Covered Out-of-the-Money Put: The speculator goes short the 6-month futures contract at a price of $400/ounce and deposits the required $2,000 futures margin in the form of 15% T-bills. At the same time the speculator grants the 6-month $380 put option, which is $20 out-of-the-money at the time it is granted, for a premium of $3,000. The roundturn commission on the futures contract is $100, and the commission on the option granting is $150.

The margin requirement on the short option is the premium, which can also be deposited in T-bills. Once the appropriate margin has been deposited, in this case $5,000 ($2,000+$3,000), the net premium of $2,750 ($3,000−$250) can be withdrawn. The new money committed to the transaction is the difference of $2,250 ($5,000−$2,750).

If the market remains unchanged, the option expires worthless. The grantor received a net premium of $2,750 plus T-bill interest on the margin deposit of $375 ($5,000×15%÷2) for a total return of $3,125 on an investment of $2,250. This is a rate of return of 138.89% for 6 months.

If the market moves higher, the option also expires, but the speculator has a loss on the short futures position. The net premium of $2,750, which is the equivalent of $27.50/ounce, serves as the protection for the short futures contract. The breakeven is $427.50/ounce. At this price, the liquidation of the futures results in a loss of $2,750, but the retained premium covers this loss. Above $427.50, each additional $1 increase in the price of the futures generates a real $100 loss on the entire position.

Were the market to go lower, two possible events occur depending on the magnitude of the decline. If the market declines to a price between $400 and $380, the option expires, but the speculator has some profit on the short futures position. Assume that, at expiration, the market is at exactly $380/ounce. The option expires, with the speculator retaining the net premium of $2,750, but the futures contract can be liquidated with a profit of $20/ounce or an additional $2,000. In addition, the T-bill interest is also earned, bringing the total profit to $5,150 ($2,750+$2,000+$375). This return of $5,150 is earned on an investment of $2,250 for a rate of return on invested capital of 228.89% for 6 months. On a decline below $380/ounce, the put option is exercised, but the rate of return is the same. The reason is that the put grantor still closes out the futures, but in this case the close-out is a result of the delivery generated by the option exercise.

While the option position is outstanding, an increase in the market price requires the deposit of variation margin on the short position, with very little reduction of the original margin on the short option because the out-of-the-money put depreciates more slowly than the variation margin on the futures appreciates. If the market declines, additional original margin is required on the short put, but this is readily supplied by the variation margin released on the short futures. Market moves that require additional margin reduce the overall rate of return, while market moves that reduce the margin requirement increase the overall rate of return.

This strategy is a bearish strategy. The speculator expects the price of gold to decline during the period of time that the option is outstanding. In addition, the speculator believes that there is very little potential for a short-term rise of any appreciable amount, because the protection supplied to the short futures position is minimal.

Example 3—Covered In-the-Money Put: The speculator goes short the 6-month futures contract at a price of $400 and deposits T-bills yielding 15% to meet the original margin requirement. The speculator then grants the 6-month $420 put option for a premium of $5,000. The commission on the futures contract is $100, and the commission on the granted option is $250. The margin requirement on the short future contract is $2,000, and the margin on the short option is the premium

$5,000. After the T-bill margin has been deposited on the entire position, the net cash premium on the option may be withdrawn. The net premium is $5,000 minus the commission of $100 and $250, or a net amount of $4,650.

In this example, because the option granted is $20 in-the-money, the option is exercised if the market remains unchanged. It is also exercised if the market is $420 or below. The option grantor is forced, through the exercise, to purchase a futures contract at $420 to cover the short position, taken at $400. Honoring this obligation results in a loss on the futures contract of $2,000 ($20×100). This $2,000 loss effectively reduces the net premium to $2,650 ($4,650−$2,000).

This $2,650, plus the interest earned on the $7,000 T-bill margin requirement, is the total profit potential. This $2,650 plus $525 [($7,000×15%)÷2], on a net investment of $2,350 ($7,000−$4,650) is the equivalent of 135.11% for 6 months.

Above $420/ounce, the option expires and the grantor has to look to the net premium for protection of the short position. The net premium of $4,650, the equivalent of $46.50/ounce, gives us a breakeven price of $446.50 ($400+$46.50). Above this breakeven price, each additional dollar increase in the price of gold results in a real loss of $100 on the overall position.

While the position is outstanding, upward movements in the price of gold generate variation margin calls which, at least initially, closely equal the reduction in original margin on the short option. Yet a major move may require a deposit of substantial additional capital. If the market declines, the increased original margin required on the short option is, most likely, offset by the excess margin on the short futures contract. Again, additional capital committed reduces the return while capital removed increases the return.

Of the three covered put granting strategies covered, this one offers the highest level of protection. The granting of an in-the-money option, and the large premium received from it, offers the greatest protection. It also offers the lowest rate of return.

Summary

Each of these three put granting strategies (at-market, out-of-the-money, and in-the-money) are valid, but each has advantages and disadvantages. Each strategy carries with it a market view that is bearish. Some views are moderately bearish, and some are very bearish. All the strategies are designed to be profitable if the market remains unchanged or goes lower. These are speculative strategies because they require that the option grantor take a market view and make a judgment. Again, markets reward good judgments and punish bad judgments.

UNCOVERED (NAKED) PUT GRANTING

Historically a small percentage of all option transactions, in both securities and commodities, have been puts. Most investors seem to believe that it is "right" to make money on rallies, but "wrong" to make money on price declines. Nothing could, of course, be further from the truth. Puts can also offer the option grantor profit potential in a rising market. These puts must, however, be uncovered or naked.

The sale of an uncovered or naked put is nothing more than the granting of a put option wherein the option grantor has not taken the appropriate short position. If the option involved is an option on futures, then the option grantor has not gone short the futures contract at the time the option was granted. The grantor still undertakes the obligation to receive delivery of the underlying futures contract at any point between the time the option is granted and its expiration. This obligation is being undertaken in exchange for the receipt of the premium. The only difference between covered and uncovered granting is that the uncovered grantor does not have a short futures position while the covered grantor does. Either strategy may be equally appropriate depending on the grantor's market view. Where covered put writing is generally a bearish strategy, naked put writing is basically a bullish strategy.

> *Example:* The option grantor grants a put option on 100 ounces of gold with a striking price of $400/ounce for a premium of $4,000 when the underlying futures contract is trading at $400/ounce. The grantor in this case does not go short the futures contract and is said to be "naked" or "uncovered." (This transaction could be the opposite side of the transaction outlined in Chapter 10 as "Buying Puts as a Speculation.") The chart in Figure 13–2 depicts the grantor's economic prospects once the naked option has been granted, depending on the direction and magnitude of the ensuing futures market move.
>
> Having granted the uncovered put, the grantor is subject to the vagaries of market movement, which may be up, down, or none at all. If the market remains unchanged, the option expires, and it makes little difference if the option was covered or uncovered. In either case, the grantor has no further liability.
>
> If the commodity moves higher, the option also expires worthless. Since the option grantor has no futures position, there is no risk of loss of the premium.
>
> If the commodity moves lower, the grantor is ultimately called upon to accept delivery of the underlying futures contract at the strike price. The potential loss is the difference between the price at which the grantor must take delivery, the strike price, and the then current

FIGURE 13–2. Uncovered Put Option Granting Chart

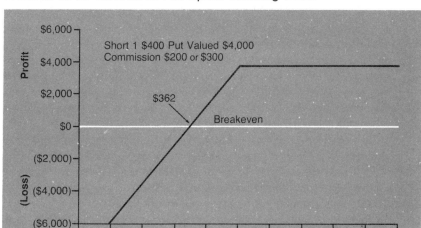

market price of the underlying commodity minus the premium originally received. This may or may not be a loss. If the difference between the striking price and the current market price is less than the premium received, the exercise may still result in a profit.

As you can see from the chart, the maximum profit is achieved at a price of $400/ounce or above. Below this price, the maximum profit is reduced by $100 for each dollar that the futures contract is below the striking price at the time of exercise. The breakeven price is the net premium in dollars per ounce subtracted from the striking price. If, at the time of exercise, the then current futures price is below the breakeven, the magnitude of the loss is the dollars per ounce below the breakeven times 100 (the quantity involved).

Uncovered Put Granting Economics

As mentioned earlier, the granting of uncovered puts is really a bullish strategy. To appreciate this fact and to determine if at-the-market, in-the-money, or out-of-the-money granting makes more sense, let's look at the economics of the various approaches. To make the differences evident, the same options that were used in the covered put writing section are presented as examples. Naturally the mathematics is based on no related short futures position.

Example 4—Uncovered At-the-Market Put: The speculator grants a put on 100 ounces of gold with a striking price of $400/ounce but does not go short the underlying futures contract. The premium on the option is $4,000, and the related commission is $200. The grantor must post margin on the uncovered short put. The margin in this case would be the futures margin of $2,000, because an uncovered short put is a contingent long position, plus the premium on the put. This original margin ($2,000 on futures plus $4,000 for premium) can and will be deposited in 15% T-bills. After the margin has been deposited, the net premium of $3,800 ($4,000−$200) may be withdrawn. This results in a new cash commitment of $2,200 ($6,000−$3,800).

If the market moves either higher or remains unchanged, the option expires, and the speculator retains the premium. This premium of $3,800 plus the interest of $450 [($6,000×15%)÷2] or $4,250, on an investment of $2,200, is a return of 193.18% for 6 months.

If the market moves lower, the put is ultimately exercised, with the speculator forced to buy the futures generated as a result of the exercise. In this case the speculator is subject to a futures commission of $100 on the futures received, thereby reducing the net premium to $3,700. This $3,700, or $37/ounce, serves as insurance on the futures received and gives one a downside breakeven of $363 ($400−$37). Below $363, each additional $1 decline in the underlying futures contract results in a loss of $100 to the speculator. This strategy, as you can see, is actually a bullish strategy, in that it generates its greatest profits in a rising market. This is, in fact, one of the most popular put strategies.

This strategy is a means of entering a limit buy order and being paid for it. Were you to wish to buy futures at $363, you would enter a limit. If the market declined to your price, you would have your long futures position. However, if the market remained unchanged or went higher, you would have nothing to show for your effort or judgment. If, instead of entering a limit order, you grant the $400 striking price put uncovered, and the market remains unchanged or goes higher, you keep the premium. This is, in fact, being paid for a limit order that was not executed. If the market goes below $400/ounce, the put is exercised, and you have your long futures position. The contract is purchased at $400, but you have received a net premium of $37/ounce. Therefore, your effective cost is $363/ounce. It is, however, likely that the option will not be exercised until it is either deep-in-the-money or in-the-money and near expiration.

When implementing this strategy, you must remember that, as the market moves lower, you will be called upon for additional original margin on the short uncovered put position. Because there is no offsetting short futures, you then have to deposit additional funds in the account. If the market moves higher, there is also a reduction in original margin because there is no short futures position.

Example 5—Uncovered Out-of-the-Money Put Granting: In this strategy, with 6-month gold at $400/ounce, the speculator grants the $380/ounce striking price call for a premium of $3,000/ounce and does not go short the futures contract. The margin on the position is $2,000 for the contingent long futures position plus the premium of $5,000 ($2,000+$3,000). After the margin, which we assume is deposited in 15% T-bills, has been deposited, the net premium of $2,850 (minus $150 assumed commission) can be withdrawn. This requires a new cash commitment of $2,150 ($5,000−$2,850). As long as the underlying futures contract remains above the strike price ($380), the option expires, and the grantor retains the premium. This $2,850 plus the T-bill interest of $375 [($5,000×15%)÷2] offers a total return of $3,225, which on an investment of $2,150 is 150% for 6 months.

Your breakeven price is the strike price of the short option ($380) minus the net premium in dollars per ounce. In this case, you have to reduce the net premium by the futures commission that would be incurred on a market decline below $380. The new net premium is $2,750 ($2,850−$100) or $27.50/ounce. Downside breakeven becomes $353.50. This strategy, which is also bullish, gives you a somewhat lower downside breakeven in exchange for a slightly lower rate of return unchanged. Overall the strategy is slightly less bullish than at-the-market uncovered put granting.

As the market moves lower, you must be prepared for increases in the original margin requirement on the short put. On rallies, you experience reductions in the original margin required.

Example 6—Uncovered In-the-Money Put Granting: In this example, with 6-month gold trading at $400/ounce, you grant the 6-month $420 striking price put option for a premium of $5,000. The margin requirement is a futures requirement of $2,000 on the contingent long position, plus the premium, or a total of $7,000 ($2,000+$5,000). The option granting commission is $250. After the margin in 15% T-bills has been deposited, the net premium of $4,750 ($5,000−$250) can be withdrawn. The new money committed to the transaction is $2,250 ($7,000−$4,750).

If the market at expiration is at or above $420, the option expires. In this case, the option grantor retains the net premium which, with the T-bill interest of $525 [($7,000×15%)÷2], is a total of $5,175 or 230% for 6 months. If at expiration that market is below $420, the grantor is obligated to purchase a futures contract at $420. This necessitates a futures commission, reducing the net premium to $4,650 or $46.50/ounce. As you can see, the downside breakeven is the strike price ($420) minus the premium ($46.50) or $373.50. This is the most bullish of the uncovered put writing strategies, since it offers the highest rate of return on market rallies and the least protection on market declines.

Again, market declines result in original margin calls, and market rallies reduce original margin requirements.

All the "speculator" granting strategies dealt with thus far have assumed that only one option was involved, and that the position was either covered or uncovered. Let's look at strategies wherein this 1-to-1 relationship is not followed.

14

RATIO WRITING

In the strategy of ratio writing, you grant a different number of options from the position held in the underlying commodity. If you hold a long futures contract, you might consider the granting of two or three call options. Conversely, if you are short two futures contracts, you might consider selling only one put option.

Ratio writing is a combination of both covered and uncovered option writing. This approach to option granting varies the risk/reward relationship, varies the upside/downside breakeven, and enhances the rate of return on invested capital possibilities. The examples in this chapter point out both the advantages and the concurrent risks.

RATIO WRITING CALL OPTIONS

The term "ratio writing" normally refers to a greater short position in the options than held in the futures. Ratio writing may therefore take the form of granting more options than your commodity position, but it may also consist of writing fewer options than your commodity position. The options that you elect to grant may be of the same or different striking prices. The option may be at-the-market, in-the-money, or out-of-the-money. Depending on the specific combination used, you affect the economics of the position dramatically.

Example 1—Granting Call Options 2-to-1 At-the-Market: For the sake of consistency and comparison, the same gold options that have been used in the previous chapters for our examples will be used here. The assumptions are that the 6-month gold futures contract is selling at $300 and the 6-month at-the-market call option on that contract is selling for $3,000. The margin requirement on a futures position is $2,000; the margin requirement on a short covered option is the premium; and the margin requirement on an uncovered option is the premium plus $2,000.

You purchase one 6-month futures contract, and, at the same time, you grant two 6-month $300 strike price call options. The commission on the futures contract is $100, and the commission on granting each of the options is $150, for a total commission cost of $400 ($100+$150+$150).

You have margin requirements on three positions: the long futures, the short covered option, and the short uncovered option. The margin on the futures contract is $2,000. The margin on the covered option is the premium of $3,000, and the margin on the uncovered option is $2,000 plus the premium of $3,000. Therefore, your total margin requirement on the position is $10,000. All this margin is original margin and, as such, can be met by the deposit of T-bills. Again let us assume that T-bills are deposited and currently yield 15%.

At the time the options are granted, you receive the net premiums in cash. This amounts to $5,600 [($3,000×2)−($150×2)−$100]. Therefore, your actual cash outlay is $4,400 ($10,000−$5,600).

As you can see from the chart in Figure 14–1, your maximum profit is achieved at the strike price of the short options. If at expiration gold is at $300/ounce, both options expire worthless. You keep the net $5,600 premium, plus the T-bill interest but minus the commission on the futures for a total profit of $5,600 on the position. The total positive cash flow is the $5,600 plus $750 interest on the T-bills or $6,350 on an investment of $4,400 for 6 months. This is the equivalent of 144.32% for 6 months or 288.64% annualized.

You have, in effect, received $5,600 as insurance on the one long futures contract that you own. This is the equivalent of $56/ounce and affords you downside protection to $244/ounce. As the chart shows, this strategy affords far greater downside protection than the 1-to-1 covered call writing discussed previously.

At any price at or below $300/ounce, the options expire. If gold happens to be at $244/ounce, you would liquidate your futures position, thereby sustaining a $5,600 loss, but this loss would be identically offset by the premium received. Below $244/ounce, you lose $100 for each additional $1 decline in the price of gold. The $5,600 net premium also serves as an insurance premium against an upward move. This too carries with it risk exposure, because you have granted two options and own only 100 ounces of gold (one futures contract). If at

FIGURE 14–1. Ratio Writing Calls 2:1 At-Market Chart

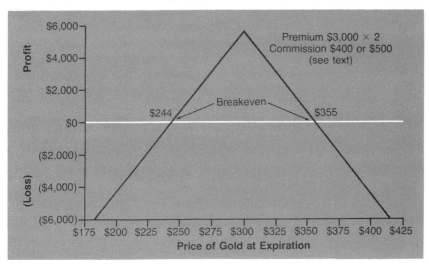

expiration gold is at $355/ounce, you also break even because you are called upon to deliver the equivalent of 200 ounces when you only own the equivalent of 100 ounces. You go into the open market and purchase a futures contract at $355/ounce and deliver this contract at $300. On the futures transaction, you sustain a loss of $5,500, and you pay a commission of $100 on the second futures for a total loss of $5,600. This loss is totally offset by the premium received. Above $355/ounce, for each additional $1 increase in the price of gold, you lose $100.

Between $244 and $355 you achieve some level of profit that cannot exceed $5,600. At each of the extremes, you break even; beyond these limits, you lose money. As the market either appreciates or depreciates, you are called upon for additional margin. If the market appreciates, the additional margin required would be additional original margin which could be met by depositing more T-bills. The additional T-bills might be purchased with the positive variation margin generated by the long futures position. If the market declines, the margin required would be variation margin on the futures and must be deposited in cash. However, the margin required on the short options would be declining and might allow the sale of some of the T-bills to meet the cash margin call.

If the delta of the short options is .5, the variation in margin on the futures and options should be substantially identical for small market movements in either direction. Substantial movements in either direction require the commitment of additional capital and reduce the overall rate of return.

In this case if the gold appreciates by $10/ounce, the futures contract appreciates by $1,000 in value and has that amount of excess margin. At the same time the options appreciate by approximately .5 times that amount and, in total, also appreciate $1,000 ($10×100×.5×2). Alternatively, if gold appreciates by $20/ounce, the futures appreciate by $2,000, and the options most likely appreciate .6 times the magnitude of the move or a total of $1,200. In the second case an additional $200 has to be committed to the strategy as the negative move of the options is $200 greater than the positive move of the futures.

This strategy also implies a market judgment. In this case the judgment is that the price of gold is subject to little change (neutral) and that the likelihood that gold would appreciate either above $355 or decline below $244 was low.

Example 2—Granting Call Options 2-to-1 Out-of-the-Money: In this example, the speculator purchases a 6-month futures contract and grants two 6-month out-of-the-money call options. The futures are at $300/ounce, and the options granted are $320 strike price calls for premiums of $2,000 each. The commission on the futures and on each of the options is $100 for a total of $300.

The margin requirements are $2,000 on the futures, the premium on the covered option, and the premium plus $2,000 on the uncovered option. Therefore, the margin requirement on the total position is $8,000 ($2,000×4). Having met the margin requirement in T-bills, the speculator can then withdraw the net premium of $3,700

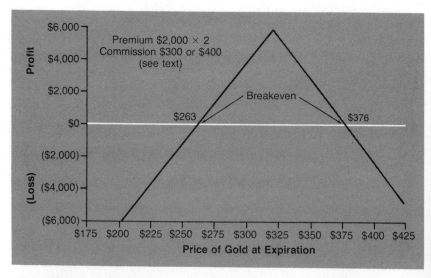

FIGURE 14–2. Ratio Writing Calls 2:1 Out-of-the-Money Chart

[($2,000×2)−($100×3)]. This results in an out-of-pocket commitment of $4,300 ($8,000−$3,700).

As the chart in Figure 14–2 shows, the maximum profit derived from the option portion of the transaction is achieved with gold at exactly $320/ounce on expiration day. This is a combination of the premium of $3,700 plus the $20/ounce appreciation on the one long futures contract for an additional $2,000. At $320, the options/future position shows a profit of $5,700 ($3,700+$2,000). In addition, the original T-bill margin, at 15% for 6 months ,has generated an additional $600 [($8,000×15%)÷2] for a total profit of $6,300 ($3,700+$2,000+$600). Both options, of course, expire worthless. Therefore, you have a profit of $6,300 on an investment of $4,300 or 146.51% for 6 months.

If the market declines, the net premium of $3,700 or $37/ounce serves as protection for your long futures position. Therefore, your downside breakeven is $263/ounce. Below this price, you lose $100 for each additional $1 decline in the price of gold.

If the market appreciates, as the chart shows, you have an upside breakeven of $376. This is because you have received a premium of $3,700, plus $2,000 appreciation in the futures contract you own. You will, however, be called upon to purchase a second futures contract above $320 to make delivery and thereby incur a second futures commission. For each $1 appreciation above $376 of the futures contract, you ultimately suffer an additional $100 loss on the total position. Anywhere between $263/ounce and $376/ounce, you sustain a profit, with your greatest profit at exactly $320/ounce.

Advances above the $300 level require additional margin. Because the delta of the short options are each less than .5, sufficient variation margin is generated by the appreciating futures to meet these calls initially. For large upward moves, additional capital has to be committed thereby reducing the overall rate of return on the position.

In this case, if the futures appreciate by $10/ounce, the futures appreciate by $1,000. At the same time, the short options most likely appreciate at about .4 times the futures, for a total of only $400 (.4×$10×100). This is true for small upward moves. For larger moves the option's rate of appreciation reaches .5, .6, or more and requires the commitment of additional capital.

Declines below the $300 level generate variation calls on the long futures position at a rate greater than the original margin on the short options depreciates. This immediately requires additional cash to keep the total position appropriately margined.

This market strategy is moderately bullish. It maximizes profit on the overall position for moderate upward moves in the price of gold.

This improvement is achieved by reducing the downside risk protection.

Ratio writing does not dictate that there must be more options short than futures long. It is just as valid an approach to be long more futures than short options. This too is a ratio.

Example 3—Granting Call Options 1-to-2 At-the-Market: The chart in Figure 14–3 portrays the situation where the speculator is long two 6-month futures contracts and has granted but one at-the-market call option. Both futures contracts are purchased at $300/ounce, and one 6-month call option is granted with a striking price of $300/ounce for a premium of $3,000. The commissions on the futures contracts are a total of $200, and the commission on the granted option is $150.

The margin requirements are $2,000 per contract on the futures for a total of $4,000, plus the premium of $3,000 on the short covered option. Once this margin requirement has been met, presumably with T-bills, the net premium can be withdrawn. Therefore, the out-of-pocket commitment is $4,350 [$7,000−($3,000−$350)].

If the market remains unchanged, the speculator realizes the net premium of $2,650 plus 15% interest on the T-bills deposited for an additional $525, or a total of $3,175 ($2,650+$525). This is an overall return of 73% for 6 months with the market unchanged. If the market moves lower, the net premium of $2,650 must supply protection to two

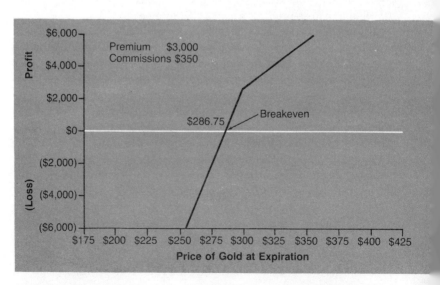

FIGURE 14–3. Ratio Writing Calls 1:2 At-the-Market Chart

FIGURE 14-4. Ratio Writing Calls 2:1 Trapezoidal Chart

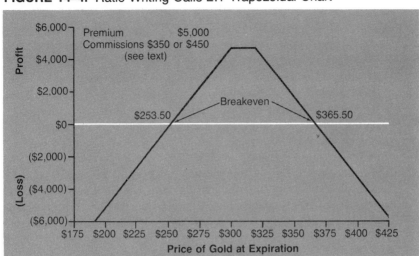

futures contracts. As a result, the downside breakeven is $286.75, because $2,650 on 200 ounces is the equivalent of only $13.25/ounce.

The beauty of this strategy is that the profit potential is limited on only one of the futures contracts, as the second futures is unencumbered by a short option. This strategy does, however, afford very little downside protection. If the market declines, the speculator must be prepared to meet variation margin calls on the long futures positions, with very little help from the short option. This is, to some degree, offset by the unlimited profit potential on the upside.

This strategy is implemented when the speculator is quite bullish, possible longer-term, but wishes some downside protection in the event of poor market entry timing.

There is no necessity that the multiple options granted against a commodity position be of the same striking price or even of the same maturity. When two call options are granted against one long position, we get what is referred to as a trapezoidal hedge. The term trapezoidal hedge comes from the graphical representation of areas of profit and loss on the position.

Example 4—Granting Call Options 2-to-1 Trapezoidal: The speculator purchases one gold futures contract of approximately 6 month's duration at a price of $300/ounce. The speculator then grants one 6-month $300 striking price call option and one 6-month $320 striking price call option. The $300 striking price call is granted for a premium of $3,000, while the $320 striking price call is granted for a premium of $2,000. The commission on the futures is $100; the commission on the $300 strike price call is $150, and the commission on the $320 strike price call is $100, for a total commission of $350.

The margin requirement on the futures contract is $2,000, on the covered call (it makes no difference which one) the premium, and on the uncovered option, the premium plus $2,000. As with all of our previous transactions, the margin is put up in 15% T-bills. Once the margin has been deposited, the net cash premium can be withdrawn. The total premiums are $5,000 minus total commissions of $350. The cash withdrawal is therefore $4,650, and the out-of-pocket requirement to institute the position is $4,350.

In this case the maximum profit is achieved at any point from the lower strike price up to and including the higher strike price. At any price between $300/ounce and $320/ounce, the $300 strike price call is exercised and the $320 strike price call expires. The profit achieved is the net premium of $4,650 plus the interest on the T-bills of $675 [$9,000×15%)÷2]. This total of $5,325 on an out-of-pocket investment of $4,350 is the equivalent of 122.41% for 6 months. The profit is identical from $300/ounce to $320/ounce. Above $320/ounce, the $320 strike price option is exercised necessitating a second futures commission, thereby reducing the net premium by $100 to $4,550. This $4,550 is the equivalent of $45.50/ounce insurance on the uncovered $320 strike price call. This gives you an upside breakeven of $365.50. Above $365.50, each additional $1 appreciation in the price of gold results in a $100 loss on the overall position.

Below $300/ounce, both options expire, but there is no second futures commission. The net option premium remains $4,650. This insurance equivalent of $46.50/ounce protects your long futures position down to $253.50/ounce. Below $253.50, each $1 decline in the price of gold results in a $100 loss on the total position.

As the market moves above $300, additional original margin is required on the two short options, but sufficient variation margin should be generated on the long futures until at least the short $300 strike price is well in-the-money. At this time additional capital most likely has to be committed to the venture. As the market moves below $300, variation margin is called for on the futures. The short option margin requirement declines, but most likely not as fast as the futures. This too requires the commitment of additional capital.

This strategy is normally implemented if the speculator believes that gold is in a fairly well established trading range from $253.50 to $365.50 with a better-than-even likelihood of remaining between $300 and $320 at expiration.

The trapezoid may be constructed with different striking prices and maturities, each of which alters the magnitude and timing of any profits and losses.

RATIO WRITING PUT OPTIONS

Ratio writing of puts is every bit as valid as calls, although it is less common, just as short positions by speculators are less common than long positions. All of the aforementioned strategies work equally well on the short side.

Example 5—Granting Puts 2-to-1 At-the-Market: You short the 6-month futures contract at $300/ounce, and you simultaneously sell two 6-month put options on the same futures contract with a strike price of $300/ounce for a premium of $3,000 each. The commission on the short futures is $100, and the commissions on the option granting are $150 per option. The margin requirement might be $2,000 on the futures, and the margin requirement on the covered call is the premium, while the margin requirement on the naked call is the premium plus one futures margin, in this case, an additional $2,000.

After the appropriate margin is deposited, which can be in T-bills, the net premiums can be withdrawn. The margin requirement in this case is $10,000 ($2,000+$3,000+$3,000+$2,000). The net premium that can be withdrawn would be $5,600 [$6,000−($150×2)÷$100]. The actual out-of-pocket requirement to margin the trade is $4,400.

If the market at expiration is at $300/ounce, the maximum profit is achieved as both options expire, and there is no profit or loss on the futures position. The total profit is the net premium of $5,600 plus 6 month's interest on the T-bills of $750 [($10,000×15%)÷2], or a total of $6,350. This is a return of 144.32% for 6 months.

This net premium of $5,600 or $56/ounce serves as protection for your short position. At any price above $300/ounce, both options expire as they serve no economic purpose to their buyer. Your breakeven is limited by the same $56/ounce. Above $356/ounce, the protection afforded by the granted options is exhausted, and for each $1 increase above this breakeven, you sustain a $100 loss on the entire position.

As the market moves below $300/ounce, you have a contingent long position as a result of the uncovered put option. Eventually you are called upon to take delivery of a second futures contract at a price of $300/ounce. Your downside breakeven is $245/ounce. At this price you would be called upon to purchase the futures at $300/ounce, which, if immediately liquidated, would result in a $55/ounce loss, as well as an

additional futures commission of $100 on this second futures contract.
For each further dollar decline below $245/ounce, you sustain a $100
loss on the entire position.

For prices between $245 and $356, at expiration, you have a profit
on the total position; however, any rise above the $300 price level
generates variation margin calls on the futures that are only partially
offset by the reduction in original margin requirements on the short
options. This requires the commitment of additional capital to the
position and reduces the overall rate of return. For market moves
below $300, additional original margin is required on the short options,
which is offset to some degree by the positive variation margin generated by the short futures. Any substantial move below $300 requires
the commitment of additional capital, with a lower return on investment consequence.

This strategy is basically a mirror image of the strategy portrayed in
Example 1 (Figure 13–1). This is basically a neutral strategy, wherein
the speculator expects relatively little movement in either direction.
This strategy holds no distinct advantage over 2-to-1 call writing at
market, unless the premium level for comparable puts is at a higher
absolute level.

Example 6—Granting Puts 2-to-1 Out-of-the-Money: You go short one
contract of the 6-month gold futures at a price of $300/ounce and at the
same time grant two 6-month gold $280 puts for $2,000 premium each.
The commission on the futures and the options is $100 each. The
margin requirements for our assumption are $2,000 for the futures, the
premium for the covered call, and $2,000 plus the premium for the
uncovered call.

After having deposited the appropriate margin in 15% T-bills, you
can withdraw the net premium. In this case the margin is $8,000
($2,000×4). The net premium is $3,700 [($2,000×2)−($100×3)]. The
actual new money committed to the transaction is the difference of
$4,300 ($8,000−$3,700).

The maximum profit is achieved when the futures are at the strike
price of the short options at expiration. In this case both options expire,
and there is a $2,000 profit on the short futures position
[($300−$280)×100]. The net premium of $3,700. plus the futures profit
of $2,000, plus the T-bill interest of $600 [$8,000×15%)÷2] gives us a
total profit of $6,300 or 146.51% for 6 months.

If the market continues still lower, you have a net premium of $3,700
plus the realized profit on the futures position of $2,000 to protect the
contingent long position created by the uncovered short put. This
protection is the equivalent of $57/ounce ($5,700÷100). Therefore, your
downside breakeven is $224/ounce ($280−$56). The reason you have
only a $56/ounce protection is that you must allocate an additional $100

to cover the roundturn commission incurred on the second futures position.

Of course, you also have a risk on the upside due to our short futures position. At any price above $280/ounce, both options expire and you keep the premium. This net premium of $3,700 or $37/ounce protects the short futures. The upside breakeven is therefore $337/ounce. Above $337/ounce, the grantor sustains a $100 loss for each additional $1 appreciation in the price of the underlying futures.

Between $224/ounce and $337/ounce, you achieve some profit at expiration, with your greatest profit occurring at $280/ounce. Any market movement from the starting price of $300/ounce generates some form of margin call. If the market moves higher, variation margin is required on the short futures, which to some degree is offset by a reduction in the original margin required on the short options. If the market moves lower, additional original margin is required on the short option, which is initially offset by the short futures.

This strategy carries with it the requirement that the speculator must have a bearish to neutral view of the market. If the view is correct, the difference between $224 and $337 is a very substantial area within which profits occur.

Example 7—Granting Puts 1-to-2 At-the-Market: The 1-to-2 ratio write with puts is designed to be most profitable when a limited degree of upside protection is sought, and when maximum downside potential is desired. Having gone short two 6-month gold futures contracts at $300/ounce, one $300 6-month gold put is granted. The margin requirement on each of the futures contracts is assumed to be $2,000, and the margin on the short put is the premium. The commission on the futures contracts is $100 dollars each, and the commissions on a $3,000 put are $150. After the margin of $7,000 ($2,000+ $2,000+ $3,000) has been met, the net premium of $2,700 [$3,000−(3×$100)] may be withdrawn. The cash out-of-pocket commitment is $4,300 ($7,000−$2,700), which would be deposited in 15% T-bills.

The maximum profit is achieved if gold at expiration is at or below $300. At $300, the option expires and the premium is retained. Based on this scenario, the net premium of $2,700, plus the T-bill interest of $525 [($7,000×15%)÷2] gives a rate of return of 46.07% [($2,700+$525)÷$4,300] for 6 months. If gold goes lower, your profit is limited only to this amount on the one futures contract. The second futures contract, unencumbered by an option, has no similar profit limitation. The risk is the possibility of gold appreciating. If gold moves higher, the net premium of $2,700 serves as your only protection. This $2,700 is the equivalent of $13.50/ounce, because you are short two contracts. Your upside breakeven is therefore $313.50.

No additional margin is necessary if the position moves lower, be-

cause the two short futures contracts supply more than enough variation margin to cover the short option. If the market moves higher,
variation margin on the two short futures is required, and very little
help should be expected from the reduction in original margin on the
short option. This is an aggressive bearish strategy.

Example 8—Granting Put Options 2-to-1 Trapezoidal: The trapezoidal hedge works as well with puts as with calls. You short one
6-month futures contract at $300/ounce. At the same time, you sell a
$300 6-month strike price put for $3,000 and a $280 6-month strike
price put for $2,000. The commission on the futures is $100, the commission on the $300 put is $150, and the commission on the $280 put is
$100. The margin on the futures is $2,000, the margin on the $300 put
is the premium, and the margin on the $280 put is the premium plus
$2,000 for a total margin requirement of $9,000 ($2,000+
$3,000+$2,000+$2,000). After this initial margin has been deposited
(assumed to be 15% T-bills), the net premium can be withdrawn.
The net premium is $4,650 ($5,000−$350).

The actual new cash committed to the position is the margin minus
the net premium or $4,350 ($9,000−$4,650). If at expiration the under-
lying futures contract is between $300 and $280, both premiums are
retained. If futures are below $300 but above $280, the $280 put ex-
pires. In either case the profit is the net premium of $4,650 plus the
interest of $675 [($9,000×15%)÷2]. This is a total of $5,325 or 122.41%
($5,325÷$4,650) for 6 months.

If the market moves higher, the net premium of $4,650 or $46.50/
ounce serves as protection for the short futures and gives you an upside
breakeven of $346.50 ($300+$46.50). Above this price, each additional
$1 of appreciation in the futures results in a loss of $100.

If futures decline below $280, you have a contingent long position
that must be protected. The net premium of $4,650 minus the commis-
sion of $100 on the second futures, serves as your protection. This
$4,550 ($4,650−$100) or $45.50 is subtracted from the strike price of
the short uncovered option ($280−$45.50) to give a downside breakeven of $234.50. Below this price, any further decline results in a loss of
$100 for each $1 decline in the underlying futures.

Moves above $300 generate variation margin calls on the short fu-
tures, which are to some degree reduced by the reduced original margin requirements on the short puts. Moves below $300 generate origi-
nal margin calls on the short puts, which are to some degree offset by
the variation margin on the short futures. Any time that additional
capital must be committed, the overall rate of return will be reduced.

Summary

Ratio writing offers the advantage that, in almost all cases, a profit is derived provided the commodity remains within a predetermined range. It is far easier to pick a range of profitable prices than an exact point of profit.

Reasonable ratios make sense. Ratios such as 1-to-2, 1-to-3, 2-to-1, 3-to-1, and in some cases 4-to-1 often have investment merit. Higher ratios generally do not serve an economic purpose. A ratio of 10-to-1 is not a ratio; you might as well not enter into the futures position at all, but just sell 9 naked options. Use the concept of ratio writing intelligently, and it should improve your overall success.

One caution: As large as a range of profitability may be, it can be violated. Be sure you have the capital and risk-taking ability for the unexpected.

COMPOUND STRATEGIES: SYNTHETIC GOLD/SYNTHETIC COMMODITIES

For centuries alchemists have attempted to create gold from lead. Today doing just that is possible through the use of commodity options. Perhaps you can't create the actual gold, but you can create all the economic benefits and risks. This, of course, is possible with any commodity; it just seems that synthetic gold has more charisma.

Example: The same price that has been used in the past for our examples is also used here. Our example uses the 6-month $300 striking price call and the 6-month $300 striking price put. These are approximately at-the-market and each costs $3,000.

To create a synthetic long position, purchase the call and grant the put. The cash flow on the transaction, assuming no commission, is $0, since the money received from granting the put is used to purchase the call. You have to deposit Treasury bills to margin the short put position, but this does not affect the ultimate utility.

If gold appreciates by $10/ounce, at expiration the call option is worth $1,000 ($10×100) and the put option is worthless. The profit or loss on the premiums is of no consequence since the purchase and sale price offset each other exactly. Therefore, your profit is the $1,000, exactly as it would have been had you owned the gold.

If gold goes lower, the premiums once again offset, but you have 100 ounces of gold put to you at $300/ounce when gold is selling at $290/ounce. You therefore sustain a loss of $1,000 as you would if you owned the actual gold.

Instead of committing $30,000 to the purchase of gold, you need only put up the appropriate margin, in the form of T-bills, continue to earn the interest, and benefit from the ownership of gold. This is, of course, an interesting idea, but more importantly, it adds greatly to all of the aforementioned strategies.

TABLE 14—1. $300 Synthetic Gold—Profit/(Loss) At Expiration

Closing Futures Price	Long Futures Profit/(Loss)	Long $300 Strike Call Ending P&L	Short $300 Strike Put Ending P&L	Synthetic Gold Profit/(Loss)
$250	($5,000)	$ 0=($3,000)	$5,000=($2,000)	($5,000)
$275	($2,500)	$ 0=($3,000)	$2,500=$500	($2,500)
$300	$0	$ 0=($3,000)	$ 0=$3,000	$ 0
$325	$2,500	$2,500=($500)	$ 0=$3,000	$2,500
$350	$5,000	$5,000= $2,000	$ 0=$3,000	$5,000

You can "synthesize" gold and then grant out-of-the-money call options against the synthetic gold. You can create a short position in synthetic gold (buy put, sell call) and then grant out-of-the-money put options against the synthetic position.

15

THE SPECULATOR—
STRADDLE AND
COMBO GRANTING

Because both a straddle and a combo include a put and a call, granting either of these options covered is impossible. You cannot be both long and short the same futures contract and achieve a position with any economic utility. Therefore, you either grant straddles and combos naked or cover only one side. Depending on the intent of the investment, both approaches are equally valid.

NAKED STRADDLES

The grantor of a naked straddle assumes the responsibility to both purchase and sell the underlying commodity at the striking price of the options involved. The examples point out that although you are obligated to both buy and sell, you normally fulfill only one of these obligations via exercise. This position is taken without a corresponding long or short position in the futures market. The motivation to undertake this kind of obligation varies. One of the more common motivations is the speculator who would be willing to buy at a lower price or to go short at a higher price. Let's look at some numbers.

Example 1: Gold for 6-month delivery is trading at $300/ounce, and both the $300 put and call on the 6-month futures contract are trading at $3,000. The option grantor sells both the put and the call for a total premium of $6,000 and takes no offsetting position in the futures market. The commission on the sale of each option is $150. The margin is the premium plus one futures contract margin. In this case the speculator must deposit $2,000 as the assumed futures margin, plus $6,000 as the original margin on the options. This is an out-of-pocket new commitment at $2,300 [$8,000−($1,000−$300)].

As you can see from the chart in Figure 15–1, the greatest profit is realized at the striking price of the short options. In this case, if gold is at exactly $300/ounce on expiration day, the net premium of $5,700 ($6,000−$300) is realized. The return, if achieved, is 247% for 6 months ($5,700−$2,300). The probability of gold being at exactly $300 at expiration is extremely small.

For prices above $300/ounce, the call option is in-the-money; below $300/ounce, the put option is in-the-money. Because both options cannot be simultaneously in-the-money, only one futures margin is required. The total net premium, though received on two options, protects each option individually because moves in opposite directions result in a reduction of profit on the corresponding option or possibly a loss. If at expiration gold is at $357/ounce, the call is exercised, and the grantor is called upon to deliver 100 ounces of gold or a gold futures contract if the option were granted on an exchange. The grantor could purchase the gold at $357/ounce for a total cost of $35,700 and deliver the gold to the call buyer for a total price of $30,000. This results in a loss on the gold portion of the transaction of $5,700 ($35,700−$30,000). This loss is

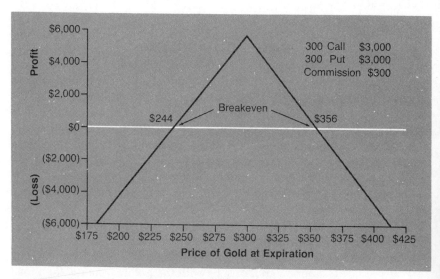

FIGURE 15–1. Naked Straddle Granting Chart

exactly offset by the two net premiums received for granting the options. In reality a futures commission is involved, which reduces the upside breakeven to $356, assuming the futures commission is $100. The put, of course, is worthless.

If, at expiration, gold is trading at $243, the owner of the put delivers the underlying gold futures contract to the put grantor at $300/ounce or for dealer option 100 ounces of physical gold. The grantor is forced to buy gold at $300/ounce and is able to liquidate it at only $243. This, too, is a $5,700 loss [($300×100)−($243×100)]. This amount is equal to the net premiums previously received. Therefore, the downside breakeven is $243. Again, assuming a $100 commission on the futures transaction, the actual breakeven is $244. The call, of course, expires worthless.

The speculator has created a position where the maximum profit of $5,700 is achieved at $300/ounce. At the same time, the upside breakeven is $356, and the downside breakeven is $244. In this range of $112/ounce, if gold trades at expiration, the option grantor cannot lose money.

Compare this strategy with 2-to-1 at-the-market ratio writing. This position is economically identical to either long one futures/short two at-the-market calls or short one futures/short two at-the-market puts. In option granting, there are many identities, that is, different positions with identical economic benefits. Note, however, that the original margin on the naked straddle is lower than the margin on the 2-to-1 ratio writing positions.

At prices either above $356 or below $244, the speculator loses $100 for each dollar's move in gold. If gold is at $366 or $234, the investor has a $1,000 loss at expiration.

T-bills are also an acceptable form of margin on this type of transaction. As a result, T-bill interest could be included, as we did in the last chapter, in any computation of overall rate of return on invested capital. T-bill interest is not, however, normally included in the breakeven computation because this yield could be achieved without the option positions.

As gold moves either higher or lower, the margin requirements on the position change. As gold moves higher, the margin on the uncovered call increases. To some degree, the margin requirement on the put decreases, but not sufficiently to overcome the necessity for the deposit of additional margin. If gold moves lower, the margin requirement on the put increases. Even though the margin requirement on the call also decreases, additional funds have to be added. This addition of capital reduces the overall rate of return on the total position.

NAKED COMBO GRANTING

Example 2: The grantor of a naked combo option also agrees to either make or take delivery of the underlying commodity, but at two different striking prices. The grantor might, for instance, grant a $320 call and a $280 put. In this case, the grantor is agreeing to make delivery at $320/ounce or to take delivery at $280/ounce.

Let's assume that both the $320 call and the $280 put are selling for $2,000 if the underlying 6-month futures contract is trading at $300/ounce. The margin requirement, which can be deposited in T-bills, is one futures margin ($2,000) plus the total of the two premiums $4,000 ($2,000+$2,000). The initial commission is only on the option granting, and, for the sake of this example, it is assumed to be $100 on each option. This results in a net premium received by the grantor of $3,800 ($4,000−$200). The out-of-pocket expense to institute the position is therefore $2,200 [$4,000−($4,000−$200)+$2,000].

As you can see from the chart in Figure 15–2, the maximum profit is achieved anywhere between the striking prices of the two short options involved. Within this range, both options expire, and the net premium of $3,800 is retained. The total return on investment is the net premium of $3,800 plus the interest on the T-bills. Assuming the bills are 15%, this adds an additional $450 [($6,000×15%)÷2]. With an out-of-pocket expense of $2,200, a return of $4,250 is 193% for 6 months.

At prices either below $280 or above $320, one of the options is

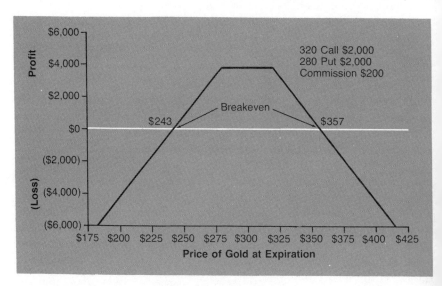

FIGURE 15–2. Naked Combo Granting Chart

ultimately exercised. Depending on the magnitude of the move out-side these extremes, we can compute the reduced profit or loss in-volved. If at expiration gold is at $243, the grantor receives gold at $280 as a result of the puts being exercised. Having purchased at $280 and then liquidated at $243, the grantor realizes a loss of $3,700 on the futures, plus an assumed commission of $100. This loss of $3,800 is offset by the net premium received. If at expiration gold is at $357, the grantor is called upon to deliver gold at $320. A purchase at $357 with a sale at $320, plus $100 in commissions, also results in a loss of $3,800. This too is offset by the net premium. For each $1/ounce move of gold either above $357 or below $243, the speculator sustains a $100 loss at expiration.

Possibly, with either a straddle or combo, both sides of the option will be exercised. This is not, however, very likely. It is unusual for options to be exercised before expiration because the purchaser is thereby giving up any remaining time/extrinsic value and, by assuming a futures position, is ex-posed to unlimited risk. For this reason either the put or call must be out of the money when the other option is exercised. Premature exercises occur when one of the options is so deep in-the-money that it trades at a discount to its intrinsic value by an amount sufficient for an arbitrageur to make money. Premature exercises may also take place when the underlying fu-tures contract has been either bid up the limit or offered down the limit. In this case, the futures contract trader may buy an option and exercise it immediately to offset an unprofitable futures position which he or she is otherwise unable to close out due to the illiquidity caused by a limit move in futures.

The speculator, in deciding whether to grant a naked straddle or a naked combo is normally influenced by the economics. Naked straddle granting normally offers a higher rate of return if the underlying commodity is close to the striking price of the options at expiration. The combination option normally offers a lower rate of return with the range of profitability, but it has higher upside breakevens and lower downside breakevens.

Review the section on trapezoidal option granting, noting the similarity to naked combo granting. Depending on the striking prices used, a naked combo can be economically identical to trapezoidal ratio writing.

PARTIALLY COVERED STRADDLES

Example 3: It is not possible to have a covered straddle, but it is possible to have an offsetting position for either the put or the call. With 6-month gold trading at $300/ounce, the speculator grants both the put and the call, which happen to be each trading at $3,000, and at the same time goes long one 6-month futures contract at $300. The commissions on the option are $150 each, and the commission on the futures is $100.

The margin requirements are: $2,000 as margin on the long futures contract, the $3,000 premium on the covered option, the $3,000 premium on the uncovered option, plus $2,000. The total margin of $10,000 can be deposited in T-bills. The grantor has received a net premium of $5,600 [($3,000×2)−$400].

The maximum profit on this position is achieved at $300 or above. It makes no difference to the grantor if the call is exercised or expires with gold at $300, as the futures contract is liquidated anyway. At or above $300, the profit realized is the net premium of $5,600 plus T-bill interest (if you include it in the calculation) on the margin of $10,000. This equals $750 for a total of $6,350 on an investment of $4,400 or 144.32% for 6 months.

If the market goes lower, risk exposure results because the speculator is both long a futures contract and short an uncovered put option. The protection is the net premium received. The $5,600 dollars received protect the equivalent of two long futures contracts, as a naked put is a contingent long position. Therefore, the $5,600 is the equivalent of $28/ounce of protection. In reality, if the market, at expiration, is $28 below $300 (or at $272), the actual loss is $100 because a second futures commission has to be paid on the put exercise. The downside breakeven is actually $272.50. At this price the put is exercised, forcing the speculator to purchase 100 ounces of gold at $300/ounce and liquidate it at $272.50, thereby realizing a loss of $2,750 [($300−$272.50)×100]. The long futures contract previously owned is also liquidated at the same price for the same loss. Therefore, the total loss is $5,500. Below $272.50/ounce, each additional $1 decline in the price of gold results in the loss of $200 to the grantor.

Again the subject of identities comes up. A long futures contract and a short call are identical to an uncovered short put except for the added commission on the futures contract if no exercise takes place. Therefore, a long futures contract and a short straddle is identical to two short uncovered puts except for the futures commission in the event no exercise takes place. Review the section on uncovered put granting if you don't see the identity (Chapter 13).

This particular position is instituted in few instances because the economics are the same as naked put granting and the commission on naked put granting is lower. This position sometimes comes about when a speculator is already long a futures and wishes to improve on an already profitable position. The transaction may be done for one of two purposes: First, if the market goes higher, the speculator is effectively selling the futures contract at a price $56/ounce higher than gold's price at the time the straddle was granted. Second, if the market goes lower, it allows the speculator to add to the long position at a price below the current market price (see section on being paid for limit orders).

Notice that the margin requirements on the granting of two naked puts, which would be two futures margins plus the two premiums, are identical to the margin requirements on the granting of a straddle against one long futures contract. They are the same due to the identity relationship. In both cases, variation margin is released if the market moves higher, and it has to be added if the market moves lower.

Example 4: You can also grant a straddle and cover the put side of the position with a short futures contract. In this example, our speculator grants both a put and a call with striking prices of $300/ounce on the 6-month futures contract for $3,000 each when the underlying futures contract is trading at $300/ounce. The speculator at the same time goes short one 6-month futures contract.

The margin requirements on the position are: $2,000 on the short futures contract, the premium on the covered put ($3,000), the premium on the uncovered put ($3,000), plus a $2,000 margin requirement on the contingent long position. All of this margin can be met with T-bills. To institute this position, the speculator has to put up a total of $10,000. The net premium received is $5,600 ($6,000−$400). The new out-of-pocket commitment is the difference, or $4,400. If the market at expiration is at $300 or below, the call expires and the put is exercised. The exercise of the put effectively closes out the short futures at the same price it was put on; the profit is therefore $5,600. This is the same rate of return as in Example 3.

If the market moves higher, either profit is reduced or a loss is realized. Above $300/ounce, the put expires, but both the futures contract and the naked call show a loss. Above $300/ounce, the call is ultimately exercised, resulting in an additional $100 futures commission reducing the maximum potential profit to $5,500. This $5,500 protects the equivalent of a 200-ounce short position. The short futures is the first 100 ounces, and the naked call is a contingent short position of an additional 100 ounces. This is a protection of $27.50/ounce as in our last example. On this position, $327.50/ounce becomes the upside breakeven. Above $327.50 the speculator loses $200 for each additional $1 of appreciation in the underlying futures contract.

This strategy also has an identity: It is equivalent to the sale of two naked calls. Both positions have the same economics except for the commission related to the short futures contract, in the event that no exercise takes place. The margin requirements on both strategies are identical.

Again, it would be unusual for someone to implement this position due to the economic advantages to the granting of naked calls. Yet the position might be implemented if the speculator already had a profitable short position in the underlying futures contract. In that instance, the granting of the straddle might be viewed as a means of incrementing an already existing profit or adding to the short position in the event of a market rally.

PARTIALLY COVERED COMBOS

It is difficult to discuss the range of possibilities related to partially covering a combo, because you can cover either the call or the put. The call or the put could be at-the-market, out-of-the-money, or in-the-money. Depending on the actual strategy involved, the results vary dramatically. There is almost no limit to the possible combinations that can be constructed within this general strategy.

> *Example 5:* You can grant a combo with both the put and the call out-of-the-money and simultaneously go long the underlying futures contract. This strategy might be implemented if your market view is that, if the market goes higher, the profit realized on the long futures plus the two premiums would be sufficient; or, if the market goes lower, you would mind increasing the long position at a lower price.
>
> Assume that 6-month gold is trading at $300/ounce, and you hold the previously mentioned market opinion. You would go long the futures contract and at the same time grant the $320 6-month call and the $280 6-month put for a total premium of $4,000. The commission on the futures contract is $100, as is the commission on each of the options granted. Therefore, you receive a net premium of $3,700.
>
> The margin requirements are $2,000 on the long futures contract, the premium on the covered call, the premium on the uncovered call, plus $2,000 margin on the contingent long position created by the uncovered put for a total requirement of $8,000, which can be deposited in T-bills. This total requirement of $8,000 carries with it an out-of-pocket commitment of $4,300 because the net premium of $3,700 can be deducted.
>
> If at expiration the market is unchanged, the profit realized is the net premium of $3,700 plus the T-bill interest of $600 [($8,000×15%)÷2]. This is 100% on your investment for 6 months. In this case, the maximum profit is achieved at the strike price of the short call ($320). At this price or above, the call either expires or is exercised, where-

upon the long futures would be liquidated, resulting in an additional $2,000 profit on the long futures [($320−$300)×100]. At exactly $320, the total profit is the net premium ($3,700), the interest ($600), plus the futures profit ($2,000) or $6,300. This is the equivalent of 146.5% for 6 months.

If the market moves lower, the call also expires, and the $3,700 net premium must protect the long futures and possibly the uncovered put. At exactly $280/ounce, the put also expires, but you have a loss of $2,000 on the long futures contract. At $280/ounce, you still have a profit of $1,700. This is the $3,700 net premium, minus the unrealized loss on the long futures. Below $320/ounce, the put option is ultimately exercised resulting in $100 additional commission on the second futures position. This leaves you with $1,600 to protect what is now two long positions: the actual long futures plus the contingent long futures created by the naked put. This $1,600 is the equivalent of an $8/ounce protection level. Your breakeven becomes the strike price of the short put minus $8, or $272. Below $272, for each additional $1 decline in the price of gold, you sustain a $200 loss.

This position, too, is an identity or equivalency. In both economic potential and margin requirements, it is approximately equivalent to the granting of two out-of-the-money covered calls. It is slightly more attractive, however, because only one futures commission is involved unless the put is ultimately exercised.

Example 6: Suppose your view of the market is that current price levels are attractive for covered option writing, but there is some chance of decline. You might consider the granting of a combo with the short call granted and covered at-the-market, along with the granting of an out-of-the-money put. This, as you know from previous chapters, is the equivalent of covered granting plus entering a limit buy order and being paid for it.

The 6-month gold futures contract is trading at $300/ounce, the 6-month $320 call is trading at $3,000, and the 6-month $280 put is trading at $2,000. In this strategy, you could go long the 6-month futures, sell the 6-month at-the-market call covered and the 6 month out-of-the-money put naked. The commissions are $100 on the futures, $150 on the call granting, and $100 on the put granting, resulting in a net premium of $4,650 ($5,000−$350).

The margin requirement is $2,000 on the futures contract, the premium on the short call ($3,000), the premium on the short put ($2,000), plus $2,000 on the contingent long position created by the naked put. This $9,000 results in an out-of-pocket commitment of $4,350 because the net premium of $4,650 is subtracted. If the market remains unchanged or is above $300 at expiration, the total profit is the net premium plus the T-bill interest of $675 [($9,000×15%)÷2] for a total rate of return of 122.41% for 6 months.

If the market moves lower, the call expires, but the net premium must protect the long futures and the contingent long futures. At $280/ounce, both options expire, but there will be an unrealized loss of $2,000 on the long futures contract. The net premium of $4,650, minus the $2,000 loss on the futures, still leaves us with a profit of $2,650 on the total position at $280. Below $280, there is a second commission when the put is ultimately exercised, thereby reducing our potential profit to $2,550. This $2,550 must now protect the long 200 ounces. This is the equivalent of $12.75/ounce. Therefore our downside breakeven is $267.25. Below this price, each additional $1 decline in the price of gold results in a $200 loss to the speculator.

Example 7: You hold the view that a given market offers upside potential and very little downside risk. You might consider the purchase of the futures coupled with the granting of an out-of-the-money call covered and an at-the-market put naked.

The 6 month futures is trading at $300/ounce, the $320 6-month call is trading at $2,000, and the 6-month $300 put is trading at $3,000. You purchase the futures, grant the $320 call for $2,000, and grant the $300 put for $3,000. The commissions are $100 on the futures, $150 on the put, and $100 on the call. This results in a net premium on $4,650 as in our previous example.

The margin requirements are $2,000 on the futures, the premium on the covered call ($2,000), the premium on the naked put ($3,000), plus $2,000 for the contingent long position created by the naked put. This margin, as before, can be deposited in T-bills. The actual out-of-pocket expense is the $9,000 margin requirement minus the net premium or $4,650.

If the market remains unchanged, both options expire, and the same rate of return is achieved as in our previous example (122.41% for 6 months). This strategy is advantageous when the market moves higher. At $320 or above, the futures are liquidated, resulting in an additional $2,000 profit on the long futures. This increases the total profit to $7,325 on an investment of $4,350, or 168.39% for 6 months. For this greater profit potential, you sacrifice less downside protection.

Below $300/ounce, the put is exercised resulting in a second future commission ($100) reducing the potential profit to $4,550. This $4,550 also serves as protection for the resulting 200-ounce long position. The 4,550 is the equivalent of $22.75/ounce, and results in a downside breakeven of $277.25. Below this price, the speculator loses $200 for each additional $1 decline in the price of gold.

Combination granting can also be done with the short side of the position covered. These strategies result in a short futures position in conjunction with the combination option granting.

Example 8: Your view is that the market has some downside potential and at the same time some upside risk. The approach you might consider is to go short at the market and at the same time grant an out-of-the-money covered put and a naked out-of-the-money call.

Remaining with the same numbers, our speculator grants the 6-month $280 gold put for a premium of $2,000 when 6-month gold is trading at $300. At the same time, the speculator both goes short the futures at $300 and grants the 6-month $320 gold call. The commission on each of the options is assumed to be $100 and the commission is assumed to be $100. The margin requirement might be $2,000 on the short futures; the premium on the covered put, the premium on the uncovered call plus $2,000 for the contingent short position created by the uncovered call. The margin can be deposited in T-bills. After the appropriate margin has been deposited, the net premium of $3,700 ($4,000−$300) can be withdrawn. This results in the commitment of $4,300 ($8,000−$3,700) in new capital to the position.

If the market remains unchanged, both options expire because they are out-of-the-money. The resulting profit is a combination of the interest earned on the T-bills of $600 [($8,000×15%)÷2], plus the net premium of $3,700 for a total of $4,300 on an investment of $4,300 or 100% for 6 months.

If the market moves lower, the total profit is increased, as the speculator's profit is enhanced via the profitable short futures position. At $280 or below, the short futures are closed out, most likely as a result of the exercise of the put. This close-out results in an additional $2,000 profit [($300−$280)×100]. This raises the total profit to $6,300 or 146.51% for 6 months.

If the market moves higher, the short futures position reduces the potential profit from the option granting. With futures at $320, there is a $2,000 loss on the futures, and this reduces the total profit to $2,300 ($4,300−$2,000). Above $320, you must assume that the call is ultimately exercised, thereby creating a second futures commission of $100. Above $320 the remaining $2,200 ($2,300−$100) must protect the 200-ounce short position. This $2,200 is the equivalent of $11/ounce; therefore, the upside breakeven on the total position is $333. Above $333, each $1 increase in the price of gold results in a $200 loss to the speculator.

This strategy, except for the commissions, is economically similar to the granting of two uncovered calls. Because the granting of uncovered calls would normally have a related futures commission without a related exercise, uncovered call granting is more common. This strategy might be employed if the speculator already has a profitable short futures position and is using the granting position as a means either to increment the profit on the short futures on a further market decline or to add to the short position were the market to rally.

You should expect to have to add additional funds to the margin account if the market rallies, and to be able to withdraw some funds if the market moves lower. Increased funds deposited, of course, reduce the overall rate of return, while withdrawal of funds have the opposite effect.

Example 9: If your market view is that a given market has substantial downside potential and limited upside risk, you might grant an uncovered at-the-market call and a covered out-of-the-money put. This strategy offers attractive rates of return on market declines, with little protection on the upside.

With 6-month gold at $300, our speculator, having gone short the 6-month futures contract at $300, grants a 6-month $300 call uncovered for a premium of $3,000 and a 6-month $280 put for a premium of $2,000. The commission on the futures is $100, the commission on the $3,000 call $150, and the $2,000 put $100 for a total of $350. The margin requirement is $2,000 for the futures, the premium for the put ($2,000), the premium for the uncovered call ($3,000), plus $2,000 for the contingent short position created by the uncovered call. This is a total margin requirement of $9,000. The cash necessary to institute the position is the margin requirement of $9,000 minus the net premium of $4,650 or $4,350.

If the market remains unchanged, the total profit is the net premium of $4,350 plus the interest on T-bills that would have been used for margin. The T-bill interest is $675 [($9,000×15%)÷2], which, added to the net premium of $4,650, gives us $5,325 on an investment of $4,350 for a total return of 122.4% for 6 months.

If the market moves lower, initially the total profit is increased as a result of the short futures. At $280, there is an additional profit on the total position of $2,000 as a result of this short. At or below $280, the total profit is the net premium of $4,650 plus the $2,000 futures profit, or $6,650 on an investment of $4,350 for a total return of 152.87% for 6 months.

If the market moves higher, the call is ultimately exercised, resulting in an additional futures commission and reducing the total profit to $4,550 ($4,650−$100). This $4,550 serves as the protection on the 200-ounce short position. The $4,550 is the equivalent of $22.75/ounce on the 200-ounce short position. This gives us an upside breakeven o

$322.75 ($300+$22.75). Above this price, each $1 additional increase in the price of gold results in a $200 loss to the speculator.

Example 10: A third market view is that the market offers attractive rates of return for covered put granting but has the risk of a meaningful rally. In this instance, the better strategy might be the granting of an at-the-market covered put and an out-of-the-money uncovered call.

Assume our speculator goes short the 6-month futures at $300, simultaneously grants the $300 6-month put covered for $3,000, and the 6-month $320 call uncovered for $2,000. The commissions may be assumed to be the same as in our last example, $350. The margin requirements are also $9,000 as above, and the net premium is the same, resulting in the same out-of-pocket expenses. What changes is the potential profits and losses for given market moves. If the market is unchanged, the profit is the same as in Example 9.

If the market moves lower, our profit is only the net premium due to the at-the-market short put. This $4,650, plus the $675 in T-bill interest, is an attractive rate of return of 122.4% as above. The attraction is also the upside. In this case, because the call is granted out-of-the-money, you do not see an exercise of the call without an upward move of some degree. At $320 or above, you can expect the call to be exercised and have a $2,000 unrealized loss on your short futures. At $320, you still have a profit of $2,650 as a result of the net premium minus the futures loss. Above $320, you incur a second futures commission of $100, thereby reducing our profit to $2,550. This $2,550 protects our now 200-ounce short position. This is the equivalent of $12.75; therefore, your upside breakeven becomes $332.75. Above this price, each $1 additional increase in the price of gold results in a $200 loss on the total position.

CONCLUSIONS

The number of possible strategies that may be implemented with partially covered and uncovered straddles and combos is almost limitless as a result of the potential striking prices. No clearcut strategy is best. The most rational approach for speculators is first to take a view of the market. Having made a market judgment, they can then, by empirical analysis of the different potential strategies, determine which is best if their market judgment is correct. In this sense, "best" is the strategy that offers the greatest return for the dollars invested.

Risk is important and cannot be overemphasized. Most straddle and combo positions are the equivalent of multiple naked options. This factor limits the number of people who have the risk-taking ability and temperament to deal with these strategies. For those of stout heart and substantial risk capital, the potential rates of return are very attractive. In many cases there are identities, as has been discussed. In some cases the identity is less costly to employ than the straddle or combo. Be sure to review the identities to determine where the commissions and possible margin requirements are lower.

16

THE SPECULATOR—
SPREADING OPTIONS

The term "spreading" has been well defined as it applies to futures contracts, but, because options have greater flexibility than futures, the definition must also be expanded. *Spreading*, in the option sense, is the purchase of an option of a given type (put or call) and the sale of the same type of option on the same commodity in either a different month or at a different striking price. Spreading is normally considered to be a 1-to-1 relationship; that is, you buy one call and you sell one call. This view is predicated on the exchanges' margin rules, which do not give any special consideration to multiple positions

Spreads may be done intermarket or even intercommodity, but these approaches deal less with option strategy and more with arbitrage. Arbitrage is beyond the scope of most investors due to the commission and margin costs involved.

Spreads fall into two general categories: vertical and horizontal. In a vertical spread, only the striking prices are different. In a *horizonal spread*, the only difference is maturity. Vertical spreads are also sometimes referred to as either "bull" or "bear" spreads, where horizontal spreads are sometimes referred to as "calendar" spreads. Varying both the striking price and the maturity is also possible, with the resultant position being referred to as a *vertical* or *diagonal calendar spread*.

Spreads may be composed of calls or puts but not of both. That is not to say that both puts and calls are not used together in some strategies, but that such strategies are not referred to as spreads. Using relationships other than 1-to-1 is also possible, and, even though these strategies do not qualify for special margin treatment, they are spreads and are referred to as *ratio spreads*.

VERTICAL SPREADS

Vertical spreads are referred to as either bull spreads or bear spreads depending on the type of market environment in which they are designed to be profitable. If the spread is designed to be profitable in a rising market, it is referred to as a *bull spread*. If the spread is designed to generate its profit in a declining market, it is referred to as a *bear spread*.

Example 1—Call Bull Spread: You are bullish on the price of gold, and 6-month gold futures are trading at $300. You might purchase the 6-month $300/ounce striking price call and at the same time sell/grant/write the 6-month $320 striking price call. As you can see, spreading is a combination of both option purchasing and option granting. In fact, some people view spreading as covered option writing, with the long option position being the cover for the short option position.

The $300 call is trading for $3,000, and the $320 call is trading for $2,000. To do this transaction, you have to deposit funds (margin) into your brokerage account. (Because margin requirements vary from firm to firm and from exchange to exchange, the numbers used in these examples are purely for illustrative purposes.)

If you purchase the $300 call and sell the $320 call, you must pay for the one, and you are paid for the other. In this case your purchase costs $3,000, and your sale generates $2,000; therefore your cash outlay is the difference or $1,000. To this $1,000 must be added the commission charged by the brokerage firm. Let's say that the commission on this transaction is $100; therefore your total dollar outlay is $1,100. This is also your total exposure. You cannot lose more than the $1,100 regardless of what happens to the price of gold. If at expiration gold is at or below $300/ounce, both options expire worthless, the result of which is the loss of your $1,100, but nothing more.

If the market goes higher, your long option serves as cover for your short option; that is, if the short option is exercised, you can exercise your option as a means to satisfy the requirement of delivering against the short. It is also possible that gold at expiration is between $300 and $320, whereupon the long option has some value and the short option expires worthless.

The easiest, though not necessarily best, method of determining the profit potential of a given spread strategy is to look at what the options should be worth on expiration day. To approach projected profits in any other fashion requires some sort of econometric model as well as many assumptions.

If, on expiration day, gold is at $300 or below, both options expire and you lose $1,100. If, on expiration day, gold is at $311/ounce, your long option ($300 call) is $11 dollars in-the-money and therefore worth $1,100, at which point it is liquidated and you break even.

If, on expiration day, gold is at $320/ounce, your long option ($300 call) is $20/ounce in-the-money and therefore worth $2,000. The short option is worthless and expires. The liquidation of your long option for $2,000—less a commission of perhaps $100—leaves you with $1,900 on an investment of $1,100. Or an $800 profit on an $1,100 investment. This is the equivalent of 72.7% for 6 months.

Above $320/ounce, both the long option and the short option increase in value by $100 for each $1 increase in the price of gold. Therefore, any additional profit realized on a further increase in the price of the $300 call is offset by a loss on the appreciation in the $320 call that you are short.

To appreciate the advantages of spreading, look at spreading in comparison to other approaches to the same market view. In this instance, the bull spreader held the view that a market rally of perhaps $10 to $15/ounce was likely. We have seen the results of a correct judgment. Compare the outcome to the outright purchase of perhaps the $300 call without the spread.

If you purchase the $300 call outright, it costs $3,000 as opposed to only $1,000 for the spread. The commissions are likely to be higher on the call than on the spread. If the market moves lower instead of higher, the risk is $3,000 instead of $1,000. The breakeven price on the spread is approximately $311, where the breakeven price on a $300 call with a premium of $3,000 is approximately $330.

What the spread does not offer that the call does, is unlimited profit potential. If gold goes to $400/ounce, the spreader realizes only an $800 profit, while the outright call buyer is able to liquidate the option for approximately $10,000 because it is $100/ounce in-the-money.

The margin requirement on this type of spread is merely the difference in the premiums because the short option has a higher striking price than the long option; as a result, the risk is defined and limited to the difference in premiums.

Example 2—Call Bear Spreads: This type of transaction is instituted at a time when the speculator feels that the market will move lower and wishes to profit from that downward move.

The approach might be the purchase of the $300 6-month gold call and the simultaneous sale of the 6-month $280 gold call. Assuming that 6-month gold is at $300/ounce, the $300 call might be trading for $3,000 and the $280 call might be trading for $4,000.

If, at expiration, gold is trading below $280/ounce, both options would expire. In this case, the option that you purchased is worthless, and the option that you granted is worthless; but the option you granted costs $1,000 more than the option you purchased. As a result you have approximately a $1,000 profit minus any commissions.

If, at expiration, gold is at $300, your long option ($300 call) expires worthless with the resultant loss of $3,000. The short option ($280 call) is $20 in-the-money and therefore worth $2,000. Presumably, you will repurchase that option for $2,000 versus its original sale at $4,000. This results in a profit on that portion of the spread of $2,000. The $3,000 loss, plus the $2,000 profit, leaves you with a net loss of $1,000 plus commissions.

At any price above $300, both options gain in value. Further losses incurred in the short $280 call are offset by profits in the $300 call.

The breakeven point on this transaction is that price where the profit on the short option offsets the cost of the long option. This price, neglecting commissions, is $290/ounce. At $290, the $280 call can be repurchased for a cost of $1,000 versus a sale at $4,000, which results in a $3,000 profit. At $290, your $300 expires worthless for a $3,000 loss. At any price below $290, you have a profit, with a maximum potential of $1,000 at or below $280.

As you can see, the initial cash flow on this position is positive. That is, you are receiving $4,000 for the option you are granting, and you are paying only $3,000 for the option that you are purchasing. This results in a positive $1,000 cash flow. The risk is that the option you have granted will be exercised, and the option you are using to cover the short has a higher striking price. The difference in striking prices times the quantity, minus the cash flow, is the true risk. If you are forced to deliver at $280 and you have to exercise your $300 call, you sustain a loss of $2,000 [($300−$280)×100]. This $2,000 potential loss, minus the positive cash flow of $1,000, leaves you with a true exposure of $1,000.

The exchanges recognize this exposure and margin accordingly. After giving you the cash flow credit, the exchanges require that you deposit the difference in the striking prices times the quantity involved. In this case, you can withdraw the $1,000 positive cash flow, but you have to deposit original margin equal to $2,000 [($300−$280)×100]. On the surface this appears logical, and in most cases it is. Occasionally when the striking prices involved are very far apart, this becomes an enormous amount of money and unrealistic in relationship to the risk. The exchanges limit the maximum amount that must be deposited to normal futures margin plus the premium of the short option. The logic is that the risk of a spread can't be any greater than an outright futures position. If any other approach is used, you face a penalty for having the long option, and there is no way that the long option can increase the overall risk of the spread.

VERTICAL PUT SPREADS

The logic that applies to calls also applies to puts. That is, it is possible to do both bull and bear spreads using puts. As with call spreads, put spreads are normally implemented when limited moves are anticipated, and limited profits are acceptable in exchange for limited risks.

Example 3—Put Bear Spread: The speculator who anticipates a limited downward move in the price of a commodity might consider instituting a put bear spread. In this instance, the speculator purchases the higher striking price and sells the lower striking price.

The 6-month gold is currently trading at the $300/ounce level, and the speculator believes that the possibility of a $20 to $30 decline exists. The 6-month $300 gold put is trading at $3,000, and the 6-month $280 gold put is trading at $2,000. The speculator purchases the $300 put for $3,000 and grants the $280 put for $2,000. The cash flow in this instance is negative by an amount of $1,000. The speculator has agreed to purchase 100 ounces of gold at $280 and at the same time acquired the right to sell 100 ounces of gold at $300/ounce. As you can see, if the short option is exercised, the speculator can exercise the long option and realize a profit; therefore no additional margin is required

If, at expiration, gold is at or above $300/ounce, both options are worthless and expire, exposing the speculator to nothing more than the loss represented by the difference in premiums originally paid, namely $1,000.

If, at expiration, gold is at exactly $280/ounce, the long option ($300 put) is $20 in-the-money and can be liquidated for $2,000. The short option ($280 put) is worthless and therefore expires. The speculator paid $1,000 to institute the position and receives $2,000 on the liquidation of the $300 put. The gross profit is therefore $1,000. Several hundred dollars in commission is likely to be involved in this type of transaction.

If, at expiration, gold is below $280, the profit is still $1,000, because for each additional dollar the speculator realizes on the long $300 put, he or she loses a like amount on the short $280 put.

The breakeven price on this transaction is the market price where the value of the $300 put is exactly $1,000 more than the market price of the $280 put. In this instance it is $290. At that price, the $300 put is worth $1,000 and the $280 put is worthless.

This transaction involves an investment of $1,000 and has a $1,000 risk. The breakeven price is $290 and has a maximum profit potential of $1,000 if gold declines to $280. Compare this with the outright purchase of the $300 gold put. That position has a dollar commitment and risk of $3,000, with a downside breakeven of $270. The advantage of the outright put purchase is that there is no meaningful limit to the profit potential.

Example 4—Put Bull Spread: The following type of transaction is implemented if the speculator feels that an upward move in the price of the commodity is imminent, and the magnitude of the move is not anticipated to be large. In this case the speculator might buy the 6-month $280 gold put and grant the 6-month $300 gold put. The $280 put is trading at $2,000, and the $300 gold put is trading at $3,000.

If, at expiration, gold is trading at $300 or above, both options expire worthless, and the speculator achieves the difference in cash flow as the total profit. In this instance, the speculator bought for $2,000 and sold for $3,000, thereby receiving a net premium of $1,000.

If, at expiration, gold is at $280, the $280 option purchased for $2,000 is worthless and realizes a loss of $2,000. The $300 put, however, which the speculator is short, is $20/ounce in-the-money and therefore worth $2,000. The speculator repurchases that option for $2,000. On this portion of the transaction, he has realized a $1,000 profit, since the option was originally sold for $3,000. The net result is a $2,000 loss and a $1,000 profit for a total loss of $1,000. At any price below $280, additional profit that accrues on the $280 put is offset by losses on the $300 put.

Margin on bull spreads done with puts is conceptually the same as margin on bear spreads done with calls. That is, the margin required by most exchanges is the lesser of the price difference represented by the strike prices times the quantity, or normal futures margin plus the premium on the short option.

Conclusions

In attempting to structure a spread position, first make the market judgment as to the direction and the magnitude of move. Then, by empirical observation, compute which spreads offer the greatest profit potential in light of the projected market move. In many instances, if the projected move is bullish, a spread constructed of calls generates a higher rate of return due to the more attractive margin requirements versus the profit potential. Similarly, for bearish moves, structuring a bear spread with puts may tend to be advantageous.

Call bull spreads and put bear spreads tend to offer the greatest profit potential with the long side approximately at-the-market and the short side out-of-the-money by the magnitude of the projected move. Bear spreads with calls and bull spreads with puts generally offer the greatest profit potential with the short side at-market and the long side out-of-the-money by the magnitude of the projected move.

When doing bull spreads with calls and bear spreads with puts, there is generally little economic justification to using options whose striking prices are more than two apart. This is because the out-of-the-money option becomes so inexpensive that it does not materially reduce the dollar commitment and risk, but it does inhibit the profit potential. In that instance, just purchasing the long option and forgetting about the spread may be better.

In spread trading, you are usually working with potentially relatively high rates of return but, in many cases, with small dollar investments. Commission can be a very significant factor. Even though some of the examples eliminated commissions for the sake of clarity, do not neglect taking them into consideration before actually instituting a position. Always consider the possibility that the short option may be exercised, and consider the risks and costs of that exercise.

In doing bull spreads with puts and bear spreads with calls, you have a greater exposure to premature exercise because, as the position moves into-the-money, the short option has the greater probability of going to a discount to its intrinsic value.

HORIZONTAL SPREADS

In *horizontal spreads*, also referred to as calendar spreads, you purchase an option of a given type (either put or call) on a given commodity, and at the same time sell the same type of option on the same commodity, with the same striking price but with a different maturity.

Calendar spreads are done for numerous reasons. One of the most common reasons may be your perception of the projected price change of a commodity over a given period of time. Let's say you believe that the price of a commodity might appreciate long-term, but that it was likely to remain unchanged short-term. You might purchase a long-term call option and grant a short-term call option. If you happen to be correct, the short-term option expires before the projected move takes place, and the premium received for granting reduces the premium of the option that you have purchased.

Another reason, which is more mechanical, is that the time value of options depreciates as a function of the square root of time (see chapter on option pricing). In this case, if you purchase a long-term option and grant a short-term option, the option granted should depreciate at a rate greater than the option owned.

Possibly you believe that short-term the price of a given commodity will increase, but long-term it will remain unchanged. You might consider purchasing the short-term call and granting a long-term call. The logic behind this approach is that the short-term option has less time value and appreciates more rapidly than the longer-term call. If you are correct, your long option should gain in value at a slower rate than the loss on the longer-term short option.

The classic calendar spread is economically viable due to the square root function of time/extrinsic value. To put it another way, options of greater duration do not cost more money in proportion to the time involved.

> *Example:* If a 1-month at-market option costs $1,000, common sense would tell us that a 4-month at-the-market option would cost $4,000, and a 9-month at-the-market option would cost $9,000. This, on the surface, appears logical, but it is not the case. The increase in the extrinsic value of an option is not proportionate to the increase in time, but rather to the square root of the increase in time. Therefore, if a 1-month at-the-market option costs $1,000, a 4-month at-the-market option costs $2,000, and a 9-month at-the-market option costs $3,000. The reason is that the square root of 4 is 2, and the square root of 9 is 3.

These phenomena give rise to the profit potential of the calendar spread. Using this fact, the speculator purchases a long-term option and grants a short-term option, because the short-term option depreciates more rapidly than the long-term option. This assumes that nothing else changes, such as the price of the underlying commodity.

> *Example 1:* Using the aforementioned price, let's assume that the speculator purchases the 9-month at-the-market option and at the same time grants the 1-month at-the-market option. Further, the price of the underlying commodity remains, and one month passes. With the price of the underlying commodity remaining unchanged and one month passing, the 1-month option expires, and the 9-month options is still at-the-market with 8 months remaining
>
> To determine the loss on the 9-month option, look at the relationship of the square root of 9 to the square root of 8. The square root of 9 is 3, and the square root of 8 is 2.828. Divide the square root of 8 by the square root of 9 (2.828−3). This gives us .943. This tells us that the time value portion of an 8-month option is worth 94.3% of the time value portion of the 9-month option. If a 9-month at-the-market option

is worth $3,000, then an 8-month at-the-market option is worth $2,829 ($3,000×.943). In other words, we have lost $171 ($3,000−$2,829) on our long option and made $1,000 on our short option, leaving us with a profit before commissions of $829.

Very few people employ this strategy in its pure sense, because its basis is in mathematics, not in market judgment. It is important to understand the mathematical concept because this understanding helps in the application of tactics to market strategy. The example was composed of at-the-market options, because they are the most expensive in terms of time value, and they best portray the example.

It is also important to understand that these options would have substantially different striking prices due to their maturity and still be at-the-market. If our 1-month at-the-market option were a call on gold with a striking price of $300, and if the prime rate were 10%, then the 4-month at-the-market call option on gold would have to have a striking price of approximately $307.50 to be at-the-market. This is because of carrying charges. If gold for delivery in one month is trading at $300, to compute the 4-month price, which is three months later, you have to include the interest, storage, and insurance cost to come up with the at-the-market price. With gold, the major cost is interest. Therefore, $300 times 10% for three months is $7.50. A 4-month at-the-market option therefore has a striking price of $307.50. Such a striking price does not exist, but it is important to remember carrying charges when thinking about calendar spreads. Note: Storage and insurance on gold costs only approximately ½% per year, but the same costs are significant with bulky commodities such as heating oil.

Calendar spreads may be done just as easily with puts as with calls. The only difference is in the definition of relative striking prices. In calls, an at-the-market option on a deferred maturity has a higher striking price than a nearby maturity. With puts, the more distant at-the-market option has a lower striking price than the nearby maturity.

Example 2: The calendar spread has practical application in addition to its mathematical possibilities. Suppose you believe that, in the next two to three months, the price of gold could appreciate substantially, but over the near term the market might only rally or decline slightly. You could always await the rally or buy now and waste the initial month's cost of premium. An alternative is to use the calendar spread.

You can use exactly the same tactics as in Example 1 to meet this market view. Purchase the 9-month at-the-market call option for a premium of $3,000, and grant the 1-month at-the-market call option for a premium of $1,000. If you happen to be incorrect in your market judgment, and if the price of gold remains unchanged or goes lower for the balance of the nine months, your initial commitment is only $2,000. If, on the other hand, you are correct, and gold is relatively inactive ending the first month unchanged, you now own an 8-month call at a real cost of only $2,000. In fact, if gold rallied $10 dollars during the first month that the spread was in existence, the 1-month option at expiration would be worth only $1,000 (its in-the-money value). At that point, it can be repurchased at no loss, while your 9-month option shows a profit of perhaps $500.

The major risk to this type of position is a major market rally over the short term. In this instance, the 1-month option, due to its limited time value, appreciates more rapidly than the 9-month option. If, for instance, over the short term gold rallies $30/ounce, the 1-month option might go up to $3,500, while the 9-month option might go up only to $2,500. This exposes you to a $1,000 loss over the short term.

Example 3: Let's say that you hold the same market view as in Example 2, that you are worried about the possibility of a short-term rally, and that you are reluctant to grant even a short term at-market option. You might consider buying the 9-month at-the-market call and granting a 1-month out-of-the-money call. A 1-month $320 striking price call might be selling for $500 with 1-month gold trading at $300.

In this case you purchase a 9-month at-the-market call option for $3,000 and grant a 1-month $20 out-of-the-money call option for $500. Your total downside exposure is only $2,500. This is a slightly larger commitment than in Example 2, but your short-term upside exposure is far less. If one month later gold rallies by $20, your granted option is still worthless since it is only at-the-market. If gold rallies by $25, the option is only $5 in-the-money, and it can be repurchased for the price originally granted. In addition, your 9-month option would be $25 in-the-money.

Example 4: Another market view that lends itself to the use of the calendar spread is a view of short-term decline, followed by longer-term rally. If you believe that over the short term, perhaps one month, the market may decline and then rally, you might consider the sale of a 1-month in-the-money call and the purchase of a 9-month at-the-market call. The 1-month $280 call might be selling for $2,500, with 1-month gold selling for $300. Sell the 1-month $280 call for $2,500, and purchase the 9-month at-the-market call for $3,000. If your judgment is correct and gold declines by, say, $20 over the month, the $280 call expires worthless. The 9-month call, on the other hand, declines but to a much lesser degree due to its remaining time value (8 months), Even though the 9-month option is now $20 out-of-the-money, it is still probably worth about $1,200 to $1,500. In fact, you could close the position out at that time with a profit. You would make $2,500 on your short option and lose only $1,500 to $1,800 on your long option. Or you can continue to hold your long option on the assumption that your market view is correct. Another alternative is to grant another short-term option against your long-term option, and once again take advantage of the more rapid decline in the time value of short-term options.

REVERSE CALENDAR SPREADS

Most calendar spreads are done with the purchase of the more distant maturity and the sale of the nearby, but the reverse is possible.

Example 5: You believe that the market could sustain a short-term rally of perhaps $20 to $30, but the longer term does not hold much promise. You might purchase the 1-month at-the-market option and the sale of the 9-month at-the-market option. If you are correct, the 1-month option on a $30 rally appreciates to somewhere between $3,000 and $3,500, while the 9-month option most likely appreciates to perhaps only $3,500 to $4,000. The total position can be closed out at a profit at that point, or you might consider liquidating the profitable long and retaining the naked short to profit by your projected market decline.

This strategy can also be implemented with the nearby in-the-money and the deferred at-the-market, or with the nearby at-the-market and the deferred out-of-the-money if a higher degree of protection is desired.

Short-term events can have a very positive or negative effect on the performance of calendar spreads. For example, were you short a nearby option and long a deferred option on gold, any major political upheaval would cause the nearby option to rally more dramatically than the deferred. If conversely, you were long the nearby and short the deferred, the political event would work to your benefit. Negative events may also have an equivalent effect on the underlying futures contracts. A speculator, for instance, who is short a futures contract that locks up the limit is more likely to buy a nearby option as protection; this, too, could cause a disproportionate rally in the nearby and possibly even a premature exercise.

It goes without saying that a calendar spread is only a spread as long as both sides of the transaction remain open. This is not a problem when the deferred position is the long position, because the short expires before the long. Yet if the calendar spread is a reverse calendar spread, the short expires first and exposes the spreader to the risks and margin requirements normally associated with an outright naked option.

RATIO SPREADS

As with option granting, either vertical or horizontal spreading is normally done on a 1-to-1 basis, but with some strategies, it is more advantageous to use ratios of other than 1-to-1. Ratio spreading is conceptually identical, when done as vertical spreads, to ratio writing against either a futures or physical commodity position.

Example 1: Six-month gold is trading at $300/ounce, and you believe that there is potential for perhaps a $20 to $30 move on the upside over the next 6 months. This is basically a bullish view but with upside limitations. A strategy you might consider is the purchase of 6-month futures and the granting of one or two out-of-the-money calls. This is a valid approach, but it entails the risk of a market decline below the level of protection provided by the premiums received for the option granting.

Perhaps more attractive is the purchase of an at-the-market call versus the sale of two out-of-the-money calls. The six-month at-the-market gold call is selling for $3,000, and the 6-month $20 out-of-the-money call is selling for $2,000. If you purchase the at-the-market for $3,000 and sell two out-of-the-money calls at $2,000 each, you have a positive cash flow from the premiums of $1,000. Let's say that the at-the-market is struck at $300, that the out-of-the-money calls are struck at $320, and that at expiration gold is trading at $320. In such a case, your $300 call is worth $2,000 because it is $20/ounce in-the-money, and the two $320 options that you sold are worthless and expire.

Your $300 call can be liquidated at a $1,000 loss ($3,000−$2,000), and you keep the premiums for the two $320 options previously granted. You have received a total of $3,000.

If the market goes lower, and at expiration gold is at or below $300/ounce, all three options expire. You lose the $3,000 that you paid for the $300 call, and you keep the $4,000 that you received for granting the two $320 calls.

As you can see from the chart in Figure 16–1, your maximum profit is achieved at $320/ounce. This profit is the $4,000 from the two expired short options, less the $1,000 loss on the long option, or $3,000. On market declines, your profit is never less than $1,000, and your exposure is at a price $30/ounce above the strike price of the short uncovered $320 call.

Even though you may view this package as a 2-to-1 ratio spreading transaction, the exchanges view it as a bull spread plus a naked short call. As a result, that is the way the position is margined. The $300

FIGURE 16–1. 2:1 Call Ratio Writing $300/$320

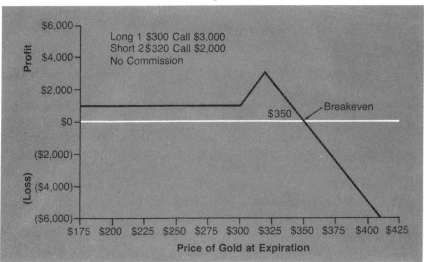

versus the first $320 is a bull spread, and the second $320 is a naked call. For the bull spread you pay the $3,000 for the purchase of the $300 call and receive the $2,000 for the $320 granted. The transaction is a cash transaction, and there are no margin calls regardless of what happened in relation to that portion of the position. The second $320 short is margined as a naked option. Your original margin is the premium ($2,000) plus a futures margin of, say, $2,000. Because this is original margin, it can be deposited in T-bills. As the market moves lower, the margin required on the second $320 call is reduced and can be withdrawn. As the market moves higher, the margin required on the second $320 call increases and must be deposited. Yet, because it is variable original margin, it can be deposited in the form of additional T-bills.

The rate of return on this type of strategy tends to be high under ideal market circumstances. If at expiration, gold is at exactly $320/ounce, the maximum profit of $3,000 is achieved. To institute this position, you have an out-of-pocket cash expense of only $3,000 ($1,000 paying for the bull spread and $4,000 margin on the naked $320 minus a $2,000 premium). In addition, you earn interest on the $4,000 T-bill deposit. If T-bills yield 15%, this is an additional $300 for a total of $3,300 on an investment of $3,000, which is 110% for 6 months.

Example 2: The same strategy works equally well with put options. Assume that your view of the market is the exact opposite of that in Example 1. You believe that the market, over the next 6 months, can sustain a decline in the area of $20 to $30, and there is little potential on the upside. Again you can go short the 6-month futures contract and grant one or two out-of-the-money puts against this position. Your exposure, however, is that the market does, in fact, rally to a degree greater than the protection afforded by the premium from the two short option.

Six-month gold is trading at $300/ounce, with the 6-month $300 put trading at $3,000 and the $280 put trading at $2,000. A satisfactory strategy is to purchase the $300 put for a cost of $3,000 and grant two $280 put options for $2,000 each. If, at expiration, gold is at exactly $280/ounce, the two short options expire, and you realize the $4,000 from the granted position. The $300 put option is $20 in-the-money and it is liquidated for $2,000, thereby realizing a loss of $1,000 ($3,000−$2,000). On the overall position you have a profit of $3,000.

If, at expiration, gold is at or above $300/ounce, all of the options expire. You lose the $3,000 that you invested in your $300 put, but you realize the $4,000 from having granted the two $280 puts. At $300 or above, your profit is $1,000.

Below $280/ounce, the naked $280 put begins to become a problem. The profit of $3,000 achieved at exactly $280/ounce serves as your protection on the naked position. This $30/ounce protection gives you a downside breakeven of $250. Below $250/ounce, you lose $100 for each additional $1 decline in the price of gold.

The margin requirements are exactly the same as in Example 2. The only difference is that calls for additional margin result from market declines as opposed to market advances.

Again the rate of return is attractive, not only from the potential premium earnings, but also from the interest earned on the T-bills used to meet the margin requirements.

Example 3: As with ratio writing, there is no limitation of 1-to-2 relationships. In many cases, implementing strategies that call for 3-to-1, 4-to-1, or perhaps 3-to-2 are advantageous.

When the ratios involved exceed 2-to-1, it is normally advisable to grant a more out-of-the-money option because the increased exposure of the multiple grant can, to some degree, be offset by the greater move necessary to incur a loss.

Were technical and fundamental indicators to project a market with both limited upside and downside potential, but with a slight upward bias, the following strategy might be used. If 6-month gold is trading at $300/ounce, and the likelihood of a rally much above the $340 level is little, you might consider the purchase of the $300/ounce call and the sale of three of the $340 calls. One of these options is part of a $300/$340 bull spread, and the remaining two options are naked.

If 6-month gold is trading at $300, the 6-month $300 call might be about $3,000, and the $340 call would be about $1,200—depending on market conditions. The maximum profit is achieved at the strike price of the short options, in this case $340/ounce. Your $300 call, which was purchased for $3,000, can be liquidated at expiration for $4,000 because it would be $40 in-the-money. The three $340 short options expire worthless, thereby generating an additional $3,600 ($1,200×3).

If, at expiration, gold is below $300/ounce, all of the options expire, and you still have a profit of $600 because the premium lost on the long option ($3,000) is more than offset by the premiums earned on the short options ($3,600).

As with any multiple call granting strategy, the exposure is above the strike price of the short calls. In this case the profit of $4,600, achieved at $340, must protect the two uncovered $340 calls. The $4,600 is the equivalent of $23/ounce on each option; therefore, your upside break-even becomes $363/ounce. Above this price, you lose $200 for each additional $1 increase in the price of gold.

Both the margin requirements and the economics of this position are more closely related to naked option writing than they are to spreading. The $300/$340 portion (1-to-1) is margined as a spread; that is, the dollar difference must be paid for in cash. The two $340 calls are margined as naked. Upward moves in the commodity generate calls for additional original margin, which can be met with the deposit of T-bills. Downward moves result in the reduction of original margin and the possibility of T-bill removal.

Example 4: The ratio strategies thus far discussed have involved a limited profit in one direction and an open-ended risk in the other direction. The flexibility of the ratios themselves also offer the possibility of reversing this relationship.

You believe that the price of gold is headed substantially lower from its current level of $300 on the 6-month futures contract. As a result, you would like to purchase several at-the-market put options, but you would also like a means whereby you could reduce your potential loss if you were incorrect. If you purchase three $300 puts at $3,000 each and at the same time grant two $280 puts, you bring about your desired objective. This strategy is really two bear spreads coupled with an outright long put.

The three options you purchase cost a total of $9,000, and the two options that you grant generate a total of $4,000 in premiums. If the market moves higher, contrary to your expectation, with gold above $300 at expiration, all the options expire, and you have a loss of $5,000. Although this is not attractive, it is still a smaller loss than if you had just purchased the three puts and lost $9,000.

If, at expiration, gold is at exactly $280, the short options expire with

the $4,000 in premiums yours to keep. Your three $300 puts are liquidated for a total of $6,000 (being $20 in-the-money). You have a $3,000
loss on your long puts and a $4,000 profit on your short puts.

Below $280, you have one $300 put without a short option outstanding against it. For each additional $1 of decline in the price of gold, you
realize an additional $100 profit on the entire position.

This position does not have margin requirements in the true sense.
You put up total dollars equivalent to the exposure. Thereafter, you are
not exposed to margin calls of any kind because no naked option position is involved. The imbalance is a ratio of 2-to-3, with the difference a
fully paid-for long put.

TRAPEZOIDAL RATIO SPREADING

Whenever in any ratio writing strategy more options are granted than
are purchased, the strategy has a naked writing component. This naked
component carries with it an open-ended risk, which can, to some degree,
be controlled by careful selection of striking price. The granting of more
out-of-the-money options increases the magnitude of negative moves necessary to create a loss. This also tends, however, to reduce the overall
maximum rate of return at the strike price of the short options. Great flexibility can sometimes be achieved by using options of different striking prices on
the short side. This approach is called *trapezoidal ratio spreading* or *step
hedging*. By so doing, you create a larger area of safety and profitability, with
little reduction in overall rate of return at the optimum price.

Example 5: If an upward move is projected in the price of gold from
the $300 level, but the magnitude of the move is hard to forecast, the
following strategy might be appropriate. Purchase the 6-month $300
gold call at $3,000 and at the same time grant one 6-month $320 gold
call for $2,000 and one 6-month $340 gold call for $1,200. The $300/
$320 portion of the total position can be viewed as a bull spread, with
the $340 short as an outright naked option.

The chart in Figure 16–2 clearly depicts that the maximum profit is
achieved with gold at $320 at expiration. At this price, the long option
is worth $2,000, which when liquidated results in a $1,000 loss from
the original purchase price of $3,000. The remaining two short options,
however, expire because one is now at-the-market, and the other is
still $200 out-of-the-money. These two premiums totaling $3,200 offset
the loss on the $300 call, leaving a profit of $2,200. This $2,200 also
serves as the protection on the naked $340 call. If gold continues to
appreciate above the $340 level, the $340 call is ultimately exercised.

FIGURE 16–2. Trapezoidal Writing $300/$320/$340

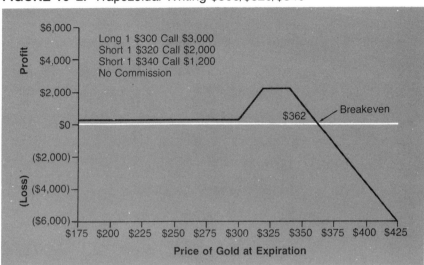

The $2,200 provides $22/ounce protection above $340, or $362 becomes your upside breakeven price. Above $362, you lose $100 for each additional $1 appreciation in the price of gold.

Below $300, all the options expire. You sustain a $3,000 loss on your $300 call, but you keep the $3,200 ($2,000+$1,200) generated by the option granting.

The $340 option, being well out-of-the-money, is at least initially somewhat insensitive to upward moves in the price of gold. As a result, it does not initially generate major margin calls for small price changes. The $340 is, however, a naked option, and on substantial price increases, calls for meaningful original margin increases.

A similar type of transaction can, of course, be done using put options with a bearish view of the market.

Example 6: In a downward trending market, you might purchase the gold 6-month $300 put for $3,000 with 6-month gold at $300. At the same time, you grant two 6-month $280 puts at $2,000 each and perhaps one $260 put for $1,200. This is about as extreme a strategy as you would consider when it is logical to purchase an option at all. Any further concentration on the short side becomes almost a totally naked position, and the premiums expended on a purchase are wasted and somewhat self-defeating.

This strategy is so heavily weighted toward naked puts, it is almost a bullish strategy. The maximum profit occurs with gold at $280 at expiration. At the price, the $300 put can be liquidated for $2,000, which creates a loss of $1,000. The remaining three options all expire, generating premium income of $5,200 [($2,000×2)+$1,200]. The net profit on the position is $4,200. If gold continues to decline, initially each dollar decline below $280 results in a reduction of the total profit by $100. At $260/ounce, the remaining profit is $2,200 as the naked $280 put is $20 in-the-money. Below $280, the remaining $2,200 profit has to protect both the naked $280 put and the naked $260 put. This $2,200 is the equivalent of $11 protection on the two naked options, and it results in a downside breakeven of $249. Below $249, each additional $1 decline in the price of gold results in a loss of $200 due to the two naked puts.

RATIO HORIZONTAL SPREADS

Ratio spreading need not be confined to options of the same maturity and of different striking prices. It is quite possible, and often profitable, to take advantage of calendar spreading when using the ratio approach to the commodity options market.

Example 7: A common type of ratio calendar spread is used because the speculator likes to purchase a longer-term option and has someone else pay for it. If your market timing and judgment are correct, this can sometimes be accomplished. What you would do is to purchase a deferred option of a given striking price, granting sufficient shorter-term options so that the premium received equals the premium paid.

In the earlier section on traditional calendar spreads, I said that, if a 1-month at-the-market option on a given commodity costs $1,000, then a 4-month option at-the-market costs $2,000, and a 9-month option at-the-market costs $3,000. So if you purchase the 9-month at-the-market option and sell three of the 1-month at-the-market options, the cash flows are equal. If you are correct, and the market remains unchanged for the first month, the three 1-month options expire, and your now 8-month option costs you nothing.

As attractive as this strategy appears, it is a very high-risk strategy for a number of reasons. The first and most obvious reason is that you have two totally naked options of short duration that are at-the-market and carry with them the normal risks associated with naked at-the-market options. Second, even a minor increase in the gold price generates substantial margin calls on the short-term options, with almost no relief supplied by the longer-term option due to its substantial time value. Fortunately there is a means whereby this objective may be achieved with a lower level of risk.

LATERAL RATIO SPREADS
DIAGONAL RATIO SPREADS

The lateral spread is normally used in one of two fashions: Either the nearby is the premium, or the deferred is the premium option.

Example: In our previous example, where the objective was to purchase a deferred option and use the sale of the nearby to either reduce or eliminate cost, you could do the following transaction.

Either purchase the 9-month at-the-market call option and sell several short-term out-of-the-money options, or purchase a longer-term out-of-the-money option for a smaller premium and then sell a limited number of at-market or slightly out-of-the-money nearby options. Either of these strategies brings about the desired result provided that there was no short-term rally in the underlying commodity.

As you can see, lateral spreads can be done with either puts or calls, and it doesn't matter whether the higher striking price is the nearby or the deferred. What does matter is the time/extrinsic value of the options involved in the lateral spread. Use caution when granting short-term options, especially when they are at-market because they have so little extrinsic value that they are very sensitive to even minor market fluctuations.

BUTTERFLY SPREADS

A butterfly spread is a type of vertical spread consisting of two long options and two short options. It is occasionally possible to institute this type of spread on a truly riskless basis. When this is possible, there is no necessity for a view of the market.

Example: Six-month gold is trading at $300/ounce, the $300 call is trading at $3,000, the $320 6-month call is trading at $2,000, and the $340 6-month call is trading at $1,200. This set of prices does not allow the construction of a riskless butterfly, but in some cases they allow this possibility.

There is always both a bid/offer spread, and commissions on these tend to limit the riskless possibilities. Rarely is a butterfly instituted on a totally riskless basis.

Example: To implement this strategy, purchase one $300 6-month call for $3,000, sell two $320 6-month calls for $2,000 each, and purchase one $340 6-month call for $1,200. As you can see, the total premium paid is $3,200 ($3,000+$1,200), and the total premium received is $4,000 ($2,000×2). Your net cash outlay is the difference of $200 ($4,200−$4,000). What you have done is created a $300/$320 bull spread and at the same time created a $340/$320 bear spread.

The maximum profit from this type of transaction occurs at the strike price of the short options comprising the butterfly spread, namely $320. If at expiration gold is at $320, all the options but the $300 are worthless and expire. The $300 is liquidated for a price of $2,000, being $20 in-the-money. This results in a loss of $1,000. The $340 expires, resulting in a loss of $1,200, and the two $320 expire, resulting in a profit of $4,000. This profit, coupled with the $2,200 ($1,000+$1,200), leaves a net profit of $1,800 ($4,000−$2,200).

As the market moves away from the maximum profit point, profits begin to decline. If the market moves lower, the profits decline because the value of the $300 option declines. If the market moves higher, the profits decline because, for each $1 increase in the price of gold above $320, you lose $200 on the short $320 options, and you make only $1 on the long $300 option. The breakeven points on this butterfly are $320 on the downside and $338 on the upside. Our maximum exposure in either direction is $200. If the market moves to $300 or below, all the options expire, and your loss is the amount by which your total purchases cost more than your total sales, or $200. If the market moves higher, above $340, both the $300 call and $340 appreciate $100 each while you lose a like amount on the two $320 short calls.

This strategy is implemented if the speculator believes that the greatest probability of market activity would lie between $320 and $338. Even if the speculator is wrong, the risk exposure is limited to $200 plus any related commissions.

This type of spread is referred to as a *butterfly* or V spread because you are long the outside and short in the middle. It is a strategy designed for a sedentary market. The butterfly can also be applied as an A spread, wherein you are long in the middle and short on the outsides. This strategy is designed to be profitable when the market makes a major move in either direction.

This particular strategy appears to be riskless, but it disregards the bid/offer spreads and commissions. In this instance, you purchase two $320 6-month calls at $2,000 each, sell one $300 6-month call for $3,000, and sell one 6-month $340 call for $1,200.

The net cash flow from this transaction is positive. You purchase for a total premium of $4,000 ($2,000×2), and you sell for a total premium of

$4,200 ($3,000+$1,200). The maximum profits occur at any price because the net premium of all the options purchased is less than the net premium received. Your maximum profit, however, is limited to this net cash difference because, below $300, they all expire, and, above $340, they all appreciate point for point.

LEGGING INTO AND OUT OF SPREADS

All the examples presented thus far either implied or said that both sides of the spread are implemented at exactly the same instant, which is often the case. This assumes that the investment strategy is one where the immediate implementation of a spread is the best way to maximize a profit. In many instances, an outright position is implemented immediately and is later transformed into a spread by a subsequent transaction, or a spread is liquidated by offsetting one leg at a time. This is referred to as *legging into*, or *legging out of*, a spread.

Example 8—Follow-Up on a Profitable Long Call: You are bullish on the price of gold, and the 6-month futures contract is currently selling for $300. You make the decision that the most attractive speculative purchase is the 6-month $320 call, which is selling for $2,000. Having made the purchase, you are rewarded with an almost immediate move to the $320 level. Most likely, your $320 option is now selling at about the $3,000 level.

Several alternatives are open to you. First, you can liquidate your option and thereby realize the $1,000 profit. Second, you can do nothing and hope for further market appreciation. Third, probably one of the more attractive approaches is to sell the $340 option short against the long $320 you currently own. With gold at $320 and about 6 months remaining on the option, you can reasonably assume the $340 call to be trading at about $2,000.

This transaction does several things. It converts an outright long position into a bull spread. In effect you leg into a bull spread. If the market goes back down, and gold at expiration is at $320 or below, both options expire, but you break even because your total purchase price equals your total sale price. If the market moves up to $340 at expiration, your $320 is worth $2,000 and may be liquidated for its original cost. The $340 option you granted expires worthless, adding an additional $2,000 to your total profit. If the market continues higher, you accrue no further profits because your long option ($320) and your short option ($340) both appreciate point for point and offset each other.

Example 9—Follow-Up on a Profitable Long Put: This strategy works equally well with puts if your market outlook is bearish. You believe that the market is likely to go lower, and you purchase the $300 6-month gold put for $3,000 with 6-month gold trading at $300/ounce. You elect to sell the $240 for $1,200. If the market remains unchanged at expiration, your $300 put is worth $2,000 and can be liquidated for a $1,000 loss ($3,000−$2,000). The $240, however, is worthless, and you keep the $1,200 premium offsetting your $1,000 loss on the $300 put for a small profit of $200.

If, at expiration, gold is at $260, your $300 put can be liquidated for $4,000 for a $1,000 profit ($4,000−$3,000). The $240 is still worthless, adding a $1,200 profit to the total position or $2,200. If gold is at $240 at expiration, your $300 put can be liquidated for $6,000 or a $3,000 profit, plus the premium of $1,200 from the expired $240 put. The total profit is $4,200. Below $240, your profit does not increase further because both the $300 and the $240 increase at the same rate, with the increasing profit on one offset by the increasing loss on the other.

This, too, is legging into a spread. In this case, the spread involved is a bear spread done with puts as opposed to a bull spread done with calls. These two examples show instances wherein the legging is designed to protect or enhance a profit. Sometimes the legging is done to minimize a potential loss.

Example 10—Salvaging a Bad Call Position: Six-month gold is trading at $300/ounce, and you believe that the market is headed higher. You purchase the $320 6-month call for a premium of $2,000. As luck would have it, some piece of negative news is released that changes your view on gold and causes an immediate $10 drop in the price of gold. Your $320 option is now trading at $1,500. You could admit your error, liquidate the option, and realize the $500 loss. Another alternative is to convert the long call option into a bear spread. The $300 call, with 6-month gold trading at $290, might be trading for $2,500. You could grant this call for $2,500 and leg into a bear spread. You would now be long the $320 at a cost of $2,000, and short the $300 for a $2,500 premium. If the market continues its decline, or at least remains at or below $300, you have a profit at expiration of $500 based on the difference in premiums.

If, at expiration, gold is at $305, your short $300 call has to be repurchased at $500. You make $2,000 on your short $300 call and lose $2,000 on your long $320 call, therefore breaking even. At $320 at expiration, you have to repurchase your short $300 call for a premium of $2,000, realizing a $500 profit but losing $2,000 on your long $320 call. Your point of maximum loss is $320, because at $320 or above, any further losses on the short $300 call are offset by concurrent profits on your long $320 call.

This strategy, though not outstanding, makes the best of a bad situation. You assume the potential to lose no more than the remaining value of your $320 call, but made it possible to realize a profit on a further market decline.

The "legging in" thus far discussed is somewhat strategic in nature. A position has been established, and, as a result of a market move, the creation of a spread is undertaken to either enhance a good position or to improve on a bad position. Spreading is a popular approach to speculating, but it is often difficult to accomplish at the price that appears in the newspaper or on the various types of quotation equipment. The reason is that the trades necessary are either taking place at different times or at different locations in the pit/post on the floor. To implement a position at specific prices, it is sometimes necessary to leg into a spread at the time it is implemented.

Example: You wish to implement a spread that calls for the purchase of the $300 6-month gold call at $3,000 and the sale of the 6-month $320 gold call for $2,000. You enter an order to do this transaction at a 10-point debit. This tells the floor broker not to pay more the $1,000 greater for the $300 call than he or she is able to receive for the $320 call. You may get a response like "unable at 10 points, market at 12 or 13 points." The broker is telling you that you may have to pay a $1,200 or $1,300 difference to implement the spread. You always have the privilege of attempting to leg into the spread yourself by entering separate buy and sell limits on the two options. If you are successful, you have your spread at your price. The risk is that one leg is filled and the other not, ultimately exposing you to a greater risk than the originally quoted 12 or 13 points.

Legging into and out of spreads is often advantageous with calendar spreads also. In some instances, a position is taken and the market does not move as rapidly as expected. This results in the time depreciation of the long option. In some cases, a shorter-term option may be granted to defray some of the costs of owning the longer-term option.

Example: For either fundamental or technical reasons, you purchase a 9-month, at-the-market call option on gold for $4,000 in anticipation at a gradual upward move of substantial proportions. At the end of the first month, the price of gold is virtually unchanged. You have the problem that each day you own the option it becomes worth less as a result of the passage of time. You originally paid $4,000, a month has gone by, and now your option is worth several hundred dollars less. If your view is that the market may remain unchanged for some time, the eventual move may not be enough to offset the losses resulting from the passage in time.

The 1-month option is trading for $1,000. If you create a calendar spread by selling the 1-month option, and the market remains virtually unchanged for the ensuing month, the short-term option expires and defrays your time losses on the longer-term option. This can be repeated as many times as necessary, until the market finally makes its projected move. If in fact the move never comes and you succeed in selling 1-month options eight times against the 9-month option, you still have a profit—having been wrong on the projected move. This is a possible approach but requires that you used both exchange and dealer options to be able to sell 1-month options eight times. You would have received eight $1,000 premiums from the expired 1-month options and have lost $4,000 on the 9-month option. A more conservative approach is to grant slightly out-of-the-money short-term options and continue to hold your longer-term at-the-market option.

CONCLUSIONS

Spreading is a fascinating area and offers a tremendous amount of flexibility to option investing. In fact, it accounts for a very large percentage of the total option volume, but it has some weaknesses. There is always the temptation to construct very complex spreads because the mathematics assure a profit. After all the costs are calculated, in many instances, there is almost no profit left. It is often better, having made a market judgment, to stick with a simple strategy such as outright purchases or sales of covered or uncovered options.

In passing, also remember that all brokers are not specialists in option trading, let alone in option spreading. If your intention is to pursue some of the more sophisticated option strategies, make sure that your broker is knowledgable in these areas.

Commissions and margin requirements vary dramatically from firm to firm. You generally get what you pay for with commissions. If you need a lot of advice and service, the brokers who charge the higher commissions generally provide the more sophisticated services. These commissions may, however, preclude your doing certain types of transactions because the commission makes the projected profit a projected loss. Margin can be very important because the dollars committed to any transaction form the basis for computing the overall rate of return. The more dollars committed, regardless of the ultimate profit, the lower the overall rate of return. No brokerage firm can charge less than the exchange minimum margin, but many charge a great deal more. Brokerage firms normally charge lower margins on well diversified accounts from well capitalized customers.

17

THE HEDGER—
OPTION BUYING
STRATEGIES

THE SPECULATOR VERSUS THE HEDGER

The strategies used by the speculator do not vary from those used by the hedger. The tactics are different. The differences are the manner and means of implementation. The preceding chapters have all assumed that the speculator is not in a business related to the specific underlying commodity. The following chapters are directed at the hedger. These chapters take the view that the hedger is a user in one form or another of the underlying commodity. Hedgers may also speculate, and all of the strategies they may choose to employ are not necessarily hedging in nature. "Hedger" is used to mean someone who has restricted choice in determining whether or not to purchase or sell the commodity. Now let's look at how the hedger uses exactly the same option markets.

Many commodity textbooks define hedging as the taking of an equal and opposite position in the futures market to whatever your position is in the physicals market. The textbooks go on to say that virtually all commercial entities hedge. This definition causes certain problems because people assume that this is how hedging is actually done. Nothing could be further from the truth. In actual practice, the commercial entities that could make use of the futures markets in various degrees and with various strategies don't. There are, in fact, many commercials who do not hedge at all.

Hedging is really the avoidance or minimization of risk through the transference of this risk to a second party. This is not always possible or even desirable in some cases. Potential profit is always a corollary of the acceptance of risk. Many commercials, as part of their normal business practices, take the risks involved with price changes in exchange for the potentially larger profit available. Traditionally, risk is accepted by the commercial until such time as the risk becomes disproportionately large in relation to the incremental profit that might be achieved. Most businesspeople are risk-takers. Hedging is not always a necessity, but in many cases it is desirable.

The traditional view of the use of options by the hedger is that the speculator is the option buyer and the commercial hedger is the option grantor. In the traditional context, the option buyer transfers the risk, and the option grantor accepts it. Option granting is not hedging, but option buying is. In reality, the commercial entity has use for both sides of the option market, as this market supplies a great deal more than pure hedging possibilities.

BUYING CALL OPTIONS AS A HEDGE

The purchase of a call option is an alternative to the purchase of a futures contract on the same underlying commodity. The purchase of an option need not be done as a direct alternative, but it may be used in conjunction with normal futures hedging practices.

It is probably easier to look at the uses of options after having selected a specific industry. Let's use the costume jewelry business as our case example. In this industry, which is highly competitive, there is a large lead time between when a new line of jewelry is created and when it is ultimately purchased by the final consumer. When the line is created, it is priced, and orders with fixed prices are taken by the manufacturer. One of the major risks is the price fluctuation in gold, which is used for either plating or alloying. This fluctuation is dangerous because the manufacturer does not know what quantity of jewelry will ultimately be sold.

How does the manufacturer hedge? Several approaches are possible. The manufacturers may look at the prior years' sales, and forecast sales for the same average amount. If last year the manufacturing process consumed 10,000 ounces of gold, the manufacturer would go long 100 gold futures contracts to fulfill this year's expected demand. As long as the usage forecast is correct, the hedge solves the problem. The jewelry that is ultimately delivered, using 10,000 ounces of gold, is a short physical position, and the 100 gold futures contracts is the hedge.

Two major problems can arise. The price of gold can go up dramatically, and sales can far exceed projections. Or gold prices can go down dramatically, and sales can drop well below the forecast level. In the first case, manufacturers lose money because they do not have sufficient gold to fabricate the jewelry at the price they used in cost calculations. In the second case, they have not used all the gold purchased via the futures, and the excess must either be held or liquidated at a much lower price, resulting in a loss.

An alternative to the purchase of futures is the purchase of call options, either alone or in conjunction with futures.

> *Example 1—Purchasing Call Options to Hedge a Forward Sale Commitment:* To expand on the prior discussion, let's look at the use of options in lieu of futures contracts to hedge the protected risks discussed. If, instead of purchasing 100 futures contracts, the manufacturer purchases 100 at-the-market call options, the results are different. The implication is not that options are in themselves better, but only that the situation changes. The only direct cost to the owner of a futures contract is the interest lost as a result of the carrying charges on the contract. The purchase of an option carries with it the cost of the premium. In evaluating the cost of the premium, subtract the cost of the carrying charges on a like futures position to determine how much the option really costs. If you were to purchase a 6-month futures contract on gold at \$330/ounce, while spot is selling at \$300, the carrying cost of the futures is \$30/ounce. If at the same time a 6-month at-the-market option cost \$35/ounce, then *the real cost of the option is only \$5/ounce (\$35—\$30)*.
>
> If you purchase the proper amount of futures contracts to hedge the anticipated need for gold, the options offer no advantage. The excess premium is actually a disadvantage of options over futures. However, if the purchased quantity turns out to be too large, there is almost no limitation to the loss if the market declines. If options are used as the hedge, the total loss can never exceed the premium, which in this case is \$35/ounce.
>
> In a declining market, the purchase of options as a hedge actually offers the possibility to improve the overall profit margin where futures do not. Assume that 100 options are purchased to cover an expected demand for 10,000 ounces of gold, that 100 ounces is the exact amount of metal ultimately consumed, but that, in the interim, the price of gold drops \$50/ounce.
>
> With gold \$50 lower, a futures hedger is obligated to take delivery of gold at a \$50 higher price than the current market. This is no disadvantage because the retail price is based on the higher cost of the metal anyway. Yet the option hedger lets the option expire and buys the gold in the open market at a \$50/ounce lower price. Also, the pricing is based on a \$50 higher cost; the hedger loses \$35 on the option but is able to buy gold \$50 lower and therefore increment the total profit by \$15/ounce.
>
> In this case the use of options is not a replacement for futures hedg-

ing, but, in conjunction with futures, it can be a more flexible overall approach. Perhaps you would hedge the portion of the commitment that you are sure of needing and use options to hedge the increment that you thought likely.

Buying out-of-the-money options is an alternative to instituting a long futures position as a hedge for a forward sale. Because options are more expensive than futures under identical circumstances, the use of an out-of-the-money option may better serve a hedging purpose. Mathematically, the probability of a price's going up is the same as of its going down. To protect against a price increase, you need only hedge with a call. The commercial is usually willing to accept some price fluctuation before purchasing inventory anyway. By purchasing an out-of-the-money option, the cost is reduced, and the risk that the commercial is unwilling to take is hedged. Commercials often delay the purchase of inventory because funds, once committed to inventory, don't earn interest, and they cost money to store and insure.

Example 2: A commercial bases pricing for the sale of costume jewelry on being able to buy gold at a price of no more than $350/ounce. Purchasing call options on gold at $350/ounce, when spot is selling at $330, is perfectly logical. If the market goes higher, the commercial is covered at the desired level. If the market goes lower, the expired option is far less costly than an at-the-market option, and the commercial earns interest on the uncommitted funds.

The commercial can also use options to replace inventory. Buying inventory in a declining market to enhance either future profits or current earnings is a good idea provided the magnitude of the decline is not too severe.

Example 3: In January 1980, it looked very attractive to purchase gold at $800/ounce on a decline from $850. It look substantially less attractive when gold later fell to $750, $700, and so on.

Instead of buying either physical gold or futures, which both have unlimited risk, the purchase of a call option serves the same purpose on a defined risk basis. Throughout the gold decline, you could have periodically purchased call options with the intention of exercising if the price stabilized. Or you could have let the options expire if the price continued to decline dramatically. You would have lost money with either approach, but your losses would have been much smaller with the options, and there are no margin calls along the way.

Example 4—Purchasing Calls to Avoid Margin Calls: If you use futures to hedge a forward short commitment, you have a long futures position. If the market moves lower, you receive margin calls on your futures position. Especially in times of high interest rates this can be very costly; either you cannot employ the capital elsewhere earning high interest, or the necessity to borrow at high interest rates can be disastrous. If a hedge is instituted using a long call option, regardless of market action thereafter, there are no margin calls and no drains on capital and the related interest costs. This is especially important in business environments, where the cost of funds to prime customers have run in excess of 22%.

Example 5—Buying Calls to Save Money: The option pricing chapter explained that option premiums go down as interest rates go up, and that premiums go up as interest rates go down. In periods of high interest rates, call options are less expensive and may be a more cost-effective means of hedging than the use of futures over any extended period of time. This becomes most important during rising interest rates because futures carrying charges go up while option premiums come down.

BUYING PUT OPTIONS AS A HEDGE

The normal view of hedging is that the hedger is long the commodity and therefore short the appropriate futures contract. The put option may be thought of as an alternative to the short hedge. In this case, the put serves the same purpose as the short futures, namely either a means of disposing of inventory or as a price protection mechanism for the same inventory.

One of the problems of being a manufacturer is that it is often necessary to purchase raw materials prior to consummating the ultimate sale of the finished goods. This is especially risky when the raw materials represent a high percentage of the final cost of the finished goods. For example, perhaps 25% to 50% of the final wholesale price of high-carat gold jewelry is represented by the gold content of the jewelry. In mid-summer the manufacturer is beginning to manufacture jewelry for delivery during Christmas. Much of the inventory purchase and fabrication is done before orders from the stores are received. Were this not done, there would be insufficient time to fabricate all the merchandise that could be sold were it available. Of course, having purchased the gold, the risk is a price decline before the final sale commitment can be made.

The manufacturer has traditionally sold futures contracts short to lock in the purchase price of the raw materials. That way, if prices decline before the goods can be sold, the manufacturer can sell the finished product at a lower price and recoup the difference from the profit on the short futures position. The manufacturer is not worried about a price increase because the realized loss on the futures position is more than offset by the higher retail price of the finished goods. These same risks are also inherent in the non-seasonal, stock item such as wedding bands that are carried in inventory and are subject to price fluctuation.

> *Example 6—Buying a Put to Hedge a Bid:* In some segments of the manufacturing and refining business, it is common to bid on contracts whether the bidding is for the construction rights to a segment of highway or for a lot of scrap gold or copper. Let's assume that you are submitting a sealed bid to purchase the jewelry out of a substantial estate for the scrap value of the gold. Very often it is several days before you are aware if you are the winner of the bid. Do you or do you not hedge? If you sell futures, the market goes up and you don't win—you lose money. If you don't sell futures, the market goes down and you do win—you lose money. This appears to be the old "caught between a rock and a hard place."

Consider the possibilities offered by put options. Instead of going short, you buy a like quantity of put options. If the market goes down and you win, your put affords the same protection as a futures contract, perhaps at a slightly higher cost. If you buy a put option, the market goes up and you win; the loss on the put is less than would have been incurred on a futures contract because a put rises more slowly due to the extrinsic value. (See the option pricing chapter.) You also have flexibility in that you have a broad selection of striking prices from which to choose. This allows you a greater degree of control of the magnitude of the actual hedge.

> *Example 7—Buying a Put to Lock in the Profit on an Inventory:* Perhaps you have acquired inventory during a substantial market de-cline, and you do not yet have commitments for the purchase of your finished product. If the market rises, you know you have a profit, but you cannot realize that profit until you fabricate and sell your inven-tory. You can go short futures to lock in that profit, but doing so would eliminate the possibility of any additional profit on the inventory were the market to continue to rise.
>
> Buying a put is a contingent short sale. If the price of the commodity remains the same or goes higher, you let the put expire and treat the premium as insurance on inventory, with this premium a cost of the flexibility of holding the inventory. If the market goes lower, you use the put to liquidate the inventory, in whole or in part, at the striking price of the long put option.

Example 8—Buying Puts During High Interest Rates and Tight Money: Traditional hedging always works, at least in the textbooks, but not always in practice. As a hedger, you go long inventory and short futures as a hedge. If the market goes higher, you hypothecate your inventory to a bank, and the bank lends you money to meet the margin calls on the short futures position. If the market goes lower, the margin released by the short futures position is paid to the bank to protect the bank from loss on the decreased value of the inventory.

This all works well until the bank figuratively or actually runs out of money. If all the hedgers in a given area use the same bank, the capital demands on the bank in a strongly rising market may be more than its capital can meet. In this case, the bank notifies the hedger that no further money can be forthcoming. The hedger has no alternative but to lift the hedge or find another bank. If the problem is widespread, no other local bank is any more cash rich. If the hedge is lifted due to an inability to meet margin calls on further market rises, the hedger is now exposed. Any major market decline can bankrupt the hedger. Had you, as a hedger, purchased a put, instead of going short futures, there would have been no margin calls on the way up. You would not have been forced to liquidate your short in the rising market, and you would not have been exposed to the subsequent market decline.

Another advantage to put hedging is that futures price increases often go hand-in-hand with rising interest rates. The additional loans made by a bank to meet margin calls often come during rising interest rates. These increased, and possibly unforecast, interest rate rises can cut into profit margin substantially.

This theoretical problem was very real to the soybean community in the early 1970s in the Mississippi valley, during a then record setting price rise. Even if the banking community has the ready capital, they may be unwilling to concentrate that large a percentage of their commodity financing in one or a group of associated commodities. Metals dealers experienced similar problems during the price rises in gold, silver, and copper during the late 1970s and early 1980s.

Example 9—Buying Puts for the Small Hedger: Hedging and the financing of hedges with banks make for an expensive operation from everyone's point of view. It is costly to set up the necessary bookkeeping and to arrange for the orderly transfer of funds from the bank to the broker and vice versa. In many cases when the quantity of the hedge is small, the costs do not justify hedging. The use of puts does not require the same complex bookkeeping and the constant transfer of funds. All the hedger need do is open a brokerage account and purchase the required number of put options.

Example 10—Buying Puts to Reduce Carrying Costs: If you are long the physical commodity and short the futures contract in a period of rising interest rates, the carrying charges between the various futures months widen to reflect this increased cost of carry. It is quite possible that an increase in interest rates will generate a margin call with no change in the price of the underlying futures contract.

Assume that the price of 6-month gold is $300/ounce and that the prime rate is 10%. If the prime rate increases to 20%, assuming the market reflected full carry, the 6-month contract appreciates by $15/ounce [($300 spot × 10%) ÷ 2]. This $15 increase generates a margin call with no increase in the value of the spot inventory. Depending on his or her cash position, the hedger either deposits capital, thereby foregoing the interest earned on that money, or goes to the bank to borrow money in a 20% prime rate market. Had the hedger instead owned a put, there would have been no call for additional funds, and any additional funds that were available could benefit from the higher interest rates through investment.

Example 11—Buying Puts to Protect a Long Hedge: When, as a hedger, you make a forward sale of a commodity and purchase futures as the hedge against that commitment, you may encounter market conditions that dictate the liquidation of the hedge. Perhaps with a forward sale of refined sugar and a dropping world price, the refiner is worried about a possible default at the time of delivery. As that refiner, you would like to lift your hedge because you feel that, if you have to buy "raws," you will be able to do so at a much lower cost but unfortunately the market is down the limit. In such a situation, you can purchase a put. This gives you two alternatives: If the market continues lower, the put hedges the long futures and may be used for its loan value to meet any margin calls. Or it may be immediately exercised to liquidate the long.

The major attraction of this strategy is that, as the refiner, you can continue to hold your long hedge. If the market once again rallies, you still have the futures as a hedge against the short forward commitment. Through the purchase of the put, you purchase an insurance policy on the possible default on the final delivery. This objective could have been met at the outset of the transaction by the purchase of a call, but at that time there was no indication of possible default.

PURCHASING STRADDLES AND COMBOS AS A HEDGE

When it comes to the purchase of raw materials, the objective is always to buy at the lowest price available. When it comes to the sale of finished goods—it goes without saying—the aim is to sell at the highest price available. Unfortunately it is not always possible or even probable that you can buy at the low and sell at the high. In inventory management, you attempt to slightly overbuy when you believe prices are lower than usual and be slightly understocked when prices are high. The purchase of straddles and combos offers this flexibility.

STRADDLE BUYING

Inventory management is perhaps the single most important short-term factor in overall profitability in many industries. Over the longer term, unions, technology, and senior management have a greater impact, but short-term cost of raw materials can spell the difference between profit and loss. The use of long straddles gives the purchasing manager a great deal of flexibility in the control of costs.

Inventory levels are normally set after reviewing the expected economic activity in the total economy, the industry, and the product. These tend to be influenced by interest rates, government policies, and the like. Unfortunately this is not an exact science. After a level of inventory has been set and established, the purchase of straddles may be advisable. Some industries, such as consumer electronics, are very sensitive to the economic levels of the economy. Part of the inventory may be gold used for the contacts in electronic circuit boards.

If the economy runs slower than anticipated due to higher-than-anticipated interest rates, the inventory is excessive in light of consumption. The cost of carrying the inventory is higher than anticipated due to higher-than-forecast interest rates. In this case the put becomes the important instrument because it allows for the disposal of a portion of the gold inventory at a predetermined price. This may be especially important with a commodity such as gold that tends to decline in periods of high interest rates. The ability to liquidate gold at a fixed price may allow the company to remain competitive during declining prices by allowing new purchases to take place at competitive levels. In a period of rising economic activity and low interest rates, the demand for consumer electronics may be higher than forecast, and the call may be exercised to supply the needed additional gold at a predetermined price. This, too, may allow the company to be more than competitive by being able to buy raw materials at less than the current market price.

Even the selection of the striking price of the straddle can be adjusted to reflect the current thinking of management without the necessity of altering the physical inventory involved.

The price of a straddle does not vary dramatically if it is struck slightly above or slightly below the current market price of the commodity. The amount by which one side is in-the-money is offset by the amount by which the other side is out-of-the-money. If management's view is that the market is more likely to decline than to advance, then the purchase of a straddle with a striking price above the current market is warranted. If the concerns are for price increase and for the purchase of materials at a better price, then a straddle struck below the current market price might be warranted. This approach can also be used when the current inventory position is thought to be too large or too small in light of projections. If the position is too large, the purchase of a straddle with the put side in-the-money allows for easy liquidation if market declines necessitate such action. If the inventory position is too small in light of market projections, the purchase of a straddle with the call side deep in-the-money might be warranted.

Straddle prices do not vary substantially for minor moves away from the at-the-market price, but, in terms of the cost of time value, a straddle that is far from at-the-market varies substantially. If the straddle is struck well above the current market, the put portion may be trading at intrinsic value and cost nothing in terms of time value. If the straddle is struck well below the market, the call side may be so far in-the-money that the call costs nothing in terms of time value. This does not mean that the straddle is cheap, but only that you are not paying much for time value.

This becomes an inexpensive inventory control tool. The deep in-the-money side is almost a 1-to-1 inventory hedge at little cost. If inventory is too large and a straddle is purchased with the put in-the-money by a substantial amount, the put fluctuates point for point with the value of the inventory on the downside. If the market moves higher, the value of the put does not decrease as rapidly as the value of the inventory increases because, as the put approaches at-the-market, it gains in extrinsic value.

If the inventory is viewed as too small, and a straddle is purchased with the call side deep in-the-money, this too acts as a 1-to-1 hedge if prices move higher due to the lack of extrinsic value on the call. If, however, the market moves lower, the call does not decline as rapidly because it gains in extrinsic value as it approaches at-the-market.

COMBO BUYING

As flexible as the straddle is as a management tool, the combo option offers even greater flexibility due to the ability to select striking prices that exactly reflect a given view at a given time. As you are aware, a *combo* is a straddle that is not a straddle, because either the striking prices or the maturities are not the same. The combo is not an entity in its own right any more than a straddle is. You may be able to purchase the straddle or combo on one order ticket for a total price, but you are, in fact, purchasing two options that may be liquidated or exercised separately.

The combo option is very well suited to the commercial entity on account of the risk-taking nature of any business venture. It is not at all uncommon to purchase raw materials without having a customer yet interested or commited to purchasing the finished product. Nor is it uncommon to agree to make delivery of finished goods at a time when the raw materials are yet to be purchased. These kinds of risk are common in business. The true exposure of this type of approach is to dramatic changes in market price that had no basis for being forecast. Against this type of exposure businesspersons would like insurance. Hence the perfect place for the combo.

> *Example 12:* A gold fabricator buys refined gold and extrudes gold wire used by a jewelry firm to fabricate chain for necklaces and bracelets. It is common practice to buy gold and to fabricate wire without orders in hand. It is equally common practice to commit to deliver the finished product without having yet purchased the gold. The gross profit margin in the business is sufficient to cover the normal fluctuation in the price of gold. However, if the market either drops or rises dramatically, the entire potential profit can be wiped out because the market move has eliminated the gross profit margin. The risk taker would not be inclined to purchase a straddle, because the straddle gives immediate protection of the inventory and any future needs. This is over-insurance. The fabricator has already included minor fluctuations in pricing, and the purchase of the unwarranted straddle would only reduce the profitability in most cases.
>
> The fabricator needs cost-effective protection against the unusual major move. If 6-month gold is trading at $300/ounce, fabricators do not care about moves from $280 to $320; these are covered in pricing. They are worried about moves above or below those prices. Below $280, they may be forced to sell finished goods at a price that results in a loss. Above $320, they may be forced to buy raw materials that, when finished and delivered, offer no profit. This is the ideal situation for the purchase of a combo comprised of a $280 put and a $320 call. With both legs of the combo out-of-the-money, the option is inexpensive and worthwhile for the protection afforded.
>
> A fabricator has bought inventory insurance with $20 deductible, in much the same fashion that individuals buy auto insurance with $100 or $500 deductible. It is too expensive in most instances to insure the risks we can afford to take.

CONCLUSIONS

Purchasing options is considered hedging if it is offsetting another risk. The transaction, as with futures, tends to be equal and opposite to the position in the physicals market. The one weakness to the purchase of options is that it is capital-intensive. It costs money to buy options whereas the use of futures is a commitment of capital, but not necessarily a cost.

Only a relatively small percentage of all options purchased are ever exercised profitably, even when held to maturity. This leads commercials to believe that the purchase of options is a money-losing proposition. This view is not correct because, if the option is purchased for the proper purpose, it is designed to be unprofitable. When purchased properly by commercial entities, most options are insurance policies, and these too are costs on which one hopes never to collect.

The view that most option buyers lose money tends to lead commercial entities to the option-granting side of the market. The only complete hedge is buying options, not granting them. That is not to say that option granting is incorrect for the commercial, but that it is not a form of hedging. Option buying reduces the risk of offsetting physical positions. Option granting increases risk.

18

THE HEDGER—
PUT AND CALL GRANTING

Both the speculator and the hedger can grant options in the dealer markets, on domestic exchanges, or on foreign exchanges. Depending on the market used for granting, the definitions of "covered" and "uncovered" vary substantially.

1. In the *dealer market*, if the grantor deposits an acceptable warehouse receipt for the underlying commodity, the granting of a call option is considered covered, the premium is released immediately, and there is no potential for margin calls. If a put is granted, and the full value of the underlying commodity is deposited in T-bills, the premium is released, and there is no potential for margin calls. In some cases, this makes the dealer market the most attractive medium in which to grant options.

2. On *domestic exchanges*, the granting of options is not quite as lucrative. The problem with exchange-traded options is in the definitions of what is covered and uncovered. If commercials have the physical, and they grant a call option, they view themselves as covered. But the exchange considers the position covered only if the cover is a long futures contract on the same exchange. If commercials are short the physicals and have sold a put option, they consider themselves covered. The exchange, however, considers the position covered only if there is an offsetting position on the same exchange.

3. Each of the *non-U.S. exchanges* has its own rules relating to what is covered and when the premium is released. If option granting is to be pursued on foreign exchanges, review the chapter on foreign options before instituting any transaction.

This chapter deals with option granting primarily on U.S. exchanges and, where appropriate, in the U.S. dealer markets. Each medium has its advantages and disadvantages.

EXCHANGE-COVERED CALL GRANTING

Under U.S. exchange rules, a call option is *covered* when a long futures contract of the same expiration is in the same account that has granted the call option. In this instance, the margin requirement is the appropriate margin on the underlying futures contract plus the premium value of the granted option. Both of these amounts may initially be deposited in the form of government securities (usually T-bills). Variation margin is charged and collected as the price of the futures contract varies, and variable original margin is charged and collected on the short option. The variation margin on the futures contract is paid and received in cash, while the variable original margin on the short option may be deposited in T-bills.

To look at the physical position that commercials must have to logically be covered call grantors, let's work back from the end result. To grant a covered call, you must be long the underlying futures contract. To logically be long the underlying futures contract, you should be short the physicals. A short call option exposes the grantor to the potential of exercise and, with it, the loss on the long futures contract. Depending on the strike price of the short option in relation to the current price of the futures contract, it is possible to determine the probability of exercise. This is another way of saying: What is the delta of the total position? (See chapter on option pricing.)

If the call option granted is at-market, the probability of exercise, or the delta, is approximately .5. This means that, over an extended period of time, 50% of all options granted at market are exercised. As the striking price of the granted option goes further out-of-the-money, the probability of exercise is lower. This position—as currently constructed, short physicals, long futures, short at-the-market call—is equivalent to short physical and long one-half of a futures contract. Therefore a true 1-to-1 hedge requires that the futures position be twice the size of the short physical position and that two covered call options be granted.

To view the position differently, the granting of a call option against a short physicals/long futures results in a reduction of the effectiveness of the futures hedge. This reduction must be compensated for by an increase in the number of futures contracts necessary to create probabilistically the same degree of hedge. You cannot create the same hedge, only the probability of the same hedge. The reason is that both the short physicals and the long futures are bilateral contracts that move point for point and offset each other. The short options, on the other hand, are unilateral contracts that move at different rates.

Let's look at the possible results of the aforementioned strategy under a variety of market situations. Again, gold serves as the example because it can be traded as a physical, a forward, a dealer option, or an exchange-traded option. (Besides, 100-ounce units make the mathematics easier!)

> **Example:** Six-month gold is trading at $300/ounce, the prime rate is 10%, and the 6-month at-the-market 100-ounce call options are trading at $3,000 each. Your short physical position is perfectly covered if gold can be purchased 6 months hence at $300/ounce. Any market environment allows only for prices to go down, remain unchanged, or go up. Each of these possibilities offers different risks and rewards.

> If the market goes lower, all three of the positions are affected to various degrees. The calls expire, and you keep the two premiums for a total of $6,000 ($3,000×2). On the two long futures contracts, you not only have the loss from market depreciation, but you also have the loss of the carrying charges on the two contracts. Lastly, your short physical position has moved in your favor by the amount of the decline plus the carrying charges on the short.

> How low can the market go before you are worse off than if you had not become involved in options at all? The answer is not that difficult. It only appears so because the total position appears more complicated than it is in reality. In a declining market, the short physicals and one long futures are true offsets, and they cancel out each other in terms of profit and loss. So the only true position is long one futures and short two at-the-market call options.

> You are effectively long one futures contract at $300/ounce and short two $300 strike price call options for a total premium of $6,000. Because the two options expire at any price below $300/ounce, you can view the $6,000 premium as protection for the one long futures contract. This $6,000 is the equivalent of $60/ounce protection on the one long futures, and it therefore gives us a downside breakeven of $240/ounce. Below $240/ounce, you lose $100 for each additional $1 decline in the price of gold.

> If gold remains unchanged at the $300 level, the two options also expire. At expiration, it is assumed that the futures contracts are liquidated at breakeven; therefore, you will keep the $6,000 premium as a profit that you would not have had, if you had not gotten involved in the options.

> Above $300/ounce, ultimately both of the options are exercised. The problem here is that one of the long futures contracts is protecting your

FIGURE 18–1. Short Physical/Long Futures/Short Calls

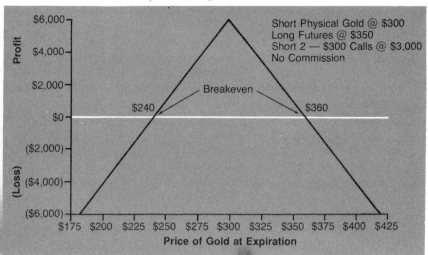

FIGURE 18–1. Short Physical/Long Futures/Short Calls

short physicals position, and you no longer have that protection if the options are exercised. The protection you have above $300/ounce is the $6,000 premium you keep, because the delivery of the futures contracts fulfills your requirement and you keep the premium. The $6,000 is the protection of your short physical position, which is the equivalent of $60/ounce upside protection. You could afford to purchase physical gold as high as $360/ounce, and the delivery at $300/ounce on your short physical is offset by the $6,000 premium. Above $360/ounce, each additional $1 increase in the price of gold results in a real loss of $100 on the total position.

There are additional items to consider in this example—commissions, the additional capital committed to buy two futures contract instead of one, and the additional capital committed for the option premiums. These items vary from commercial entity to commercial entity, depending on the commissions normally paid and the internal rate of return generated on invested capital.

The maximum profit is achieved at the strike price of the short option, which in this case is $300/ounce. To institute this transaction, you deposit an assumed margin of $2,000 for each futures contract and $3,000 for each short option. You withdraw, however, a cash premium of $6,000. So, neglecting commissions, your real deposit is only $4,000. On this $4,000, you earn a premium of $6,000 for 6 months, or 150% for the six months involved. Yet you accept a risk that you would not otherwise have, if you just hedged with futures. The risk is a price decline below $240 or a price increase above $360. The added return is there only because there is an added risk. This, however, may be a risk you are willing to assume in light of the potential rate of return involved.

This position—short physicals/long two futures/short two options—is a complex position. In reality it is identical to short physicals, and short two uncovered at-the-market put options. As mentioned earlier in the book, there is the concept of identity. That is, two apparently different positions are economically identical in reality. Let's look at this identity.

Example: You are short the equivalent on one contract of the physicals, and, instead of going long two futures and short two call options, you sell two uncovered at-the-market puts. If the puts are also trading for $3,000 each, you have an identity. If the market moves lower, the options are ultimately exercised, and you are called upon to take delivery of two futures contracts at $300/ounce, the striking price of the short puts. You are contingently long two futures contracts at $300/ounce. One of the futures contracts on which you take delivery may be thought of as an offset to the short physicals position that you hold. The other futures contract is protected by the premiums ($6,000) that you receive as a result of exercise. Therefore the $6,000 protects this one futures contract, which results in a downside breakeven of $240/ounce. Below this price, you exhaust the protection afforded by the premium and begin to realize a real $100 loss for each additional $1 decline in the price of gold below $240.

If the market remains unchanged, it makes no difference what strategy you employ—either a put or a call expires—not to mention the lack of necessity for hedging in the first place. At exactly $300/ounce, the option expires, and you have neither a loss nor a gain on your physical position; therefore, you have just the $6,000 premium as a profit on your investment.

Above $300/ounce, your options expire, but you begin to realize a loss on your unhedged physical position. The protection for this unhedged position is the $6,000 premium. The $6,000 gives you an upside breakeven of $360/ounce, above which you lose $100 for each additional $1 advance in the price of gold.

As you can see, the two positions are almost economically identical. They are "almost" identical because, if the market remains unchanged or goes higher, you do not have to pay two commissions on the futures contract used in the earlier portion of the identity.

According to the textbook approach, futures hedging is normally a passive strategy; that is, the basic intent is to transfer risk, and not attempt to increment profits. In reality, great care is normally taken as to the timing and the price at which the hedge is instituted. Option granting is also an attempt to transfer risk, but only a portion of the risk can be transferred. The total risk transference is the premium received by the grantor.

Once a future hedge has been established, it is usually not lifted until the offsetting side is also liquidated; therefore, once established, it becomes passive. Option granting from the commercial's point of view should not be a passive strategy. Option granting should be dynamically managed, once the position has been granted. For example, suppose the strategy used is the first wherein there were two futures contracts long and two calls short. In such a case, as the price rises and the probability of exercise improves, either the number of futures contracts should have been increased or the number of short options reduced. (The tactics of dynamic option management are discussed later in the chapter.)

USING DIFFERENT STRIKING PRICES

Our prior examples used at-the-market options and a ratio of 2-to-1 because the probability of the exercise of an at-the-market option is generally 50%. The further out-of-the-money the strike price of the option granted, the lower the probability of ultimate exercise.

Example: A 6-month $320 call option is trading when 6-month gold is trading at $300. If the market is relatively quiet, this particular option might have a delta of .25, which means the probability of ultimate exercise is 25%. If you elect to implement the aforementioned strategies with this option, you have to grant four of the $320 to achieve the same probabilistic result.

These positions are probabilistically identical, not necessarily identical in terms of potential profit or risk. The probability of the exercise of two options with a delta of .5 is identical to the probability of exercise of four options with a delta of .25. The expected profit on both transactions, in an efficient market, is also identical. That is, the potential profit times the probability of the profit's occuring is identical if the options are efficiently priced.

In this assumed position, you are short the equivalent of one contract of futures due to your physical position. You are long two contracts of futures and short four of the $320 6-month call options, because the probability of exercise is .25. Mathematically, .25 times four options has the probability over an extended period of time of resulting in one exercise. Therefore one futures contract protects the short physical, and the second futures contract protects the four short out-of-the-money calls.

The $320 6-month call option is trading at $2,000. The same three possibilities of market action exist. If the market remains unchanged, all the options expire, the futures contract is liquidated unchanged, and the physical contract is fulfilled through an open market purchase at the projected normal profit.

If the market goes lower, the option expires, and one futures contract is offset, in the loss sense, by the profits on the short physical. The second futures contract is protected by the premium received from the premiums on the expired options. This $8,000 ($2,000×4) gives us a downside breakeven of $220. Below $220, each additional $1 decline results in a $100 loss on the unhedged futures contract.

At exactly $320, the options expire. The losses on the physical contract are offset by the profits on one of the futures. The other futures contract has shown a profit of $2,000 [($320−$300)×100]. Therefore at $320, the total profit is $2,000 from the futures and $8,000 from the expired options. Above $320, the physical is hedged by one futures contract. The second futures contract hedges one of the short options. The three remaining options are naked. The $10,000 achieved at $320 serves as protection for the three short uncovered options. This is the equivalent of $3,333 per option, or $33.33/ounce. You have therefore an upside breakeven of $353.33 ($320+$33.33). Above this price, each additional $1 appreciation in the price of gold results in a $300 loss on the entire position.

This position is also an identity, and it can be duplicated by the sale of four $280 6-month put options provided that the $280 put is also trading for $2,000. The commercial is also not limited to changing the striking prices granted but has the flexibility of different markets in certain commodities. For comparison sake, look at the strategies available on the same commodity in the dealer markets.

DEALER-OPTION-COVERED CALL GRANTING

Commercials are commonly short the physical in the form of a forward delivery obligation. For example, when jewelry fabricators contract to deliver a given quantity of high-carat gold jewelry, they usually have not actually purchased the gold from which the jewelry is to be fabricated. Another example is a leverage contract dealer who has sold forward gold to one of its customers. Normally, in such instances, the commerical purchases an offsetting forward contract from a bullion dealer to hedge this short obligation.

If the commerical happens to purchase the forward contract from a bullion dealer who also deals in options, the forward contract purchased can also serve as a hedge against a short call option. The same problem exists with dealer options as exists with exchange-traded options: The granting of an at-the-market option to the dealer has a .5 probability of exercise, and it therefore reduces the effective hedge by one-half.

The same solution exists in this instance as on exchanges. The commercial has to purchase a second forward contract and grant a second at-the-market option. Two at-the-market options have a probability that, on average over an extended number of transactions, only one is exercised. Therefore, one of the forward contracts serves as a hedge for the short physical commitment, and the second as a hedge for the two short at-the-market options.

Option granting in the dealer market is truly a commercial activity. The margins involved are not set by an exchange, but they are individually negotiated between the commercial and the dealer. No original margin may be required of commercial counterparts, depending on their creditworthiness, or substantial margin may be required. It is common to require a margin of perhaps 15% of the value of the metal involved as initial margin, and perhaps 110% of the premium, but this margin can be deposited in the form of T-bills. The advantage is that the margin serves a double purpose. First, it finances the forward that is serving as a hedge for the short forward held by the commercial. Second, it serves as the basis for granting a covered option. The premium on the covered option is released to the grantor immediately.

> *Example:* Six-month gold is trading at $300/ounce, and 6-month dealer call options are trading at $3,000. If you purchase two forward contracts, you might have to deposit 15% of the current value of the gold. If spot gold is trading at $280, then 15% of 200 ounces is $56,000×.15 or $8,400. You then grant the options for a total premium of $6,000 ($3,000×2) and withdraw the premium. Your total commitment is $8,400−$6,000 or $2,400, which we deposit in T-bills. This is a substantially smaller margin than with exchange-traded options, and it is possible only because of the commercial relationship between the two parties involved.

The dealer most likely marks the total position to the market, only to limit exposure. It is impossible to be more specific, because the margin requirements are a function of the entities involved.

The breakeven prices are identical to the exchange example because the forwards are assumed to be done at the same price as futures, and the options are assumed to be granted for the same premiums. This arrangement was made for simplicity, and it is not necessarily indicative of a relationship that always exists. There is also a difference between the prices offered and those bid by different dealers.

The exchange environment gives rise to prices that are directly proportionate to the supply and demand at the time of the transaction. They are not necessarily "fair" prices in the theoretical sense. They are neither good nor bad, just different. The market that is used to grant the option should be the market that offers the best economics.

The dealer market also offers out-of-the-money options, as well as put options. So the alternative identity transactions are equally viable in the dealer markets. Both dealer and exchange options offer fungibility. In other words, there is generally a two-way market, although the dealers are not obligated to maintain one. This allows for a dynamic approach to option portfolio management.

Foreign option granting may offer the same or possibly better rates of return in the granting of commodity options, but the option itself is not fungible. This characteristic carries with it the disadvantage that, once an option has been granted, it cannot be liquidated at the pleasure of the grantor. The option either expires or is exercised by the purchaser. Grantors may adjust their risk and breakeven price only by altering the futures or forward contracts that are held as a hedge against the short options.

EXCHANGE-COVERED PUT GRANTING

The U.S. exchanges view a covered put option as one wherein the same account that has granted a put is also short a futures contract of a like expiration on the same exchange. In that instance, the margin requirement for the position is the normal futures margin on the short futures contract plus the premium of the short option. Both of these margin requirements may initially be met on most exchanges by the deposit of T-bills. Normal variation margin is charged on the short futures contract, which must be met in cash; and a variable original margin is charged on the option, which may be met in T-bills.

To be the grantor of a covered put, the commercial must be short the underlying futures contract. To be short the underlying futures contract, the commercial logically has an offsetting long in the physicals market.

The granting of the covered put reduces the effectiveness of the short futures position as a hedge for the long physical position. Depending on the striking price of the put, the probability of exercise can be determined. Options that are at-the-market have a probability of exercise of approximately 50%. Over an extended number of transactions, probabilities indicate that the put option is exercised about 50% of the time. This means that the effectiveness of the hedge has also been reduced by 50%.

To maintain the mathematical equivalent of a full hedge, after the granting of an at-the-market covered put, a second short futures contract has to be instituted and a second at-the-market put granted. The further out-of-the-money the strike price of the covered put, the lower the likelihood of exercise, and the greater the effectiveness of a 1-to-1 hedge. Conversely, the further the covered put is in-the-money, the greater the likelihood of exercise, and the greater the number of futures/put positions necessary to maintain an effective hedge. Following is the approach that we elect to follow.

Example: You are long the equivalent of one contract of physicals, short two exchange futures contracts, and short two at-the-market puts of the same duration as the futures. The physical is gold. Six-month gold is trading at $300/ounce, and the 6-month at-the-market puts are trading at $3,000 each. What are your prospects for various changes in market price?

If, at expiration, gold is exactly $300/ounce, both options expire and the futures contracts are liquidated at neither profit nor loss. The only economic impact is that you keep the $6,000 ($3,000×2) received for having granted the options.

If, at expiration, gold is above $300/ounce, the options also expire, and you keep the $6,000 premium. But the futures contracts are moving against you. One of the contracts is no problem since it is a hedge against our long physical position; therefore, losses on the futures are offset by profits on the physical. The second futures contract is offset by nothing. The $6,000 premium serves as your protection on this second futures contract. This $6,000 which is the equivalent of $60/ounce on the one contract, protects you up to a price of $360/ounce. At $360, you have a $6,000 loss on the futures, but you also have the premium as an offset. Above $360, each additional $1 increase in the price of gold results in a real loss of $100 on the total position.

If, at expiration, gold is below $300/ounce, both put options are exercised, resulting in the delivery of the two short futures contracts out of your account. This removes the hedge you had against your long physical gold position. Your only protection is again the $6,000 premium. This premium now serves as protection for your physical position. The $6,000 on the 100-ounce physical position is $60/ounce, and it gives you a downside breakeven of $240. Below this price, each additional $1 decline in the price of gold results in a $100 loss.

While the position is outstanding, you are exposed to margin calls, as with any futures position. If the market moves lower, you receive cash variation margin on the futures and have to deposit additional T-bills on the short options. In a declining market, the cash flow from the futures almost always exceeds the increased margin on the short options. The excess by which the cash variation on the futures exceeds the increased original variation on the short puts can be used to meet any additional margin requirements charged by a bank if the physical gold is also financed. Eventually, as the put options become deep in-the-money, the additional margin required on the options increase at the same rate, because positive variation margin is being generated by the short futures and no free capital is available for bank financing.

As the market rises, cash variation margin is required on the short futures contracts, and this variation increases at a rate greater than the reduction of the original margin requirements on the short options. The physical gold, however, appreciates, and it should be a source of additional capital through bank loan if necessary.

The examples involving the commercial have omitted commissions not only for the sake of clarity, but also because commercial commissions vary dramatically depending on the broker involved. In some cases, they vary also according to whether the commercial is also an exchange member and executing its own orders. Commissions can be significant and should be considered in any actual calculations of breakeven and rate of return.

The $6,000 premium and the interest generated by the T-bills deposited as margin are positive factors in this form of transaction. It is difficult, if not impossible, to compute a rate of return without knowing the final outcome of the transaction. However, the actual margin deposited at the outset is the margin on two futures contracts (assume $2,000 each), plus the premium on the two options of $3,000 each. The option premium is, however, at the same time withdrawn in cash. The actual deposit is only on the futures, or $4,000. If you can earn 15% interest ($300) on the T-bills for six months, and receive a $6,000 premium, your potential profit is $6,300. On a $4,000 investment, this is 157.5% for six months.

This potential return exists only because there is also a risk. Had you just hedged with futures, there is no risk. The example entails risk above $360 and below $240. That is why there is the potential for return.

USING DIFFERENT STRIKING PRICES

The prior example uses at-the-market options in a ratio of 2-to-1 because the probability of exercise is 50%, and this figure is as close as you can come to a neutral hedge. By using different striking prices and different neutral ratios, you can alter the rate of return in proportion to the risk inherent in the strategy.

Had you picked out-of-the-money options wherein the probability of exercise is only 25%, you could have used a 4-to-1 ratio and achieved a higher profit potential. In that case you would have gone short four futures contracts and granted four out-of-the-money covered puts.

Example: You are long the quantity equivalent of one 6-month futures contract in your physical position, and you go short four 6-month futures contracts at $300/ounce. It is reasonable to assume that a $280 put option on the 6-month futures might be trading for about $2,000. You therefore grant four 6-month $280 puts at $2,000 each for a total premium of $8,000.

Your actual margin deposit is $8,000 to cover four futures contracts at an assumed original margin of $2,000 each. Even though you must deposit the premium, you can do so in the form of T-bills and remove the cash equivalent immediately.

If, at expiration, the market is at exactly $300, the options expire, and the futures contracts can be liquidated at neither a profit nor loss. Therefore, you make $8,000 in premiums plus the interest on the T-bills deposited for the futures contracts. That is $8,000 in premiums plus $600 [($8,000×15%)÷2], or $8,600 on $8,000 committed for six months.

If, at expiration, the market is at $280, the options still expire, because they are then at-the-market. You keep the premium and also have an $8,000 profit on the short futures position [($300−$280)×400 ounces], but you have a loss of $2,000 on your physical position. Your total profit is the interest ($600), plus the futures profit ($8,000), minus the physicals loss ($2,000), plus the premium ($8,000), for a total profit of $14,600.

Below $280, the put options are exercised, and your short futures are taken away. Below $280, the $14,600 serves as protection for your 100-ounce physical position. This is substantial protection since gold has to decline an additional $146/ounce to reach a downside breakeven. Below $134/ounce, you lose $100 for each additional $1 decline in the price of gold.

Your real exposure is to a market advance. Above $300, you are losing money on your short futures. You have a real net short position of three contracts, since one is offset by your physical position. This net short position is protected only by the premiums received. The $8,000 premium protects three short futures contracts. This is the equivalent of $26.67/ounce ($8,000÷300 ounces). Your upside breakeven is only $326.67. Above this price, each additional $1 increase in the price of gold exposes you to a $300 loss.

Although both of these strategies have the same probability of exercise and affords a mathematically neutral hedge, their potential risks and profits are entirely different. The second strategy is biased toward a downtrending market, and the commercial who employs this strategy is superimposing a negative market view on a normally neutral hedging approach.

This strategy offers very little exposure to margin calls in a declining market, as the variation margin released by the short futures positions accrues at a much faster rate than additional margin is required on the short options. However, in a rising market the net short position of the futures contracts generates margin calls very rapidly, and the reduction in margin required on the short options is minimal in comparison.

DEALER OPTION
COVERED PUT GRANTING

The definition of a covered put is clear and concise when it comes to exchange-traded put options, because the only thing that the exchange considers good cover is an offsetting futures contract. The same is not true in the dealer market. The dealer may consider a properly margined short forward or total cash/T-bills both as good cover.

The Short Forward Contract

Commercial entities are logically short a forward (that is, have the obligation to deliver) to the dealer, if they have an offsetting long position in the physicals market. This long physical might very well be future mine production in the case of a commodity such as gold or silver. This is the traditional hedge—long the physical, short the forward. A short forward is also the offsetting side for granting a covered put. As with futures, if the put granted is struck at the market, the probability of exercise is approximately 50%. To incorporate covered put granting into its hedging strategy, the commercial goes long the equivalent of 100 ounces of gold, shorts forwards equal to 200 ounces of gold, and grants two 100-ounce at-the-market put options.

> *Example:* Gold for delivery six months hence is trading at $300/ounce. The commercial is short two forward contracts that call for the delivery of 100 ounces of gold, each at $300/ounce. The commercial is also the grantor of two put options struck at $300/ounce for $3,000 each.
>
> If, at expiration, gold is at exactly $300/ounce, both put options expire, and the grantor retains the $6,000 ($3,000×2). The long physical gold position can be either sold in the open market or delivered against one of the short forwards. Regardless of how the commercial disposes of the gold, it does not affect the economic outcome because the forwards are at-the-market also. The commercial has, in fact, en-

hanced the sale of its gold by the receipt of the $6,000 option premium.

If, at expiration, gold is above $300/ounce, the two put options expire because they are out-of-the-money and worthless. The 100-ounce physical position is delivered against one of the short forward contracts, leaving the second forward uncovered. The commercial has sold the dealer a second 100 ounces of gold at $300/ounce as a result of the second forward contract. The $6,000 premium received from the sale of the options serves as the protection for the second forward contract. This $6,000 is the equivalent of $60/ounce protection for the second forward. The commercial's breakeven price is $60 above the price of the forward, or $360/ounce. For each $1 increase in the price of gold above $360/ounce, the commercial sustains a real $100 loss on the total position.

If, at expiration, gold is below $300/ounce, the put options are exercised. The 200 ounces of gold received as a result of the exercise of the puts are used to offset the short forward position. This delivery against the forward eliminates the economic impact of the short forward. What is left is a 100-ounce physical gold position and a $6,000 premium received from the puts. This $6,000 serves as protection for the 100-ounce long physical gold position. This $6,000 is the equivalent of $60/ounce on the 100 ounces and gives you a downside breakeven of $240/ounce. Below $240/ounce, the commercial loses $100 for each additional $1 decline in the price of gold.

As with the futures, it is also possible to grant put options of a different striking price than the forward price of the underlying commodity. Another example is the granting of out-of-the-money puts with striking prices of $280/ounce. These out-of-the-money puts might be trading for $2,000 each if 6-month gold is trading at $300/ounce. Let's assume that the probability of exercise for these options is 25%, and as a result you use a hedge ratio of 4-to-1. We are long 100 ounces of physical gold, short four forward contracts at $300/ounce, and short four $300 strike price covered puts.

If, at expiration, gold is at $300/ounce, there is no economic impact to any of the positions except that the puts expire and you keep the $8,000 ($2,000×4) premium. Above $300/ounce, the puts also expire, and one of your short forwards is covered by the physical gold. The remaining three forwards are now uncovered and protected only by the $8,000 premium. This $8,000 is the equivalent of $26.67/ounce ($8,000÷300) protection. Above $326.67/ounce, each additional $1 increase in the price of gold results in a $300 loss.

If, at expiration, gold is below $300/ounce, the puts are exercised and offset the short forward positions. The $8,000 premium serves as protection for the remaining 100-ounce physical position. This is the equivalent of $80/ounce and gives a downside breakeven of $220/ounce.

As you can see, this approach, though mathematically neutral, is superimposing a bearish investment judgment on the overall hedging strategy. There is nothing wrong with this approach as long as the effect is understood.

Cash/T-Bills Position

Covered put writing, in the dealer market, may also be done against a cash/T-bill position. In other words, if the dealer is holding either cash or T-bills that are the equivalent of the market value of the commodity times the striking price, the position is considered covered. This offers not only a method of earning interest, but greater flexibility in a hedging/writing program.

COVERED DEALER PUTS
VERSUS CASH/T-BILLS

The use of puts alone, as a quasi hedge, does not carry with it a forward position. Therefore, the put must be the opposite of the position in the physicals market. The granting of a put is a contingent long position, and so the physical position should be short. If the put granted is at-the-market, the probability of exercise is approximately 50%. As a result, a neutral hedge is one-half the size of the put, or two puts must be granted against a given amount of gold.

Example: The commercial entity is short 100 ounces of gold and wishes to grant an at-the-market put as a hedge. Two at-the-market puts have to be granted. Assuming that the short physical position is to be delivered in six months, then the granting of two 6-month at-the-market options is a logical approach. Assuming that 6-month gold is trading at $300, it is equally logical to assume that two 6-month at-the-market puts might be sold for $2,000 each or a total of $4,000.

If, at expiration, gold is at $300/ounce, the put expires, and the gold to be delivered versus the short physical can be purchased in the open market at neither a profit nor a loss. The result is that the $4,000 premium is received for having done nothing. Assuming that $60,000 in T-bills is deposited as security with the option dealer, they too are released and the interest is earned. The $60,000 in capital earned an assumed 15% on the bills or $4,500 [($60,000×15%)÷2], in addition to a $4,000 premium. The total on invested capital is $8,500

($4,500+$4,000) or 14.17% for 6 months. Only the premium should be thought of as additional earnings, since the T-bill interest could have been earned at no risk.

If the market goes higher, the puts also expire, and the commercial retains the premium. The risk, in this instance, is that the commercial has no true hedge against the short physical commitment. The $4,000 received in premium is the exposure coverage. If gold, at expiration, is at $340/ounce and the commercial must buy at that price, he or she incurs a $4,000 loss versus the physical short at $300. This loss is offset by the premium retained. Above $340, there is no further protection afforded by the premium, and any further rise results in a $100 loss for each additional dollar of appreciation in the price of gold.

If, at expiration, the price of gold is below $300/ounce, both of the put options are exercised. The commerical receives delivery of 200 ounces of gold at $300/ounce. The first 100 ounces poses no problem, since the commercial has a short commitment for this 100 ounces. The second 100 ounces is protected by the $4,000 retained premium. This $4,000, which is the equivalent of $40/ounce, protects the position down to a price of $260/ounce. Below this price, the protection afforded by the premium has been exhausted, and each additional $1 decline results in a real loss of $100.

As with our prior examples, the granting of options may be done at-the-market, out-of-the-money, or even in-the-money. Let's look at the possibility of granting out-of-the-money put options covered by T-bills.

Example: Six-month gold is currently trading at $300/ounce, and our commercial has a short commitment equal to 100 ounces. Consider the granting of the $280 put versus a T-bill hedge. The $280 put is trading at $2,000 per option. Because this particular option has a 25% probability of exercise, the neutral hedge is the sale of four options against a 100-ounce short forward commitment.

Having granted four $280 put options covered by T-bills, you receive the $8,000 ($2,000×4) premium. If the market remains unchanged, the options expire, and you have the premium plus the interest on $120,000, which represents the deposited T-bills. The T-bills earn $9,000 [($120,000×15%)÷2]. This $9,000 plus the $8,000 premium is a return of 14.17% on the commited capital for 6 months, or 28.34% annualized.

If the market goes higher, the puts expire, thereby removing the hedge from the physical short commitment. The $8,000 premium serves as the protection for the now uncovered short. On 100 ounces of gold, this is the equivalent of $80/ounce. Gold could appreciate by

$80/ounce before the protection afforded by the premium is exhausted. Above $380/ounce, each additional $1 increase in the price of gold results in a real $100 loss on the total position.

If gold declines to $280/ounce, the options still expire because, at expiration, these options are only at-the-market; but there will be a profit of $2,000 [($300−$280)×100] on the short physical commitment. At exactly $280, the total profit is the premium of $8,000 plus the physical profit of $2,000 or $10,000.

Below $280, all the puts are exercised. One of the puts is no problem because the 100 ounces of gold received are delivered against the short physical commitment. The remaining puts are your exposure. The $10,000 realized profit at $280 becomes the protection on the remaining 300-ounce long position. The $10,000 is the equivalent of $33.33/ounce protection on the 300 ounces. This affords us protection down to $246.67 ($300−$33.33). Below this price, you experience a $300 loss for each additional $1 decline in the price of gold.

When there are both active exchange and dealer markets for a commodity, the commercial entity has much greater flexibility than on the exchange alone. The exchange is the major market for most commercials, but the dealer market allows for the custom tailoring of the options in regard to strike, quantity, and quality to the specific needs of the user.

CONCLUSIONS

Although the granting of puts and calls is not technically hedging, it has many advantages that appeal to the commercial entity. Put option granting may be thought of as a method of acquiring inventory when the uncovered put is granted. Options granting may be used for incrementing the total profit earned on manufacturing through the sale of out-of-the-money calls. Option granting may be a means of generating additional working capital through the premiums received. *Option writing does not, however, eliminate risk; it increases it.*

The sale of options carries with it an obligation that did not exist prior to the granting of this option. The acceptance of the obligation associated with the granting of the option offers the incremental profit of the premium. Commercial entities may be best equipped to be option writers due to their knowledge of the industry in which they operate, as well as their ability to acquire and dispose of the physical product. Option writing itself, however, is only a tool that, if used correctly, may be of substantial help to commercials.

Option writing has serious consequences, both positive and negative.

As much as it has benefits, it can also cause profit or losses at times when they are most damaging. Don't assume that an option-granting program is something that can be approached lightly and is of little consequence. Before entering into an option writing program, be sure you understand not only the concepts involved, but the ramifications of any strategy employed under the worst of circumstances.

The granting of puts and calls, especially in conjunction with a futures hedging program is a very complex business operation. It should be handled only by someone who is thoroughly familiar with both media and the concepts involved. Many institutions became involved in option granting in the early days of CBOE, initially achieving outstanding results, but, over extended periods, they became disillusioned with their longer-term results. Option granting imposes a finite limit to the profit that can be achieved, and it does not totally limit risk. It is important that the magnitude of this seemingly simple statement is understood.

19

THE HEDGER— STRADDLE AND COMBO GRANTING

The granting of straddles or combos obligates the grantor to either make or take delivery of the underlying commodity, since both a straddle and a combo consist of a put and a call. A position in which you simultaneously want delivery and are willing to make delivery is, at least on the surface, illogical. Yet, depending on the economics of the position, both transactions may be acceptable.

EXCHANGE STRADDLE GRANTING

Commercial straddle grantors obligate themselves to either receive or deliver one contract of a specific commodity at a predetermined price. Commercials, by the nature of their business, are either long or short the underlying commodity. It is technically impossible to have a hedged position against a straddle because the exercise of either side of the straddle creates a position opposite to the type of position that would be created were the other option exercised. If you are long the underlying commodity, the call side of the straddle is hedged, whereas if you are short the underlying commodity, the put side is hedged.

The term "hedged" is used in the economic sense because the commercial may be long or short the physical commodity, not necessarily the underlying futures contract. The physical commodity is not considered hedged for an exchange-traded option, but it may be considered a hedge for a dealer option.

If the commerical is long the physical commodity and grants a straddle, the exercise of the call results in a reduction or elimination of the long position. The exercise of the put results in an increase of the long position. If the commercial is short the underlying commodity, the exercise of the call results in an increase of the short position. The exercise of the put decreases or eliminates the short position.

STRADDLE GRANTING—LONG FUTURES

Being long one futures contract and short a straddle whose striking price is the same as the current futures price is the equivalent of being short two at-the-market puts. This is an identity. If the market goes higher, the put portion of the straddle expires, and the call portion of the straddle is exercised. There is no economic impact to the exercise of the call because the call is covered by the long futures position. Were you short two at-the-market puts, with no futures position, and the market rises, the puts expire without economic impact. In either case, the only effect is the retention of the premiums, with no further liability.

The granting of an at-the-market straddle or two at-the-market uncovered puts carry with them a 50% probability of exercise. So, the economics of granting two at-the-market uncovered puts, or of being long one futures contract and short an at-the-market straddle, is probabilistically the equivalent of being long one futures contract.

This position is used as an offset to a short physical position because it is the equivalent of being long the futures. The granting of a straddle, while being long the futures and the physicals, is a complex way of accomplishing a very simple transaction. If the intent is to hedge the short physical position, it is better to:

1. buy an at-the-market call,
2. go long the futures, or
3. grant two at-the-market puts.

STRADDLE GRANTING—SHORT FUTURES

If you grant a straddle and are short the underlying futures contract, another identity is created. The granting of an at-the-market straddle with a short futures position is the equivalent of granting two uncovered at-the-market calls. The granting of two at-the-market uncovered calls is probabilistically the equivalent of being short one futures contract. This position is then a potential hedge for a physical position that is the equivalent of long one contract of the underlying contract. If you intend to hedge a long position, it would make more sense to:

1. go short one futures contract,
2. grant two at-the-market uncovered calls, or
3. buy an at-the-market put.

Neither of these two strategies are normally encountered because there are much simpler ways of accomplishing the desired investment objective. They are covered, however, because they appear to be logical strategies when, in fact, they are not.

STRADDLE GRANTING—NO FUTURES

Straddle granting by a commercial is normally done in lieu of the use of futures. If you have a long position and grant a straddle, the exercise of the call portion of the straddle eliminates or reduces the long position. This may be perfectly acceptable if the straddle is being used for this purpose. It is conceivable that a given commercial has acquired excess inventory, in light of projected business levels, and is granting a straddle in anticipation of the exercise of the call. If this happens, the commercial winds up short the futures and ultimately delivers off the excess inventory. In this case, the straddle is normally granted with the call portion of the straddle well in-the-money to improve the chances of exercise. The reason that a straddle is granted instead of just an in-the-money call is that, if the call is exercised, the put probably expires and the commercial retains a second premium. The risk, of course, having entered into this strategy, is that the market comes down, and the put, not the call, is ultimately exercised. This results in an increase in inventory through the long futures position at a time when the objective is to reduce inventory. Lower prices may, however, justify adding to inventory.

Straddle granting might also be considered when an inventory position is considered too low. In this case, the granting of the straddle is undertaken in anticipation of the exercise of the put portion of the straddle, and the expiration of the call portion. To enhance the probability of the "proper" outcome, the straddle should be granted with the put portion of the straddle well in-the-money. If the put is ultimately exercised, the commercial winds up long the futures and can ultimately receive delivery of the underlying commodity. If the market rises and the call, instead of the put, is ultimately exercised, the risk is that it would result in being short the futures. The short futures position, in effect, reduces the inventory still further. This might be acceptable in light of higher prices.

The granting of straddles on the exchanges without a futures position is considered to be uncovered granting and is margined accordingly. In this case, the margin is the equivalent of one futures margin plus the equivalent of both premiums. Fortunately, the total margin required is original margin, and it can be deposited in the form of T-bills. In addition, as the straddle position moves either higher or lower, small moves tend to offset each other. That is, if the market moves higher and the call is appreciating, the put is depreciating by approximately the same amount. As a result, for small moves the requirement for the deposit of additional margin is unlikely. Large moves, however, tend not to be offset. If a market were to move substantially higher, there would be ever increasing demands for increased original margin on the short call portion of the straddle, without a commensurate decline in the put. The put can never generate more than its total value as potential profit. Eventually the put is worthless, and the call continues to appreciate. The converse is true in a declining market. For small moves, the decrease in the call value offsets the increase in the put value. For a major move, however, the put can continue to appreciate even after the call is worthless. In these instances, the grantor is called upon to deposit additional original margin to cover the short option position. This additional margin can also be in the form of T-bills, since it is additional original margin, not variation margin.

EXCHANGE COMBO GRANTING

In many industries the demand for the finished goods produced is elastic. That is, as the price goes higher, the demand declines; as the price goes lower, the demand increases. This is a well understood phenomenon, and it is well provided for by careful purchase of raw materials in light of projected prices. Either the major price increase or the major price decrease defies planning. The granting of combo options may help in the solution to this kind of problem.

Example: You are a refiner of gold whose purchase commitments are set in relation to your projections for future gold prices. As prices go higher, you purchase less gold because the ultimate users demand less for their finished products. As prices go lower, you have committed to the purchase of more ore because your customers will demand more refined product. A major price increase could cause you a problem because you would have refined gold and not have the normal demand. At the same time, a major decline would make your customers demand more refined products than you are prepared to deliver.

A possible solution to this problem is the granting of a combo option on gold. Let's say that 6-month gold is currently trading at $300/ounce. You have made your forward purchase commitments with thought to possible price fluctuation both upward and downward. Your only concerns are the major rally or the major decline. To protect yourself, you grant a 6-month $340 call option and a 6-month $260 put option.

As long as gold remains between $260 and $340, both options expire and you retain the premium, having done nothing. If, however, gold rallies above the $340 level, you can be assured that your call is ultimately exercised, leaving you short the futures as a means to dispose of your excess inventory. If gold drops sharply to below $260, the put is ultimately exercised and you are long the futures awaiting delivery of the physical commodity to meet your projected shortfall.

This strategy works at almost any level of the manufacturing and distribution process. The results of strategy can be varied depending on the actual striking prices used.

Example: You are a jewelry fabricator who has made a physical metals purchase in anticipation of a given level of demand. If the price rises, the demand for the finished product declines. Your purchase of gold was made at a price of $280/ounce based on the consumer demand at a price of no more than $300/ounce. Gold is now at $300 and climbing. You could sell at-the-market call options to reduce your current inventory and at the same time sell perhaps $280 put options to replace that inventory, were the price of gold to once again decline.

DIFFERENT STRIKING PRICES

In a given strategy, not all striking prices have to be the same. In commercial transactions, it is unlikely that transactions involving only one lot of the commodity would be done. It is more likely that quantities of 10 or 20 lots would be more common. This offers more flexibility than the commercial whose volume is limited to one lot.

Our earlier example involved elasticity of demand, which varies with price. The implementation of strategy can take various levels into consideration if multiple positions are possible.

Example: Six-month gold is at $300, and, as a commercial, you feel that there will be an ever decreasing demand as prices rise. You can sell options of ever increasing striking prices. Perhaps one call is granted at $320, a second at $340, and a third at $360. Conversely, if the market declines, and you believe there will be an increasing de mand, you might grant one put at $280, a second at $260, and a third at $240. This strategy has the effect of reducing the inventory when prices appreciate and of increasing the inventory when prices decline.

ALTERING QUANTITIES

All the examples thus far in this chapter assume that an equal number of puts and calls are sold. Altering the quantity may add even greater flexibility. If more calls are sold than puts, you have either granted a straddle or a combo with additional naked calls. If more puts are sold than calls, you have granted either a straddle or combo with additional naked puts.

Example: Your raw materials purchasing is slightly behind projected demand, and your greater exposure is from a price decline. In such a case, the granting of a surplus number of puts might make sense. If, on the other hand, you have a slightly excess inventory, the granting of excess calls might be the best method of disposing of the excess inventory during price rises.

OPTION GRANTING—OUR OTHER BUSINESS

Option granting can of itself be a business. Commercial entities that deal in the physical commodity are often in a better position to be option grantors than any other individual. They normally pay smaller commissions due to their size. Their hedging costs are lower due to exchange rules, and they have greater in-depth knowledge of the pricing (supply/demand) of the commodity. Thus commercials have the opportunity to grant options as a totally separate business within the corporate structure itself. To successfully do so over an extended period of time, the company is underwriting someone else's risk in exchange for accepting a premium, in much the same way that an insurance company writes insurance.

To do so *effectively*, it is necessary to understand the "fair value" of options. Our next chapter deals with econometric models used for option evaluation. That chapter should serve as the basis for determining whether or not to become a professional option writer.

20

ECONOMETRIC MODELS

An econometric or option pricing model is a mathematical algorithm that, based on a history of similar or related events, attempts to either evaluate a current event or predict a future event. In both security and commodity options, option evaluation models are used for both price evaluation and price forecasting. When using a model, remember that is is just a model—a "best guess" using sophisticated mathematical tools. A model tells you what the price of an option *should* be, not what it *will* be. An option model tells you when a given option is mathematically overpriced or mathematically underpriced.

Models can never be more accurate than the quality of the model or the data supplied. The model is a tool to be used in conjunction with other recognized tools of price evaluation, such as fundamental or technical analysis. An econometric model never made anything happen. The model can only predict the likelihood of the occurence of an event or price. Mathematicians can prove that a bumblebee can't fly; how fortunate that a bumblebee can't read.

Econometric models have been used for years in many industries as a tool in pricing and long-range planning. Until options began trading on the Chicago Board Options Exchange (CBOE), the data was insufficient for option evaluation models to be of any worth. With listed option trading now a major market in both securities and commodities, the option model has come into its own. Many sophisticated investors and institutions have access to, and regularly use, options models in their decision-making process. Let's first look at how option models work for securities, and then see what the differences are for commodities.

THE BLACK-SCHOLES MODEL

Although a degree in higher mathematics is not necessary to trade commodity options, the formulas are useful. In many cases, the models are available as a subscription service or prepackaged for use on a home computer (both discussed later). The actual Black-Scholes formula is as follows:

$$\text{Theoretical option price} = pN\ (d_1) - se^{-rt}N(d_2)$$
$$\text{where } d_1 = \{\ln(p/s) + [r + (v^2/2)] + \}/v \times t^{-1/2}$$
$$d^2 = d^1 - v \times t^{-1/2}$$

The formula variables are:

p = commodity future price

s = striking price

t = time remaining until expiration,
  expressed as percentage (%) of year

r = current risk-free interest rate

v = volatility (normally measured by annual standard deviation)

ln = natural logarithm

$N(x)$ = cumulative normal density function

One of the by-products of this formula is the hedge ratio, which is $N(d_1)$. The terms "hedge ratio" and "delta" are used throughout the book and may be assumed to be interchangable.

As complicated as the formula appears, in reality it is very simple and contains nothing more complicated than exponential and square root functions. It can be used on most scientific calculators, and it is sold by some manufacturers as a packaged program ready for use. As useful as a pocket calculator is, it is no substitute for a computer. A home computer, for this purpose, is very useful as it can do many Black-Scholes calculations rapidly.

The cumulative normal distribution, a statistical function, can be found in statistics books containing normal distribution tables. A normal distribution graphically generates a "bell-shaped" curve (discussed in Chapter 4). This curve, when applied to stock or commodity price distributions, indicates that most of the time prices change very little, but once in a great while they change dramatically. For calculation purposes, it is possible to derive the cumulative normal distribution function by the following formula.

$$x = 1 - z(1.330274y^5 + 1.781478y^3 - .356538y^2 + .3193815y)$$

where $y = 1/(1 + .231641 | s |)$ and $z = .3989423e^{-s^{1/2}}$
  Then
  $N(s) = x$ if $s > 0$ or $N(s) = 1 - x$ if $s < 0$

When this model is used for the evaluation of security options, the price of the option increases as the risk-free interest rate increases because there is no forward price of the underlying security. If the model is used for commodity options, the forward price (futures price) of the commodity is used. In this instance, the price of the option declines as the risk-free interest rate increases. This is perfectly logical since using the current price of a security for a forward evaluation disregards an important fact: The cost involved in the ownership of the underlying security is unrelated to risk, but it is related to the risk-free interest that could be achieved if the funds were alternatively invested. Futures price includes this amount in the "carry."

USING THE MODEL

This model, although designed for securities, works perhaps better for commodities. This is because many of the securities on which options trade pay dividends, and the model does not take dividends into consideration. Commodities do not pay dividends, and, even with the commodities that have accrued interest, it is easy to interpolate an appropriate forward price that includes this interest.

The model is based on a lognormal distribution of prices. The model is basically a normal distribution, but, with the exponentialization, it becomes lognormal. Both normal and lognormal distributions are bell-shaped distributions, but a normal distribution considers the downside distribution to be equivalent to the upside potential. In other words, with a normal distribution, negative commodity prices are possible. Although this is theoretically possible, it is highly unlikely that someone will ever pay you to take a commodity off their hands. The lognormal distribution is also a nonsymmetrical bell-shaped curve, skewed toward the upside to eliminate the negative price of the underlying commodity or security. This is not only convenient, but it is also practical as the volatility of a commodity is also a function of price in absolute terms. Commodities tend to make small moves at lower price levels. The lognormal distribution takes this into account.

The use of a lognormal distribution also tends to slightly overprice in-the-money calls and slightly underprice out-of-the-money calls because observed actual market distributions have a slightly larger tail to the distribution. This must be taken into consideration if the option model is to be used as the sole investment decision maker.

VOLATILITY

As used in the Black-Scholes formula, volatility is a function of the average price of the security, the daily price change and the number o observations. These variables, when used with the standard textbook "standard deviation" formula, are quite workable for securities, despite some minor problems. This formula assumes that volatility is a constant, which it is not. As a general rule, the volatility of a security changes over time, but in most instances it does not change dramatically rapidly. This is certainly not the case with commodities. Commodities tend to have more rapidly changing volatilities than securities, and this capability must be mathematically acknowledged.

This one variable causes perhaps the greatest problem to the option modeler. Experience has shown that a volatility that gives equal weight to all price changes will understate volatility in markets of high volatility, and overstate in markets of low volatility. Of the several possible solutions to the problem, none is anywhere near perfect.

It is, of course, possible to attribute greater importance to more recent events and thereby have recent price changes more significant than more distant prices.

> *Example:* You could take yesterday's price change and weigh it 20 times the effect as a 20-day-old price change. This approach appears to be used by most modelers today, especially in commodities. Realize that different futures months are not different commodities, and as a result there should be a correlation between the volatility for each of the different contracts. The problem is that a futures contract does not exist forever. It has a definite life, that is, from the time it is initially listed until the time delivery takes place. This adds the additional problem that the more distant months trade inactively with large price changes, and the nearby months trade actively with small price changes. It has been common practice to use the volatility of the most actively traded month as the basis for all volatility calculations. The contract normally used is the most nearby contract, until such time as first notice day arrives. After first notice day, the next contract month should become the basis for volatility establishment.

The most common approach, assuming a large data base is not available, is to use only the last 20 days of price change as the basis for calculations. This approach gives a weighted average for the last 20 days, with yesterday's change 20 times as important as 20 days ago. This approach must be watched carefully to be sure that the results generated bear a close resemblance to current prices over a period of time. This approach has the potential to introduce as much error as the use of the lognormal approach if it is not monitored carefully. The accurate computation of volatility is critical because, individually, it has the greatest potential short-term effect on the model's pricing.

IMPLIED VOLATILITY

It is possible to allow the market to determine the volatility for the option modeler. The Black-Scholes formula is designed to solve for the price of the option. If, however, the price of the option is known and the volatility is what is desired, the formula is just rewritten to solve for v. Whatever the markets say the volatility is, it is. This is implied volatility.

The logic of this approach is that, if there is sufficient volume in the option itself, the market is efficient, and the implied volatility is the actual volatility. This volatility must be computed for each option trading. In some cases, the differences between the volatilities of different options on the same commodity are substantial. In many cases, these differences can be attributed to the volume levels in the different striking prices and different maturities. This can, to some degree, be eliminated by weighting the various volatilities derived by the volume traded. For instance, after having computed the implied volatility for all the options traded, you would first multiply the implied volatility of each option by the number of options that traded for that series. Having done so for all the options traded, you would total all the multiplications, and then divide this number by the total volume. This gives you a weighted implied volatility for that commodity. Caution must be used not to include options that are so far out-of-the-money that market movement in the underlying commodity does not affect their price, or the weight average will understate the implied volatility. To make the implied volatility a still more accurate tool, the time to expiration must be considered in the weighting.

In securities, the different expirations of a given option call for the delivery of the same underlying security. In commodities, each maturity, from a mathematical point of view, must be considered a different commodity. It is necessary to compute the implied volatility for each maturity. This still leaves some error as the more inactively traded back months have an implied volatility that, in most cases, is slightly higher than the actual volatility due to the inactivity.

This approach to the computation of volatility is quite accurate and, with some minor adjustment, may be used in lieu of standard deviation in option models. Unfortunately, not all options have sufficient activity for the market to be efficient; therefore, the day-to-day change in the option may give an implied volatility that is unrealistically high in light of the volatility of the underlying commodity. One approach is to weight the implied volatility as we did standard deviation; that is, we attribute a greater weight to today's volatility than to yesterday's volatility.

Another problem that does not have an ideal solution is intraday price moves. This is a double problem because the commodity exchanges report only price changes on the tape as opposed to every trade. In very volatile markets, the highs and lows are more indicative of the volatility than the day-to-day closing price change. At the present time, there is insufficient data to determine how this possible discrepancy should be included in commodity option evaluation.

Still another problem that has no ready solution is that of limit moves. Some of the commodity options currently traded have daily price limits and some don't. This causes computational and accuracy problems.

LIMIT MOVES

If the futures contract is trading at the limit and the option does not have a limit, the volatility, from a short-term point of view, is far higher on the option than on the future. The only apparent solution to the problem is to compute the volatility on the option in the aforementioned manner and compute the volatility on the future by using the spot month, which in most cases has no limits. Then add to the spot price the carrying charges that are evident in that market, to come up with a fantasy future price for the futures contract that is trading at the limit. The option value may be slightly overstated due to the fact that more one-sided volume is in the option by traders who are unable to trade the futures contract because it is trading at the limit.

Having computed the implied volatility for both the commodity and the option, it is a relatively simple matter to insert the value in the Black-Scholes (or other) model and come up with a true value for the option. Option volatility tends to lag commodity volatility and give rise to overpriced and underpriced options in terms of their econometric value. This fact gives rise to two situations:

1. A given option is overpriced or underpriced in terms of its fair value.
2. Some options are overpriced or underpriced in relation to other options on the same commodity.

These two facts become additional input to the speculator or hedger in determining the advisability of implementing a specific option strategy. To the professional option investor, these are the basis for the total decision process.

PROBABILITY OF PROFIT

Probability of profit is also referred to as *expected return*, which is an especially important concept for the consistent investor. Statistics are used routinely to predict the outcome of given situations. For statistical projection to have a high degree of correlation with the observed outcome, however, there must be a large number of events and/or a very high probability of occurence.

> *Example:* If you go to a Las Vegas or Atlantic City casino and play roulette, there are 18 black numbers, 18 red numbers, and a green "0" and "00." You can bet, for instance, red or black and receive 2-to-1 odds. If you bet red, and the number comes up red, the casino pays you twice what you bet. If you bet black and red comes up, you lose. Were there only red and black on the wheel, you could not lose because, each time that you were wrong, you would just double your bet. If you could play forever, you would eventually win. This would work because with a 50-50 chance (only red or black) and doubling your bets, you walk away when you have won. The "0" and "00" change the odds. The odds of being correct by picking red or black are not 2-to-1; they are actually 19-to-9, because there are 38 possible outcomes and only 18 chances of winning. For occasional gamblers, the fact that the odds are slightly against them are of little statistical importance. They either win or lose depending on their "luck" on that particular evening. To the casino, however, the slight edge is statistically significant because they are infinite gamblers. This slight edge times an infinite number of rolls guarantees that they will make money. The casino may lose on a given evening or to a given player, but over time they make money. If you doubt this fact, look at the hotels and casinos; they are not making all those profits on their hotel rooms and the bar bills.

The professional option investor is in much the same position as the casino. The purchase of an option is the purchase of term insurance, and the granting of an option is the sale of term insurance. The premium level necessary to insure profitability to either party is a function of probability. If the individual investor or corporate entity invests in commodity options with sufficient regularity to become statistically significant, the profit achieved should closely parallel the profit projected by statistics.

For each particular strategy, there is a potential profit or loss for each price level at expiration. This potential profit or loss times the probability of that price occuring is the expected return or probability for a given strategy.

> ***Example—Expected Return on the Purchase of a Gold Call Option:*** Six-month gold is currently trading at $300/ounce, and the $300 striking price 6-month call option is trading at $3,000. In theory, the price of gold can decline to $0 or rise to infinity. In true option evaluation, these possibilities and all the intervening price possibilities are subject to our computational analysis. For the sake of simplicity, how-

ever, let's assume that gold can do only three things: (1) remain un-changed, (2) go up $100, or (3) go down $100. Let's assign probabilities to each of these three possibilities: a 25% chance of a $100 decline, a 50% chance of remaining unchanged, and a 25% chance of going up $100. This assumption covers all of the possibilities.

If gold remains unchanged or goes down $100, the option expires worthless, and you lose the entire premium. If gold goes up $100, at expiration, the option is $100 in-the-money and therefore worth $10,000 ($100×100). So the expected return is computed as follows:

1. For down $100, the expected return is the loss ($3,000) times the probability of occurrence, or .25 for an expected loss of $750 ($3,000×.25).
2. For unchanged, the expected return is the loss ($3,000) times the probability of .50 or $1,500 ($3,000×.50).
3. For up $100, it is the expected profit of $7,000 ($10,000−$3,000) times the probability of .25 or $1,750 ($7,000×.25).

Therefore the total expected profit is the total of the individual ex-pected profits: minus $750, minus $1,500, plus $1,750, for an expected profit of minus $500. Statistically, you should lose $500 on this transac-tion.

In reality, the numbers do not tell us anything about what will happen on this or on any other transaction. The number tells us that, if you purchase this option an infinite number of times, you should lose $500 times the number of purchases made on average. On an individual transaction, you may make money, break even, or lose money—regardless of what the statis-tics say. The expected profit or loss becomes important over a number of trades. The more trades that are done, the greater the likelihood that the expected profit will approach the actual profit (loss) that is forecast by the probability model.

Our example serves the purpose of explaining the logic behind ex-pected return, but it is too simplistic to be of value in actual operation. Obviously, the critical portion of this approach is the assignment of prob-abilities of outcome to the various prices. It is not only important that the assignment be accurate, but it must also be all-inclusive. That is, each possi-ble price must have a probability assigned to it.

The price distribution chart in Figure 4–1 shows that the probability of the price of a commodity falling between two prices is, in fact, proportionate to the area under the curve of the chart as it relates to the area between the two points. No matter what the projected distribution of project price (log-normal or otherwise), the area between two points under the curve gives the probability of being between those two points. The peak of the distribution for both stocks always lies to the left of mean, which is generally considered to be the current price of the commodity. According to "random walk" (Chapter 4) logic, the probabilities are equal that commodity prices will either appreciate or depreciate in the future.

In a lognormal distribution, however, the area to the left of the mean is larger than the area to the right of the mean, based on the assumption that price cannot go below $0. Depending on the distribution used, perhaps 40% of the total area lies to the left of the mean and 60% of the area lies to the right of the mean. If a normal distribution were used, 50% of the area under the distribution line would be on each side of the mean. The probabilities being discussed apply only at expiration, and nothing said concerns the probability of a given price occurring before expiration.

The height, width, and consequently area are a function of the volatility of the underlying commodity, when volatility is expressed as standard deviation. When used in this context, volatility must be converted to the time period involved, since the volatility thus far discussed has been presented in terms of volatility for one year.

Time and the related volatility are square-root-related functions in the option sense. To determine the volatility for the period involved, the following formula works nicely:

$$v_t = v \times t^{-1/2}$$

where $v =$ annual volatility
       $t =$ time in years
       $v_t =$ volatility for time t

With the volatility for the time period involved, all that is necessary is to solve for the price of the commodity being at various price levels at expiration. This is done by solving individually for the probabilities of a commodity below or above a given price at expiration. This goes back to the area under the curve discussion.

The following formula gives us the probability P of a commodity being below price q at the end of time period t:

$$P = N\{[\ln(q/p) + (v_t{}^2/2)]/v_t{}^{-1/2}\}$$

where $N =$ cumulative normal distribution
       $P =$ current price of the futures contract
       $q =$ price in question
       $\ln =$ natural logarithm
       $v_t =$ volatility for the time period in question

To determine the probability of the commodity being above a current price at expiration, you need only subtract P (as solved for above) from 1. Therefore: $P(\text{above}) = 1 - P(\text{below})$.

To determine the overall probability of profit for a given strategy, start at the lowest price of consequence, compute the probability, and then, by the minimum price fluctuation, compute each succeeding probability times the expected profit at that level. To do a meaningful number of computations, this is best done on a computer.

With sufficient computer power, it is possible to evaluate a wide number of strategies on a large number of commodities. Most individuals do not have access to the magnitude of computer power necessary to evaluate a large percentage of the strategies available, but common sense may first be applied to limiting the number of possibilities that are to be investigated in depth. Speculators might rule out option-granting strategies, due to a lack of capital. Hedgers might rule out granting strategies, as they are not true hedges. If the number of strategies can be limited to a reasonable number, a good pocket calculator may suffice for the necessary calculations. If, on the other hand, you are a professional option investor or an investor who would implement any and all strategies, you need the full range of strategies evaluated in order to make appropriate business decisions.

A computer program that is designed to look at all possibilities ultimately generates a list of calls or puts to buy, a list of calls or puts to write, and a nice assortment of bull spreads, bear spreads, and calendar spreads. From this menu, speculators or hedgers can pick strategies that offer a high expected rate of return and that are in alignment with their fundamental or technical views of the market. A by-product of having a view of the market is that it is not necessary to investigate mathematically strategies that are contrary either to your view of the market or to your investment objective and risk-taking ability.

OPTION SERVICES

Depending on your needs and your budget, a wide variety of option services are available to you as an option investor. The same types of services that are available to investors in security options are also available to commodity option investors. These services run the gamut from very costly and very sophisticated to very inexpensive and very simplistic.

At the top end of the list is the custom-designed, in-house, on-line, user-modifiable system. This type of system is normally used by either large commercial hedgers or portfolio managers of large commodity trading advisors. This type of system is normally employed when the entity has made the commitment to the use of the options markets in large volume. Typically the option model and a related bookkeeping service are programmed by the user's in-house computer system development department, and they are routinely enhanced as additional needs are defined. Again, with this type of commitment, there is usually an option department or at least several people who are making the firm's decisions in options only. The type of person or people varies depending on the entity involved.

This type of system also requires access to on-line prices. This requirement can be met by subscribing to one of the quotation vendors such as Ultronics, Bunker Ramo, Quotron, and the like. It can also be met through direct subscription to the exchanges through their price dissemination networks. This type of system, while the most sophisticated, is also the most demanding in terms of dollars and personnel. Other approaches work nearly as well, but they are less demanding.

The next step down is the use of an option consulting firm, such as the Options Group in New York, who are specialists in every phase of both the security and commodity options markets. Depending on the consultants and the services they provide, most of your needs can be met. Typically, consultants can write custom-tailored programs and even supply the on-line capability through their own hardware. This allows you most of the same benefits as doing it yourself. What is lost is the flexibility of an in-house system that, at very little incremental cost, may be modified by your own staff.

The use of a consultant is probably the best choice for the user who intends to do a substantial amount of business but does not today have a staff of knowledgable people in both options and options programming. The costs to implement this type of system are large and, with future modifications, ongoing.

The next step down is the out-of-house, user-modifiable programs. In the security options business, two of the largest such vendors are Monchek Webber and Bridge Data. These services are normally sold on a subscription basis. The vendor installs a terminal on the user's premises and supplies the data via data lines. Available are on-line services that evaluate the various options according to a model, and they usually allow the user to alter the strategies and the parameters of the model. Typically, interest rate, volatility, and market price are the kinds of variables that the user can change to investigate the results of the various changes. The program itself is not subject to modification. The program remains the property of the vendor, and it is leased on an as-is basis without any liability. The weaknesses of this arrangement are that the program is not custom-tailored to your needs and that the costs are on-going without ownership of either the hardware or software.

The next step down is the packaged program. This type of program is normally supplied by brokerage firms to their account executives and to selected large customers. This type of program generally is a batch processed program and an off-line service. At the end of a trading day, the brokerage firm runs a program that evaluates all the options according to their model, along with a group of strategies including buying, granting spreading, and so on. This data is then either printed and mailed to the various branches and customers, or it is transmitted in hard or soft form to the ultimate users. This method is very cost-effective because it is done off-line and during nontrading hours. The weakness is that the data is based on closing prices and is a day old at the time it can be used. It does, however, identify options that appeared attractive at the close as well as the related strategies, both of which can be looked at during market hours the following day. This type of data service lends itself to the smaller user, where high costs are not justified.

Another type of product that may be of use to the option investor is the packaged program designed to be used on a personal computer. Software Options, Inc. of New York currently offers an option trading system called COTS for use on either the IBM or the Apple personal computer. In its basic form, this system is designed to be used by the individual investor at home for option evaluation. It is an interactive system that, given the daily futures prices, calculates true option values. This price entry can be done either manually or via subscription to a data base service such as CSI Inc. in Boca Raton, Florida. The system is designed to evaluate individual options, as well as option strategies. It will, with available enhancement, do the necessary calculations on various strategies such as bull, bear, or calendar spreads. If you currently own the appropriate hardware, or if you are looking for an excuse to buy a personal computer, the program is not especially costly and quite usable.

The last commercially available alternative is the programmable pocket, scientific calculator, such as the Hewlett Packard HP-41CV or the Texas Instrument TI55 or TI56. These types of calculators may be programmed with the necessary formulas to allow option evaluation on a rapid basis. Traders and clerks on the floors of the various exchanges use this type of calculator to do option calculations during trading. This, of course, is the least costly of the vended approaches, but it also requires the entry of all data by the user. Many of the calculator manufacturers sell program packages that are designed to evaluate options.

Beyond the commercial avenues, there are other alternatives, including writing your own programs for either a home computer or a pocket calculator. Many of the home computer users have "user's groups" in which you will probably find other option devotees. Very often these user groups have programs available that have been written by their members. The writing of a program to evaluate options is not a major undertaking if you have some experience in programming. You might elect to do such a program on a home computer or on a programmable calculator. The nice thing about doing your own program is that it does exactly what you want it to do, and you can change it any time you want.

For those of us who have given up the use of paper and pencil for calculations, even a simple calculator with a square root function can be used to evaluate options. All you need is the basic model and the necessary time to do the calculations.

Depending on your proposed usage and your projected volume, you can determine which approach appears best. I have not listed all the alternatives, nor have I listed all the potential vendors. The vendors listed merely represent various levels of information available. Whether an individual vendor is any "better" for you than another depends only on your intended usage. You have to evaluate what they offer in light of your own needs.

21

USING MATHEMATICS IN TRADING

Given that option modeling should be part of the basis for using the options market, how do you fit econometric models into a trading strategy or business plan? The use of mathematics can be applied to option trading in two distinct manners. First, it can be the only tool. In other words, the applied strategies rely totally on the mathematics of the situation, with no view toward fundamental or technical analysis at all. Commercial option trading firms follow this approach. Option professionals are as ready to buy as they are to grant or to spread. Everything depends on the price and the price alone. Large investors or commercial entities that follow this approach enter a business and, depending on how good they are at their business, determine their level of profit or loss. This type of enterprise depends on the quality of the mathematics, the control of execution, margining costs, and the diversity and number of positions for the statistics to work to their benefit. As valid as this approach is, only a limited number of entities use it.

The vast majority of users of econometric models, whether individuals or corporations, use the models as another tool for making investment judgments, in much the same fashion as fundamental and technical analyses are used.

APPLICATION OF MATHEMATICS

Models may be used as either the first tool or the last tool. That is, you can use the computer to identify the strategies that offer the highest potential expected return, and from that point consider only strategies that agree with your fundamental and technical analysis. Or you can do the fundamental and technical analyses of the market involved, and then call on the computer to generate the strategies that offer the greatest expected return in light of your investment judgment.

Either approach has its advantages and disadvantages. Using the computer as the first tool requires a great deal of computer power and "number crunching." It does, however, show you all the strategies, some of which you might not have investigated in light of your market view. Using the computer as the last tool requires a lot less computation, but it offers the possibility of overlooking some potentially very profitable strategies. Whichever approach you use, the ultimate application is the same.

CALL WRITING

In the chapters on call writing for both the speculator and the hedger, several examples demonstrated covered and uncovered writing both in- and out-of-the-money. The minute a commodity has more than one striking price and one maturity, the question arises as to which option should be written. One approach is to evaluate all the possibilities first by rate of return exercised, then by rate of return unchanged, and lastly by upside or downside breakeven. Once this list of possible candidates has been compiled, it can be compared against a list of acceptable criteria. Investors establish their own criteria in light of their risk-taking abilities and available capital. Such criteria might include the granting of no option unless the rate of return unchanged was 20%, or having a minimum downside breakeven of at least 15%, or some other alternatives.

With the addition of the econometric model, the criteria can become less subjective. Having culled the potential opportunities down to a list of prospective call-granting strategies that meet the subjective criteria, it is now possible to compute, using the model, the strategies that offer the least likelihood of being below the breakeven point, in the case of a covered call, at expiration. This approach carries with it no guarantees, since all you have is a list of the "covered writes" with the least likelihood of being below the breakeven point at expiration. This ranking is based on probability. The probability that the commodity would be below the breakeven has been computed, but it can still happen despite the probability. What you wind up with is a list of the most conservative covered writing possibilities, based on probabilities. The formula in Chapter 20 on computing the probability of being below a given price P can be used to ascertain the probability of violating the downside breakeven.

The ability to measure risk protection in terms of probability, quantified by volatility, is a very useful tool. It allows the prospective option writers a criterion by which they can realistically compare the advantages of out-of-the-money, at-the-market, and in-the-money options objectively. By setting subjective minimum guidelines, as stated before, and then using the models to cull the list of potential option-granting strategies, it is possible to have the best of both worlds. You create a window that includes options that have both an acceptable degree of risk and an acceptable rate of return in light of established parameters. These parameters have to be periodically adjusted in light of interest rates, volatility, and the commodity itself as conditions and personal judgment change.

CALL BUYING

The purchasing of calls either as a speculation, with or without T-bills, is one of the limited risk strategies that tends to appeal to the largest audience of investors. The degree that the option is out-of-the-money, at-the-market, or in-the-money affects the probability that at exercise it will be profitable.

The computer model can be used for two purposes in evaluating call-buying strategies. First, it can evaluate the probability that any call purchased will be sufficiently in-the-money at expiration to have a value. Second, given the volatility, the computer can rank the various calls in order of their degree of overvaluation or undervaluation. This allows the speculator to buy the call that offers the greatest probability of success. In many cases, options are overvalued in light of their profit potential. If call buying is the strategy that best meets your investment objective and risk-taking ability, however, then the computer can evaluate which option has the best potential for profit, despite the fact that it may be overvalued.

This philosophy also works for the hedger, since it evaluates the option that is the least costly in terms of overvalued/undervalued when used as an alternative to futures hedging. Based on the expected profit, or more likely loss in the case of call buying, the hedger can compare the real cost of owning the option versus the advantages of not being exposed to variation margin calls on a futures position. The ability to compare options of different striking prices and different maturities allows the hedger a means of determining the real cost, over time, of the "insurance."

PUT WRITING

As with call writing, the writing of puts may be considered purely from a mathematical point of view. With such a point of view, writers write any put that offers a positive expected rate of return, and they use the computer model to rank the potential of each put-granting strategy.

The writing of puts covers such a broad range of possibilities that the computer becomes very useful to both speculators and hedgers. Puts can be written both covered and uncovered for all of the reasons outlined in the strategy chapters. The put is especially useful in determining the expected rate of return as opposed to the purchase of a futures contract. An earlier chapter discussed the use of the naked put option as an alternative to the entry of a limit order on a given futures contract. This strategy can be compared to the expected rate of the granting to the rate of return, if the projections on the underlying commodity itself are correct. That is, if the projection is for a price appreciation in the underlying commodity to generate a given profit versus a given risk, this can be compared with those same parameters for the uncovered put writing. The probability of occurrence can also be superimposed on the potential profit of both strategies and compared in terms of expected return.

If uncovered put granting is to be used by a commercial entity, the model can determine the likelihood of the commodity being at a given price at expiration. The model can thereby inform the commercial of the probability of acquisition of additional inventory based on the striking price of the option granted. The model can also be used to determine if the underlying commodity will be at a given price, and this information can be used to forecast the need for additional capital for margin requirements. This feature may be the deciding point for using futures, uncovered put granting, or even call buying.

PUT BUYING

The buying of puts can be ranked in exactly the same manner as calls. The model can be used to evaluate puts of different maturities and different striking prices according to the degree of overvalue or undervalue, ranking them accordingly. From a hedger's point of view, the ranking can be used to determine the real cost of the option based on expected loss (profit) when used as a hedging medium. It also serves the purpose of comparison to a future hedging strategy where only a portion of the position is hedged with that cost related to the cost of the purchase of out-of-the-money puts. Speculators can use the models to determine what striking price should be purchased as protection for a long futures position, and they can realistically evaluate the potential versus purchase of a call as an alternative.

Because, at any given price of the commodity, the exchanges have only certain striking price trading, there is the possibility of higher striking prices on the upside for calls and lower striking prices for puts. This situation may give rise to the desire to create synthetic put or calls. The model allows speculators to compare the expected return from the creation of the desired synthetic put versus the purchase of an existing, less desirable put. In general, synthetic puts are more expensive than real puts due to the additional commission costs and committed capital, but it is possible, based on a market projection, that the synthetic put may be economically desirable.

CALENDAR SPREADS

The strategy section on calendar spreads presented calendar spreads both from a mathematical point of view and with the imposition of investment judgment. The implementation of a calendar spread from a mathematical point of view is difficult to evaluate without a computer. The computer gives the user the ability to project the expected return at any time that the spread is outstanding. Without the computer, you know only the magnitude of the potential profit or loss possible. Due to the calendar's limited profit and unlimited risk, it is important to evaluate the probability of the commodity being either above or below predetermined price at different given points in time.

In a mathematically attractive calendar spread, the striking prices involved are normally close to the current market price of the underlying commodity. The computer allows us to evaluate the relative effect that a given price move has on both the longer-term and shorter-term options, as well as the probability of that move occurring. Having made this evaluation, it is possible to determine, based on expected return, if the granting of a calendar spread with both legs at-the-market makes more sense than granting the shorter-term option 2-to-1 or more out-of-the-money. Expected return is the great equalizer, in that it allows us to compare apples to oranges.

This use of the model also allows us to quantify the effect of short-term moves of the underlying commodity while both legs of the spread are open. It allows us to compare lateral calendar spreads where the long leg is at-the-market and the short leg out-of-the-money or vice versa.

From a speculator's point of view it allows the test of various "what if" situations. For example, what if the market rallied short term and I had to close out the short option? What would I have lost? What is the expected return on the remaining long option? If the market were to achieve the levels that I forecast, what is the expected profit of the calendar strategy compared to, perhaps, reverse calendar spreads or the outright purchase of a call or put?

Commissions are generally very significant in spread transactions, and they should definitely be considered when comparing the bottom-line potential of alternative strategies.

BULL AND BEAR SPREADS

Trading bull spreads and bear spreads carries with it limited risk and limited profit compared either to the outright purchase or to granting options. Yet, as mathematics show, it is more important over an extended period of time to have a high expected profit as opposed to a high potential profit.

The computer offers several uses for bull and bear spreads. The computer can be used to determine the overall expected profitability of the spread, as well as the probability of the commodity itself being above or below a specific price at expiration. In addition, the computer can tell the worth of individual options within the spread at any point in time. The ability to compare one spread with another is particularly important because it is possible to implement bull or bear spreads with either puts or calls. The computer is the easiest way to make this comparison and consequently to make the correct decision. In doing bull spreads with calls or bear spreads with puts, the long option loses its time value more rapidly than the short option. Without the use of the computer, determining the profit at a given point in time for a given level of price change is difficult. The computer allows us to selectively determine the correct strike price to use in the formulation of the bull spread or bear spread depending on the timing of a market move.

The ability to project value over time based on volatility allows us to determine whether to grant a bull spread with calls or puts if we are bullish. The computer also allows us to then look at the two alternative strategies and evaluate the ramifications of a given strategy in light of expected profit. This "what if" in many cases deters the investor from implementing a strategy that could spell disaster if the appropriate move does not take place within a given time frame.

RATIO WRITING

When in ratio writing the number of granted options is greater than the number of purchased options, there is an open-ended risk. In other words, if you ratio write calls, there is an upside breakeven above which the magnitude of the risk has no limit. Ratio writing puts generally has the same exposure on the downside. Occasionally there is also a risk of market move in the opposite direction if the value of the options granted does not exceed the value of the options purchased.

The computer, with its ability to evaluate the probability of a commodity being at a given point in time, allows you to evaluate the expected rate of return of any ratio strategy. Based on market projection, you can custom-tailor the exact ratio to correspond to the market projection envisioned. If, for instance, your market projection calls for a 10% increase in the price of a given commodity, the computer can evaluate the expected return from an assortment of ratio-writing strategies and rate them in order of expected return. In addition, the computer can also evaluate the advisability of comparable naked put- or call buying strategies. With the computer, you can tailor a ratio writing strategy whose graphical representation closely parallels the graphical representation of a lognormal distribution. If this is done, the highest profit also occurs at the point of highest price probability.

If in the ratio writing strategy the number of options purchased exceeds the number of option granted, then there is no naked component to the strategy. Yet it is still important to ascertain the expected profit of the overall position. This is very often a go/no-go decision. The computer can evaluate the expected profit of the additional options purchased in conjunction with the 1-to-1 spreads and determine if additional options reduce or increment the expected return of the overall position.

BUYING STRADDLES AND COMBOS

A market can be at only one price at a time, but the purchase of a straddle or combo is done in anticipation of the market being either above or below a given price at some point in time. If the straddle or combo has been purchased with no related futures position, the investor can very quickly compute both the upside and downside breakeven of either position. The computer is of value because it can compute the probability of the price exceeding those breakeven prices, as well as generate an expected rate of return on the purchase. If either of the positions are taken in conjunction with a long or a short futures position, it is easiest to convert the complex option/futures position to its option identity, and then enter the specifics of the synthetic option position for evaluation. These complex option/futures positions have both upside and downside breakevens, with one of the sides having unlimited risk. The computer can realistically evaluate the risk and present it in the form of expected return.

GRANTING STRADDLES AND COMBOS

The granting of straddles and combos is in many cases identical to the ratio writing relationship. All the comments made with respect to ratio writing, of course, hold true for straddles and combos. The combo offers the possibility to alter the range of profitability to a larger degree of commodity price change than does the straddle. In addition, it is more common to find price aberration in deep-in-the-money or deep out-of-the-money options. This combination often facilitates the construction of a combo whose graphical profit picture closely approximates the probability distribution, with a commensurately high expected rate of return.

PROFESSIONAL STRATEGY—
THE NEUTRAL HEDGE

Options, in many cases, are overpriced in relationship to their evaluated worth as determined by an econometric model. The degree of overpricing varies from moderate to extreme depending on market conditions and the commodity involved. No option grantor would consistently enter a market where the probability of profitability is not a positive number. On the other hand, buyers are willing to overpay for an option because they are paying a premium in much the same fashion as they pay an insurance premium on a house. Life insurance is overpriced actuarially, and everyone still buys it because the insurance insures the risk they are unwilling or unable to take. Options function in much the same manner. Options allow speculators to trade commodities with a predetermined risk; and this limitation of risk is the reason they overpay for the option.

The fact that options are usually overpriced gives rise to profit potential for the professioanl option writer. The concept of the neutral hedge is related to the term "delta." According to the mathematics of option writing, for every option, there is an offsetting hedge that could be put on, in which any loss realized on the short option is exactly offset by a corresponding profit on the hedge. Conversely, any profit realized on a hedge held against a short option is offset by a loss on the option.

The neutral hedge is not a constant quantity. In general, an at-the-market option is neutrally hedged when an offsetting futures or physical long is held equal in quantity to about half of the quantity covered by the short option. As the option moves further in-the-money, the quantity of the underlying commodity necessary to maintain the neutral hedge increases. As the option moves further out-of-the-money, the quantity of the underlying commodity necessary to maintain a neutral hedge is reduced. The actual quantity necessary to maintain the neutral hedge can be determined by solving for delta through the Black-Scholes model.

The logic behind neutral hedging is that the professional option writer hedges all positions properly, that the true value earned from option granting offsets the losses sustained on the hedge positions, and that therefore the amount by which the options are overpriced remain as the option grantor's profit. This mathematical approach to profitability works only over an extended period of time in a variety of market circumstances. As with all statistical approaches, it takes a large number of transactions for the real result to approach the statistically forecasted outcome.

To implement this strategy, the option grantor must use an econometric model to determine the true value of the option to be granted. After the options have been valued according to the model, each option must be revaluated to determine the degree to which it is overpriced. The computer program should rank the various options according to their degrees of being overpriced. The program must evaluate every situation carefully because the degree of overpricing must be sufficient to cover all the commissions involved and still generate a profit. For example, short-term options appear to be the most overpriced because returns are computed on an annualized basis; therefore an option with one day to run that is overpriced by 1% will appear to be 365% overpriced. It is highly unlikely that this option could be granted and return a profit after all the costs are covered. In addition to being mathematically correct, the program must also be rational.

If the neutral hedging concept is followed in the granting of call options, the strategy requires the purchase of additional quantities of the commodity as the price increases, and the sale of portions of the hedge as prices decline. The grantor does not make money on the hedge but loses money at a controlled rate. You don't make money by buying high and selling low.

Assuming that the model is correct and that the hedging is implemented properly, the dollars lost on the hedging should equal the fair value of the option at any point in time. At expiration, the losses on the hedge equal the fair value, and the overpriced portion of the premium remains as the profit. This approach to hedging requires a very sophisticated computer system that is especially sensitive to market conditions especially in terms of volatility. If the computer is not working with a real volatility number, it is unable to accurately evaluate options in rapidly changing market conditions.

Several other factors come into play with this type of strategy. Let's say the hedge of an at-the-market call is approximately 50% of the long position covered by the call, and the hedge for an at-the-market put is 50% of the quantity of the commodity underlying the put. The hedge for an at-the-market straddle is no position in the underlying commodity at the time the option is granted. Having granted a straddle, as the market moves higher, a portion of the underlying commodity is purchased, and, if the market moves lower, a short position in the underlying commodity must be taken. This appears simple, and it is—provided only one option has been granted. As the number of options increases, the computer must keep track of the neutral hedge on the entire position. This task is further complicated if you are granting both puts and call with different striking prices and different maturities. If you happen to be a commercial entity dealing in the underlying commodity as either a physical or a future, the problem is further complicated, and the computer system must be even more sophisticated. As you grant call options on an exchange and implement a neutral hedge, you are purchasing futures contracts. This purchase of futures contract may not be creating a long futures position, but it may be liquidating a short futures position held by your firm against a long physical position. This is neither bad nor good; it is a fact of the strategy. You are, in fact, substituting a short option as a hedge for the long physical in lieu of a short futures position.

The more complex the business involved, the more sophisticated the computer system required. To implement this type of system, the computer must be able to keep track of the firm's entire inventory position as well as its entire hedge position. The computer system should be able to keep track of positions as they relate to the options separately from positions instituted for hedging the commercial business. This control becomes important when you attempt to evaluate the overall profitability of option granting as well as the efficiency of the option model itself.

Approaching professional option granting on a small scale is not economically rational. The support systems necessary to be competitive in this market are substantial. The computer must be able not only to do all the strategy work for individual options, but it must also be able to handle spreads and all of the back-office bookkeeping required if the system is to be successful. For neutral hedging to work efficiently, the hedge must be capable of being altered in very small percentages as the market changes. This is possible only when multiple options have been granted and the hedges can be altered in full futures contract amounts. It is physically impossible if one option has been granted, requiring a 50% hedge, and the market appreciates to the point that the hedge should be increased to 55% to be able to add the required additional 5% if 5% does not represent a full contract. It probably does not make sense to enter this type of program if you are not going to have short option positions requiring 50 to 100 contracts of the underlying commodity necessary in the hedge.

Neutral hedging is a bona fide strategy, but it works only when done in large quantities on a very sophisticated level. It is not necessary to use the neutral hedging concept for the commercial to use the market on the granting side. Neutral hedging is a business—a separate business that requires the commitment of people, time, and money to be successful.

The concept of the "neutral hedge" is tied directly to the concept of "the probability of profitability" and "delta." Because the probability of either an upward or downward move in the price of a commodity is 50/50, the proper hedge on an at-market option is 50%. That is, an at-market option has a 50% chance of being in-the-money at expiration and thus being exercised. It also has a 50% chance of being out-of-the-money and thus expiring. As an option becomes further in-the-money as a result of commodity price change, the probability of exercise at expiration increases and therefore necessitates a larger hedge percentage. Conversely, as market change causes an option to become out-of-the-money, the probability of exercise declines, necessitating a less-than-50% hedge.

CONCLUSIONS

Commodity options serve an important function to the professional, whether it is a form of hedging, when approaching the markets from the buying side, or a method of incrementing rate-of-return when approaching from the granting side. Econometric models constitute sophisticated tools to help in evaluating options. It is not absolutely necessary that mathematics be used in the evaluation process, but it is helpful. The markets themselves are as efficient as they are because many individual and commercial entities use models in their decision-making process. A model doesn't resolve all the problems; in many cases, it causes more problems than it solves. Yet it is, when properly employed, a very helpful tool in using options.

22

TAXES

In 1973, when the Chicago Board Options Exchange (CBOE) opened its doors, there were no published Internal Revenue Service (IRS) rulings on exchange-traded security options. The CBOE, at that time, requested rulings from the IRS. The IRS, not ready to issue rulings, issued only a private ruling to the CBOE itself. A private ruling can be relied upon only by the person to whom it was granted. The CBOE, at that time, reasoned that the IRS in issuing the private ruling was aware that that private ruling would be widely disseminated. The CBOE cautioned investors to get their own private rulings before acting on what had been given to the CBOE. Several years later, the IRS issued its final published ruling on exchange-traded security options.

Today the commodity industry finds itself in much the same position that the CBOE did in 1973. Exchange-traded commodity options are a new investment from the IRS's point of view. The exchanges realize that the importance of tax rulings cannot be underestimated. The Coffee, Sugar and Cocoa Exchange, in conjunction with the Commodity Exchange, Inc. have formally requested ruling from the IRS on exchange-traded commodity options. In addition, as did the CBOE, these exchanges have asked that, if the IRS is unwilling at this time to publish rulings, they issue private rulings to the exchanges themselves.

It is imperative that individual investors discuss the tax consequences of various option strategies with their accountants or tax advisors. The intention here is not to give tax advice, but only to make the investor aware of some of the tax rulings that have been requested, along with the logic used in the formulation of those requests.

In requesting both public and private rulings, the exchanges are doing their best to help individual investors in their tax planning. A private ruling, of course, appeals only to the exchange itself, but it may serve as a guide to individuals in requesting their own private rulings.

From the tax point of view, there are basically two participants in the commodity options market: the individual and the commercial. Usually commercials use the market as a business tool; therefore, all profits and losses represent ordinary income or loss to the corporation. Taxes are of greater importance to the individual who is treating options as an investment.

The tax rulings that have been requested deal only with the nonmargined option, as proposed by CSCE, COMEX, Mid-Am, and CBOT. The proposal does not deal with a margined option as proposed by the CME. The differences are substantial: No true variation margin passes from the buyer to the seller or vice versa in the nonmargined option, and no economic benefit accrues to either party until the transaction is ultimately liquidated or expired.

In total eleven rulings have been requested that deal with a broad list of possible transactions. Let's look at the individual ruling requests.

HEDGING OPTIONS

Ruling 1: Except as provided in section 1256(e)(3) relating to syndicates, transactions by holders in long CSCE options and by grantors in short CSCE options which qualify under section 1256(e)(2) will be treated as "hedging transactions" for purposes of sections 263(g), 1092, and 1256.

This ruling is requesting the IRS to confirm that, subject to the normal interpretation, options used by commercials as part of their normal hedging program are to be treated in the same manner as futures (ordinary income or loss).

INVESTMENT (NONHEDGING OR SPECULATIVE) OPTIONS

Holders: Long CSCE Options

Ruling 2: The cost of a long CSCE option to the holder is a nondeductible capital expenditure.

This ruling request is asking that options be treated like other speculative investments, that is, as a capital expenditure wherein the gain or loss is capital in nature as opposed to a deductible expense, such as interest.

Ruling 3: In the case of the holder of a long CSCE option who holds such option as a capital asset, gain or loss on lapse or offset will be considered gain or loss with respect to a regulated futures contract in accordance with section 1234(a) and will be subject to tax in accordance with section 1256(a)(3).

This rule request asks that long options receive the same ultimate treatment as futures contracts from a tax point of view, that is, 60% long-term capital gain/loss and 40% short-term gain/loss.

Ruling 4: No gain or loss will be recognized to the holder of a long CSCE option upon its exercise. For purposes of sections 1256(a), the CSCE futures contract will be deemed to have been entered into at the striking price set forth in the option; and for purposes of determining gain or loss with respect to the CSCE futures contract, the premium paid for the long CSCE option will be treated in the same manner as an amount of gain previously taken into account as provided under section 1256(a)(2).

This ruling asks that the exercise of the option does not, of itself, create a tax liability. The premium paid for the option should be treated as an increase in the purchase price of the underlying futures contract; in the case of a call and thereafter, the futures contracts receive normal tax treatment. The converse would hold true for a put, where the premium would be treated as a reduction in the sale price of the futures contract. This is very similar to the tax treatment of long options in the securities markets.

Ruling 5: Section 1256(a) (1) will not be applicable to a long CSCE option which is unexercised at year-end.

Commodity futures contracts have a tax liability at year-end due to the variation margin passed daily from the long to the short or vice versa. This ruling requests that that portion of the regulation not be applicable to long option holders because no variation margin is passed between the long and the short.

Grantors: Short CSCE Options

Ruling 6: A short CSCE option will qualify as a regulated futures contract within the meaning of section 1256(b), and is to be taxed under the rules in section 1256(a) and (c).

Because the grantor of an option both pays and receives variation margin in the same manner as futures, the ruling requests the same treatment as futures.

Ruling 7: The premium received by the grantor of a short CSCE option is not to be included in income at the time of receipt.

Even though the grantor receives the premium in cash at the time that the option is granted, there is the offsetting liability of depositing a like amount of original margin with the clearing corporation. Therefore, the grantor does not receive an economic benefit at the time the option is granted. This lack of benefit should not give rise to a concurrent tax liability, as the premium is earned over time.

Ruling 8: Upon lapse of a short CSCE option by passage of time, the full amount of the option premium received by the grantor shall be treated as gain under section 1256(c) and shall be taxed under section 1256(a)(3).

As the vast majority of granted options are granted covered, it would be grossly unfair, taxwise, to treat the option differently from the tax treatment of the hedge. This ruling requests that the option premium receive the same treatment as a gain realized from a futures contract transaction.

Ruling 9: Upon termination of a grantor's obligation under a short CSCE option by offset, gain or loss shall be recognized to the grantor under section 1256(c). Such gain or loss shall be calculated by reference to the amount of premium received on granting the option and the amount of premium paid to enter the offsetting transaction. Such gain or loss shall be taxed under section 1256(a)(3).

The logic behind this ruling request really falls into two categories. First, the option grantor, if covered, also has a futures position that, as a result of simultaneous offset, has a tax liability. It is logical to apply the same tax treatment to both sides of the same transaction. Second, if the option is used in a hedging fashion as opposed to futures, it should still have the same treatment as futures, in that it is serving the same purpose.

Ruling 10: Upon exercise of a short CSCE option, gain or loss to the grantor shall be recognized under section 1256(c). Such gain or loss shall be calculated by reference to the amount of premium originally received on granting the option and the amount of variation margin required to be posted under the futures contract on the day the option is exercised if the futures contract is not liquidated on the day the option is exercised. The amount by which the premium received, adjusted as required under section 1256(a)(2), exceeds the required variation margin, or the amount by which the required variation margin exceeds the premium received, adjusted as required under section 1256(a)(2), shall be recognized as gain or loss respectively. If the futures contract entered into on exercise of the option is liquidated on the day the option is exercised, the amount of gain or loss shall be calculated by reference to the premium originally received by the grantor of the option and the amount paid (or received) on liquidation of the futures contract. Such gain or loss shall be taxable under section 1256(a)(3).

This ruling requests that, because the option results in the creation of a futures contract, the tax treatment should be the same as futures. If the exercise results in the deposit of margin equal to or greater than the premium, there should be no tax liability at the time of the exercise. If the premium is greater than the initial margin requirement on the futures, the grantor realizes an economic benefit and should therefore have a tax liability. If the position is immediately liquidated, the total profit or loss is realized and the appropriate tax liability should than be incurred. In all cases it was a futures transaction and should qualify for futures tax treatment.

Ruling 11: If the short CSCE option is held open at the end of the grantor's taxable year, the short CSCE option shall be treated as liquidated for its fair market value on the last day of the year and any gain or loss shall be taken into account by the grantor in accordance with section 1256(a)(1). The amount of such gain or loss shall be calculated by reference to the premium received on granting the option and the fair market value of the option at the end of the taxable year. Such gain or loss shall be taxable under section 1256(a)(3).

The logic behind this ruling request differs substantially from securities, but it is very logical from a commodities point of view. Commodity positions are taxed at year-end despite the fact that they have not been closed out. The reason is that position holders have either paid variation margin or received the economic benefit therefrom, and therefore they should have the tax liability. This is not the case in securities, and this is the reason why an open position does not have a tax liability. Commodity options fall in between securities and commodity futures. Purchasers of options have not received any economic benefit, even if a position has moved substantially in their favor. Yet grantors have put up variation margin and thereby sustain an economic loss. From the grantor's point of view, the consequences are identical to being in a futures position. Variation margin (although called variable original margin) is received and paid; therefore it is logical that grantors should have both tax liability and treatment equal to futures.

CONCLUSIONS

All these rulings appear logical, but you cannot rely on a ruling unless it is either issued to you personally or is a published ruling. It would not be uncommon for the IRS to delay action on these ruling requests. In the case of the CBOE, the IRS wanted a substantial period of trading before they ultimately issued rulings. In the interim, investors who have not requested and received their own private rulings are in a state of limbo.

These requested rulings also do not deal with the more complex strategies such as spreads, straddles, and combos. The tax questions related to these types of strategies are far more complex than they are for similar strategies in securities. As much as it would seem logical to apply the same reasoning that applies to outright long and short options to the more complex strategies, this can be most disadvantageous from a tax point of view.

Spreads, for example, are a combination of both a long and a short option. Yet the margin that might be released if the short option moved in the grantor's favor might be required to remain in the account. If so, the spreader might incur a tax liability on the short premium earned and not yet have received the economic benefit. This might require the payment of taxes without the funds necessary to do so. There are also questions related to the striking prices of options involved in the spreads. Depending on the striking prices, the transaction may have different tax liabilities due to the relative risks involved.

Conversions are another problem. The sale of a call, coupled with the sale of a futures and the purchase of a put, is economically identical to the granting of a put with no offsetting futures position. There is logic to treating this position identically to option granting. But what if different striking prices are used? Only time and experience will give us some indication of what is logical. For the time being, the best we have is the request rulings as potential guidelines. Discuss the possibilities with your accountant or tax advisor before making any investment.

23

TRADING TECHNIQUES

You now have all the tools necessary to deal in commodity options. Before you enter the market, however, consider a number of things. How you enter the market, to some degree, is governed by your investment objectives and your risk-taking ability. If you are a commercial entity entering the market, your decisions are based more along the lines of techniques of hedging and money management.

Speculators have far more complex questions to answer. Speculators must determine what type of risk they are willing to accept. If they wish to limit risk to defined amounts of capital with no possibility of margin calls, then they compile a list of acceptable strategies that include option buying and 1-to-1 spreading. These strategies both offer speculators profit potential but do not expose them to a loss greater than the dollars originally committed. If speculators are capable of accepting a greater risk, the whole range of option strategies is open to them. In addition to buying and 1-to-1 spreading, there is ratio spreading, covered and uncovered writing, ratio writing, and the host of other strategies.

Risk entails more than the dollars committed. Well capitalized option investors must also look to their general knowledge of the market. If their experience with commodities and options is generally limited, the defined risk strategies may be the best place to start. Time also contributes risk to trading. If speculators do not have a substantial amount of time to devote to the management of an option portfolio, and the account is not managed by a professional money manager, defined risk strategies are also best. Lastly, temperament plays an important role in the decision-making process. Speculators must be able to make rational decisions and not become emotionally involved in their decisions. If you cannot rationally decide to liqui-date a bad position before the losses become extreme, then the limited risk strategies are probably also best.

WORTHWHILE CONSIDERATIONS

1. *Use only risk capital:* Never commit money to any form of investing that you cannot afford to lose. Do not commit an amount of money that, if lost, would affect your style of living.

2. *Do not use temporary money:* In commodity trading, in many cases, the most profitable strategies are longer term. Do not commit funds that are destined to be withdrawn at a specific point in time.

3. *Don't over-commit based on profits:* If your trading strategies prove profitable, do not commit all your profits or change the types of risk you are willing to assume. Larger positions generate larger losses. See rule 1.

4. *Establish a formal plan for trading:* Determine your objective and your risk-taking ability. Having done so, formalize a plan and follow it.

FORMALIZED PLANS

People lose money trading commodity futures and commodity options for numerous reasons. Finding out how to lose is not important; developing a plan that improves your chances of winning *is* important. No two people have exactly the same approach to trading. Having a formalized plan puts your investment procedures in a logical order.

Decide whether your approach to trading will be fundamental, techni-cal, mathematical, or possibly a combination of all three. Prior to making any investment commitment, review the fundamental, technical, or mathemati-cal factors that you have decided to include in your plan. It is also wise to evaluate those factors even if you are not an adherent to that form of analysis. For example, it is foolish to be a buyer, based on your fundamental analysis, when all the subscribers to technical analysis are selling. It is also foolish to buy a specific option, having made a fundamental and technical decision, when that option is mathematically the most overpriced.

Establish a trading plan that not only tells you when to get into a position but that also tells you when to get out. One of the greatest mistakes that speculators make is getting into market on a tip, rumor, or market news, and then getting out for the same reason or because they have a "nice" profit. If you follow a plan, all entries into and exits from the market are done for just cause.

Liquidating a position at a loss is emotionally difficult and taking a profit very easy emotionally. A trading plan that defines risk and profit potentials in conjunction with fundamental and/or technical analysis removes a great deal of the emotion from investment decisions. Generally, once a position has been established, it should not be liquidated until either the objective has been reached, or until some fundamental or technical consideration justifies taking the loss. You do not have to be right in commodity investing 50% of the time provided the profits are greater than the losses. It is generally well advised to remain with profitable positions (let the profits run), and to liquidate unprofitable positions (cut the losses short).

If nothing else, the adoption of a formalized trading plan keeps you from overlooking important facts. A formalized "checklist" of thing to be done before a trade is made forces you to consider all the relevant facts before acting.

Stay with your plan. If you are a technical trader, follow technical guidelines. If technical analysis dictates that a position should be liquidated, don't look for fundamental reasons to justify remaining with the plan.

Give the plan time to work. Over the short term, evaluating a trading plan is impossible. It is not unusual in commodities to have over 50% losses. If your plan is not generating the desired results, reevaluate the plan, but don't change it unless you find a flaw in the basic plan. Good plans take time to construct and time to work. You may take many small losses before you have a large winner. If, after some time, your plan appears to be limiting your profits and not minimizing your losses, consider redoing the plan. Talk your plan over with someone more experienced in this type of trading, but remember that the other trader's investment objective and risk-taking ability may not be the same as yours.

RISK CAPITAL

In security options, the exchanges' suitability rule says that the broker should not recommend a transaction that is unsuitable for customers in light of their risk-taking ability and investment objectives. The first part of this rule is a good guide for the speculator in commodity options. You should never invest more than you can afford to lose without affecting your life style.

Having decided on the type of transaction that best meets your investment objectives and that falls within your risk-taking guidelines, realize that it is not always necessary to trade. The corollary to making money is not losing money. You do not lose anything by not being in the market. There will not always be an investment that is fundamentally, technically, and mathematically attractive. When nothing is attractive, don't trade. Remember even a fair trade carries with it commission costs. If the trade does not offer a reasonable chance for return, don't invest.

Don't commit all your funds at one time. The most attractive-looking trade today may not even appear attractive in comparison to what might be available tomorrow. If the strategies that you are following have margin requirements, and if there may be calls for additional margin, don't commit more than 50% of your risk capital. If the market moves against you temporarily, you don't want to be in the position of having to liquidate to meet a margin call; worse yet, you don't want to have to commit additional funds that you did not wish to place at risk.

In a way, margin calls are a blessing. Take advantage of them. If a position has moved sufficiently against you to generate a margin call, it is time to reevaluate the position. Any position that cannot stand up to the scrutiny of reevaluation should be liquidated. Do not blindly meet margin calls. Meeting margin calls without due consideration may be throwing good money after bad. Meeting margin calls on a given position may also concentrate too much of your risk capital in one position.

Diversify your position. Do not commit a large percentage of your risk capital to any one position or group of positions that respond similarly to the same fundamental news. Diversification does not mean buying gold options, buying silver options, and buying platinum options. In considering diversification, consider positions on the same side of the market in this evaluation. The purchase of a call on gold and the sale of a put on gold are on the same side of the market and may result in an overconcentration of assets.

Don't let success change your concentration of assets. If, for example, you have been very successful trading sugar options, with no more than 10% of your risk capital in sugar, don't let your success in sugar allow your commitment to rise above your previously decided percentage.

Regardless of how good a given situation looks, don't commit all your assets to one position. Options trading is a probability game. You have to be able to play consistently to win. If one loss wipes out your risk capital, that is enough reason not to make that commitment.

If you are an option buyer, consider several additional kinds of risk. If you have purchased an option and the market has moved in your favor, as the option gets more expensive, the leverage is reduced and the absolute dollar risk is increased. Consider taking profit when your options have gone in-the-money and possibly replacing the position with an out-of-the-money substitute.

Long at-the-market options are all time value. This time value depreciates as a function of the square root of time. This depreciation becomes most evident in the last 30 to 45 days of the option's existence. Consider liquidating long positions with substantial time value remaining while the option still has one month or more to expiration.

Don't exercise options and continue to carry the futures position unless your investment objective and risk-taking ability include futures trading. Bad option positions become worse futures positions once exercised.

Market actions should be dictated by some fundamental or technical factor, not by your need for additional capital for some other venture. Don't use funds to trade that you may need for some other purpose. In the long term, it is unprofitable to be forced to liquidate what ultimately may be a very profitable position because you need the capital for other purposes.

TACTICS

Once a potential position has met your criteria for investment, how do you institute the position? Don't rush in at all costs. Use limit orders to institute positions that are sensitive to precise execution. If your strategy calls for execution at a specific price or better, the use of a market order may result in the execution at a price that makes the position unprofitable. Use common sense in making price determinations. It is generally not possible to buy at the then current bid, or to sell at the then current offer. In computing the potential for a position consider the effects of paying several "pips" higher or receiving several "pips" lower. If the profitability is still there, give the broker some discretion as to price.

If the position you wish to implement contains both option and futures contracts, remember that they are traded at different pits/posts. This can result in a time delay between the execution of the various legs. This time delay is risk. Ask your broker before you enter an order, where the "floor" believes the position can be executed. Some firms, on larger positions, take contingent orders, by which they do not execute one side unless they can execute the other. If this service is available, use it.

It is usually far easier to institute a position than it is to liquidate it. Once you are in the market, and a position is moving in your favor, it is difficult to force yourself to take a profit and decide how to take the profit. Try not to liquidate positions that are moving in your favor unless there is a justified reason for taking the profit. It is too easy to let losses run and cut profits short. Where possible, use stop orders as a means of exiting the market. If you are long an option, and the position is moving in your favor, put in a stop to protect the profit. As the position continues to move in your favor, move the stop to further increase the profit. Place your stop order where there is a technical reason to place them—such as just below a support level on a long position. If you have placed a stop sell, for instance, to protect a long position, and the stop was placed in a valid technical position, don't lower the stop if the market declines. If the stop was in the right place and you get stopped out, you should be out.

PICKING A BROKER

How to pick a broker starts with the brokerage firm. If you are a totally self-reliant investor, and you want nothing from the broker but an execution, you should shop for price. Look for the lowest commissions and the lowest margin requirements. Be sure that the broker is well capitalized because commodity investments are not federally insured as are security investments. Be prepared to do your own research, watch your own positions, make your own recommendations, and supply your own services such as technical charts and price evaluation models.

If you are the type of investor who is looking for advice and support facilities, think through your choice carefully and ask a lot of questions. What option research facilities does your firm offer? Do you have a price evaluation model? How are its results disseminated to customers? What are your commissions and margin requirements? Do you execute your own orders or do you use someone else's floor brokers?

If you receive acceptable answers to all these questions, the big question remains. Who will be your account executive? Most people believe that they want to deal only with a well established successful broker. There is nothing wrong with this if that broker specializes in commodity options. Most brokers specialize in one or two products. Over the years they develop a clientele whose investment objectives closely parallel their specialty. Most well established brokers are not particularly interested in new products because they are generally not appropriate for their existing clients. Your best choice is probably a broker who today specializes in security options. The strategy and tactics are very similar, and most of such a broker's security option knowledge will serve both of you.

The one problem you might encounter is that the broker must be licensed to trade commodities. Some brokerage firms license their account executives to trade either commodities or securities, but not both. If you encounter this problem, your best choice is probably a commodity broker who is younger in terms of experience. The reason is that a new broker does not have a well established client base and is willing to concentrate on a newer product. Well established commodity brokers are so involved in the day-to-day trading of their existing accounts that they seldom have the time to become involved in something new. The best approach is to discuss with the resident branch manager who your broker should be. Each brokerage office has a "man of the day" who is designated to handle incoming calls and prospective accounts. It is unlikely that the man of the day is the broker best qualified to counsel you in commodity option transactions. Also don't hesitate to change brokers if you don't have an affinity for the person with whom you are dealing.

There are very few experts in commodity options today. The product has not been trading long enough for there to be "old timers." Your best choice in brokers is an individual who has an interest in the product and who has both the time and the inclination to work with you.

The CFTC regulations required that for a brokerage firm to deal in exchange-traded commodity options, that firm must either be a member of the exchange on which the options are traded or a member of a self-regulatory body, such as the National Futures Association (NFA). If the brokerage firm does not meet this requirement, they may not deal in commodity options. In your investigation of potential brokerage firms, be sure that the firm you choose is an appropriate member, or you may find that the broker feels that commodity options "aren't right for you" because he or she can't trade them.

MANAGED ACCOUNTS

As much as you may be fascinated with commodity options, maybe you weren't meant for each other, at least directly. To be successful in any investment, you must be willing to devote the time, have the necessary funds, and possess the proper temperament. If you find yourself lacking in any of these areas, or if your trading shows a weakness in any of these three key ingredients, consider having your money managed.

Managed money falls into two general categories: trading advisors and pools. Either approach is viable, and the decision is based on your circumstances.

COMMODITY TRADING ADVISORS

Commodity trading advisors are individuals or companies that specialize in managing other people's money in the commodity markets. Individual advisors may manage only the money of a few friends, or they may be large management organizations with tens of millions of dollars under management. The smaller advisors sometimes manage accounts as small as $25,000 but most of the larger advisors require between $100,000 and $500,000. Most of the larger advisors have been in the business for at least several years, with an investment history and track record that can be reviewed.

Since exchange-traded commodity options are a relatively new form of investing, any trading advisor is unlikely to have figures to show any performance history in the option markets. However, a successful history of commodity futures trading or security options trading may indicate future potential.

Each of the advisors has a particular approach to investing—fundamental, technical, or mathematical. There are enough advisors that finding one whose approach to investing is compatible with your own should not be difficult.

Realize that, because exchange-traded commodity options are new, you will most likely not be able to find an advisor who manages only commodity option money. In most cases, the advisor uses the option markets in conjunction with the futures markets. This may give rise to a level of risk that is greater than you wish to assume based on your risk-taking ability.

Commodity trading advisors charge a management fee that is usually based on the amount of your money being managed. Many advisors also charge a performance fee; that is, they charge a part of your profits as a fee. In general, a smaller management fee and a higher performance fee is the most attractive to the investor, since the advisor makes a substantial amount of money only if the customer also makes a substantial amount of money.

Locating a suitable trading advisor is not as easy as it sounds. It is unusual for brokerage firms to suggest trading advisors because there is potential liability if the trading advisor does not perform as advertised. Most brokerage firms, however, supply a list of advisors from whom to choose. Another alternative is the annual commodity directory published by *Commodities Magazine*. Once each year they publish a directory issue that lists many of the commodity trading advisors, as well as brokers and other services available to the brokerage community. If all else fails, the larger trading advisors are required to be registered with the Commodity Futures Trading Commission. For a small fee you can request a list of all the registered commodity trading advisors.

In addition, many brokerage firms have in-house advisory services that they make available to their customers. Often there is no fee for the service because the brokerage house is getting the commissions generated by the account. These types of services are no better or no worse in general than the out-of-house services, and they should be evaluated by the individual investor in the same manner.

Trading advisors ask an account to sign numerous forms in opening the account. Some of the forms may be from the brokerage firm who will be executing the order and holding the customer's funds. Others are forms prepared by the advisors themselves. One of the forms you are asked to sign is a power of attorney. Read the form carefully; you should sign only a limited power of attorney. A limited power of attorney gives the trading advisor the right to make transactions in your account but nothing else. Some limited powers of attorney also authorize the brokerage firm to pay advisors their management fees out of your account; this is not uncommon. Generally you should not sign a full power of attorney because doing so gives the trading advisor the right to withdraw assets from your account. I am not presuming to give legal advice. If you have any questions, discuss these documents with your attorney before you sign them.

COMMODITY POOL OPERATORS

A commodity pool is just that. Individual investors put their money under the management of an advisor, and the advisor manages the money as a unit instead of as individual accounts. The use of the pool concept allows individuals with smaller amounts of money access to professional management. Generally commodity pools have minimum investments of $5,000. All commodity pool managers are registered with the Commodity Futures Trading Commission as commodity pool operators. Some pools are offered to all investors through brokerage firms, while others are established for an individual group of investors.

Most pools are created by brokerage firms to allow smaller investors to participate in the commodity markets. Each pool has a specific investment objective and method of operation. Generally a disclosure document is furnished outlining the goal of the pool, as well as its method of operation. It is unlikely that you will find a pool that specializes in commodity options, but, quite conceivably, such a pool may be formed by one or more brokerage firms.

Some pools are legally securities, and, as such, they are registered with the Securities and Exchange Commission. In this case the disclosure document you will receive is a prospectus.

How the pool is organized determines how management and related fees are paid. Generally, commodity pools have a small initial sales charge, but brokers continue to participate in the commissions generated by the pool in direct proportion to the amount their customers have invested in the pool. Pools that are organized as securities generally have a higher initial sales charge, but they may have lower ongoing commission because the broker does not participate after the initial sale.

The pools themselves are normally managed by independent commodity advisors. If the pool is a new pool or a securities pool in its initial offering, there is no track record to investigate. Some managers of the larger pools manage more than one pool. Although there are no guarantees, if the pool investment advisor has had a good track record with other pools, you may be more comfortable with the new offering.

Some pools offer limited risk. The pool guarantees investors that they will never be called upon to deposit additional funds regardless of how the pool performs. Some pools also have a mandatory period for the initial investment. In other words, investors may be required to remain in the pool for a period of one year or be allowed to liquidate only on given dates, usually quarterly.

24

GETTING STARTED

Now that we have gotten through all the fundamental and advanced concepts and discussed our trading plan, it is now time to do your first transaction.

WHICH OPTION TO BUY?

If your first transaction is to be the purchase of a call or a put option, the question becomes: What maturity and what striking price. Let's assume the market is projected to go higher and we are looking at calls. A fundamental or technical decision carries with it a time frame in which you anticipate the projected move to take place. Needless to say, you must purchase an option that does not expire prior to the happening of your forecast event. The key to the maturity decision is that you should pick a maturity that still has 30 to 45 days remaining at the time the option is to be liquidated (see chapter on option pricing).

The selection of striking price is a function of breakeven. It is ideal to purchase an option that is out-of-the-money, and to liquidate that option when it is in-the-money. You should purchase the option that is out-of-the-money by slightly less than the magnitude of the move you anticipate.

Example: You are going to purchase a 6-month call, and 6-month gold is trading at $300/ounce. If you anticipate a $50 upward move, you should purchase the option that is $40 out-of-the-money. This generally offers the highest rate of return on invested capital if the move is realized, and there is a reasonable amount of time remaining at the time of liquidation.

In picking a striking price, predetermine the breakeven. To do so, you might wish to use the following format:

Total premium in dollars	$ _____
Plus total commission in dollars	$ _____
Equals total outlay for option	$ _____
Divide by contract size (ounces, pounds, etc.)	$ _____
Equals cost of option per units volume	_____
Add (in case of call) or subtract (for put)	
to striking price to determine breakeven	_____

Note: This form disregards that a commission will be paid at the time that the option is liquidated. This number is not included because some brokerage firms do not charge a second commission, some charge a fixed amount, and some charge a percentage of the option's value.

WHICH OPTION TO GRANT?

An approach to the market that entails granting requires some computations. Determine upside or downside breakeven, along with rate of return unchanged or rate of return exercised. Although these numbers are important, option granting is normally based on the fundamental or technical view that a market is going either higher or lower. These specific numbers become important only in that they should show the greatest profit if the commodity makes the projected move. The logic is to grant the option that offers the greatest rate of return if the commodity reaches the projected price.

SPREADING

Generally, spreading strategies offer a higher probability of profit in exchange for a lower total profit. Especially with ratio spreading, the points of maximum profit and breakevens are most important. Spreading is not normally a "first-time" strategy.

CONCLUSIONS

As you enter these markets, proceed slowly. You do not lose money by not trading. As you gain confidence and experience, you can engage in more strategies. A textbook can teach only so much; beyond that point experience is the only teacher. As you gain experience, reread the chapters covering the strategies that you are then employing. They will make more sense and be more useful.

Lastly, I wish you good luck and many profitable trades.

25

THE PILOT PROGRAM AND THE FUTURE

In the fall of 1982, the Commodity Futures Trading Commission authorized a "pilot" program for the trading of commodity options on commodity futures contracts. This program was given a duration of three years. During that period, the CFTC is evaluating the necessity for commodity options and the economic impact that commodity options have on the commodity futures markets as a whole. Whether or not the "commission" will reach any conclusions is questionable. The Securities and Exchange Commission authorized a similar program in security options in 1963, and that program is still a "pilot" program.

Assuming that the pilot program in commodity options is not terminated, where do we go from here? What does the future hold?

Several commodity exchanges did not initially apply to trade commodity options because they did not trade a commodity on which option trading was allowed. The Commodity Exchange Authority (CEA) had banned the trading of options on certain commodities during the 1930s. When the CFTC was reauthorized in 1982, Congress provided for the lifting of the 50-year-old ban. Now such exchanges as the New York Cotton Exchange and possibly the New Orleans Commodity Exchange may elect to file for permission to trade options on some of their commodities.

The CFTC reauthorization also cleared the way for exchanges to trade options on such commodities as wheat, soybeans, cattle, and hogs. This may prove to be of particular interest to such exchanges as the Chicago Board of Trade and the Chicago Mercantile Exchange.

In early 1982, the CFTC published proposed regulations for "dealer options." The early eighties should see these regulations become effective in some modified form. Their appearance will allow for both the expansion of the dealer option market by existing participants and the entry of new participants. It is not unreasonable to assume that large commercial and industrial entities might become both grantors and buyers of commodity options on the products in which they are specialists. Such areas as currencies, coffee, cocoa, and petroleum products are likely candidates for this type of market.

It is not unlikely that the CFTC will lift its temporary ban on foreign options and that American speculators will once again have access to options on copper, silver, lead, tin, zinc, aluminum, and nickel on the London Metals Exchange. They should also have the opportunity to trade options on all the "soft" commodities traded in London. The lifting of this ban might also prove interesting to speculators who are interested in Canadian, French, Swiss, or Bermudian options.

The last area with apparent growth potential are in commodity options that are traded subject to securities regulation. The Chicago Board Options Exchange is already trading options on fixed income securities (GNMAs). The Philadelphia Stock Exchange is currently trading options on British pounds, Swiss francs, German marks, and Japanese yen. The Pacific Coast Stock Exchange has expressed interest to the SEC in the possibility of trading option on gold coins, and the American Stock Exchange has asked the SEC for permission to trade options on a gold-denominated notes.

Where do we go from here? It is hard to say. But, with the interest from both the public and the exchanges, we could well be entering a period of growth that could parallel or exceed the growth of the CBOE during its early years of existence.

REFERENCES

OPTION CONSULTANTS
AND SOFTWARE VENDORS

THE OPTIONS GROUP, INC.
50 Broadway
New York, New York 10004

SOFTWARE OPTIONS, INC.
19 Rector Street
New York, New York 10048

MONCHIK WEBER, INC.
111 John Street
New York, New York 10038

STEWART DATA, INC.
11 Broadway
New York, New York 10004

IDENTITIES—EQUIVALENT POSITIONS

This Position Equals. . .	. . .This Position
Long Call	Long Commodity/Long Put
Long Put	Short Commodity/Long Call
Long Commodity	Long Call/Short Put
Short Commodity	Long Put/Short Call
2-to-1 Ratio Call Grant	Naked Straddle
2-to-1 Ratio Put Grant	Naked Straddle
Short Call Naked	Short Futures/Short Put
Short Put Naked	Long Futures/Short Call
Covered Call Granting	Short Put Naked
Covered Put Granting	Short Call Naked

SUGGESTED READING

Commodities

Gibson-Jarvie, Robert. *The London Metal Exchange*. Woodhead-Faulkner.

Gold, Gerald. *Modern Commodity Futures Trading*. Commodity Research Bureau Inc.

Horn, Fredrick F. and Farah, Victor W. *Trading in Commodity Futures*. New York Institute of Finance.

Teweles, Richard J., Harlow, Charles V., and Stone, Herbert L. *The Commodity Futures Game*. McGraw-Hill.

Technical Analysis

Edwards, Robert D. and Magee, John. *Technical Analysis of Stock Trends*. John Magee.

Options

Classing Jr., Henry K. *The Dow Jones-Irwin Guide to Put & Call Options*. Dow Jones-Irwin Inc.

McMillan, Lawrence G. *Options as a Strategic Investment*. New York Institute of Finance.

GLOSSARY

Arbitrage The simultaneous purchase and sale of substantially identical commodities in the same or different market for the purpose of profiting by the price difference.

Assign or Assignment Notice The determination of which grantor will be called upon to perform on a granted option. Normally done on a random or other nondiscriminatory basis. Term applies to both the clearing corporation and to the brokerage firm.

Automatic Exercise A policy of some of the exchanges that all options in-the-money by a certain amount are exercised at expiration unless the option owner has instructed elsewise.

Back Month A more deferred month of futures contract trading.

Bearish A market view toward lower prices.

Bear Spread An option strategy wherein one option is bought and another is sold. The entire position is designed to be profitable if prices decline. This position can be implemented with either puts or calls.

Beta The volatility of a given item (a specific commodity) in relation to a group of items (all commodities).

Breakdown In technical analysis, a market's violation of a support level, indicating lower prices.

Breakeven Point The point at which a given strategy neither makes nor loses money.

Breakout In technical analysis, a market's penetration of a resistance level, indicative of higher prices.

Bullish A market term indicative of higher prices.

Bull Spread An option position composed of both long and short options of the same type, designed to be profitable in a rising market. It may be composed of either puts or calls.

Butterfly Spread A position composed of two long and two short options. Generally designed to be profitable if the market remains in a narrow trading range. This strategy is a combination of a bull spread and a bear spread. Also referred to as a "V" spread. Can also be designed to be profitable for major moves in either direction and is then referred to as an "A" spread.

Calendar Spread A transaction involving the purchase and sale of options of different maturities with either the same or different striking prices.

Call An option that gives its owner the right but not the obligation to take delivery of the underlying commodity at a fixed price either during or at a specific time.

Carrying Charges The cost involved in the ownership of a physical commodity or the futures contract. These normally include interest, storage, and insurance.

CBOE The Chicago Board Options Exchange.

CBOT The Chicago Board of Trade.

CME The Chicago Mercantile Exchange.

Closing Transaction A transaction wherein a previously established option position is liquidated.

Collateral An amount of money or physical property, such as T-bills deposited as good faith money to guarantee performance on a short option position.

Combination A short or long option position consisting of a put and a call of either different striking prices or maturities.

COMEX The Commodity Exchange Incorporated.

Contango *see* Carrying charges.

Contango Option An option (put or call) that allows its owner to benefit from the widening or narrowing of the carrying charges.

Contingent A type of order that is to be executed only upon the occurrence of a given event, such as sell March gold contingent September trading at $300 or greater.

Conversion A combination of transactions wherein one option is effectively converted to another type; for example, buy put, purchase futures, sell call converts a long put to a short call.

Cover　(Verb) To close out a previously established position. (Noun) The physical property held as a hedge against a short option.

Covered　A granted option position wherein the appropriate underlying commodity position is held, such as long futures, short call.

Covered Call　A position of long futures/short call.

Covered Put　A position of short future/short put.

CSCE　The Coffee, Sugar and Cocoa Exchange Inc.

Day-Trade　A transaction wherein the institution and liquidation of the position take place within the same trading day.

Debit　To remove money from an account. A type of transaction wherein the cost of purchase exceeds the proceeds of sale.

Delta　The amount by which the price of an option changes for a given change in the price of the underlying commodity. Mathematically the same as hedge ratio in neutral hedging.

Diagonal Spread　The purchase and sale of either put or calls with both different maturities and different striking prices.

Dint　Also referred to as a "lookback" option. A lookback call gives its owner the right to purchase the underlying commodity at the lowest price that commodity achieves over a given period of time. A "lookback put" gives its owner the right to sell the underlying commodity at the highest price it achieves over a given period of time.

Discount　An option is said to be trading at a discount if its current market price is less than could be realized if the option were exercised neglecting commission.

Dont　(From the French word *donner*, to give) A dont call or a dont put option are identical to regular calls and puts except the buyer does not pay a premium. If the option is not exercised, the option buyer pays a cancellation fee.

Down-and-Out Option　Generic term for a limited price option. An option that expires either through the passage of time or as a result of an adverse price move of a predetermined amount, usually 10%. "Down-and-out" refers to calls; "up-and-out" refers to puts.

Downside Breakeven　The price below which a further market decline results in a loss on the position(s) outstanding.

Downside Protection　The price below which the grantor of a cover call has exhausted the protection afforded by the premium received.

Downtrend　A technical analysis term used to indicate that market prices have a downward bias. The market would normally be traded from the short side during a downtrend.

Earnest Money   The money deposited to assure performance of a contractual commitment, also called margin in futures and options trading.

Early Exercise   The exercise of an option prior to its expiration date. Options are normally exercised very near or at their expiration.

Econometric Model   A mathematical algorithm that attempts to simulate a physical situation as in the Black-Scholes model used to forecast option prices.

Equity Requirement   A dollar requirement imposed by a brokerage firm, exchange, or clearing corporation as a prerequisite for certain types of transactions. For example, you might be required to have a $5,000 equity in your account before being allowed to trade commodity futures.

Equivalent Position (Identity)   Two apparently different option/commodity positions that have the same economic benefit, such as 2-to-1 ratio writing and naked straddle granting.

Exercise (Assignment)   The exercise of an option by its holder is the act of either taking (in the case of a call) or making (in the case of a put) the delivery of the underlying commodity or futures contract.

Exercise Limit   The maximum number of options that may be exercised during a given period of time.

Exercise Price   The price at which the commodity underlying the commodity option changes hands, also referred to as the "striking" or "strike" price.

Expected Return   The mathematical profit, in percentage terms, that should be realized from a given strategy based on probability and an infinite number of transactions.

Expiration Date   The last day that a holder of an option may exercise the option.

Expiration Time   The time on the expiration date that the option ceases to exist and the rights of exercise are terminated.

Extrinsic Value   (Also called "time value") The amount by which the market price of an option exceeds the amount that could be realized, were the option exercised and the underlying commodity liquidated.

Fair Value   A price determined by an econometric model that indicates what a given option "should" be trading for, with a given set of parameters.

First Notice Day   The first day on which the holder of a short position in a commodity futures contract can notify the clearing corporation of his or her intention to deliver.

Floor Broker   An exchange member who executes orders on the floor of an exchange.

Fundamental Analysis   A method of commodity price forecasting based on the effects of supply and demand upon price.

Good-Till-Cancelled (GTC)   A qualification on the duration of time allowed until an order entered to an exchange floor expires. GTC orders are good until cancelled or until the related option or futures contract ceases trading.

Hedging   The taking of an equal and opposite position in the futures market to one's position or commitment in the cash market. Or, holding the appropriate futures position to offset an option commitment.

Hedge Ratio   The appropriate commodity position held to offset any losses on a related short option position.

Holder   The individual who is the owner, such as the long, in a commodity option transaction.

Horizontal Spread   Long and short the same type of option (either puts or calls) with different maturity dates.

Identity (or Equality)   Two or more option or option/futures positions with the same economic attributes.

Implied Volatility   A measurement of the volatility of a given commodity based on the price of the option, as opposed to the historical price of the commodity itself.

In-the-Money   A call is said to be in-the-money when the commodity price is greater than the striking price of the option. A put is in-the-money when the striking price of the option is greater than the current price of the underlying commodity.

Intrinsic Value   The portion of an option's current market price that could be immediately recovered were the option exercised and the underlying futures position simultaneously liquidated.

Lag   The market phenomenon of the current price of a commodity option responding more slowly to price change than the change in the "fair value."

Last Trading Day   The last day on which an option of a given maturity or a futures contract may be bought or sold.

Leverage   The ability of a given amount of money to control property of substantially greater value. For example, a $3,000 margin requirement for gold futures might give one the control of $30,000 of the metal.

Limit Order   A buy or a sell order that instructs the floor broker to execute at a given price or a better price, if available, but not at a worse price.

Lognormal Distribution A statistical distribution that is normally applied to stock and commodity prices with the implication that the price can rise to infinity but cannot decline below zero.

Margin In commodities, an amount of money deposited to insure performance of an obligation at a future date.

Mark-to-Market A process whereby each customer's commodity account is evaluated daily in relation to the current market prices, of the commodities contained therein, to determine the appropriate margin.

Market Order A buy or sell order that tells the floor broker to immediately execute the order at the then best available price.

Model *see* Econometric model.

Naked Option A short option position without the appropriate underlying futures position.

Neutral Hedge A hedging strategy wherein profit or losses on a short option are exactly offset by profits and loss on the related hedge.

Open Interest The total number of futures or options contracts outstanding on a given commodity.

Opening Transaction A transaction that creates a new option position either long or short.

Option Price Curve A graphical representation of projected option prices based on possible prices of the underlying commodity.

Out-of-the-Money A call option is said to be out-of-the-money when the striking price of the option is higher than the price of the underlying commodity. A put is out-of-the-money when the commodity price is higher than the strike price of the option.

Overvalued A market condition wherein the price of a given option is higher than an econometric model projects the fair value to be.

Parity A market price for an option that is identical to its intrinsic value.

Position The specific commodity(ies) or option(s) held either long or short in an account.

Position Limit The largest position of a given type that may be held by an individual customer or group of customers acting in consort.

Premium The price of an option excluding any related commission.

Profit Range A range of prices of the underlying commodity in which the option customer sustains a profit.

Put An option that gives its owner the right but not the obligation to sell a given quantity of a certain commodity either during or at a specific point in time.

Pyramiding   The use of the profit generated by a position to add to the same position.

Resistance   A technical analysis term that indicates a market price where sellers become more aggressive than buyers.

Return If Exercised   The rate of return sustained by an option grantor if the option in question is exercised.

Return If Unchanged   The rate of return sustained by the option grantor if the market price of the underlying commodity remains unchanged.

Return on Investment   The percentage profit that an option grantor realizes based on the dollars commited to the position.

Rolling Down   The act of liquidating an option position and reinstituting a substantially identical position with a lower striking price.

Rolling Forward   The act of liquidating an option position and reinstituting a substantially identical position with a more distant maturity.

Rolling Up   The act of liquidating an option position and reinstituting a substantially identical position with a higher striking price.

Spread Order   An order that instructs the floor broker to buy and sell options of the same type (either puts or calls) with either different maturities, striking prices, or both.

Standard Deviation   A statistical measurement of the volatility of a commodity in terms of price over a period of time.

Stop Order   An order placed away from the current market price that becomes a market order depending on specific trades, bids, or offers.

Straddle   An option that gives its owner the right but not the obligation to both buy and sell a given commodity at a given price either during or at a specific point in time.

Strategy   A plan of action for the initiation and follow-up of a position in the market.

Striking Price   The market price at which the owner of an option has the privilege of either taking or making delivery depending on the type of option.

Support   A technical analysis term that defines the market price at which buyers become more aggresive than sellers.

Synthetic Put   A put created through the short sale of the underlying commodity and the purchase of a call on the same commodity.

Synthetic Commodity   The artificial creation of the economic benefits of owning a commodity through the purchase of a call and the sale of a put.

Technical Analysis An approach to commodity price forecasting based on the prior history of price, volume, and open interest—all displayed graphically.

Theoretical Value The projected market price of an option as computed by an econometric model, also referred to as "fair value."

Time Value *see* Extrinsic Value.

Uncovered A granted option position without a related commodity position that would be offset were the option exercised.

Undervalued A market price of a commodity option that is less than the market price predicted by an econometric model.

Variable Ratio Writing An option granting strategy wherein the quantity of the hedge is varied in relationship to the probability of the option's exercise.

Vertical Spread A spreading transaction where the options outstanding have different striking prices and the same maturity.

Volatility A historical measure of the price change of a commodity over a period of time.

Write The act of granting an option, also known as "selling" and "making" an option.

INDEX

Valeur First Boston Corp., 92 (*see* "Dealer
    options")
Variable ratio option writing, 81–83
Variation margin in commodities, 12, 15
Vertical line chart, 42, 43
Vertical spreads, 26, 225, 226–229
    butterfly, 243–245
    put spreads, 229–231

Volatility, 288–289, 294
    implied, 290–291
    pricing of options, 70–72
Volume, 60–61

Winnipeg Commodity Exchange, 107
Writers of commodity options, 112